State-Owned Enterprises in the Middle East and North Africa

World-wide privatization has expanded rapidly but in the Middle East and North Africa (MENA) region progress has been markedly slow. The two main obstacles to privatization in the MENA region are seen to be the high level of overstaffing in public enterprises and the inability of economies to create jobs fast enough.

This volume is divided into two parts. The first addresses key issues of an institutional and political economy nature to explain pressures for and against state-owned enterprise (SOE) reform and privatization. The second part of the book presents empirical studies of Egypt, Jordan, Sudan and Turkey to illustrate the specific roles played by the state and by interest groups in the pace of SOE reform, as well as to analyse the negative impact on productivity and financial performance of an inflated public sector.

The conclusions drawn from these studies are that social protection and effective labour redundancy policies should be addressed prior to privatization, and that there is a prerequisite for increased private sector investment in SOEs to accelerate MENA's integration with the world economy via trade-related programmes and infrastructure.

Merih Celasun is currently Dean of the Faculty of Economics, Administrative and Social Sciences at Bilkent University in Ankara, Turkey. He previously worked with the World Bank and with Turkey's State Planning Organization. He is a Research Fellow and a member of the Board of Trustees of the Economic Research Forum, a Cairo-based regional think-tank and networking institution.

Routledge Studies in Development Economics

State-Owned Enterprises in the Middle East and North Africa

Privatization, performance and reform

Edited by Merih Celasun

London and New York

First published 2001
by Routledge
11 New Fetter Lane, London EC4P 4EE

Simultaneously published in the USA and Canada
by Routledge
29 West 35th Street, New York, NY 10001

Routledge is an imprint of the Taylor & Francis Group

© 2001 The Economic Research Forum for the Arab Countries,
Iran and Turkey

Typeset in Galliard by
Curran Publishing Services Ltd, Norwich
Printed by
TJ International Ltd, Padstow, Cornwall

All rights reserved. No part of this book may be reprinted or
reproduced or utilized in any form or by any electronic,
mechanical or other means, now known or hereafter invented,
including photocopying and recording, or in any information
storage or retrieval system, without permission in writing from
the publishers.

British Library Cataloguing in Publication Data
A catalogue record for this book is available
from the British Library

Library of Congress Cataloging in Publication Data
  State-owned enterprises in the Middle East and North Africa:
  privatization, performance and reform / edited by Merih
  Celasun.
     p. cm.
  Includes bibliographical references and index.
  1. Government business enterprises–Middle East–Case
  Studies. 2. Government business enterprises–Africa–Middle
  East–Case studies. 3. Privatization–Middle East–Case studies.
  4. Privatization–Africa, North–Case studies. I. Celasun, Merih.
  HD4276.5 .S73 2000
  338.956'05–dc21   00-032208

ISBN 0-415-23609-6

Contents

PART I
Broad issues and region-wide perspectives   1

Figures

Tables

Boxes

Contributors

Ismail Arslan is an economist in the World Bank's Poverty Reduction and Economic Management Department in the Europe and Central Asia Region. Before joining the World Bank he worked as senior adviser in the State Planning Organization of Turkey. He specializes in macroeconomics, trade policy and public finance. His work has been published in a number of books and international journals.

Peter H. Aranson received his Ph.D. from the Department of Political Science, University of Rochester in the United States. He was published in the areas of public choice, law and economics, and regulation and industrial organization and served on the editorial boards of the *Cato Journal, Constitutional Political Economy* and *Advances in Austrian Economics.* Prior to joining Emory University in Atlanta, Georgia in 1981 he taught at the University of Miami, the Georgia Institute of Technology and the University of Minnesota. At the time of his death in August 1999 he was Professor of Economics at Emory University.

Ragui Assaad holds a Ph.D. in city and regional planning from Cornell University in the United States and is currently Associate Professor of Planning and Public Affairs at the Humphrey Institute of Public Affairs, University of Minnesota. His teaching and research are in the areas of labour markets and labour policy in developing countries, poverty and poverty alleviation strategies, the informal economy and the role of institutions in development.

Merih Celasun is Dean of the Faculty of Economics, Administration and Social Sciences at Bilkent University in Turkey. He was previously Professor of Economics at the Middle East Technical University in Ankara. His research interests lie mainly in the areas of macroeconomic management, development planning, structural reforms and income distribution.

Ahmed Galal holds a Ph.D. in economics from Boston University in the United States. He is currently the Executive Director and Director of Research of the Cairo-based Egyptian Centre for Economic Studies (ECES), a position that he also held from 1996–8. He is on leave from the World Bank where he has worked in various capacities since 1984. His research and extensive writings have included issues relating to privatization and regulation and industrial and trade policy. His current work is focused in the areas of education, regionalism and small and medium enterprises (SMEs).

Taher H. Kanaan is a Jordanian national of Palestinian origin and holds a Ph.D. from Trinity College, Cambridge University in the United Kingdom. He is currently a private consultant in economics and business and also serves as a member of the United Nations Committee for Development Policy. His professional activities have included positions with the United Nations Secretariat, the Arab Fund for Economic and Social Development, and he has twice served as a cabinet minister in the Jordanian government. His research and writing have focused on a variety of areas including agricultural development, the social effects of economic adjustment on Arab countries and state and private enterprise issues in Jordan.

El-Khider Ali Musa is a Sudanese national and holds a Ph.D. from the School of Management, University of Bath in the United Kingdom. He is currently with the School of Management Studies at the University of Khartoum, Sudan. He has also served as a research fellow at the University of Magdeburg in Germany and his current work is focused on privatization and private sector development.

Mustapha K. Nabli is a Tunisian national and holds a Ph.D. in economics from the University of California, Los Angeles. His fields of interest include international trade, economic integration, applied econometrics, macro and monetary economics, institutional economics and economic development in general. He has recently taken on the position of Chief Economist and Director, Social and Economic Development Group in the Middle East and North Africa region of the World Bank.

Suleyman Ozmucur has taught at Bogazici University in Turkey and at Vassar College in the United States. He is currently a visiting professor at the University of Pennsylvania, Department of Economics. His current research areas include income distribution, issues in productivity measurement, prediction of economic and financial vulnerability and macroeconomic model-building.

John Page holds a Ph.D. in economics from Oxford University in the United Kingdom and is currently Director, Economic Policy and Senior Advisor, Development Policy at the World Bank. Before joining the World Bank in 1980 he taught at Princeton and Stanford Universities and currently is Professorial Lecturer at the Paul Nitze School of Advanced International Studies of the Johns Hopkins University. He has written extensively on trade policy, industrial economics and policy and the economics of developing countries including the Middle Eastern economies as well as on the causes of East Asia's economic success and the subsequent crisis.

Jamal Saghir is currently Sector Manager in the Infrastructure Development Group, Middle East and North Africa region of the World Bank. He has worked at the World Bank in various capacities since 1990 on projects in Africa, Latin America, the former USSR and the MENA region. His work has been in the areas of privatization and restructuring, private participation in infrastructure (PPI) and global water and waste water development issues.

Fatma Taskin holds a Ph.D. in economics from Boston University in the United States and is currently an associate professor of economics at Bilkent University in Ankara, Turkey. Her research and extensive publication list has been in the areas of comparative analysis of developed and developing economies and on various applications of productivity measurement.

Sahar M. Tohamy is a senior economist at the Egyptian Centre for Economic Studies (ECES) in Cairo. Her research and writing have included the issues of prospects of a free-trade agreement between Egypt and the United States, tax administration and transaction costs in the Egyptian tax payment system and barriers to service trade liberalization in Egypt. Her current research focuses on the economic impact of tourism on the Egyptian economy and the impact of the Euro-Mediterranean Agreement on Egypt's food processing industry.

Osman Zaim holds a Ph.D. in economics from Washington State University in the United States and is currently an associate professor of economics at Bilkent University in Ankara, Turkey. He has also taught at Washington State University and at Oregon State University. His areas of research and numerous journal contributions include the areas of applied microeconomics, environmental economics and measurement of efficiency of production.

Preface

Privatization is sweeping the globe, but the controversy about the appropriate role of the public and private sectors rages on. What determines whether a good or service should be produced by the state or by the private sector? Should civil servants manufacture clothing, generate electricity or deliver health care? And should the private sector be responsible for educating children, operating prisons or providing social insurance? Societies have drawn the line between the public and private in very different ways and have used government regulation of private activity as a means to blur the distinction.

In the Middle East and North Africa (MENA) region, the state has traditionally been large, in part because of ideology and in part because the existence of rents from resources such as oil made the state an important tool for political patronage. State-owned enterprises (SOEs) provided a particularly useful vehicle for populist policies, especially for employment of a rapidly growing labour force. Until recently, the topic of privatization was almost taboo in most MENA countries. The political constraints were greater than in many other parts of the world and there were not the severe economic dislocations that necessitated reform elsewhere, such as the collapse of communism in Eastern Europe or the debt crisis in Latin America.

However, the debate about privatization in the MENA region, as in the rest of the world, has evolved considerably in recent years. On the economic side, there is a growing body of evidence that ownership matters. There is strong evidence that in competitive markets private firms will tend to be more efficient than public ones. In markets that are regulated or oligopolistic, both private and public firms are likely to be inefficient, but the evidence on the relative degree of inefficiency is mixed. The key determinant of the degree of inefficiency relative to the economic ideal is the degree of competition introduced in the market.

Is it possible to disentangle the effects of ownership, competition and regulation? Much of the academic literature has tended to take a more purely economic view that assumes the separability of ownership, competition and regulation. Many practitioners of privatization, however, would argue that you cannot separate ownership from competition and regulation: that bureaucratic capture of SOEs is inevitable because of the nature of the relationship and incentives that exist between politicians and SOEs. While temporary improvements in performance may result from restructuring SOEs or toughening the regulatory environment, governments cannot sustain these unless they are linked to privatization. This 'backsliding' argument implies that because governments are more willing to encourage tough competition and regulation when firms are privately owned, privatization is more likely to lead to sustained improvements in the performance of firms. Furthermore, while there is now vast experience with implementing privatization programs around the world, the key obstacles are most often political. The privatization decision is driven by the trade-off that politicians face between the political benefits of patronage that SOEs offer and the political costs of higher taxes that SOEs require to remain afloat. It is these political trade-offs that have become the central issue in much of the world.

This book makes an important contribution to this debate in showing how far the thinking on the issues of SOE reform and privatization has evolved in the MENA region. The cross-country studies define the new frontiers of the debate on privatization: the need for institutions, the implications of globalization, the impact on national savings and the movement of private participation to new areas such as infrastructure. The papers on individual countries add another dimension, providing important evidence on how privatization has worked in practice and how key issues such as interest groups and labour redundancy have an impact. This volume is also particularly timely because the political consensus for SOE reform and privatization has never been greater in the region. The analysis here can certainly play an important role in informing decisions about future policy on the appropriate role of the state and of the private sector.

Nemat Shafik
Vice-President for Private Sector Development and Infrastructure
World Bank

Part I
Broad issues and region-wide perspectives

1 Perspectives on state-owned enterprise reform and privatization in the MENA region

An overview

Merih Celasun

Introduction and background

In the mid-1990s, a more reformist and outward-looking policy perspective has emerged in the Middle East and North Africa (MENA) region. While this may partly be viewed as a response to the unsatisfactory growth record in the previous decade, it also seems to reflect coalition realignments seeking a faster trade integration with the world economy, greater scope for private sector development and wider access to international capital. In the new policy setting, the revitalization of state-owned enterprise (SOE) reform and privatization gains a critical importance. The unprecedented surge in world-wide privatization also provides a supportive international context for robust public-sector reforms in the MENA region.

In Western Europe, privatization has become a socially acceptable policy element in the reform agendas of governments after the vigorous implementation of the United Kingdom's (UK) privatization programme in the mid-1980s, the rationale of which is now endorsed by the British Labour Party. In Latin America, where state entrepreneurship has a long tradition, privatization was introduced as part of fiscal adjustment to the debt crisis in the early 1980s, following the early start in Chile in the post-Allende period. In the 1990s, privatization has come to be viewed as the cornerstone of structural policies in Latin America, which aim to improve resource allocation in a rapidly changing world economic environment.[1]

After the collapse of communist regimes in Central and Eastern Europe and the former Soviet Union, the SOE reforms and privatization, together with a wide range of liberalization measures, have become central elements of a comprehensive transformation process to create market economies based on private property rights. Notwithstanding the unchanging nature of its political regime, China is considered as 'one of the leading practitioners of infrastructure concessions, in both electric power and toll roads' (Poole Jr 1996: 1–2). It is also reported that China endorsed in the Fifteenth Party Congress in September 1997 'radical reform for state enterprises, including outright divestiture of the state's stakes in all but the biggest firms' (Lieberman and Kirkness 1998: 1).

These world-wide trends in privatization imply a massive transfer of ownership and/or control rights to the private sector, which may be under-scored by the estimated value of US$468 billion worth of state asset sales around the world (excluding give-aways under voucher schemes) over the ten-year period from 1984 to 1994 (Poole Jr 1996). In conjunction with other major trends (such as political liberalization, deregulation and advances in communications technology), the world-wide privatization has set in motion a far reaching dynamic process that is likely to induce deep changes in institutional relationships, behavioural patterns and market conditions at the local and global levels.

For developing economies, a notable consequence of this process has been the sharp rise in their long-term external finance from private sources, and diminishing role of official development assistance. Net long-term private flows to all developing countries increased from US$42 billion in 1990 to US$247 billion in 1996, reaching 87 per cent of total net flows. Foreign direct investment (FDI) has become the dominant form of net private flows, exhibiting a strong response to active privatization programmes in developing countries, mainly in Latin America and East Asia. During 1990–6, foreign investors (including FDI and equity investors) provided nearly 45 per cent of the total proceeds (US$156 billion) from privatization sales in all developing economies (World Bank 1998).

For advanced market economies, the *ex-post* assessments of privatization point to its notable impact on the efficient functioning of markets and enter-prises, widening share ownership and rebalancing of control between trade unions and management.[2] It is also stressed that privatization facilitates a more precise identification of the public-good elements of state enterprises (Bishop, Kay and Mayer 1994). This is an important contribution to the redefinition of the role of the state in a rapidly transforming economic envi-ronment. In practice, fiscal relief appears to have been an objective of secondary importance. The UK privatization experience also provides a strategic lesson to late reformers. The post-privatization regulatory control is generally inefficient, and the benefits of privatization are more fully realized when competition is introduced into 'previously monopolized and regulated network utilities' (Newberry 1996: 1).

In the transition economies, the impact of privatization has been more difficult to assess, because the process started within the unfavourable setting of trade disruptions and macroeconomic disorder, which resulted in the collapse of output and disarray in sectoral structures in the early 1990s.

The big-bang approach to privatization received considerable criticism in much of the earlier research, which stressed the merits of incremental reforms and the start-up of new private enterprises (Milor 1994, Akyuz 1994). In turn, proponents of rapid privatization were more concerned with the risks of reform reversals, diversion of state property (by managers and workers) in an ownership vacuum and prolonged drift in corporate governance in the course of slow and hesitant privatization (Sachs 1991).

More recent analysis of former socialist economies indicates that consistent policies for financial discipline, domestic competition and macroeconomic control have fostered a more rapid growth of private firms as well as improved performance in state enterprises (World Bank 1996 and Sachs 1996). In this context, Stiglitz makes a noteworthy observation: 'China has sustained high growth by extending the scope of competition without privatizing state enterprises. In contrast, Russia privatized extensively without doing much to promote competition, and the economy suffered' (Stiglitz 1997: 3).

As for developing countries, the evaluation of their SOE sectors and reform experiences has always been a tricky and challenging task for researchers. In most cases, the SOE sectors have been established to serve a multiplicity of objectives in political, economic and social spheres, calling for interdisciplinary approaches to their analysis. A heavy reliance on SOEs as an institutional vehicle of national development has typically resulted in extensive political patronage, labour redundancy, highly segmented financial and labour markets, and firmly entrenched interest groups. Thus, the SOE reform initiatives have encountered more intense opposition in developing country environments.

The SOE reform experience of the developing world is comprehensively evaluated in the World Bank (1995) report entitled *Bureaucrats in Business: The Economics and Pollitics of Government Ownership* (briefly, the BIB Report). This study conceptualizes SOE reform as a broad process, entailing five components: divestiture (asset sales, liquidation or giveaways), competition, hard budgets, financial reforms and changes in institutional relationship (or incentive structure) between SOEs and governments. The political desirability, political feasibility and credibility of reforms are explicitly explored, and the issue of contracting is accorded a special treatment.

By using the SOE financial returns, productivity and saving–investment deficits as indicators of success, the BIB Report evaluates the performance and reform record of sample countries. It major conclusion is: 'The more successful reformers (Chile, Korea and Mexico) made the most of all five components' of the SOE reform process and divested more (World Bank 1995: 5). The attempt to increase managerial autonomy and improve the incentive structure were common to all reformers, but their impact has not been significant in the absence of reform accomplishments in other areas. The less successful reformers have been mainly constrained by political difficulties in maintaining the government's support base and overcoming legal and administrative obstacles in the implementation process.

The BIB evaluation also discloses a number of noteworthy trends. Despite increasing divestiture, the share of SOEs in developing countries gross domestic product (GDP) (excluding transition economies) has not declined in the 1980s and remained around 11 per cent. The relative size of the SOE sector is higher in low-income countries (14 per cent of GDP). The available evidence shows that large SOE sectors tend to hinder the growth process at the aggregate level.

The MENA countries generally have large SOE sectors as well as large civil service and military establishments. During 1978–91, the GDP share of non-financial SOEs was 17 per cent in Morocco, 30 per cent in Egypt, 31 per cent in Tunisia, 48 per cent in Sudan and 58 per cent in Algeria, markedly exceeding the 11 per cent average for all developing countries (World Bank 1995: 268–71). Although the GDP share of SOE sectors is not a fully satisfactory measure of their relative position and significance, the above-average size of SOE sectors in the MENA region points to the existence of acute structural constraints on aggregate growth as suggested by the cross-country evidence marshaled in the BIB Report.

Conventional wisdom emphasizes the low productive efficiency and inferior financial performance of SOE sectors in order to explain their adverse impact on the growth process. While such an emphasis is justified, the unique nature of the MENA region's vulnerability to external shocks should also be considered carefully.

In various episodes of the post-1980 era, the region's economies faced severe shocks stemming from declining oil revenues and associated fall in remittance incomes and other financial transfers. The growth momentum could have been preserved by a strong structural response to external shocks through a major effort to reallocate resources toward tradable sectors, the expansion of which provides a greater scope for productivity improvements as well as non-traditional export earnings. The region's response to new challenges has been inhibited, however, by the heavily protected productive structures of public industries, and private sector's preference for investments in non-tradable sectors (such as housing and real estate) as aptly stressed by Page (1998). The stagnation of per capita income has been avoided in countries (notably, Morocco and Tunisia), where export performance has been relatively stronger.

From the mid-1980s to early the 1990s, the region's inability to restore long-term growth resulted in an unfavourable domestic context for SOE reforms. Depressed real wages and limited new job opportunities reduced the political desirability of scaling down overstaffed SOEs. The SOE reform attempts through modified institutional arrangements were generally ineffective in the absence of other reforms (Ayubi 1997).

Notwithstanding the important differences in country conditions, a more reformist policy approach was observed in the MENA region from the mid-1990s onward.[3] This seems to have coincided with strong signs of output recovery, which benefited from macroeconomic stabilization that has been achieved with considerable support from international financial institutions (El-Erian *et al.* 1996, Economic Research Forum (ERF) 1996). In the new setting, reforms need to be sequenced in such a way as to yield tangible gains in the earlier phases, build credibility and avoid overloaded reform agendas for policy institutions and legislatures. If trade reforms are firmly introduced at the outset, a greater public concern with competition, market efficiency and trade logistics will generate additional pressures for SOE reforms and privatization.[4]

The present volume brings together a number of scholarly articles on SOE performance, reform issues and the changing context of privatization in the MENA region. The volume originated from a workshop on 'The changing size and role of the state-owned enterprise sector in the MENA region', organized by the Economic Research Forum for the Arab Countries, Iran and Turkey (ERF) in cooperation with the World Bank at Amman (Jordan) in May 1996. Besides offering a selection of articles based on papers presented at the workshop, the book also includes invited contributions that report the findings of empirically based original research.

The book is divided into two parts. Chapters 2–6 in Part I contain research contributions on broad reform issues, cross-country perspectives and strategic approaches to privatization as they relate to the MENA region. In turn chapters 7–12 in Part II present country-specific research on various aspects of SOE performance and reform in Egypt, Jordan, Sudan and Turkey.[5] The case studies do not cover the entire region, but are highly representative of policy approaches and outcomes in most MENA countries.[6] The salient features of this volume's contributions are highlighted in the following section of this introductory chapter.

Overview of contributions

Broad issues and region-wide perspectives

Why has there been a status quo bias in SOE reforms? How can more pressure be generated for privatization? In Chapter 2, Mustapha Nabli develops a unified conceptual framework for the institutional economics analysis of SOE reform, which ingeniously combines the approaches based on transaction costs and political economy considerations. In Nabli's framework, the welfare cost of the SOE sector plays a crucial role in explaining interest group pressures for or against the reform. This cost is considered to be a function of not only the relative size of the SOE sector but also it costs and inefficiencies in the wider economic context.

Upon a careful review of factors that impact on the welfare cost of the SOE sector, Nabli delineates possible ranges of this cost, over which pressure for or against reform may dominate. Nabli observes that most of the countries in the MENA region display SOE characteristics that indicate a strong bias in favour of little or no privatization. Within his unified conceptual framework, Nabli also explores interactions of SOE reform and other reforms, and suggests that reforms should be sequenced in such a way as to produce maximum results with least resistance and make the SOE sector's costs more transparent to the general public. In his chapter, Nabli also argues that a substantial amount of divestiture is 'itself a prerequisite for possible improvement of the performance of what may remain in the public sector'.

Despite the rapid expansion of data based on world-wide privatization, the subject has not been sufficiently researched as a positive economic problem.

In Chapter 3, Sahar Tohamy and Peter Aranson make a novel contribution to the literature by developing a theoretical model and testing its predictions in a world-wide context. In their theoretical model, politicians maximize the net total surplus (or support) of workers and investors in making choices on privatization under different methods. Their model differentiates a number of institutional arrangements for public firms and generate varying patterns of support for, or opposition to, privatization. The empirical testing of the authors' model shows that the likelihood of privatization increases as public firms' debt becomes smaller and government spending for social security and welfare gets larger.

For the MENA region, the empirical findings of Tohamy and Aranson suggest that issues surrounding hard budget constraints (implying low SOE debt) and adequate social security arrangements (or unemployment benefits) should be addressed prior to privatization. Their theoretical model predicts that restrictions against employment cuts reduce the likelihood of enterprise sales to private investors, but increase the probability of worker or manager buy-outs. Workers' gain would be larger in profit maximizing firms, implying less labour resistance to privatization after market liberalization. These results provide support to the inferences drawn from Nabli's conceptual framework regarding the appropriate sequencing of reforms, which suggested policy-regime changes to enhance domestic competition in earlier phases of the overall reform process.

The unsatisfactory pace of new job creation has been a major source of political difficulties faced in the earlier episodes of privatization. In Chapter 4, John Page presents a coherent reassessment of the MENA region's previous privatization attempts in the context of its sluggish employment performance, narrow trade orientation (excluding oil) and limited fiscal resources for labour redundancy policies. Page's assessment establishes a clear link between faster trade integration and accelerated economic growth, which is a prerequisite of more supportive labour market conditions for divestiture of large SOEs with redundant workers.

Page notes that the potential benefits of a greater trade orientation have been recognized in almost all countries in the region, where substantial trade liberalization is already in progress. The trade agreements with the European Union also offer new opportunities for export promotion. While strongly endorsing the direction of recent trade reforms, Page argues, with a great deal of supportive evidence, that infrastructure deficits are substantial in lower-income economies of the region. Infrastructure bottlenecks are 'the primary impediment' to increased investment and nontraditional exports. Page recommends that the generalized privatization programmes of the mid-1990s be 'strategically reoriented' toward trade-related infrastructure with a view to accelerate the MENA's integration with the world economy.

In response to a variety of strategic considerations, the size and signifi-cance of infrastructure privatizations have indeed shown an unprecedented rise in the 1990s. During 1990–6, infrastructure-related sell-offs (mainly in telecommunications and power) accounted for 42 per cent of the total privatization proceeds (about US$156 billion) in all developing countries (World Bank 1998). What lessons can we draw from the world-wide practice in infrastructure privatization, and how can they be applied to the MENA region?

In Chapter 5, Jamal Saghir provides a thorough evaluation of the objectives, methods and principles of infrastructure privatization, and examines their significance for the MENA economies. The contributions of Page and Saghir have strong complementarities, and crystallize the strategic benefits of infrastructure privatization in strengthening trade performance, capital market development and mobilizing additional resources for domestic investment.

At a more operational level, Saghir distills useful lessons from the world-wide experience in infrastructure privatizations and private participation in infrastructure projects. Previous experience shows that it is much more difficult to introduce changes in sectoral structures after privatization, 'when there are private shareholders with contractual rights'. In the pre-privatization stage it is a sensible strategy to identify potentially competitive elements and separate them from natural monopolies; establish regulatory frameworks, where necessary; and resolve issues concerning labour redundancy, tariff adjustments and consumer protection. In the post-privatization stage the distinction between policy and regulation is crucial.

For the MENA region, Saghir puts an emphasis on legal reforms for property rights protection and dispute resolution mechanisms, including international arbitration. The private investors need to be solidly assured of their contractual rights in order to enable them to take risks that are not unduly high by cross-country standards. Otherwise, they will demand 'higher returns to compensate for higher risks', which are ultimately financed by higher prices for the consumers. Effective guarantees from the governments and international financial institutions can further improve the creditworthiness of long-term infrastructure projects.

In a long-term perspective, savings mobilization and productivity improvement are central to a sustained growth process. While foreign savings, official grants and remittance income contribute to economic growth through a number of channels, domestic savings normally constitute the bulk of total savings available for domestic investment. The countries that have large SOE sectors are typically characterized, however, by low domestic savings ratios. In this context, the relevant question is: what are the potential gains in savings from enterprise reforms and privatization? This question and related issues have not been explicitly examined in the recent literature. In Chapter 6, Ahmed Galal presents an empirically-based analysis of savings and privatization, using the Egyptian database for public enterprises. Although his numerical results apply to Egypt, his innovative methodology and general findings have wider implications.

In his review of the initial conditions, Galal notes that the savings–investment gap of his sample, which represents about a third of the value added of Egypt's public enterprise sector, declined in the post-1987 period and turned into surplus in the early 1990s. This has been achieved, however, by investment reduction rather than increased saving, which is hardly conducive to increased productivity performance. For the analysis of possible future paths of savings, the author defines two counterfactual scenarios in addition to the no-reform (or factual) scenario. His two counterfactuals are the commercialization and privatization scenarios.

In Galal's simulations, future profits of enterprises, and hence their savings, are influenced by assumptions on productivity improvement and additional investment beyond the benchmark paths specified for the no-reform scenario. Galal exercises considerable caution on the numerical assumptions that crudely reflect reform outcomes observed elsewhere. A hypothetical reform programme combining 50 per cent commercialization and 50 per cent privatization yields an annual increase in savings with a magnitude of 2.4 per cent of the base year (1994) GDP. If these savings are extrapolated to the rest of the sector, additional savings could be as high as 7 per cent of GDP.

In his chapter, Galal also undertakes a sensitivity analysis, which underscores the potential benefits of new investments in privatized enterprises. The author concludes that 'care must be taken to secure, where appropriate, the commitment of new owners to an investment program'. In the privatization of large and overstaffed SOEs, the investment initiatives of the new owners may be constrained, however, by a number of factors, including the extent to which the authorities have addressed labour redundancy issues in the pre-divestiture stage.

Country studies

As emphasized by Page and by Tohamy and Aranson in their chapters, labour redundancy is a major impediment to privatization, especially in economies that cannot absorb new labour force entrants. In most cases, the existing labour legislation makes involuntary layoffs impossible. In Chapter 7, Ragui Assaad presents an in-depth research on the design of voluntary severance programmes for redundant workers in Egypt's public enterprise sector. These programmes aim to achieve the target exit rates while remaining voluntary in nature. This can be done by 'compensating workers for the rent they receive by being in the public enterprise sector'.

In the absence of survey data on actual displaced workers, Assaad carefully pursues indirect approaches to determine worker-specific rents that are based on sectoral earnings equation estimates and plausible assumptions on non-wage benefits. A worker's rent is defined as 'the difference in the expected streams of total compensation in the public and private sectors up to the age of mandatory retirement'. The author's calculations show that the average rent of a public enterprise sector worker is equal to 108 average monthly wages in 1988 prices. Rents for female workers are found to be 68 per cent higher than those of males, because of their less promising employment prospects in the private sector.

In his chapter, Assaad also gives estimates of alternative compensation programmes that achieve a 30 per cent reduction (366,000 workers) in the total public enterprise labour force (1.21 million workers in 1988). The estimated total fiscal cost ranges from 4.6 per cent of GDP (for the programme that matches compensation payment exactly to the worker-specific rents) to 8 per cent of GDP (for the flat payment scheme, where no indexation is used). These findings show that fiscal cost of providing voluntary severance packages are substantial in Egypt's highly overstaffed public enterprise sector.

The case of Jordan is presented in Chapter 8 by Taher Kanaan. Jordan has a large public sector, but the GDP share of SOEs, excluding the government services, remained around 14 per cent in the early 1990s. While Jordan's SOEs have dominant positions in public utilities and natural-resource-based monopolies, two major government institutions hold a wide range of minority shareholdings in commercial enterprises. The available evidence shows weak performance in public utilities and inferior financial efficiency in government-associated enterprises. Kanaan observes serious weaknesses in the management and control pattern of public shareholding companies in which the government has high equity participation.

In his chapter, Kanaan outlines Jordan's privatization strategy (announced in 1996), which places an emphasis on restructuring and divestiture of substantial capacity in power and telecommunications, and selling large equities to strategic partners in other sectors.

While favouring the restructuring of SOEs with modern management systems, the author argues that change of ownership patterns should be considered 'only if and when they can help liberalize markets or reduce their imperfections, and/or contribute significantly to the improvement in the efficiency of enterprise management'. Kanaan observes that market-supportive reforms may also be applied to certain government services, and proposes such a reform for official universities, taking into account social policy objectives in financing well-defined categories of students.

The case of Sudan poses enormous challenges to researchers, who have to contend with sparse information on policy and performance in an economy that has suffered from civil strife since the mid-1980s (Elbadawi 1998). The protracted political conflict has also sharply reduced the country's access to international assistance.

Public enterprises have played a major role in Sudan's historical development process, and contributed about 48 per cent of its GDP in 1978–91 (World Bank 1995). In Chapter 9, El-Khider Ali Musa evaluates Sudan's experience with the reform of public enterprises, drawing upon available data on recent privatization transactions. In his retrospective on public enterprises, Musa stresses the multiplicity of their goals, including regional development and the provision of social services in rural areas, which have not been conducive to commercial operations. As part of the policy response to acute fiscal crisis, privatization was initiated in the early 1980s under international pressures. However, the process proceeded on a purely *ad hoc* basis, and was disrupted by political instability and outbreak of civil war in the South.

In his chapter, Musa gives a detailed account of Sudan's privatization drive in the 1990s in the context of the government's comprehensive adjustment strategy, which emphasized economic liberalization and private sector development. Although the necessary legal and institutional frameworks have largely been established, the author reports that 'the implementation has been flawed in several respects': lack of transparency, under-valuation of state property and excessive official leniency with delayed payments from private investors. For low-income economies with large public sectors, Sudan's experience shows that the effectiveness of privatization suffers from political instability and the absence of international technical and financial assistance.

Because of extensive data availability, Turkey's experience with public enterprises provides a greater scope for empirically-based analysis. From the policy standpoint, the Turkish case is also interesting, because Turkey has switched to an outward-oriented growth strategy with notable success, notwithstanding the sluggish progress in privatization. The various facets of Turkey's SOE sector and its performance are examined in three chapters contributed by different authors.

In Chapter 10, Merih Celasun and Ismail Arslan present a broad evaluation of Turkey's non-financial SOE sector against the background of major shifts in economic strategy and policy regimes. The available indicators show that the SOE sector has fallen behind the private sector, which played a leading role in Turkey's export drive in the post-1980 era. In the mid-1980s, the SOE investments were shifted from manufacturing to energy, telecommunications and transport sectors to break the infrastructure bottlenecks in the outward-oriented growth process.

Despite their narrowing contribution to aggregate output, Turkey's SOEs have, nevertheless, remained a convenient vehicle for populist policies of a political nature. The authors' analysis brings out the strong sensitivity of SOE financial performance to changes in policy stance on income distribution, real wages and modes of deficit financing. After the 1994 financial crisis, SOE deficits have been substantially reduced under hard budget constraints. During 1995–7, Turkey's high inflation persisted, however, mainly due to the government's inability to deal with growing social security deficits and a high interest burden on the budget.

In their chapter, Celasun and Arslan also assess the legal setbacks and administrative weaknesses that have impeded the process of privatization, which yielded only US$2.8 billion in total gross revenues in 1986–95 (and a cumulative US$3.7 billion by the end of 1997). With the establishment of a more enabling legal framework in 1996, growing public support and closer attention to labour issues, Turkey's privatization is likely to accelerate, in conjunction with more extensive private sector participation in infrastructure projects.

In Chapter 11, Suleyman Ozmucur provides a comparative analysis of productivity and financial performance of public and private enterprises, utilizing a rich database on the 500 largest industrial firms in Turkey, which collectively generated 43 per cent of value added in Turkish industry (mining, manufacturing and power utilities). The author's study shows that labour and capital productivity are, respectively, 65 and 83 per cent higher in private enterprises than corresponding levels in public enterprises over the 1982–94 period. The analysis of profitability indicators reveals the inferior financial efficiency in public enterprises.

Furthermore, Ozmucur's study finds important differences in the behavioural response of private and public enterprises to changes in macroeconomic conditions. During inflationary periods, the private sector lowers its output, and increases its mark-up and sales profitability. During periods of GDP expansion, private enterprises increase their production. No such systematic behaviour is observed in the public sector.

Ozmucur's findings point to the existence of considerable potential for additional domestic savings in response to improved productivity and the financial performance of public enterprises as suggested by Galal's simulation study (in Chapter 6) on savings and privatization. The measurement of potential gains in savings requires, however, further research on public enterprises that generally operate in more capital-intensive sub-sectors, which reflect on their comparatively lower output–capital ratios.

In Chapter 12, Osman Zaim and Fatma Taskin adopt a highly elaborate methodology to explore the possible effect of ownership on efficiency trends in Turkish manufacturing (excluding mining and electricity output). Zaim and Taskin employ stochastic and non-stochastic techniques of production function estimation, which views deviations from the frontier as measures of technical inefficiency. The authors use an extensive data set on twenty-eight sub-sectors in large manufacturing, where public and private production are registered separately from 1974 to 1991.

The empirical results of Zaim and Taskin show that the pure technical efficiency in large manufacturing is on a declining trend in Turkey. The performance of the public sector was somewhat superior relative to that of the private sector prior to 1982, but the efficiency level of public enterprises exhibited a decline after 1982. The latter decline may be attributed, as noted by the authors, to reduced investments in public manufacturing in the post-1980 era of economic liberalization and relatively high trade-orientation.

Viewed as a whole, the research findings on Turkey have an important implication. The post-1980 changes in the sectoral structure of public investments warrant a more integrated framework of analysis. Reduced investments in public manufacturing provided room for increased public investments in infrastructure sectors, which facilitated Turkey's export-led recovery from its severe debt crisis in the late 1970s. On the other hand, the structural deficiencies in manufacturing investments have been offset mainly by real exchange rate depreciations and real wage reductions that enhanced the price competitiveness of Turkish exports at a considerable social cost. The related issues concerning the sustainability of Turkey's export expansion are important, but have been explored elsewhere (Togan 1998, Arslan and Celasun 1995).

Concluding remarks: the way ahead

The available evidence shows that the productivity and financial performance of the SOE sector is generally low in the MENA economies. The experiences of Egypt and Turkey indicate that the SOE deficits can be lowered under hard budget constraints, but this has usually been achieved by investment cuts and real wage reductions, which cannot be regarded as long-term remedies. The attempts to improve SOE performance through changes in institutional relationships have not been successful in the absence of robust reforms in trade and finance. In the future, the SOE reform directions are deeper commercialization and privatization that primarily aim at increased market efficiency, improved savings performance and more efficient capital allocation to support a trade-oriented growth process.

In the MENA region, privatization gained a considerable momentum in the mid-1990s in conjunction with the emergence of a relatively more supportive social and political environment. The cross-country evidence suggests that privatization proceeds more rapidly when labour issues are addressed in earlier phases and enterprises operate under competitive conditions.

Given the more favourable political conditions in the region, the limited size of domestically held private wealth and relatively narrow capital markets will pose a major constraint on large-scale divestitures. The attraction of the return of flight capital, foreign investment and private capital flows from the Gulf remains, therefore, a key challenge to the region's reforming countries with low savings. This challenge can be met more effectively in a dynamic growth environment supported by macroeconomic stability and sound legal and institutional frameworks that are compatible with contemporary norms and practices at the international level.

To accelerate aggregate growth, the region's economies need to move much faster to increase their non-oil trade integration with the world economy. This requires a well-coordinated policy effort in a number of directions.[7] Robust trade reforms are needed upfront to realign incentives in favour of export-oriented sectors. A greater emphasis is warranted on the improvement of the quality of human capital and technological capabilities. In the intermediate run, it is also essential to remove infrastructure bottlenecks that impede trade-oriented activities in the growth process. The new policy setting offers strategic opportunities in infrastructure privatization and private sector participation in infrastructure to improve trade logistics and enable a wider access to international finance.

Infrastructure privatization requires, however, rigorous structural, legal and regulatory arrangements in the pre-privatization stage. Capacity building in the economics of regulation is a region-wide challenge. International technical cooperation and assistance can play a highly fruitful role in this direction.

From the perspective of long-term development, it also needs to be emphasized that outward-oriented growth strategies and privatization should be complemented by internal reforms to promote 'the development of human resources, equality of opportunities, transparency in governance, strong local demand and sustainable environment' (Sirageldin 1998: 1).[8] In the final analysis, it is up to the citizens of the region to choose and implement reforms that will integrate them with the global economy in a rewarding manner. Hopefully, research presented in this book will contribute to a broader understanding of issues surrounding SOE performance and reforms that are an important component of the overall reform process in the MENA region.

Notes

I am indebted to the contributing authors of this volume, and wish to express my gratitude to Gillian Potter, Maureen Moynihan, Abda El-Mahdi, Ismail Arslan, Cevdet Denizer, Kudret Celebi and Oya Celasun for their valuable support and contributions.

1 See Glade (1991) for comprehensive assessments of privatization experiences in Latin American economies.
2 The literature of the country experiences with privatization is vast. See, for example, OECD (1996) for reviews of various aspects of privatization in selected OECD and non-OECD countries; Vickers and Yarrow (1988) and Bishop *et al.* (1994) on the UK's privatization experience and policy lessons; Anderson and Hill (1996) on world-wide privatization; World Bank (1995) on SOE reform and privatization in the developing world; Akyuz (1994), Milor (1994), Sachs (1991, 1996) and World Bank (1996) on privatization and related issues in transition economies and reforming communist states; and Ayubi (1997), Anderson and Martinez (1998) and Luciani (1997) for previous contributions on etatism, privatization and private sector development in the MENA region.
3 See Handoussa (1997) and Shafik (1998a, 1998b) for in-depth assessments of the MENA region's economic future, social issues and policy perspectives on closer integration with the world economy. Sirageldin (1998) argues for the adoption of coordinated internal and outward oriented development strategies, and examines the nature of deeper internal reforms needed in Arab countries. Waterbury (1998) critically explores feasible reform paths in the context of political issues and institutional patterns.
4 As argued by Rodrik (1996) and Safadi (1997), international disciplines and restrictions placed on domestic policies by membership in the World Trade Organization and trade agreements with the European Union will present opportunities to lock in trade reforms and provide stable and transparent incentives for the domestic industry.
5 Some of the contributing authors of this volume use the acronym 'PE' for public enterprise (rather than SOE for state-owned enterprise), reflecting the common usage in their countries.

6   The aggregate World Bank statistical database for the MENA region does not cover Turkey, unless indicated otherwise.
7   For a coherent analysis of the nature of growth-oriented economic reforms in the process of global integration see Sachs and Warner (1995).
8   See, for example, Handoussa and Kheir-El-Din (1998) for a case study on Egypt's long-term development vision, which treats external and internal reform perspectives in an integrated manner.

Bibliography

Akyuz, Y. (1994) 'Reform and crisis in the transition economies', in *Privatization in the Transition Process: Recent Experiences in Eastern Europe,* United Nations conference on 'Trade and Development' (UNCTAD/GID/7) United Nations Publications.

Anderson, R. E. and Martinez, A. (1998) 'Supporting private sector development in the Middle East and North Africa' in N. Shafik (ed.), *Prospects for Middle Eastern and North African Economies: From Boom to Bust and Back,* London: Macmillan: 173–93.

Anderson, T. L. and Hill, P. J. (1996) 'The political economy of privatization' in T. L. Anderson and P. J. Hill (eds), *The Privatization Process: A Worldwide Perspective,* Lanham, Md. and London: Rowman and Littlefield: xi–xiii.

Arslan, I. and Celasun, M. (1995) 'Sustainability of industrial exporting in a liberalizing economy: the Turkish experience', in G. K. Helleiner (ed.), *Manufacturing for Export in the Developing World: Problems and Possibilities,* London: Routledge: 11–166.

Ayubi, N. (1997) 'Etatism versus privatization: the changing role of the state in nine arab countries', in H. Handoussa (ed.), *Economic Transition in the Middle East: Global Challenges and Adjustment Strategies,* Cairo: American University in Cairo Press: 125–66.

Bishop, M., Kay, J. and Mayer, C. (1994) 'Introduction: privatization and economic performance', in M. Bishop, J. Kay and C. Mayer (eds), *Privatization and Economic Performance,* Oxford: Oxford University Press: 1–14.

Economic Research Forum for the Arab Countries, Iran and Turkey (1996) *Economic Trends in the MENA Region,* Cairo: Economic Research Forum.

Elbadawi, I. A. (1998) 'Sudan: toward a strategic vision for peace and development', in N. Shafik (ed.), *Economic Challenges Facing Middle Eastern and North African Countries: Alternative Futures,* London: Macmillan: 178–201.

El-Erian, M. A., Eken, S., Fennell, S. and Chauffour, J-P. (1996) *Growth and Stability in the Middle East and North Africa,* Washington, D.C.: International Monetary Fund

Glade, W. (ed.) (1991) *Privatization of Public Enterprises in Latin America,* San Francisco: ICS Press.

Handoussa, H. (1997) 'Adjustment and beyond: the Middle East in transition', in H. Handoussa (ed.), *Economic Transition in the Middle East: Global Challenges and Adjustment Strategies,* Cairo: The American University in Cairo Press: 3–16.

Handoussa, H. and Kheir-El-Din, H. (1998) 'A vision for Egypt in 2012', in N. Shafik (ed.), *Economic Challenges Facing Middle Eastern and North African Countries: Alternative Futures,* London: Macmillan: 53–77.

Lieberman, I. W. and Kirkness, C. D. (1998) *Privatization and Emerging Equity*

Markets, Washington, D.C.: World Bank and Flemings.

Luciani, G. (1997) 'Privatization as a policy for development' in H. Handoussa (ed.), *Economic Transition in the Middle East: Global Challenges and Adjustment Strategies*, Cairo: American University in Cairo Press: 107–21.

Milor, V. (1994) 'Changing political economies: an introduction', in V. Milor (ed.), *Changing Political Economies: Privatization in Post-Communist and Reforming Communist States*, Boulder and London: Lynne Rienner Publishers: 1–21.

Newberry, D. M. (1996) 'Privatization and regulation of public utilities', presidential address to the European Economic Association Eleventh Annual Congress, Istanbul, 22 August.

Organization for Economic Cooperation and Development (OECD) (1996) *Privatization in Asia. Europe and Latin America*, Paris: OECD.

Page, J. (1998) 'From boom to bust – and back? The crisis of growth in the Middle East and North Africa', in N. Shafik (ed.), *Prospects for Middle Eastern and North African Economies: From Boom to Bust and Back*, London: Macmillan: 133–58.

Poole, Jr. R. W. (1996) 'Privatization for economic development', in T. L. Anderson and P. J. Hill (eds), *The Privatization Process: A Worldwide Perspective*, Lanham, Md and London: Rowman and Littlefield: 1–18.

Rodrik, D. (1996) 'Trade policy can improve transparency in governing', in *Economic Trends in the MENA Region* (Box 2.1), Cairo: Economic Research Forum: 33.

Sachs, J. D. (1991) 'Accelerating privatization in eastern Europe', paper presented at Annual Conference in Development Economics, Washington, D.C., 25–6 April.

—— (1996) 'Reforms in eastern Europe and former Soviet Union in light of the East Asian experiences', NBER Working Paper Series no. 5404, Cambridge, Mass.: National Bureau of Economic Research.

Sachs, J. D. and Wagner, A. M. (1995) 'Economic reform and the process of global integration', *Brookings Papers on Economic Activity*, no. 1, Washington, D.C.: 1–95.

Safadi, R. (1997) 'Global challenges and opportunities facing MENA countries at the dawn of the twenty-first century', in H. Handoussa (ed.), *Economic Transition in the Middle East: Global Challenges and Adjustment Strategies*, Cairo: American University in Cairo Press: 19–41.

Shafik, N. (ed.) (1998a) *Prospects for Middle Eastern and North African Economies: From Boom to Bust and Back*, London: Macmillan.

—— (ed.) (1998b) *Economic Challenges Facing Middle Eastern and North African Countries: Alternative Futures*, London: Macmillan.

Sirageldin, I. (1998) 'Globalization, regionalization and recent trade agreements: impact on Arab countries, rapid exogenous change – slow endogenous response!', keynote address at international conference on 'The New Economic Development and their Impacts on Arab Economies', Arab Planning Institute, Tunis, 3–5 June.

Stiglitz, J. (1997) 'More instruments and broader goals: moving toward the post-Washington consensus', *WIDER Angle*, no. 2, Helsinki: World Institute for Development Economics Research: 1–3.

Togan, S. (1998) 'Determinants of economic growth in Turkey', in N. Shafik (ed.), *Economic Challenges Facing Middle Eastern and North African Countries: Alternative Futures*, London: Macmillan: 159–77.

Vickers, J. and Yarrow, G. (1988) *Privatization: An Economic Analysis*, Cambridge, Mass.: MIT Press.

Waterbury, J. (1998) 'The state and economic transition in the Middle East and North Africa', in N. Shafik (ed.), *Prospects for Middle Eastern and North African Economies:*

From Boom to Bust and Back, London: Macmillan: 159–77.

World Bank (1995) *Bureaucrats in Business: The Economics and Politics of Government Ownership*, Oxford and New York: Oxford University Press.

—— (1996) 'From plan to market', *World Development Report 1996*, Oxford and New York: Oxford University Press.

—— (1998) *Global Development Finance 1998*, Washington, D.C.: World Bank.

2 Institutional analysis of state-owned enterprises reform and the MENA region

Mustapha K. Nabli

Introduction

One major characteristic of the Middle East and North Africa (MENA) region economies is the large size of the state-owned enterprise (SOE) sector. Compared with other regions, except former communist countries, it is striking how pervasive has been the role of the SOE sector in most countries of the region. This characteristic has significant implications both for SOE sector reform itself and for the overall process of reform since powerful interactions exist between them. The interactions are complex, they are often strong and sometimes decisive for the success of the programme. Very often the interactions go both ways between overall reform and SOE sector reform.

The analysis of these interactions poses, however, the problem of what is meant by SOE sector reform. In the World Bank BIB Report (World Bank 1995) this term is used to encompass a large spectrum of actions including privatization and divestiture, privatization with regulation, management contracts, performance contracts, and improved public ownership and management.[1] Obviously, the type and content of interaction between any of these types of SOE reform and other aspects of reform may be different and has to be assessed carefully.

The BIB Report finds that the success of reform shows a strong positive correlation to success in the different types of a SOE reform package. Criteria for success are related to basic financial and economic indicators, namely financial performance, productivity and the savings–investment deficit. The report shows that the effects of the different components of SOE reform tend to be in the same direction. This finding helps simplify the analysis in as much as one does not have to look into the interactions of reforms and each type of SOE reform action separately. This issue will be returned to later.

This chapter presents a complete summary of the various interactions between SOE sector reform and other reforms, based on the BIB Report which emphasizes the effects of other reforms on SOE reform, but with a more comprehensive assessment of the interactions. It also presents an institutional economics analysis of SOE reform based both on transaction costs and political economy considerations. The focus will be on the importance of the size of the

SOE sector and the extent of inefficiencies and costs associated with it. These factors are crucial for understanding the interactions between other reforms and SOE sector reform. Finally, the chapter looks into some of the implications of the analysis for SOE sector reform in the MENA region.

Overall reform and SOE reform

The BIB Report deals extensively with the interactions between SOE reform and other aspects of overall reform programmes. The focus of attention, however, is on the influences of the latter on SOE reform. SOE reform has in itself important effects on other aspects of a reform package and can play a significant role in the implementation process of overall reform programmes. Before turning to these issues it will be useful to have at hand a brief description of a global reform programme of the type implemented in developing countries in the recent past. This will help in analysing the interactions between the various aspects of reform packages and SOE sector reform.

A prototype global reform programme

A typical encompassing programme of reform includes a set of policies and the building of institutions designed to achieve macroeconomic stability on one hand, and a complete framework for the efficient functioning of a market system in an open economy on the other hand. SOE reform is part of such a global package with the aim of improving overall efficiency and developing the role of the private sector. The design, initiation and implementation of such programmes have to take into consideration the specifics of countries, but some general features have been found to be crucial in the improvement of the performance of developing countries, even though issues of the timing and sequencing of reforms continue to be debated.

The macroeconomy

At the level of the macroeconomy institutional reform is basically concerned with a few major issues that are crucial for attaining the basic objectives of macroeconomic stability and creating overall favourable conditions for growth and development.

The issue of choosing a nominal anchor for domestic money in order to establish price stability is of primary importance in the design of macro policy. It often takes the form of choosing an exchange rate system, that is, pegging domestic money to one currency or a basket of foreign currencies. Closely related issues are the independence of the central bank and the credibility of fiscal policy.

The credibility of fiscal policy is largely dependent on the enforcement of hard budget constraints in the public sector. Whether for the government, the central bank or the banking sector, mechanisms and controls have to be established so as to actually enforce hard budget constraints. Those constraints in turn have strong implications for the enforcement of hard budget constraints on firms, and on state-owned enterprises in particular.

The development of an efficient tax administration is another major component of a successful framework for macro management; it is a prerequisite for a good and credible fiscal policy.

Bank supervision is another aspect of institutional reform at the macro level. The elaboration, publication and enforcement of rules and norms of prudent management and behaviour by the banking system are important for the establishment of a stable system and the implementation of an effective monetary policy.

Opening the economy

Trade liberalization is a central component of the programme, and implies elimination of quantitative restrictions on imports, the reduction in the level and variance of tariffs on imports, and a pro-export policy. It aims at making the economy integrated in the world markets with domestic producers facing foreign competition.

Capital account liberalization allows integration of the domestic capital market into world markets, and implies the lifting of controls on capital movements. The extent and content as well as the timing and sequencing of the lifting of controls have been variable in practice and contentious in theory.

Developing competitive markets

An institutional framework for competitive markets, requires a set of laws, rules and regulations that eliminate restrictions to entry, enforce anti-monopoly and anti-dominant position conditions, and enhance liberalized price competition. Price controls are to be lifted, investment is to be liberalized and the institutional framework for competitive markets developed.

If there are to be incentive mechanisms aiming at affecting resource allocation, through investment in particular, they should be made so as to imply the least distortions, and address directly the various market failures they are supposed to remedy.

Financial sector reform

This aspect of reform packages includes a large set of measures and policies with the following important components:

- Improved supervision and regulation; discussed above in the context of the macroeconomic framework.
- Reduction or elimination of the direct role of government in credit allocation and overall resources of the banking system; and of control of interest rates.

- Strengthened capacity of financial system to allocate capital on a commercial basis; development of capital markets, for debt or equity, in order to diversify sources of finance and create a favourable environment for financial innovation; monitoring of performance of firms and managers; and efficient mobilization of savings.

Labour market reform

The objective of labour market reform is usually to reduce the prevalent rigidities and increase the capacity of adjustment by firms in a competitive environment.

Poverty and social protection

Reform programmes may include policies for poverty reduction and protection of the less favoured segments of society. Social policies may vary considerably from country to country, but they can provide for minimum health coverage and work interruption insurance schemes.

Institutions for the firm and the private sector

The development of an adequate institutional framework for the development of the firm and the private sector includes a wide range of laws, rules and regulations relating to the delimitation and enforcement of property rights, a well functioning judiciary, modern company law, and so on.

SOE reform

The SOE sector reform involves at least three components: divestiture or transfer of ownership of assets from the public to the private sector, imposition of hard budget constraints on state-owned enterprises which remain in the public sector, and efforts at improved performance of management.

Effects of other reforms on SOE reform

The main effects of various components of an overall reform package on SOE sector reform, extensively discussed in the BIB Report, can be analysed in terms of political economy considerations and effectiveness of reforms. The following sections summarize the arguments found in the report and point out a number of other effects that may be relevant for the implementation of SOE reform.

Political economy considerations: desirability and feasibility of SOE reform

The implementation of reforms in other areas is supposed to unleash pressures that are of significance for SOE reform, and which take place mostly in the political arena.

Desirability of SOE reform from the political leadership point of view can be promoted through positive pressures for reform from groups that benefit from it or from wide ranging gains that can be of value for the leadership. In the BIB Report, four types of reform are found to be of importance in this context. The requirements of a credible fiscal policy as well as the initiation of financial reform induce pressures for reduction of public deficits in general and deficits of public enterprises in particular. Easing of trade restrictions and removal of barriers to entry create a more competitive environment which makes more explicit the costs of protecting SOEs and subjects them to the constraints of market competition.

Additional effects not discussed in the BIB Report can also be relevant. The introduction of a nominal anchor such as exchange rate pegging, which often requires prior adjustment, eliminates the implicit subsidies from foreign exchange overvaluation, if price stabilization is firmly achieved. Favourable discounting windows from the central bank become more strict or non-available. Fiscal policy reform implies also more effective tax collection, especially with respect to SOEs, which would make them more effectively subject to payment of taxes as well as social security contributions.

The feasibility of SOE reform is related to the costs of reform and to the political pressures opposing it. The concern here is with accompanying reforms that may help withstand and dilute the opposition, especially from employees of the public sector. Some measures are part of a reform package for the SOE sector, such as compensation schemes to reduce overstaffing, or measures to make SOE jobs more demanding by punishing all kinds of labour shirking or siphoning of goods and property; but some other reforms may help mitigate the opposition, such as the elimination of obstacles to private job creation so as to give employment opportunities for SOE employees. The development of alternative social security schemes which encourage labour mobility and decouple the link between SOE jobs and social services also help to reduce opposition to reform. The development of training programmes to help retrain workers who lose their jobs is also important.

Effectiveness: making for success in SOE reform

A number of factors are pointed out in the BIB report as contributing to the success of an SOE reform package some of which are directly part of SOE reform. First, divestiture is found to be strongly related to the success of SOE reform. Second, the imposition of hard budget constraints on SOEs through the phasing out of direct transfers, the improvement of pricing mechanisms, the curbing of hidden subsidies and of easy access to credit are also important. A further important component consists of the reform of the relationship between government and SOE managers through improved supervision institutions, increased management autonomy and explicit performance agreements.

However, of even more importance are two other forms of reform that are found to be highly significant for the success of SOE reform, namely competition policy and financial sector reform.

The development of competition in the internal markets and through outside opening creates pressures and mechanisms that enhance the success of SOE reform, first by making divestiture appear as the most attractive option of reform in order to avoid protection and subsidies to SOEs in a competitive environment. Second, competition creates pressures for the improved performance of remaining SOEs by making explicit the costs of supporting them, and by providing information on managers' performance as compared to other firms operating in the same markets.

Financial sector reform has probably the most significant impact on SOE reform, for it encourages enforcement of hard budget constraints on public sector enterprises. It also makes privatization easier by making mobilization of resources through the financial system more readily available and plays a role in the assessment of entrepreneurs and the better overseeing of managers. More indirectly, financial sector reform helps develop competition through easier entry into markets, thereby affecting SOE reform.

SOE reform effects on other reforms

SOE reform can be an important vehicle for the successful adoption and implementation of other reforms. The interactions are of a dynamic character and may produce positive feedback in reform processes.

First, SOE reform, when successful, eliminates one major source of fiscal instability, through the reduction of fiscal deficits and their better predictability. Since financing of public enterprise deficits is often disguised or hidden, this gives more transparency and credibility to fiscal deficit figures whether actual or predicted. If divestiture results in significant revenues for the government this may help improve the fiscal position and even allow public debt reduction.

Second, since the banking system is often burdened by an important SOE non-performing portfolio, reform of public enterprises contributes to the improvement of the financial situation of banks and to the respect of prudential regulations and ratios. Hence, financial sector reform is positively affected by SOE reforms.

Third, when SOE reform includes the sale of equity to the public through the stock market it often contributes very effectively to the development of capital markets and the visibility of their role in the allocation of financial resources. The emergence of a large shareholder group allows the deepening of the stock market and contributes to its maturity.

Fourth, competition in domestic markets is enhanced by SOE reform, since it implies the disappearance of open or covert discrimination in pricing policies, public procurement, taxation and so on. Private firms thereby find themselves operating on a level playing field and are less prone to ask for special treatment and market-distorting favours.

Fifth, reform of the public enterprise sector may also contribute to the improvement of the labour markets if it results in weakened labour unions and a greater acceptance of labour flexibility. Since SOE reform itself often includes an important component of labour shedding it helps actors to more readily understand the needs of restructuring even by private firms.

However, it should be noted that botched SOE reforms can also give rise to negative feedback on other reforms. Its implementation may cause the postponement, change and even reversal of reforms. When public enterprise reforms are found to imply high costs of adjustment in the labour markets and lead to strong opposition by labour unions, they may thwart the reform of labour markets in general. Also, when privatization leads to the development of private monopoly positions in some activities, this reduces the credibility of government policy in support of competition and its acceptance by the private sector which has vested interest in non-competitive markets.

Size, inefficiencies and SOE sector reform

The discussion in the previous section shows many interrelations between the various aspects of a reform programme and SOE reform. The initiation, implementation and success of SOE reform programmes are to a large extent a function of the other reforms; However, the discussion, as in the BIB Report, is only suggestive of the types of interactions and does not give any indication about their possible strength and significance which obviously vary from country to country.

One hypothesis suggests that major determinants of the power and significance of the interactions with other reforms are the size of the public sector and the extent of the inefficiencies and costs that are associated with it. These factors are particularly important for the MENA region where they are especially prominent and play a crucial role in the reform process.

The analysis of these factors can be made using the two main approaches found in institutional economics literature, namely transaction costs and collective action or political economy considerations.[2]

Transaction costs and SOE reform

The state-owned enterprise

The arguments and rationale for SOEs were based, in early development economics literature and the practice of development policy, on market failures and the limitations of a private sector decentralized market process. The validity of these arguments has been questioned and ways of dealing with them were developed which mostly show that public enterprises are not the most efficient mechanism. This chapter does not review this debate, but only uses these arguments about SOEs as a starting point in its analysis.

From the perspective of transaction costs theory, institutions such as firms or markets or contracts, appear or are created as arrangements for minimizing transaction costs.[3] The latter concept is used in the broad sense of the total cost of organizing, monitoring and enforcing the rules of an institutional arrangement

(Lin and Nugent 1995). These costs may be *ex-ante* to the arrangement or *ex-post*, and they can be directly or indirectly related to the arrangement.

In terms of transaction costs theory a SOE can be seen as an institutional arrangement that is cost-minimizing. In addition to the basic factors behind the emergence of the firm in general as a cost-minimizing arrangement in the sense of Williamson (1985), SOEs are also meant to minimize coordination costs stemming from a number of market failures and costs of achieving some distributional objectives.

First, they allow the benefits to be realized of externalities that are difficult to capture by privately-owned firms and for the provision of public goods. While not captured by the firm itself these benefits accrue to society with such an institutional arrangement. This happens in developing countries at the early stages of development, for instance, when a new activity is undertaken with the required training and innovation. This applies also for the provision of public goods which would require otherwise more costly arrangements for their production and consumption.

Second, in the context of developing countries with non-existent or weak capital markets and strong aversion to risk at low levels of income, a comprehensive public enterprises creation programme may be a vehicle for pooling risk and overcoming the failures of the private sector in undertaking new activities.

Third, SOEs may be a vehicle for attaining distributional objectives at lower cost than the usual tax and transfer arrangements. Costs and difficulties of tax collection are known, but also targeting of transfers to the preferred groups is not easy through budgetary means. Public enterprises can be a convenient arrangement for the distribution of such benefits by generating employment, higher wages, various side-benefits, and so on.

While helping to solve the preceding problems and economizing in this sense, a state-owned enterprise creates its own incentive system because of its ownership. Ownership by the state gives rise to effective interest by a variety of stakeholders in addition to the state: its management, employees, suppliers and customers and the political establishment. This implies costs due to the prevalence of asymmetries of information and opportunistic behaviour involving the various stakeholders. The institutional framework of the SOEs has to be completed in order to deal with these problems.

Completing the arrangement

Dealing with the opportunistic behaviour and the specific incentives created by public ownership requires a complete institutional framework for SOEs. Besides the usual rules relating to firms in general, there is a need for specific additional constraints regulating relations within the firm, between managers and owners or the state, and the firm and the market environment.

Within the firm various rules and regulations have to be instituted in order to reduce the costs due to opportunistic behaviour from the different groups. Such controls apply to recruitment, procurement and sales, wages and pay incentives.

The controls and rules tend to become increasingly rigid and complex as ways are found to get around them. While helping to deal with opportunistic behaviour, these rules and regulations reduce the ability of the firm to adapt easily and rapidly to changing market conditions.

The extent of autonomy of managers in decision-making is controlled through submission of various decisions and activities such as investment, borrowing, expansion and contraction of activities and so on, to prior approval. Specialized committees or direct government approvals are required. Attempts are made to find incentive systems for managers and to reach a clear delimitation of responsibilities. Various institutional schemes for the management of public enterprises are tried such as holding organizations of different types.

The absence of domestic as well as foreign competition in many situations provides opportunities for SOEs to exploit dominant market positions through higher price or lower quality. The institutional framework is then completed with regulations including price controls, detailed quality rules, relations with suppliers and customers.

Inefficiencies and costs

While the setting-up of state-owned enterprises initially aims at minimizing some transaction costs, it is the complete institutional set-up that is relevant. This set-up implies additional costs of different kinds.

X-inefficiency has received the most attention and relates to the choice of inefficient techniques and the waste of resources. Leibenstein (1989) applies this approach to state enterprises in developing countries, but other costs, such as those of monitoring inside and outside the firm, are also important. The existence of possibilities for above market rewards stimulates rent-seeking whether for jobs in public enterprises, for procurement, social benefits, the finance of sales, and so on. The costs to society of rent-seeking rises with the extent of competition for such rents and their resulting dissipation.

Other indirect costs of public enterprises include those resulting from the macroeconomic effects of financing deficits, the labour market rigidities that develop in the public sector, and the crowding-out of more productive private investment.

As for other kinds of administrative controls and regulations, it has been observed that this set-up tends to become increasingly complex and costly. The number of rules, regulations, and administrative bodies increases in order to deal with the more sophisticated forms of opportunistic behaviour. The complexity and cost thereof also increase with the size of the public sector itself. The increases in costs and in inefficiency lead to demands for changes in institutional arrangements.

Other reforms and costs

The implementation of different reforms can have an impact on the costs and inefficiencies of the SOE sector. Some of the effects may be cost reducing while others may be cost increasing, but in most cases they make them transparent.[4] This enhances the demand for changing the institutional arrangements.

Trade liberalization and competitive domestic markets may induce greater efficiency and improved performance of public enterprises.[5] They allow possible reductions in the costs of monitoring of managers performance by comparing their performance with that of competing private firms. Reduced rents because of competition or labour market reform, may result in less rent-seeking and welfare gains. Financial sector reform induces better screening and controls from banks and improved decisions and performance, since banks are more commercially oriented in their decisions and less likely to be influenced by political decisions.

These gains are found empirically relevant, as the performance of SOEs is generally superior under conditions of competition. However, these reforms may also result in increased costs when enterprises turn out to be non-competitive, lose market share and show decreased productivity.

The most significant effect, however, of other reforms is to make costs of the public sector more transparent. A number of these costs are often hidden and non-apparent and the various reforms through different channels make them more apparent. A number of hidden subsidies disappear or have to be supported by the budget directly: lower than market interest rates, higher prices paid by the government or consumers through the protection or administered prices, unpaid taxes and social security contributions, government guaranteed domestic or foreign credit, overvalued exchange rates and fixed exchange rate foreign debt. Inversely, contributions of SOEs to the finance of government activities become more transparent such as unpaid bills or unpaid subsidies due to government decisions to support reduced prices for some goods and services.

The political economy of privatization

While the various mechanisms in the political economy of SOE reform were suggested earlier, a complete framework of analysis of use for understanding such interactions is now presented. This section will emphasize one aspect of SOE reform, namely privatization. The political economy arguments discussed are essentially applicable to this type of reform and are based on the theory of collective action. In this approach interest groups play a central role in influencing policy, but their success in collective action depends on their ability to overcome the free-rider problem and on the costs of coordination and monitoring of the groups.[6] Some favourable factors for successful collective action are group characteristics such as limited size, homogeneity in origin and goals, an even distribution of benefits, geographical concentration, and the possibility of using selective incentives.

The analytical framework will be couched in terms of political pressure for and against reform, and it is the relative strength of these pressures that determines the outcome in terms of policy decisions for privatization. The approach and the features of this analysis are very similar to the type of analysis found in the context of many policy choices like trade liberalization or exchange rate policies and so on. The main characteristic is the asymmetry found in the determinants of pressures for and against change. This asymmetry implies a bias in favour of the status-quo in general, and has been widely applied in the context of trade reform.[7] The application to SOE reform has been less common, but has increasingly been used (Suleiman and Waterbury 1990b). An important issue that has received quite a lot of attention in the discussion of reforms is that of gradualism versus the big-bang type of approach. The arguments hinge on a number of considerations such as complementarities between different reforms costs of reversibility of reforms and the possibilities of building constituencies in favour of reform.[8] The following discussion can better be understood in the context of a gradualist programme of reform, and many of the arguments are on how to build pressures for reform.

Pressure for privatization

There are very few organized groups that lobby for SOE reform and privatization. The large size, non-homogeneity and dispersion of the beneficiaries of SOE reform are not favourable to the appearance of organized pressure groups. The beneficiaries include such diverse components of society as consumers who support the costs of state-owned enterprises, in terms of the higher price and lower quality of products and services; the private sector which is discriminated against in various ways; investors and firms crowded-out from the financial system by SOEs; taxpayers who have in the final analysis to pay for the deficits; and so on.

Only two groups are potentially active in favour of privatization. The first are foreign creditors who are interested in improved performance in order to increase the likelihood of reimbursement. The second are private domestic and foreign investors who are potential buyers of state-owned assets, and who perceive profitable investment opportunities. These possess some favourable characteristics, in particular they tend to have information about SOEs not available to other groups, and may be active in promoting privatization.[9]

An interesting issue is whether the banking sector can be an active promoter of privatization. Since banks often support a large part of the financial burden of public enterprises in the form of non-performing loans, they may be interested in their reform and in particular privatization. However, they are more likely to be ambivalent about the process since they would prefer the government to bail out public firms and thereby reduce the extent of provisions and loss-taking that is needed to clean their balance sheets.

It is through political leadership that pressure for privatization is most likely to be effective, since it can better assess the benefits from privatization and – since they are widely dispersed – can better internalize them in the form of political capital. Such benefits can take various forms such as overcoming a financial crisis or improved overall economic performance. However benefits can also be essentially in the political arena with a change of the support base from that of previous regimes who catered to SOEs, to a new support base including a wide shareholders group, or the reduced power of unions (Starr 1990). The leaders' ability to constitute new coalitions to replace the preceding dominant one is of crucial significance to the success and irreversibility of SOE and other reforms.

The extent of the pressure for privatization as essentially perceived by the political leadership, as well as a restricted group of bureaucrats, and supported by such groups as foreign creditors or the domestic private sector would depend essentially on the potential benefits of privatization. But these benefits are inversely related to the welfare cost of the public sector. This cost is a function of the relative size of the sector and of the extent of the costs and inefficiencies. The relative size of the public sector may be measured by its share in gross domestic product (GDP) for instance. The costs and inefficiencies associated with the public sector can be measured by the social welfare cost per unit of resources (unit of value added can be a proxy) used in the public sector and includes all of the costs discussed above. The total relative cost would then be the product of the relative size and the unit cost, and is equal to the total welfare cost as a share of GDP.

The relationship between this variable and pressure for reform is shown in graphical form in Figure 2.1.[10] When the cost of the public sector is low, there are no perceived political benefits from privatization, and pressure in its favour is limited. As the relative cost increases the pressure for reform might even decrease initially for some range of the cost as the leadership may feel that it does not want to face the beneficiaries of SOEs who are becoming well organized and effective in defending their interests. Then as costs become significant and as they increase, the political leadership more clearly perceives the benefits of reducing these ineffi- ciencies and of improving performance in order to strengthen their power base and make it more enduring. At some point, the pressure for reform starts to increase very rapidly as illustrated in the figure. The process that allows the pressure to be effective may vary according to the nature of the political regime, whether demo- cratic or authoritarian, but the effects should remain relevant.

Pressure against privatization

Contrary to the benefits from privatization, the costs are more concentrated and groups opposing it are more readily organized.

The group most likely to be opposing reform, particularly privatization, are public sector employees and the labour unions. SOE reform, whether in the form of divestiture or improved management and reduced deficits, often implies labour shedding, reduced wages and benefits – open or hidden – and more work discipline. Since unions are readily active in the public sector, homogeneity is present and costs of organizing are low, political pressure opposing privatization will therefore be present.

Other groups which may oppose privatization are the political groups that use SOE as a vehicle for distribution of favours and patronage whether in the form of jobs, social benefits or political contributions. Whether political parties or the politico-administrative establishment, such groups are likely to be opponents of privatization.

Pressure

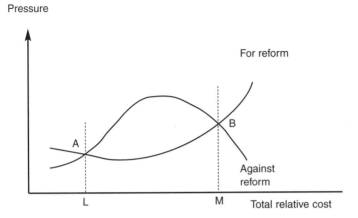

Figure 2.1 The political economy of privatization

There has been some debate as to whether managers of state-owned enterprises might constitute an active group opposing privatization (Suleiman and Waterbury 1990a). One could argue that the group is homogeneous, interacts easily and is linked to the political establishment that opposes privatization, and may lose jobs or benefits. On the other hand, another argument shows managers less likely to oppose privatization, since they themselves may benefit from it, whether by acquiring enterprises themselves or working for private investors. They may also favour modifying the relationship between the capital owner of the enterprises, the state, and themselves in order to insulate themselves from excessive interference and be able to perform their management tasks more effectively.

The pressure against privatization is represented in Figure 2.1 as a function of the total relative cost to society of the SOE sector. At the low end both the size of the public sector and its inefficiency are small. The dominance of the private sector means strong competition and not much scope for rents for the SOEs, and little reason to work hard to protect them. The small size of the SOE sector allows better monitoring and transparency, which again reduces the opportunities for rents: groups of beneficiaries would be too small to be effective, and pressure would be weak. However, after some threshold of cost, which would be relatively low, opposition would increase rapidly. The size of the public sector and the inefficiency, which is in part captured as rent by the beneficiaries, become larger and the pressure stronger. Group characteristics favour strong action by the beneficiaries. However, as the total cost increases, such pressure may start diminishing at some point. The size of the public sector becomes too large and the groups lose their homogeneity and effectiveness to organize. Conflicts may arise among groups who may perceive that they are not receiving their fair share of the rents. The increased inefficiencies become so high they reduce the potential gains, as enterprises become unable to provide the benefits that make them useful.[11]

Outcomes

Figure 2.1 is useful for understanding the political economy of privatization, but it calls for more explanation. It is important to point out that the curves are meant to apply to a given country with a given set of characteristics that determine the respective positions of the curves. Such characteristics may pertain to the political structure of decision making, the level of development, the extent of competition in the economy and so on. For instance, even at the low end of cost, if private monopolies are dominant in the country, pressure against privatization may be stronger because of worries about increased monopoly power by the private sector.

From Figure 2.1, it can be seen that for a given country in a given situation there are two threshold levels of relative cost of the public sector along the X-axis. If costs are sufficiently low, that is, lower than L, or are sufficiently large or higher than M, the pressure for reform dominates and privatization is highly likely to be initiated and to be successfully implemented. However, for the large range of cost from L to M, opposition to reform is very strong and there is a tendency for the status quo to prevail.

The significance of the two points of crossing of the curves is interesting. At both points pressures for and against are of equivalent strength and the outcome is indeterminate, but they have different dynamic characteristics. Even though they cannot have the significance of market equilibria, one can interpret them in a similar way in a kind of political market. Point A, at the lower end, can be characterized as 'unstable', for movements away from it are reinforcing. For instance, if there is a movement to the right, opposition to reform dominates and the size or unit cost of the public sector would tend to increase, moving farther away from A. On the other hand point B is 'stable', in the sense that there is a tendency for such situations of 'desired but not implemented change' to prevail. For instance, a movement away from B towards the left, means that some reform reducing the size or the cost of the public sector is undertaken. But this initial step of reform reinforces opposition, reform is blocked and either the size or the cost will tend to increase again. Point B can be interpreted as a 'large public sector trap' situation, and breaking away from it may require 'revolutionary changes'.

While strictly speaking a graphical representation, such as in Figure 2.1, is valid for a given country we can use it to illustrate cross-country experience. Assuming that relevant country characteristics are not too different, the threshold levels L and M would apply for describing possible outcomes in different countries.[12] When the total relative cost of the public sector is low, there is high likelihood for initiation and the success of privatization. In a country such as Japan – where the public sector was small and inefficiencies not important – privatization was not a significant issue, and the leadership was able to carry its programme without difficulty.

Let us consider, as a useful hypothesis for discussion, that the lower limit of the middle range is associated with a share of SOE activity in GDP of 10 per cent.[13] While this ratio measures only the relative size of the SOE sector, we suppose that the associated unit costs are appropriate to make for this threshold. The below 10 per cent range would include such developed countries as Japan, Belgium, Spain, the United Kingdom and Germany.[14] The privatization programme of the UK is well known, but significant programmes have also taken place in the other countries. Among developing countries belonging to this range, privatization transactions were very active: Argentina, Turkey, Brazil and the Philippines.

On the other hand, when the total relative cost of the public sector becomes very large, and exceeds a level which we may suppose to be associated with a 50 per cent share of SOE sector in GDP, pressure for reform becomes sufficiently strong to overcome resistance. A political consensus may appear in favour of reform because of the large potential gains that outweigh the short-term costs of the opposition by specific interest groups. This may describe the situation of East European countries and the reforms undertaken after the fall of communist regimes. However, as the discussion about the 'stability' of point B suggests, mass privatization reform requires a large political shift in order for it to be implemented without reversal.

An interesting aspect of this analysis is the existence of a large range of total relative cost where the status quo of no-privatization prevails. It includes many countries in Latin America, Africa and the MENA region. Pressure against reform is sufficiently strong as to make the likelihood of reform very small even when the benefits from it are perceived to exist at the level of the leadership.

Affecting the likelihood of privatization

We can now recast the arguments about the interactions between other reforms and SOE reform in terms of Figure 2.1. Various types of measures and policy reforms can be used in order to shift the curves shown in the diagram and increase the likelihood of privatization. The objective is to shift the curve of 'pressure for reform' up and the curve of 'pressure against reform' down so as to reduce the range of the no-privatization outcomes.

From our analysis of the costs and inefficiencies of the SOE sector and the way they are influenced by reforms, we can infer some political economy effects. The most significant impact is the enhanced transparency of the costs and inefficiencies which helps shift upward the curve of 'pressure for reform' through more awareness from the leadership of the potential gains. It has been observed also in the analysis of various kinds of reform that the appearance of economic crisis helps focus the attention and clarify the significant benefits from reform. This factor applies to privatization.[15]

The reduced inefficiencies due to reform have also the implication of reducing the stakes for the beneficiaries from the SOE sector rents and benefits, thereby reducing opposition. This shifts the 'opposition to reform' curve downwards. The net outcome for a given country would depend both on the shift in the curves and the movement along the horizontal axis of the country due to the changed size of the public sector and of its inefficiency.[16]

For most countries in the no-privatization range the effect of a reduction of the range dominates and privatization becomes more likely. It is in terms of the association with other significant reforms that explains why some countries with a larger than 10 per cent share of SOE have carried out strong privatization programmes, such as Chile, Mexico and Pakistan.[17] We can also interpret the strong privatization programmes in France and Portugal as being associated with the implementation of the single market in Europe in the late 1980s and early 1990s, despite the size of the SOE sector.[18]

Implications for the MENA region

The previous analysis cannot be used to make predictions about the outcomes for specific countries, since it is difficult to have the precise positions of the curves about the political economy of privatization and even to have an exact measure of the total relative cost of the SOE sector. However, it can be used to infer some general implications for SOE reform in the MENA region.

Privatization

The importance of the SOE sector in countries of the MENA region is one of its characteristics, and it has been associated with below average overall economic performance in terms of total growth and productivity growth, compared to other developing countries. In terms of Figure 2.1 and the assumptions used above, most MENA countries would be found in the intermediate or upper range as the figures in Table 2.1 for countries for which data on the share of SOE sector in GDP are available show.

If the figures of the relative size are weighted by the extent of the inefficiencies and costs of the SOE sector they would clearly confirm that most of the MENA region countries are to be found in the middle range, with possibly two countries, Algeria and Sudan, in the upper range.

The first implication is that there is a strong bias in favour of the status quo in the region and maintenance of the SOE sector with little or no-privatization. The strong role of the SOE in the existing political coalitions and the high level of unemployment in the region make for strong opposition to reform.

The second implication is that it is crucial to associate SOE sector reform with other reforms in the region, in order to overcome resistance to privatization and induce a stronger commitment by the leadership. The various mechanisms discussed in the chapter have to be brought to bear in order to increase the likelihood of privatization. It is not surprising that the limited privatization that took place in the region was mostly in Morocco and Tunisia, and was strongly associated with comprehensive reform programmes. Algeria provides an interesting case for analysis given the size and the well-known costs of the Algerian public sector.[19] There have been repeated declarations of political commitment in that direction, but little action has taken place in terms of privatization until recently. This suggests that Algeria may be trapped in the 'large public sector no-

Table 2.1 Share of the SOE sector in GDP, various countries

Algeria	64.6
Egypt	34.1
Mauritania	25.0
Morocco	18.0
Sudan	48.2
Tunisia	30.2

Source: World Bank 1995: 268–71.

reform' situation discussed above. Also the oil factor has to be taken into account in this case, for the existence of important oil revenues reduces the incentives of the leadership for reform. Such revenues, like foreign aid, allow the government to support the cost of the inefficiencies longer and imply post-ponement of privatization. The decline in the oil and gas revenues in the late 1980s and early 1990s was associated with increased interest in SOE sector reform, but the recent improvement in expected revenues may again lower interest in reform.

The example of Algeria brings out the oil factor in the MENA region. The existence of oil revenues and the ever present expectation of their increase biases even more the situation in favour of no-reform. This applies to the many countries of the region where oil revenue is the most significant resource.

Other SOE reforms

While the analysis of the political economy of reform was made for privatization, the other aspects are relevant for SOE sector reform in general. It has been pointed out in the introduction that the BIB Report found an association between divestiture and other components of SOE reform such as the enforcement of hard budget constraints or the introduction of institutional arrangements for the improvement of performance of management.

This distinction is particularly relevant for MENA countries, where contrary to privatization, attempts at other kinds of SOE reform have been numerous. The size and extent of the costs in the region have long been noticed by political leaders, who in the face of resistance have attempted to improve the performance without significant divestiture. These attempts are numerous and were sometimes wide ranging in many countries. In some cases they included limited privatization or more often liquidation of the worst performing enterprises. While no complete review and assessment of these attempts is available, reference to a few cases such as Egypt or Tunisia show that the gains from such attempts have been minimal.[20]

The transaction costs approach as well as experience world-wide and regionally show that not much can be expected from SOE reform if it does not include privatization on a large scale, at least of firms operating in competitive markets. The significant reduction of the size of the SOE sector is itself a prerequisite for possible improvement of the performance of what might remain in the public sector.

The sequencing of reforms

One major implication of the analysis is the existence of 'positive feedbacks' or 'virtuous circles' of reform between privatization and other aspects of structural reform. The question arises then as to the appropriate sequencing of reforms and particularly the issue of where to start, given that each individual reform would be subject to resistance and opposition. While the answer would be specific for each country depending on the relative strength of the various interest groups and the impact of the reforms, some general propositions may be made. In addition to the economic arguments about sequencing, from the political economy point of view the design of the reform package should aim at giving priority to reforms that have the most impact and with the least resistance. It follows that foreign trade liberalization and domestic competition would come first in a country with a large public sector and strong opposition to privatization. In addition to the fact that such reforms are simpler and can be implemented more easily and faster, the opposition to them may be overcome more readily. Financial sector reform is the next most crucial component of the package, and may usefully be implemented prior to privatization. These reforms help to a large extent to make privatization and SOE sector reform possible and contribute to their success.

Notes

This chapter is based on a paper presented at the Economic Research Forum (ERF) workshop on 'the changing size and role of SOEs in MENA region' held in Amman, Jordan in May 1996. Useful comments and discussion by participants at the workshop are gratefully acknowledged. We are also indebted to Jeffrey Nugent for useful comments and suggestions.

1 The term 'BIB Report' is used in this chapter to designate the World Bank (1995) document, *Bureaucrats in Business: The Economics and Politics of Government.*
2 For surveys of the approach see Nabli and Nugent (1989) and Lin and Nugent (1995). Rodrik (1996) gives an up-to-date survey of the issues of political economy of reform.
3 Institutions are defined by Lin and Nugent (1995) as 'a set of humanly devised behavioral rules that govern and shape interactions of human beings, in part in helping them to form expectations of what other people will do'.
4 It is noticable that some of the reforms undermine the validity of the use of SOEs as an institution for transaction costs minimization discussed above. For example, the case of the development of capital markets and financial sector reform.
5 Leibenstein (1989) discusses some of these effects for the reduction of X-inefficiency.
6 Demand factors for policy change are emphasized here, based on Olson (1965) and Hardin (1982). A complete analysis would also take into consideration supply factors by politicians. The framework presented here takes account of these factors but in a different way.
7 The standard arguments can be found in Baldwin (1985), Bhagwati (1988) and Nabli (1990). Alternative theoretical arguments are presented by Fernandez and Rodrik (1991) who explain the bias in favour of the status-quo by the uncertainty regarding

the distribution of gains and losses from reform, and by Alesina and Drazen (1991) who explain delayed reform by attempts of interest groups to make others bear most of the costs of reform in the presence of uncertainty about those costs for each group.

8 Dewatripont and Roland (1995) give a formal analysis supporting gradualism as against big-bang approaches to reform.

9 The role of the World Bank and IMF may be cited in supporting privatization and coordinating action by foreign creditors.

10 The following graphical representation can be made separately for either the size of the public sector or the unit welfare cost of SOEs as the variable on the X-axis. The shapes of the curves of pressure for and against reform would be similar, allowing their 'aggregation' which makes the arguments stronger and the graphics simpler.

11 That the curve has to slope downwards after some point, can be seen from the following argument. The movement along the X-axis means that the public sector is becoming increasingly large, and the interest groups become more encompassing. They would then tend to internalize both the costs and the benefits of reform, and as the costs increase pressure against reform becomes weaker. See Olson (1982) for such a proposition.

12 When comparing two countries there is movement along the X-axis, but also across different curves of pressure for and against reform, and thresholds are different. But we assume here that there is a low level 'clustering' of thresholds and a high level for the various countries.

13 The limit may well be lower than 10 per cent in many cases where the SOE sector plays a larger role in the prevailing political coalitions.

14 According to the data in appendix Table A.1 of the BIB Report (World Bank 1995) and referring to the average for the period 1978–91.

15 See figure 4 in Anderson (1995). The share of SOE in economic activity for these countries is as follows: Turkey 7.5, Brazil 6.5, Argentina 4.7, the Philippines 1.9.

16 It is sometimes also pointed out that structural adjustment with stabilization, when it implies more unemployment and reduced real wages, may make the leadership less favourable to reform of public enterprises, which often includes shedding of labour.

17 Even though for these countries the share was not much different from 10 per cent.

18 Although again the size was not much larger than 10 per cent for these cases.

19 This analysis may also be applicable to Sudan.

20 Waterbury (1990) clearly arrives at such a conclusion for Egypt and the other countries in his study, namely Mexico, Turkey and India.

Bibliography

Alesina, A. and Drazen, A. (1991) 'Why are stabilizations delayed?', *American Economic Review*, December: vol. 81, no. 5: 1170–88.

Anderson, R. (1995) 'Privatization in the Middle East and North Africa', paper presented at workshop on 'Strategic visions for the Middle East and North Africa', Gammarath, Tunisia, 9–11 June.

Baldwin, R. E. (1985) *The Political Economy of US Import Policy,* Cambridge, Mass.: MIT Press.

Bhagwati, J. (1988) *Protectionism*, Cambridge, Mass.: MIT Press.

Dewatripont, M. and Roland, G. (1995) 'The design of reform packages under uncertainty', *American Economic Review,* December, vol. 85, no. 5: 1207–23.

Fernandez, R. and Rodrik, D. (1991) 'Resistance to reform: status-quo bias in the presence of individual-specific uncertainty', *American Economic Review*, vol. 81, no. 5: 1146–55.

Hardin R. (1982) *Collective Action*, Washington, D.C.: Resources for the Future.

Leibenstein, H. (1989) 'Organizational economics and institutions as missing elements in economic development analysis', *World Development*, vol. 17, no. 9: 1361–73.

Lin, J. Y. and Nugent, J. B. (1995) 'Institutions and economic development', in J. Behrman and T. N. Srinivasan (eds), *Handbook of Development Economics*, vol. 3, Netherlands: Elsevier Science.

Nabli, M. K. (1990) 'The political economy of trade liberalization in developing countries', *Open Economies Review* 1: 111–45.

Nabli, M. K. and Nugent, J. B. (1989) 'The new institutional economics and its applicability to development', *World Development*, September: vol. 17, no. 9: 1333–48.

Olson, M. (1965) *The Logic of Collective Action*, Cambridge, Mass.: Harvard University Press.

—— (1982) *The Rise and Decline of Nations*, New Haven and London: Yale University Press.

Rodrik, D. (1996) 'Understanding economic policy reform', *Journal of Economic Literature*, March: vol. 34, no. 1: 9–41.

Starr, P. (1990) 'The new life of the liberal state: privatization and the restructuring of state–society relations', in E. N. Suleiman and J. Waterbury (eds), *The Political Economy of Public Sector Reform and Privatization. Boulder*, Colo.: Westview.

Suleiman, E. N. and Waterbury, J. (1990a) 'Introduction: analyzing privatization in industrial and developing countries', in *The Political Economy of Public Sector Reform and Privatization*, Boulder, Colo.: Westview.

Suleiman, E. N. and Waterbury, J. (eds) (1990b) *The Political Economy of Public Sector Reform and Privatization*, Boulder, Colo.: Westview.

Waterbury, J. (1990) 'The political context of public sector reform and privatization in Egypt, India, Mexico and Turkey', in *The Political Economy of Public Sector Reform and Privatization*, Boulder, Colo.: Westview.

Williamson, O. E. (1985) *The Economic Institutions of Capitalism*, New York: Free Press.

World Bank (1995) *Bureaucrats in Business: The Economics and Politics of Government Ownership*, London: Oxford University Press.

3 Privatization

A positive analysis with extensions to the MENA region

Sahar M. Tohamy and Peter H. Aranson

Introduction

Privatization of government-owned enterprises has become a prominent feature of public policies for most former communist states and many other nations. International aid agencies often make privatization, along with trade liberalization, a central requirement for granting of assistance. Indeed, there appears to be widespread agreement that privatization is desirable. We nevertheless know little about the preconditions that support or retard the progress of privatization cross-nationally and in specific countries. Here we describe elements of a positive model that cross-nationally explains the rate of privatization; we also report on tests of that model and apply it to the Middle East and North Africa (MENA) region.

While recommendations for privatization are abundant in the literature on transition economies and developing countries, the number of studies that address privatization as a positive economic problem is small. None of these few empirical studies, furthermore, develops a model and tests its predictions. This study investigates economic and institutional structures that produce differing sources and intensities of support for and opposition to privatization. Our model predicts, and our empirical results show, that the presence and size of a social security and welfare system increase the probability of privatizing public sector firms, while increases in these firms' debt reduces that probability.

The second section highlights the main features of privatization programs in Eastern European countries and in Russia. The following section briefly reviews works that approach privatization as a political–economic problem. The chapter then summarizes the rent-seeking and regulation literature that underlies the theoretical model, and presents the model, its predictions, and a summary of empirical results, discussing implications of the empirical results for the MENA region.

Privatization in Eastern Europe and Russia

The literature on privatization in Eastern Europe falls into two broad categories: works outlining prerequisites for an efficient transition, and works that depict various characteristics of actual privatization programs in East European countries.[1] Examples in the first category include discussions of constitutional and institutional reform (Mueller 1991, Buchanan 1990), financial reform and fiscal policies (McKinnon 1992, Dornbusch 1993), and safety net programs (Newberry 1992). Murrell (1991a, 1991b) and Kornai (1986, 1990) compare the performance of market and centrally-planned economies and present reasons for the economic failure of socialism. Newberry (1991) emphasizes the importance of a reasonable speed for the transition. Ericson (1991), Rubin (1994), and Cooter (1992) examine the legal infrastructure for a successful transition. Lewandowski and Szomburg (1989) and Tirole (1991) demonstrate the importance of consistent laws that define property rights during and beyond the transition, while Stark (1994) criticizes the 'blueprint approach' to privatization. Recommendations on the appropriate method of privatization none the less remain abundant.

Work in the second category concentrates on the description of specific privatization programs implemented in East European countries. Kornai (1986, 1990) and Lipton and Sachs (1990a, 1990b) provide the earliest outlines of programs implemented in Hungary and Poland, respectively.[2] All public sector enterprises are 'corporatized' prior to privatization. Privatization in Hungary is sometimes referred to as 'spontaneous', implying that the manager of the enterprise, a foreign potential owner or workers can initiate the procedures for privatization. However, the state privatization agency approval is required in any of these cases.

Poland implements privatization of small and medium size businesses through public offerings, employee buy-outs and leasing. For large public sector firms, Poland relies on a mass privatization program, under which the Ministry of Privatization transforms public enterprises into joint-stock companies. National Investment Funds (NIFs) receive 60 per cent of the shares in these companies. One fund acts as a core for each company, owning around one-third of its total shares. Individual investors may buy shares in these funds.

The Czech Republic's voucher privatization program targets large public sector firms. Each citizen is eligible to bid with vouchers for shares in public sector firms that the Czech government offers for privatization. The government determines the companies that each 'privatization wave' includes. Book value figures determine share prices for each company. If there is excess demand for a specific firm, the government does not sell any shares until it adjusts share prices upward; it repeats this process until it eliminates any excess demand. Russia's privatization program divides public sector firms into small, medium and large firms. Small enterprises that employ up to 200 employees may be privatized through tender offers, public auctions, or liquidation, and privatization of these firms is generally carried out by local governments (Hill and Karner 1996). Large enterprises employing more than 1,000 employees are the target of Russia's voucher privatization program.

The voucher privatization program gives workers and managers of public sector firms a choice among three privatization options (Boycko, Shleifer and Vishny 1995). Each of these options allows workers and managers to acquire free or subsidized shares in their firms. Option one provides that workers and managers can acquire 25 per cent of the shares at no charge, and they can buy another 10 per cent of the firm's capital at a 30 per cent price discount. Option two gives workers and managers control over 51 per cent of their firm. Option three allows managers to buy 40 per cent of the shares, given that they meet certain conditions for the firm's operation after privatization. Managers and workers need a majority vote to implement options two or three. According to Linz (1994) workers and managers chose the second option in 80 per cent of the voucher privatization cases.

The political economy of privatization

A limited number of articles on Eastern Europe investigate the political economy of the transition. We review four theoretical works that address the problem of privatization, none of which tests its predictions empirically. Then we summarize two empirical studies of privatization.

Chen (1996) sets up a model in which a bureaucrat chooses firms for privatization; consumers allocate their incomes between rationed goods that public sector firms supply and those that private firms supply; and public sector firms must supply equal amounts of the rationed goods to all consumers at subsidized prices. Once a public sector firm is privatized, its goal changes from meeting a bureaucratically set output quota to profit maximization; firms that are not privatized continue to meet quota and price requirements. As a result of privatization and the change in the firm's goal, the prices of public sector firms' output rise. Chen assumes that the bureaucrat's goal is to maximize budget surplus subject to a political constraint of remaining in office. To remain in office the bureaucrat must compensate a specific percentage of the population by an amount at least equal to that percentage's loss in real income from higher prices. He shows that the bureaucrat will find it optimal to privatize firms in sectors with less market power.

An alternative goal for the bureaucrat is to maximize consumers' welfare subject to a balanced budget constraint. In this setting Chen uses the size of total budget surplus to represent total welfare of the population. If the private sector is big enough, the bureaucrat will privatize the sector with the least market power. Thus, Chen concludes that with these two different objective functions, it is 'cheapest' for the bureaucrat to privatize firms with little market power and the greatest state subsidies.

Shapiro and Willig (1989) view privatization as a means by which a welfare-maximizing framer limits public officials' discretion. The framer is a 'public-spirited' agent who seeks to maximize social welfare from the operation of enterprises. To minimize the deviation between the framer's welfare maximization goal and the goals of those running the enterprises, the framer relies on public management or a combination of private management and regulation. In the case of public management, the minister is responsible for managing the firm, while in the case of regulation, private managers of firms react to regulatory incentives as the regulator imposes them. Both the minister and the regulator may have 'private agendas' that cause their objective functions to

diverge from that of the framer. Shapiro and Willig show that privatization eliminates the minister's discretion to pursue a private agenda. Yet, privatization also
introduces an agency problem between the regulator and the privatized firm.

Shleifer and Vishny (1994) describe a game between a politician and enterprise managers, where the politician gains support from excess employment in
firms. Managers maximize profits of firms in which they own a fraction of shares.
The politician and managers bargain over an equilibrium allocation of
employment and subsidies. Shleifer and Vishny show that if the politician can
bribe managers to increase employment, the allocation of resources is independent of cash flow rights: a Coasean outcome (Coase 1960). If no bribes are
permitted, and if the politician holds control over the firm's operation, an
increase in the private sector's share in a firm results in higher excess
employment and lower subsidies. Also, the higher the firm's profitability and the
higher the surplus, the larger is the politician's ability to impose excess
employment. If managers hold control rights, however, then private owners'
shares do not affect the allocation of resources and there is no excess
employment. Furthermore, the more extensive private ownership becomes, the
more difficult it is for a politician to convince managers to dissipate their profits
on excess employment.

Boycko, Shleifer and Vishny (1996) show that even after privatization, the
politician can rely on government subsidies to compensate firm managers for
excess workers. But the political cost of subsidies for the politician is higher than
the cost of using the firm's profits to accommodate excess employment. The
tighter a country's monetary policy, the higher the cost of subsidies, and consequently the more effective is privatization.

Lopez-de-Silanes, Shleifer and Vishny (1995) show that between 1987 and
1992 there was no universal wave of shifting local services in US counties from
in-house provision to contracting out. They use cross-sectional analysis of 1987
census data to examine factors determining the choice between these two modes
of provision. Their work and this research overlap in that they hypothesize that
high unemployment rates make privatization less attractive (which coincides
with our prediction). High public wages relative to private wages, by contrast,
have an ambiguous effect on privatization. (We show that the effect depends on
the institutional arrangement prior to privatization, and the method of privatization chosen.) They find that unionization has a negative effect on
privatization. (We do not test for unionization *per se*, even though, as we discuss
in higher public sector wages may be a result of strong unions.) Finally, Lopez-
de-Silanes *et al.* (1995) show that laws that require hard public sector budget
constraints encourage privatization.[3] (Our model produces a similar prediction.)

Jones, Megginson, Nash and Netter (1996) examine under-pricing in initial
public offers (IPOs) of privatized firms.[4] They document significant under-
pricing, similar to that found in private sector IPOs. So they test to find out if
under-pricing arises because of uncertainty about share values. The authors use
as proxies for uncertainty: issue size; whether the issue is a part of a group offer;
and the size of the offer as a percentage of the company's shares. They expect

that the larger the size of the issue, the larger the percentage of shares in the company offered, and if the IPO is a part of a group offer, the less uncertainty there is about share values. In addition to uncertainty proxies, they include as variables in the regression: the percentage of each offer allocated to employees; the percentage allocated to foreigners; a dummy to represent IPOs from the UK; and a dummy to represent IPOs from former communist countries. The only variables that are significant are the percentages allocated to foreigners and the UK dummy.[5] Jones *et al.* conclude that uncertainty has little power in explaining under-pricing, and they argue that under-pricing may be necessary to market the issues and gain political support for privatization.

Rent-seeking and regulation

Privatization choices are like regulatory decisions, because they benefit some groups at the expense of others. So we draw a parallel between reliance on politicians to make privatization decisions in former communist and developing countries, on the one hand, and government allocations of regulation (or protection) to specific sectors in capitalist countries, on the other. This strategy allows us to use the extensive literature on economic regulation to model the decision to privatize or to keep firms in the public sector.

In the context of democratic or semi-democratic governments, we must examine the ability of interest groups to influence privatization policies. If property rights to public sector firms are clear and transactions costs are zero, we would predict from a Coasean perspective that market transactions will produce an efficient allocation of rights. Market allocation of shares in public firms will allow the highest valuation parties – workers or capitalists – to acquire full or partial property rights in these firms. But transaction costs are seldom zero, and other works in the literature on the interaction between economic regulation and interest group actions conclude that smaller groups are more efficient than are larger ones in advancing their interests. Our research accepts the premise that, in general, politicians ignore the interests of larger groups. Because a firm's workers and investors are smaller in size than are consumers and taxpayers as groups, we focus on the distribution of surplus from privatization to these two groups and exclude the interests of consumers and taxpayers.

Stigler (1971) and Peltzman (1976) explore price regulation in which the relevant groups are producers and consumers. Their politician accommodates the interests of various groups in an effort to increase the probability of gaining a majority of votes. Stigler (1971) provides a theoretical foundation for analysing government regulation. Various groups 'demand' regulations, and the government 'supplies' these regulations through political decisions. Competition from other political parties limits but does not eliminate a political party's ability to collect regulatory benefits for itself: competition prevents a political party from acting as a monopolistic supplier that achieves above-normal profits (Stigler 1972). Competition from 'demanders' of regulation also limits the size of surplus that groups retain from lobbying in the market for regulation (Tohamy 1994).

Peltzman (1976) mathematically formalizes and extends Stigler's model by introducing a majority-generating support function for the politician in the case where an industry benefits from price regulation. The output market displays a downward sloping demand schedule whose parameters set the extent to which the politician can regulate the industry to yield above-normal profits. Peltzman shows that in cases of government-regulated prices, both price and profits will be lower than if the industry acted monopolistically through a cartel. This result holds true because the politician balances the interests of industry and consumers in support-maximizing calculations.

In these works, and because of the nature of the regulations considered, consumers oppose entry barriers, price fixing and tariff protection.[6] But the characteristics of large groups make it difficult for consumers collectively to influence regulatory decisions (Olson 1965). In privatization circumstances, however, opposition to privatization arises from smaller, well-organized labour groups whose actions differ from those of large groups of unorganized consumers.

Model, predictions and summary of empirical results

We assume that the politician who decides on privatization maximizes the net total surplus from public sector workers' and investors' political support as the result of privatization.[7] The discrepancy between a firm's stream of profits and what an investor pays for shares in a public sector firm represents a surplus that the politician allocates to new owners of privatized firms. For workers, in addition to lower prices for shares sold or given to them, the surplus may take the form of above-market wages that continue after privatization. If they receive no surplus, neither workers nor investors will support privatization. The outcome of the interaction between workers' and investors' support for, and opposition to, privatization determines the number of firms the politician privatizes, and it affects as well his or her choice of privatization method.

Public sector workers' surplus

Here we define workers' surplus from employment in the public sector, and how privatization changes that surplus. Cases one to four present possible arrangements prior to privatization and identify what benefits (surplus) workers enjoy in each case. Table 3.1 summarizes the main features of these four institutional settings. The following sections analyse the four cases.

A profit-maximizing public sector firm   In this setting the treasury evaluates public sector managers' performance based on how successfully they maximize profits. The firm hires workers up to the point where the value of the last worker's marginal product is equal to the wage rate (see Figure 3.1). If public and private sector firms pay workers the same market wage rate w_m, the resulting profit-maximizing level of employment is at $L_{\pi max}(w_m)$ and workers' surplus

Table 3.1 Institutional setting and goals of public sector firms prior to privatization

1 A profit-maximizing public sector firm	The treasury's goal is to maximize profits from the firm's operation, and it evaluates the managers' or workers' performance in terms of how successful they are in maximizing profits.
2 A worker-managed public sector firm	Workers are responsible for management of the public sector firm. The control employment, but they have no ownership rights.
3 A break-even public sector firm	A public sector firm has no control over how many workers to hire. In this case public sector firms have no access to subsidization, and the constraint on additional hiring occurs when profits reach zero.[8]
4 A subsidy-receiving public sector firm	A firm has no control over how many workers to hire, and it need not limit the number of workers to the zero profit level. The government subsidizes the firm for the burden of excess employment.

Note: author classification

from employment in the public sector is zero. If employment in the public sector guarantees workers a wage $w_{ps} > w_m$, however, the profit-maximizing level of employment is at $L_{\pi max}(w_{ps})$. Workers' total surplus then equals the area $(V_{wps}+b)$.

Either investors' surplus from the free distribution of shares in this firm or workers' gain from converting this firm into an employee stock ownership plan

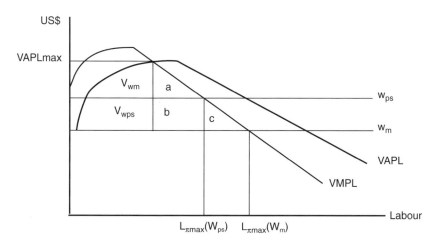

Figure 3.1 A profit-maximizing public sector firm
Source: author's calculations.

(ESOP) equals $(V_{wm} + V_{wps} + (a + b + c))$ if w_m prevails and $(V_{wm} + a)$ if w_{ps} prevails. Both groups will support privatization of an originally profit maximizing public sector firm because neither group is better off under the status-quo.[9] Yet, each group prefers to gain the whole surplus, so we cannot predict whether one or the other will end up with the entire surplus, or if the politician will decide to divide it between the two groups.[10]

A worker-managed public sector firm   In the worker-managed firm, where workers control employment levels but have no ownership rights to the firm, workers maximize the value of the average product of labour, VAPL, and limit the number of workers to $LVAPL_{max}$, with each worker earning $VAPL_{max}$.[11] Their surplus is equal to the area $(V_{wm} + V_{wps})$ or $(VAPL_{max} - w_m) \cdot L_{VAPLmax}$, as depicted in Figure 3.2. If their firm is transferred or sold to a private investor and workers get the market wage rate, w_m, they lose this surplus and the new owner hires $(L_{\pi max}(w_m) - L_{VAP}L)$ additional workers to maximize profits. His total profit equals $(V_{wm} + V_{wps} + (a + b + c))$. If public sector wages, w_{ps}, remain higher than private sector wages however, then existing workers' surplus loss from privatization is the area V_{wm} only: when public sector workers continue to earn w_{ps}, existing workers keep the fraction of their original surplus represented by V_{wps}, and the investor's surplus equals $(V_{wm} + a)$ only.

Privatization may occur through the firm's transformation into an employee stock ownership plan (ESOP) firm. The workers' goal then changes from maximizing $VAPL$ to maximizing profits. Because their objective has changed, they hire $(L_{\pi max}(w_m) - L_{VAPLmax})$ additional workers if public sector wages are equal to market wages and $(L_{\pi max}(w_{ps}) - L_{VAPLmax})$ if public sector wages are higher than private wages. New workers have no claim to the firm's assets. Therefore,

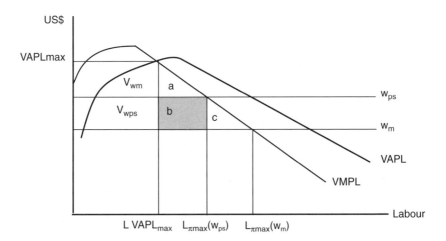

Figure 3.2 A worker-managed public sector firm
Source: author's calculations.

they receive the wage prevailing in the public (or private) sector, w_m (or w_{ps}). As owners, existing workers keep the area under the VMPL curve up to the level of employment they choose minus the cost of that level of employment. So, if the wage rate is at w_m, existing workers' surplus increases from the area (V_{wm} + V_{wps}), their surplus under worker-management, to (V_{wm} + V_{wps} + (a + b + c)), their surplus if they own shares in the firm. Similarly, if the public sector wage rate is at w_{ps}, workers' surplus increases from (V_{wm}) to (V_{wm} + a). Because the larger surplus is divided among the same number of workers, the firm's original workers are better off as stock owners than they were under worker management.

If a private investor buys the firm, and if w_m applies to public sector firms, then workers lose the total surplus they enjoy prior to privatization, (V_{wm} + V_{wps}). If the new owners must pay workers $w_{ps} > w_m$, however, then existing workers lose only the area (V_{wm}) and they continue to receive a positive surplus, V_{wps}, under private investor ownership. Workers' gain from the free distribution of shares over their gain from privatization to an investor, therefore, is larger when w_m prevails, compared to when w_{ps} continues to prevail after privatization. Investors' surplus, and in turn their support for investor privatization, is also larger when w_m prevails than when w_{ps} prevails.

A break-even public sector firm   If, prior to privatization, the firm has no control over how many workers it hires, workers will continue to work in a public sector firm until VAPL is equal to the market wage rate. Beyond this point no worker will accept a wage lower than he can earn on the market. At this level of employment, profits equal zero and the number of workers is $L_{\pi 0}(w_m)$ (Figure 3.3a). If there are restrictions against laying off workers after privatization, no private investor will be interested in buying a firm whose expected profit stream

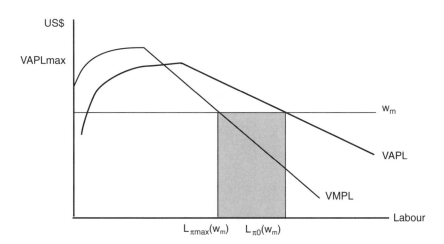

Figure 3.3a A break-even public sector firm and w_m
Source: author's calculations.

equals zero.[12] Workers, on the other hand, will remain indifferent between the status-quo and the free distribution of shares to workers. The firm will continue to break even whether or not government privatizes it.

If labour restrictions no longer prevail, then to maximize profits a private investor will reduce the labour force from $L(w_m)$ to $L_{\pi max}(w_m)$ and pay each worker w_m. Because of the expected reduction in the number of workers, each worker faces the probability of being laid off. We assume that a worker does not find employment if he gets laid off, so his income becomes zero if there is no unemployment benefits system. (We later relax this assumption). If each worker has the same probability of being laid off, p_f, which equals $(L_{\pi 0}(w_m) - L_{\pi max}(w_m))/L_{\pi 0}(w_m)$, then the probability of remaining employed is $(1 - p_f)$. If workers remain employed, they receive wm, but if the firm becomes privatized, worker's expected wage is $(1 - p_f)w_m$. The surplus per worker from remaining employed if the firm is not privatized equals the difference between w_m and $(1 - p_f)w_m$, or $p_f w_m$. The total surplus for the existing labour force equals surplus per worker times the number of workers employed under public ownership. In other words the total surplus equals $p_f L_{\pi 0}(w_m)w_m = (L_{\pi 0}(w_m) - L_{pmax}(w_m))w_m$, the shaded area in Figure 3.3a.

If $w_{ps} > w_m$, the firm's labour force equals $L_{\pi 0}(w_{ps})$. Workers' surplus prior to privatization is $[(V_{wps} + b) + [L(w_{ps}) - L(w_{ps})]w_{ps}]$. If firms cannot lay off workers after privatization, workers will be indifferent between the status quo and either privatization method (shares to workers versus shares to investors). When firms can lay off workers after privatization, workers are indifferent between the status quo and a free distribution of shares to themselves, but they will oppose the distribution of shares to private investors that causes them to lose all their surplus. Notice that if investors can lay off workers, workers' loss, and

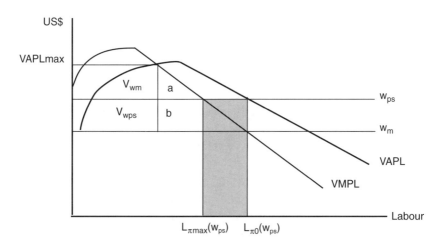

Figure 3.3b A break-even public sector firm and w_{ps}
Source: author's calculations.

consequently their opposition to investor privatization, is larger when w_m prevails than when w_{ps} prevails.[13]

A subsidy-receiving public sector firm   Prior to privatization the firm must hire L_s workers, where L_s is larger than the firm's profit-maximizing level of employment. The government subsidizes the firm to cover its losses from excess workers. The firm hires $L_s > L_{\pi 0}$ units of labour. The money-losing firm costs the government budget(s) dollars. The budget cost of workers' surplus is only equal to the shaded area in Figures 3.4a and 3.4b, which is less than or equal to the value of the surplus.[14] We calculate the surplus to existing workers in terms of guarantees against laying off workers in a manner similar to that of case three.

If w_m prevails, workers' surplus prior to privatization equals $[L_s(w_m) - L_{\pi max}(w_m)]w_m$. If there are no restrictions against laying off workers, they lose this entire surplus if the firm is privatized through investor privatization, as distinct from ESOP privatization. Existing workers only lose a fraction of that surplus, $([L_s(w_m) - L_{\pi 0}(w_m)]w_m)$ if shares are distributed to them. When restrictions against laying off workers prevail, the government will not be able to privatize these firms, and elimination of the subsidy will not be feasible because the firm relies on it to sustain any fraction of the labour force beyond the break-even level. If $w_{ps} > w_m$, existing workers' surplus is a combination of above-normal wages, w_{ps}, and the surplus from remaining employed if the firm remains in the public sector. The total surplus equals $[(V_{wps} + b) + [L_s(w_{ps}) - L_{\pi max}(w_{ps})]w_{ps}]$. Workers keep $(V_{wps} + b)$ if the firm is privatized to a private investor, while their surplus is $[(V_{wps} + b) + [L_s(w_{ps}) - L_{\pi 0}(w_{ps})]w_{ps}]$ if shares are distributed to existing workers. Similar to the w_m case, privatization or the elimination of subsidies will not be feasible unless the public sector allows firms to lay off workers.

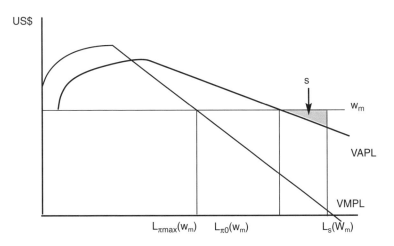

Figure 3.4a A subsidy-receiving public sector firm and w_m
Source: author's calculations.

Unemployment benefits, unemployment rates and subsidies   We turn now to the effect of the subsidy on the size of workers' surplus, and consequently, their opposition to privatization. We relax the assumption that if workers are laid off as a result of privatization, their income falls to zero. Their income will not equal zero if they can find alternative employment, or if there are unemployment benefits. Welfare payments or alternative job opportunities become relevant only when privatization entails a reduction in a public sector firms' number of workers. Privatization of worker-managed or profit-maximizing firms does not depend on the existence of such benefits or job alternatives, or on how either compares to public sector wages. But workers' expected income in a break-even or subsidized firm after privatization depends on such benefits or the availability of other job opportunities.

Let UB be unemployment benefits that a public sector worker receives if he is laid off as a result of his firm's privatization, and let $p_a(UR)$ be the probability that a laid-off worker finds alternative employment, w_a the corresponding wage rate, and UR the unemployment rate.[15] A higher unemployment rate reduces the probability that a laid-off worker finds alternative employment. Thus,

$$\frac{dp_a}{dUR} < 0$$

Each worker faces an equal probability of being laid off, p^f.[16] If the public sector wage is at w_m, then a worker's expected income after privatization is $[(1 - p_f)w_m + p_f p_a w_a + p_f(1 - p_a)UB]$. The surplus per worker from remaining employed if the firm is not privatized equals the difference between w_m and $[(1 - p_f)w_m + p_f p_a w_a + p_f(1 - p_a)UB]$, where p_f equals $(L_{\pi 0}(w_m) - L_{\pi max}(w^m))/L_{\pi 0}(w_m)$. The resulting total surplus for the firm's work force becomes:

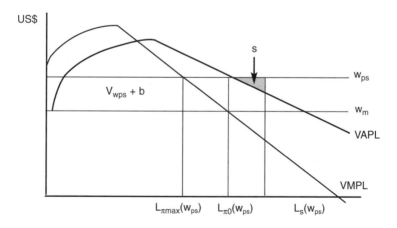

Figure 3.4b   A subsidy-receiving firm and w_{ps}
Source: author's calculations.

$$(L_{\pi 0}(wm - L_{\pi max}(w_m))[w_m - (p_a.w^a + (1 - p^a)UB] \qquad (1)$$

Differentiating total surplus with respect to UB we have

$$\frac{\partial total\ surplus}{\partial UB} = L_{\pi 0} - L_{\pi max}(1 - p_a) < 0 \text{ as long as } p_a < 1 \qquad (2)$$

and

$$\frac{\partial total\ surplus}{\partial UR} = L_{\pi 0} - L_{\pi max}(w_a - UB)\frac{\partial pa}{\partial UR} > 0 \qquad (3)$$

From equation (2), the higher the unemployment benefits, UB, the smaller the workers' total surplus from public sector employment. Similarly, from equation (3), the higher the unemployment rate, the smaller the workers' probability of finding alternative employment, and the larger the difference between workers' public sector wage and their expected income if they are laid off. The higher the unemployment rate becomes, therefore, the larger the workers' opposition to privatization.

The number of workers a subsidy-receiving firm employs prior to privatization is a function of the size of subsidies that it receives. Equation (4) defines workers' total surplus accordingly.

$$\text{Total surplus} = (L_s(w^m,s) - L_{\pi max}(w_m)).[w_m - (p_aw_a + (1 - p_a)UB] \qquad (4)$$

where $\frac{\partial L_s}{\partial w_m}$ and $\frac{\partial L_s}{\partial s} > 0$

Differentiating (6) with respect to subsidies, s, gives

$$\frac{\partial total\ surplus}{\partial s} = (w_m - (p_aw_a + (1 - p_a)UB)\frac{\partial Ls}{\partial s} \qquad (5)$$

which is > 0. Therefore, the larger the government subsidies to public sector firms, the larger the existing workers' surplus from public employment, and the stronger their opposition to privatization that entails a reduction in the firm's employment level.

Predictions and summary of empirical results

We list here three hypotheses derived from various predictions in the previous section. Then, we briefly describe the data, the empirical testing analysis, and the general results.[17] We test these hypotheses.[18]

1   Higher government expenditures on social security and welfare increase the likelihood of privatization.
2   The larger the level of subsidization the less likely it is that the policy-maker privatizes a firm through distribution of shares to investors.

3   The higher the unemployment rate, the less likely it is that the policy-maker distributes shares to investors.

To account for the possibility that governments may subsidize public sector firms through debt rather than subsidies, we use two measures of subsidization: subsidies to public sector firms and public sector firms' debt. The dependent variable is the number of privatizations per country per year, which measures the probability of privatization in a specific country in a given year.[19] Government expenditures on social security and welfare as a per centage of gross domestic product (GDP) measure the unemployment benefits of laid-off workers.[20] We divide enterprise debt and subsidies by total government expenditures to eliminate the effect of liberal government spending on the size of subsidies and debt, and to eliminate the need for exchange rate conversions.

We expect the relationship between government expenditures on social security and welfare/GDP and the probability of privatization to be positive, while we expect the relationship between the probability of privatization and each of the subsidies/government expenditures, debt/government expenditures, and unemployment rates to be negative. The data represent a total of forty-six countries over the period 1988–95, of which nine report no privatizations. Table 3.2 shows the regional distribution of the sample countries.

We use several variants of the Poisson model to estimate the statistical relationships. Empirical results show that:

1   Public sector firms' debt is the strongest of the four variables in reducing the likelihood of privatization.
2   Government expenditures on social security and welfare increase the probability of privatization.
3   Unemployment rates and government subsidies to public enterprises have limited roles in reducing the probability of privatization.

Implications of the results for the MENA region

Before extending these results to MENA countries, we must ask if such an extension is warranted. Stated differently, do they reflect merely the large number of privatizations from Western Europe or Latin America or are they more general? While MENA observations are too few for separate regression analysis, we address this question in the section by analysing the MENA countries sub-sample relative to the rest of the world (ROW) sub-sample. We examine the regional distribution of transactions, then we evaluate the mean and variance of the number of privatizations per country per year for both the MENA and the ROW. This analysis seeks to discern whether the sub-sample of MENA countries differs significantly from the entire sample.

Following this, we discuss the conditional likelihood maximization technique we use to account for country-specific effect. This technique eliminates, or at

Table 3.2 Regional distribution of sample countries

Region	Countries		Transactions		Average no. of transactions/ country
	no.	%	no.	%	
Africa	2	4.4	3	1.1	1.50
Asia	5	10.9	24	8.5	4.80
Eastern Europe and former Soviet Republics	7	15.0	17	6.0	2.43
Latin America	13	28.0	44	15.6	3.38
Middle East and North Africa (includes Turkey)	6	13.0	37	13.1	6.17
US and Canada	2	4.4	8	2.8	4.00
Western Europe	11	24.0	150	53.0	13.64
Total	46	100.0	283	100.0	6.15

Source: Privatization International 1996.

least reduces, country-specific effects, thus producing unbiased parameter estimates. Hausman, Hall, and Griliches (1984) develop this method to adjust for country specific random and fixed effects in the context of non-linear estimation models. We then focus on the strengths and weaknesses of our empirical analysis with respect to the MENA region. While our empirical testing and results are limited to the effect of variables such as government expenditures on social security and welfare, subsidies, debt, and unemployment rates; our model predicts that other variables influence the speed and method of privatization. Finally we discuss how these other variables may be of particular importance to the progress of privatization in the MENA region.

The MENA sub-sample

Table 3.2 presents the regional distribution of the data. The share of transactions from Western European countries accounts for over one-half of the sample, thanks to the large number of privatizations from the UK. Excluding UK transactions from the sample yields a different picture; the share of Western Europe in the number of transactions falls to 33 per cent of the total. Similarly, while the average number of transactions per country in Western Europe is 13.64, excluding the UK reduces the average number per country to 6.7. Therefore, while the UK's share of privatizations in the sample is over-represented, that conclusion does not characterize other regions, such as Latin America or Western Europe.

Latin American transactions and Middle Eastern shares in total transactions are similar: the first group accounts for close to 16 per cent of total transactions, while the second accounts for 13 per cent. For Eastern European countries the average number of transactions per country is only 2.43. Two reasons account for this smaller average number of privatizations. First, many Eastern European countries rely on voucher programs, while our analysis only includes cash transactions. Second, the lag with which explanatory variables are reported for former communist countries prevents us from using many transactions that these countries completed in the last two years.

To test if MENA countries' privatizations belong to the same population as transactions from the entire sample, we divide the sample into two sub-samples: MENA countries and the rest of the world (ROW). We test the hypothesis:

$$H_0: \mu_{MENA} = \mu_{ROW}$$

$$H_1: \mu MENA \neq \mu_{ROW}$$

where μ_{MENA} and μ_{ROW} are the average number of privatizations per country per year for the MENA and the ROW regions, respectively. We test also if variances are equal for the two sub-samples. Neither the mean nor the variance is significantly different for the MENA region compared to the ROW sub-sample. So, as a group the MENA sample does not differ significantly from the sample for the rest of privatizing countries.

Conditional likelihood maximization

We move now from regional differences in privatization to country-specific differences. We rely in our empirical analysis on Hausman, Hall, and Griliches's (1984) conditional likelihood maximization to address this problem. In linear regression models we adjust for unobserved country-specific effects by using dummy variables that take the value '1' for a specific country and the value '0' for all other observations. While it sacrifices degrees of freedom, this technique is widely used especially to analyse data sets whose number of countries is small, while the number of observations per individual country is large. Because of the integer nature of our dependent variable (the number of privatizations per country per year), the Poisson model is appropriate to capture the relationship between the probability of privatization and explanatory variables. But using dummy variables in non-linear regressions produces inconsistent parameter estimates.

We employ Hausman *et al.*'s conditional likelihood maximization as an alternative to using dummy variables. They use the sum of the dependent variable over each country's series of observations as a sufficient proxy for all characteristics that may influence the dependent variable, but which the explanatory variables do not capture. If, for whatever reason, conditions in a country that are not included in the independent variables are more conducive to privatization than those that prevail elsewhere, then these conditions will be reflected in the total number of privatizations per country over the period of observation, irrespective of annual variations in explanatory variables.

Strengths and weaknesses of the empirical analysis

Hausman *et al.*'s method allows us to account for each country's differences, no matter how large the number of countries may be. This advantage is important in our case because our sample consists of a relatively large number of countries, while the number of observations per country is limited to as few as two or three observations in some cases. So even though we analyse the MENA countries as a region earlier, our empirical analysis separates the region's countries.

Applying the conditional likelihood maximization technique none the less assumes that country-specific effects are constant over the period of analysis. So, we cannot adjust for a change in policy that a country adopts in the middle of that country's data series. This is a potential problem in our analysis, because if a country adopts a structural adjustment program in the middle of the study period, we still account for that country's characteristics by using its total number of privatizations over the period of analysis. Then, the predicted number of privatizations after the adoption of the structural adjustment program, will be underestimated because conditional maximization incorporates information from the pre-structural adjustment years.

In addition to the strengths and weaknesses of the econometric techniques, the unavailability of explanatory variables for MENA and Eastern European countries restricts our sample and, in the case of Eastern European countries and former Soviet Republics, limits significantly the model's predictive power. Table 3.3 shows the distribution of privatization transactions from the Privatization International Database. Compared to Table 3.2 we see that the share of Eastern Europe and former Soviet Republics rises from 6 per cent of total transactions to close to 18 per cent. The share of Western Europe, by contrast, falls from over one-half the transactions to 35 per cent of privatizations. Better representation of Eastern European and former Soviet Republics in future empirical analysis will increase our confidence in the model's ability to predict the progress of privatization in transition countries.

Restrictions on lay-offs, public–private wage differentials, and market power

Our model predicts that restrictions against laying off workers reduce the likelihood of selling public enterprises to private investors but increase the likelihood of worker or manager buy-outs. The model also predicts that workers' gain from buying shares in their firms is higher for those employed in profit-maximizing firms than it is for those in worker-managed firms. So countries that introduced market-oriented policies for public sector firms' output markets before privatization will have an easier job (encounter less political resistance) in privatizing public sector firms, even with workers enjoying above-market benefits from public employment before and after privatization. Continued wage differentials, differentials in other benefits, or in job security that persist between public and private firms in the region must encourage workers to participate in buying their firms.

The MENA region is famous for its sizeable informal sector. The existence of such a sector during privatization is a mixed blessing. On the one hand, a large informal sector increases laid-off workers' expected income after privatization even in the absence of welfare or safety-net programs, because

Table 3.3 The regional distribution of privatizations

Region/country	Number of privatizations	% of total	Value (US$ million)
MENA (includes Turkey) of which:	154	10.13	6,708
Egypt	45		1,672
Kuwait	15		1,431
Morocco	34		1,190
Tunisia	1		22
Turkey	56		2,321
Africa	56	3.68	3,829
Asia	162	10.66	146,501
Australasia	60	3.95	32,178
Eastern Europe and former Soviet Republics	269	17.70	14,249
Latin America	232	15.26	68,392
US and Canada	49	3.22	6,708
Western Europe	538	35.39	296,053
of which UK	161		117,227
Total	1,520	100.00	574, 618

Source: Privatization International (1996).

workers' probability of finding alternative employment becomes higher, compared with the probability in nations with small informal sectors. This generalization implies that privatization will encounter less political resistance. Work conditions, benefits, and wages, on the other hand, are lower in the informal sector in which labour laws generally are not enforced as rigorously as in the public sector or formal private sector. These conditions widen the gap between w_m and w_{ps} and increase workers' opposition to investor privatization.

While in some developing and Eastern European countries the relevant restrictions take the form of laws against laying off workers, in many other cases these restrictions are informal conventions, traditions and norms of public enterprise management. Understanding the intricate nature of varying labour relations in the public sector of various countries, and varying relations across sub-sectors in a single country is key to implementing a successful privatization program. While using the Hausman *et al.* method will account for some of these country-by-country differences, it would be desirable to measure their effects specifically, rather than as a generalized 'fixed effects' problem.

Tohamy (1997) analyses the effect of public sector firms' market power on the progress of privatization. Existing or potential market power, as expected, increases private investors' gains from privatization. Workers' interests in privatizing firms with market power differ depending on the institutional arrangements that govern these firms before privatization. There is a trade-off, therefore, between investors' support for privatization and the risk of privatizing firms with market power. That trade-off is not conclusively determined in the case of worker privatization.

MENA countries for many years have guaranteed public sector firms' monopoly positions in several strategic sectors. Even when they are privatized, the absence of antitrust laws in the region's economies increases the range of short term profitability of (present) public sector firms and their potential longer term profitability in the absence of antitrust laws or effective competition. Possible adoption of antitrust laws as part of structural adjustment programs increases uncertainty about a firm's market power for privatized firms. The timing of adopting antitrust laws relative to privatization highlights the importance of sequencing the transition not just for considerations of allocative efficiencies but also for considerations of efficiency in the political support maximization process itself.

The adoption of antitrust laws may be a mixed blessing, however. Bowing to substantial scholarship and the realities of international competition, over the last two decades federal courts and bureaux (the Antitrust Division of the Justice Department and the Bureau of Competition of the Federal Trade Commission) in the US have weakened the force of antitrust laws. But they also have limited the power of individual states to shelter firms from competition through entry-restricting and other forms of regulation. Hence, to achieve the benefits of privatization, MENA countries must abandon the kinds of protections that they previously have offered to both public and private enterprises.

Finally, even though we do not focus here on the welfare consequences of the privatization decision, we emphasize that accepting the politician's political support maximization goal does not mean necessarily that we argue that the politician will maximize support without regard to welfare losses. Becker (1985), for example, argues that politicians and groups that receive surpluses from the political allocations of economic rights have an interest in reducing the welfare costs of providing these subsidies. It would be interesting to test this hypothesis in the context of the politician's choice of privatization methods, especially when workers' surplus is equal among arrangements with different welfare implications.

Conclusion

We identify several institutional and economic parameters that affect the size of workers' and investors' support for, or opposition to, privatization. We summarize the recent literature that approaches privatization as a public choice problem, and we present a model in which politicians maximize (the sum of) workers' and investors' support for privatization of public sector firms. We present empirical results of the model's predictions in the context of a world-wide cross-country study of privatization. These results show that government expenditures on social security and welfare increase the probability of privatization, while public enterprise debt reduces that probability.

The role that unemployment rates and subsidies play in reducing the probability of privatization requires further investigation.

We outline the general strengths and weaknesses of our empirical analysis with special emphasis on issues related to the MENA region. We also discuss some of the model's other predictions that are of particular interest to developing countries in general, and MENA countries in particular. We argue that a closer examination of labour market conditions in MENA countries and restrictions against laying off workers will prove useful in understanding and predicting workers' opposition to privatization.

Finally, this research stresses the importance of approaching privatization as a positive economic problem where we can predict and test empirically specific patterns of privatization based on each country's economic and institutional environments. This approach of studying privatization must complement the normative literature on the welfare consequences of privatization and the superior performance of private versus public ownership. The results of positive analysis is a fascinating intellectual topic in its own right; but it also can have significant implications for real-world public policy prescriptions.

Notes

1 This presentation of the literature is by no means comprehensive. We intend it merely to shed some light on various aspects of reform that scholars on privatization in Eastern Europe judge to be critical for a successful transition.
2 See also Frydman *et al.* (1993), Fischer (1992), Mizsei (1992), Bohm and Kecskes (1992), Simoneti and Bohm (1992), Tamowicz (1993) and Mladek (1993).
3 We analyse the case where the law does not allow laying off workers following privatization. In this case it is impossible to privatize a firm that employs excess workers prior to privatization, and that firm must remain in the public sector.
4 They also examine the effect of uncertainty variables on underwriter fees as a per cent of the offer. We focus on under-pricing in our discussion of their paper because it is more relevant to our work.
5 The coefficients on these two variables are positive in the regression explaining initial returns.
6 Other groups that may have an interest in the outcome of privatization include downstream factor users, members of the government bureaucracy whose power is correlated to the size of the public sector and private suppliers of complements and substitutes of public sector output.
7 If they were fully informed, consumers would be interested in the elimination of market distortions and market power. Taxpayers, by contrast, are interested in maximizing the revenues from the sale of public sector firms to reduce taxes and government debt and to eliminate ongoing subsidies to public sector firms.
8 The only difference between cases three and four is the firm's access to government subsidization. In both cases the number of workers that the firm employs is higher than the profit-maximizing level. In case three the break-even output point determines how many workers the firm can afford to employ, while in case four it is the size of the subsidy that limits the number of workers that the firm continues to employ.
9 Workers will not oppose privatization on the basis that it will reduce the surplus they receive prior to privatization, but they may oppose the free distribution of shares to investors only.

10 Even if the politician divides the surplus between workers and investors, both groups will be better off compared to the status-quo. There may arise another level of rent-seeking, however, in which each group tries to receive the full surplus thus eliminating the other group's surplus. Both groups support privatization in general, but they do not agree necessarily on the method. (This case resembles, a gains-from-trade situation in which there exists a range of benefits that trading partners divide based on their negotiating powers.)

11 For more detailed analyses of the worker-managed firm, see Ward (1958), Furubotn and Pejovich (1973), Pejovich (1980, 1987, 1992), Furubotn (1981, 1984, 1988, 1992), Furubotn and Wiggins (1984), Gardner (1988), Burkett (1994), Sacks (1994) and Vanek (1971).

12 We assume here, contrary to conventional wisdom, that private investors cannot increase the firm's profits as a result of privatization. If we do not make this assumption, we may find cases in which money-losing firms attract private investors. In these cases the question becomes: how much more efficient is the firm under private ownership than it is under public ownership?

13 If workers can anticipate who will be laid off, those who keep their jobs will be better off under privatization, whereas those laid off will be worse off. In a future paper we intend to relax the workers' homogeneity assumption and examine whether the model's predictions will remain intact.

14 Beyond the breakeven level of employment, VAPL is less than w_m but not equal to zero. The discrepancy between the VAPL and total labour cost represents the firm's losses, and consequently its level of subsidization. The size of workers' surplus is equal to the total wage cost of employing workers beyond the breakeven level. We make this assumption because workers would not be employed if the VAPL is less than the wage rate, and therefore their surplus from employment in the subsidized firm is the total wage they receive without subtracting the value of what they add to the firm's production.

15 If unemployment benefits are larger than the alternative employment wage rate workers are better off not working at all and receiving unemployment benefits instead. If w_a < UB, therefore workers do not include alternative employment in their expected income calculations.

16 If workers are not homogeneous (see note 13), the probability of being laid off may be higher for some members of the workforce and lower for others.

17 We refer the reader to Tohamy (1997) for a more comprehensive presentation of the econometric methods and the detailed results.

18 All hypotheses concerning unemployment benefits and unemployment rates refer to the situation where there are no restrictions against laying off workers after privatization. The presence of such restrictions results in workers maintaining their surplus from public employment after privatization, and their expected income remains unaffected by privatization.

19 Data on the dependent variable come from three sources: Privatization International is a database that documents world-wide privatization transactions from 1980 to the present. The other two sources are privatization announcements in the *Financial Times*, and Jones *et al.* (1996).

20 We use government expenditures on social security and welfare as a proxy for unemployment benefits.

Bibliography

Becker, G. S. (1985) 'A theory of competition among pressure groups for political influence', *Quarterly Journal of Economics*, vol. 158, no. 3: 371–400.
Bohm, A. and Kecskes, L. (eds) (1992) *Reprivatization in Central and Eastern Europe:*

Country Privatization Reports and Specific Implementation Issues, Washington, D.C.: Economic Development Institute of the World Bank and Central and East European Privatization Network.

Boycko, M., Shleifer, A. and Vishny, R. (1995) *Privatizing Russia*, Cambridge, Mass.: MIT Press.

—— (1996) 'A theory of privatization', *Economic Journal*, March, vol. 106: 309–19.

Buchanan, J. M. (1990) 'Socialism is dead; Leviathan lives,' *Wall Street Journal*, 18 July, p. A8.

Burkett, J. P. (1994) 'Self-managed market socialism and the Yugoslav economy, 1950–91', in M. Bornstein (ed.), *Comparative Economic Systems: Models and Cases*, 7th edn, Burr Ridge, Ill.: IRWIN.

Chen, Yan (1996) 'The optimal choice of privatizing state-owned enterprises: a political economic model,' *Public Choice*, vol. 86: 223–45.

Coase, R. H. (1960) 'The problem of social cost', *Journal of Law and Economics*, October, vol. 3: 1–44.

Cooter, R. (1992) 'Organization as property: economic analysis of property law applied to privatization' in C. Clague and G. C. Rausser (eds), *The Emergence of Market Economies in Eastern Europe*, Cambridge, Mass.: Blackwell.

Dornbusch, R. (1993) *Stabilization, Debt, and Reform*, Englewood Cliffs, NJ: Prentice Hall.

Ericson, R. E. (1991) 'The classical soviet-type economy: nature of the system and implications for reform', *Journal of Economic Perspectives*, Fall, vol. 5, no. 4: 11–28.

Fischer, S. (1992) 'Privatization in Eastern European transformation' in C. Clague and G. C. Rausser (eds), *The Emergence of Market Economies in Eastern Europe*, Cambridge, Mass.: Blackwell.

Frydman, R., Rapaczynski, A. Earle, J. S. *et al.* (1993) *The Privatization Process in Central Europe*, New York: Central European University Press.

Furubotn, E. (1981) 'Codetermination and the efficient partitioning of ownership rights in the firm', *Journal of Institutional and Theoretical Economics*, vol. 137, no. 4: 702–9.

—— (1988) 'Codetermination and the modern theory of the firm: a property-rights analysis', *Journal of Business*, vol. 61, no. 2: 165–81.

—— (1992) 'Eastern European reconstruction problems: some general observations', *Journal of Institutional and Theoretical Economics*, vol. 148, no. 1: 201–6.

Furubotn, E. G. and Pejovich, S. (1973) 'Property rights, economic decentralization and the evolution of the Yugoslav firm, 1965–1972', *Journal of Law and Economics*, October, vol. 16, no. 2: 275–302.

Furubotn, E. G. and Wiggins, S. N. (1984) 'Plant closings, worker reallocation costs and efficiency gains to labour representation on boards of directors', *Journal of Institutional and Theoretical Economics*, vol. 140, no. 1: 176–92.

Gardner, H. S. (1988) *Comparative Economic Systems*, Chicago: Dryden.

Hausman, J., Hall, B. H. and Griliches, Z. (1984) 'Economic models for count data with an application to the patents–R&D relationship', *Econometrica*, July, vol. 52, no. 4: 909–38.

Hill, P. J. and Karner, M. (1996) 'Spontaneous privatization in transition economies', in T. L. Anderson and P. J. Hill (eds), *The Privatization Process: A World-Wide Perspective*, Maryland: Rowman and Littlefield.

Jones, S. L, Megginson, W., Nash, R. C. and Netter, J. (1996) 'Share issue privatizations as financial means to political and economic ends', paper presented at the Emory Business School, Emory University, Atlanta, Ga., Spring.

Kornai, J. (1986) *Contradictions and Dilemmas: Studies on the Socialist Economy and Society,* Cambridge, Mass.: MIT Press.

—— (1990) *The Road to A Free Economy: Shifting from a Socialist System: The Example of Hungary,* New York: W. W. Norton.

Lewandowsky, J. and Szomburg, J. (1989) 'Property reform as a basis for social and economic reform', *Communist Economies,* vol. 1, no. 3: 257–68.

Linz, S. J. (1994) 'The privatization of Russian industry', *Radio Free Europe/Radio Liberty Research Report,* vol. 3, no. 10: 27–35.

Lipton, D. and Sachs, J. (1990a) 'Creating a market economy in Eastern Europe: the case of Poland', *Brookings Papers on Economic Activity.*

—— (1990b) 'Privatization in Eastern Europe: the case of Poland', *Brookings Papers on Economic Activity:* 75–145.

Lopez-de-Silanes, F., Shleifer, A. and Vishny, R. W. (1995), 'Privatization in the United States,' NBER Working Paper Series, National Bureau of Economic Research, Cambridge, Mass.

McKinnon, R. (1992), 'Taxation, money, and credit in a liberalizing socialist economy,' in C. Clague and G. C. Rausser (eds), *The Emergence of Market Economies in Eastern Europe,* Cambridge, Mass.: Blackwell.

Mizsei, K. (1992) 'Privatization in Eastern Europe: a comparative study of Poland and Hungary', *Soviet Studies,* vol. 44, no. 2.

Mladek, J. (1993) 'The different paths of privatization: Czechoslovakia 1990 – ?' in R. Frydman, A. Rapaczynski, J. S. Earle *et al.* (eds), *The Privatization Process in Central Europe,* New York: Central European University Press.

Mueller, D. C. (1991) 'Choosing a constitution in East Europe: lessons from public choice', *Journal of Comparative Economics,* vol. 15: 325–49.

Murrell, P. (1991a) 'Symposium on economic transition in the Soviet Union and Eastern Europe', *Journal of Economic Perspectives,* Fall, vol. 5, no. 4: 3–9.

—— (1991b) 'Can neoclassical economics underpin the reform of centrally planned economies?', *Journal of Economic Perspectives,* Fall, vol. 5, no. 4: 59–76.

Newberry, D. M. (1991) 'Sequencing the transition', Working Paper Series, Washington, D.C.: Institute for Policy Reform.

—— (1992) 'The safety net during transformation: Hungary' in C. Clague and G. C. Rausser (eds), *The Emergence of Market Economies in Eastern Europe,* Cambridge, Mass.: Blackwell.

Olson, M. (1965) *The Logic of Collective Action: Public Goods and the Theory of Groups,* Cambridge, Mass.: Harvard University Press.

Pejovich, S. (1980) 'The costs of codetermination', *Review of Social Economy,* December, vol. 38, no. 3: 319–21.

—— (ed.) (1987) *Socialism: Institutional, Philosophical and Economic Issues, International Studies in Economics and Econometrics, vol. 14,* Boston: Kluwer Academic.

—— (1992) 'A property rights analysis of the inefficiency of investment decisions by labour-managed firms', *Journal of Institutional and Theoretical Economics,* vol. 148, no. 1: 30–41.

Peltzman, S. (1976) 'Toward a more general theory of regulation', *Journal of Law and Economics,* August, vol. 19, no. 2: 211–48.

Privatization International (1996) *International Privatization Databases,* London: Privatization International.

Rubin, P. H. (1994) 'Growing a legal system in the post-communist economies', *Cornell International Law Journal,* Winter, vol. 27, no. 1: 1–47.

Sacks, S. R. (1994) 'The Yugoslav firm' in M. Bornstein (ed.), *Comparative Economic Systems: Models and Cases*, Toronto: Irwin.

Shapiro, C. and Willig, R. D. (1989) 'Privatization to limit public-sector discretion', Working Paper, Princeton University Department of Economics, August.

Shleifer, A. and Vishny, R. W. (1994) 'Politicians and firms', *Quarterly Journal of Economics*, November, vol. 109, no. 4: 995–1026.

Simoneti, M. and Bohm, A. (eds) (1992) *Privatization in Central and Eastern Europe 1991: Country Privatization Reports & Specific Implementation Issues*, Washington, D.C.: Economic Development Institute of the World Bank and Central and East European Privatization Network.

Stark, D. (1994) 'Path dependence and privatization strategies in East Central Europe', in V. Milor (ed.), *Changing Political Economies: Privatization in Post-Communist and Reforming Communist States. Emerging Global Issues*, London: Lynne Rienner.

Stigler, G. J. (1971) 'The theory of economic regulation', *Bell Journal of Economics and Management Sciences*, Spring, vol. 2, no. 1: 1–21.

—— (1972) 'Economic competition and political competition', *Public Choice*, Fall, vol. 13: 91–106.

Tamowicz, P. (1993) 'Small privatization in Poland: an inside view', in R. Frydman, A. Rapaczynski, J. S. Earle *et al.* (eds), *The Privatization Process in Central Europe*, New York: Central European University Press.

Tirole, J. (1991) 'Ownership and incentives in a transition economy', *Working Paper Series*, Washington, D.C.: Institute for Policy Reform.

Tohamy, Sahar M. (1997) 'A theory of privatization', Ph.D. dissertation, Department of Economics, Emory University, Atlanta, Ga.

Tohamy, Soumaya M. (1994) 'Incrementalism in the US federal budgetary process: an interest-group perspective', Ph.D. dissertation, Department of Economics, Emory University, Atlanta, Ga.

Vanek, J. (1971) 'The participatory economy', in *The Participatory Economy: An Evolutionary Hypothesis and A Strategy for Development*, Itacha, NY: Cornell University Press.

Ward, B. (1958) 'The firm in Illyria: market syndicalism', *American Economic Review*, September, vol. 48, no. 4: 566–89.

4 Getting ready for globalization

A new privatization strategy for the MENA region?

John Page

Introduction

The 1990s in the Middle East and North Africa (MENA) region has have been characterized by two important – but incomplete – transformations of the region's economies.[1] The first is the increasing extent to which the MENA region had begun to integrate itself into the world economy. Trade policy reforms in virtually all countries have removed quantitative import restrictions and reduced and rationalized tariffs. Jordan, Morocco, and Tunisia have signed trade integration agreements with the European Union (EU). Egypt is in the last stages of concluding a similar agreement, and Algeria, Lebanon and Syria are at earlier stages of negotiations. Yet, despite these efforts, integration of the MENA countries into the global economy has proceeded rather slowly (World Bank 1997b). The rate of growth of trade – measured as the ratio of exports plus imports to gross domestic product – has lagged other regions of the developing world. Intra-regional trade has stagnated, and perhaps most worrisome, non-traditional exports have failed to expand rapidly.

The second transformation is of the economic role of the state. Fiscal constraints on public investments, combined with a rethinking of the statist development strategies that had characterized the region in the three decades following independence, created new space for the private sector to take a leading role in economic development. Privatization of public enterprises engaged in producing goods and services was initiated by most MENA governments, and institutional reforms designed to improve the climate for private investment were undertaken. In contrast with other regions, however, these efforts have also lagged. Privatization transactions have been relatively few, and in some important economies such as Egypt, Morocco and Tunisia the government's strategic approach to privatization in terms of the companies offered for sale and the modalities has shifted several times.

This chapter reviews briefly the experience of MENA countries with privatization and globalization. It argues that rapid implementation of across-the-board privatization has lagged behind in the MENA region because of fears on the part of governments that the labour redundancies which might occur as a consequence would exacerbate an already grave employment problem. It also argues that there is an important link between the lack of trade-related infra-structure and the growth of trade. The chapter represents a means by which the region's economies can accelerate trade integration and growth while avoiding the early stage employment problem associated with privatization.

MENA's record of privatization

Privatization of state-owned enterprises (SOEs) in the MENA region has been slow relative to other regions, especially Latin America and East Asia. Although privatization programmes in many of the region's major economies have been in place since the early 1990s it was not until 1994 that the volume of sales and revenue began to increase substantially.

Globally between 1988 and 1995 governments of developing countries sold SOEs worth about US$130 billion. the MENA region's share of those transactions was less than 3 per cent (US$3.4 billion). The region has also lagged in offering new projects for the private provision of infrastructure (PPI). Through the end of 1996 the MENA region accounted for only 4 per cent of all PPI projects world-wide.

The pace of privatization has accelerated somewhat since 1994, but transactions have been concentrated in a small number of MENA economies. In 1995 and 1996 about US$2.0 billion worth of public sector assets were sold, more than three times the volumes in 1993 and 1994. The vast majority of these transactions took place in only three MENA countries, Egypt, Kuwait and Morocco. Tunisia, which began its privatization efforts in 1986, earlier than most MENA countries, has failed to increase the momentum of its programme and has sold only US$32 million of SOE assets since 1993.

Jordan has only recently (1997) offered substantial shares in public sector companies for sale. Algeria's privatization programme – faced with growing political violence and the need to shift to the sale of larger SOEs – has stalled, while privatization efforts in Syria, Lebanon and the majority of the Gulf Cooperation Council (GCC) countries have not yet begun in earnest.

One set of estimates has placed the potential value of future privatizations in the region at an additional US$2.0 billion through 1999 (*Privatization International Magazine* 1996). Governments in Algeria (250), Egypt (100), Jordan (20), Morocco (100), Tunisia (60) and Yemen (70) have identified some 600 enterprises as privatization candidates. The estimated total value of PPI projects proposed by governments in MENA is about US$45 billion. However, while these initiatives represent a major increase over the historical record, they remain small internationally at about 3 per cent of all transactions.

Within individual MENA economies privatization efforts have been characterized by shifting political support and changing privatization strategies and techniques. The results have been equally mixed; privatization programmes have gained and lost momentum as investors have been unsure of governments' intentions with respect to the types of enterprises to be offered for sale, the methods of privatization, and the conditions of sale, including the regulatory regime. The recent experience of some of the region's economies in undertaking major privatization efforts is briefly discussed next.

Egypt

SOEs continue to dominate Egypt's economy despite a privatization programme that began in 1991. The public sector – including the administration, service and economic authorities, and public enterprises – employs about 35 per cent of the labour force, and produces nearly 60 per cent of non-agricultural output. Public enterprises in manufacturing and services employ more than one million workers and the state sector accounts for approximately two-thirds of Egyptian manufacturing.

Privatization began as part of Egypt's stabilization and structural reform programme of the early 1990s. Law 203 of 1991 reorganized the public enterprise sector into seventeen holding companies structured along sectoral lines. The law allowed for the privatization of companies held by these legally autonomous entities and established a 'public enterprise office' (PEO) to act as the liaison between the government and the holding companies. The Ministry of Industry, which had exercised line authority over the public manufacturing sector, was stripped of its decision-making power and a Ministry for Public Enterprise was created. Multilateral and bilateral donors – especially the USAID programme – provided technical assistance for the Ministry and PEO on privatization techniques.

The privatization process was slow to begin. The first transaction took place only in February 1993 and many of the early privatizations consisted of the sale of miscellaneous assets, liquidations and employee buy-outs or share distributions. Privatization was mostly limited to healthy companies, with the worst performing companies left untouched (*Oxford Analytica* 1995).[4] Moreover, Law 203 specifically prohibited the privatization of certain 'strategic industries' including public utilities, telecommunications, and military industries. Private investors and the donor community urged more aggressive action on the part of government.

In May 1993 the first initial public offering (IPO) of a public sector company – Misr Chemicals – was made on the stock exchange. The success of this transaction led to other partial privatizations through the capital market, primarily by offering 10 per cent of PE shares to employee stock options and 10 per cent on the stock exchange. While continued implementation of partial privatizations through the capital market led to some stock market volatility, the programme has been responsible for a substantial increase in stock market capitalization in Egypt.

The government of Prime Minister Kamal El-Ganzoury, which took office in January 1996, substantially accelerated the pace of privatization. In 1996 more than US$800 million in assets were privatized and by end 1996, forty-six (of the 314) Law 203 companies had been wholly or partially privatized. The programme for 1997 called for the sale of thirty-three companies to strategic investors and IPOs to be undertaken for an additional twelve companies. Several highly publicized transactions – including the sale of the nation's only brewery to a foreign anchor investor – have increased international awareness of the programme and public acceptance.

Nevertheless, there are a number of important problems remaining in Egypt's approach to privatization:

- The bulk of transactions (64 per cent by value) have consisted of minority placements through the capital market, liquidation or sale of assets and employee ownership schemes. While these transactions have increased the momentum of the programme and added to revenues, they have not fundamentally altered the governance structure of the public enterprises.
- The privatization programme has followed no coherent strategy in identifying enterprises to be brought to the market, relying instead on the decisions of the individual holding companies. Thus some holding companies have attempted to retain their most profitable enterprises and privatize loss makers which have elicited little investor interest.
- Initial steps to privatize telecommunications and power generation have proceeded slowly and have required changes in legislation. Pricing issues and the regulatory regime have not been fully addressed.
- Privatization of the major public financial institutions has lagged privatization efforts in the real sectors.

Jordan

While Jordan's public sector is large – accounting for about 55 per cent of total employment – state ownership in manufacturing and services is less pronounced than in most other MENA countries. SOEs are concentrated in infrastructure (transport, water, electricity and telecommunications) and in phosphate mining and cement manufacturing. In addition the Jordan Investment Corporation (JIC) holds minority shareholdings (mostly 10 per cent) in 60 companies listed on the Amman Stock Exchange.

Until 1996 privatization efforts were *ad hoc* and decentralized among the JIC and individual ministries. Although the JIC had announced several privatization initiatives, prior to the end of 1996 only two hotels had been sold and the telecommunications company had been corporatized. The privatization effort accelerated somewhat in 1997 with the following initiatives:

- Forty per cent of the telecommunications company was offered for sale to an anchor investor.
- The Jordan Electricity Authority was corporatized as a public shareholding company and a decision was reached to separate distribution from generation. Divestiture decisions were made for the Irbid District Electricity Company and the Jordan Electric Power Company.
- JIC advanced privatization of its holdings in cement and tourism.

- An executive authority for privatization was established in the Prime Ministry.

These actions, while a major increase over previous efforts, still primarily reflect intentions to privatize rather than transactions completed. If they proceed as planned, however, the rapid privatization of substantial capacity in power and telecommunications would be unique in the region.

Morocco

There are about 800 SOEs and public–private joint ventures in Morocco across a wide range of sectors, including finance, industry, services and agriculture. Together they produce about 12 per cent of GDP and employ 6 per cent of the urban formal labour force. The privatization programme was authorized in 1989 by an act of parliament, but began in earnest in 1991 when the institutional framework was fully in place. One hundred and fourteen public investments (seventy-seven companies and thirty-seven hotels) were targeted for privatization by the end of 1998. Since the programme began, 54 privatizations have taken place with a total asset value of US$1.22 billion. The sectoral distribution by type of company is given in Table 4.1. The government has directly solicited private participation in the power sector through an IPP, and has undertaken a water and electricity concession for Casablanca with a foreign firm.

Morocco's institutional framework is among the most well defined in the region. A privatization minister is responsible for overall programme implementation. He presides over a five member inter-ministerial transfer commission which – to ensure transparency – must approve all private placements as meeting specific social, regional or employment goals. An independent valuation authority establishes reservation prices. Transactions are also allowed to take place through the financial markets, including the Casablanca Stock Exchange, and by competitive bidding. The law does not mandate employment guarantees, but in some cases employees may be accorded preference in buying shares.

Foreign investment in privatized firms is in general allowed, and economy-

Table 4.1 Morocco: privatizations by sector

Hotels	19
Transportation	2
Gas distribution	2
Food/agro	3
Cement	3
Textiles	3
Petroleum	5
Banking/finance	3
Other	12

Source: Damji 1997.

wide there are no restrictions on foreign ownership. The government has made significant efforts to attract foreign investment, including removing restrictions on capital transfers, and allowing innovative methods, such as debt swap agreements, to encourage foreigners to invest. Ten of the twenty-seven companies and four of the eighteen hotels privatized have been sold at least partly to foreign investors. However, the law permits preference in private placements to be given to local investors for cases of 'regional' priority. In practice this preference seems to have been used in cases where firms sourced inputs locally and the domestic private investor has guaranteed to continue the practice.

A recent innovation was the public offering in 1996, of 'privatization bonds' by the treasury in the amount of approximately US$180 million. These zero coupon, two-year bonds are convertible to shares of public enterprises offered on the Casablanca Exchange with preference over other investors. They reduce the pressures on the finance ministry to accelerate individual transactions to meet fiscal targets while at the same time stimulating investor pressure to increase the momentum of the overall programme.

Tunisia

The SOE sector in Tunisia is extensive. Widespread public investment was undertaken in virtually every area of production and services from independence in 1954 to the beginning of the 1970s. State ownership in Tunisia is characterized by a complex web of minority shareholdings, subsidiary agreements and ownership by state-controlled banks. When privatization efforts began in the second half of the 1980s enterprises in which the state had an equity share of more than 34 per cent accounted for 31 per cent of GDP and 40 per cent of total investment. SOEs employed about 156,000 people, 13 per cent of total employment.

Tunisia's privatization programme was launched in 1986 as part of a larger effort at macroeconomic adjustment and structural reform, but the institutional framework was only put in place in 1989 with the promulgation of a general legal framework for enterprise restructuring and privatization. Between 1986 and 1994 approximately forty-five companies with an asset value of US$90 million were privatized, concentrated in hotels, construction, and restaurants. The majority of transactions consisted of private placements, and number of unprofitable firms were liquidated.

In 1994 a second legislative framework was enacted to permit the government to undertake privatizations through the sale of shares on the Tunis Bourse and via strategic investors for large, sensitive transactions. This second phase of privatization had been completed from a list of forty-seven eligible companies. The flagship transaction was the sale of 20 per cent of the shares of Tunis Air, the national airline, via an IPO on the Tunis Bourse. In 1997 the pace of privatization appears to have further accelerated. Sixty enterprises with total net assets of approximately US$1.5 billion have been identified for sale, including key public companies such as cement plants and banks.

Nevertheless, Tunisia's privatization programme has several limitations which will constrain its scope and speed of implementation:

- The institutional framework for the programme has changed several times since 1989.
- Identification of the number and value of privatizable public enterprises is made difficult by a maze of direct ownerships, cross-holdings, and mixed public-private ownership.
- In an effort to minimize worker resistance the government has refused to make public the enterprises to be privatized, and the process by which transactions are carried out is not well understood nor is it transparent.
- Government has required new owners to maintain existing staffing levels in privatized firms and to avoid whole or partial closure of the enterprise.
- The Tunis Bourse needs modernization and reorganization to handle an increased volume of transactions.

Why has privatization lagged in MENA?

Although it is no longer growing rapidly, the public sector continues to dominate the MENA region's economies to a greater extent than in other

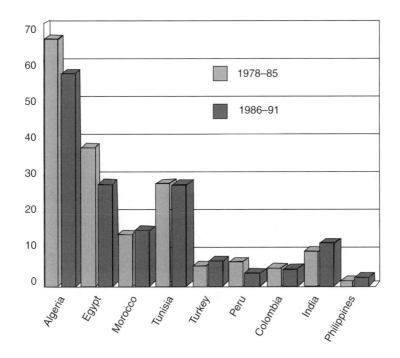

Figure 4.1 Share of state-owned enterprises in economic activity (as % of GDP)
Source: World Bank 1995b.

regions of the developing world. Both the share of total assets owned and the share of output produced by the public sector in the MENA are high by international standards (Figure 4.1). And – perhaps more important to understanding the lack of dynamism in the privatization process – the share of the total labour force employed in the public sector is also high (Figure 4.2).

During the post-independence period public sector salaries and benefits in the MENA region were established largely without reference to alternative wages in the private sector. The public sector became the wage leader in the labour market. Civil service (and public enterprise) jobs paid better wages, offered more fringe benefits, gave better job security, and assured more social status than those in the private sector. In a number of MENA economies the government guaranteed public employment to university graduates, and frequently acted as employer of last resort for graduates at lower educational levels (World Bank 1997c).

One result of this pattern of employment, wages and benefits was that MENA countries are now endowed with one of the largest – and relatively best paid – public sectors in the world (Table 4.2). MENA countries devote a larger share of their GDP (9.8 per cent) to civil service salaries than any other region. They are the only grouping of countries internationally in which the ratio of public sector wages to wages in the private sector exceeds one (1.3).

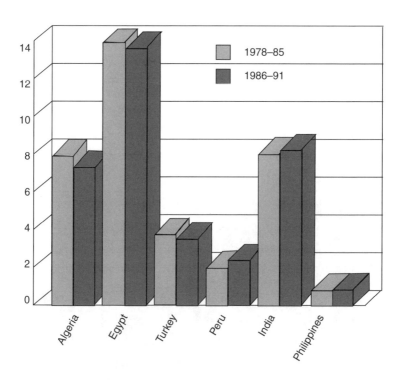

Figure 4.2 Share of state-owned enterprises in employment (% of total employment)
Source: World Bank 1995c.

Table 4.2 Central government wages, early 1990s

Region	Number of countries	Central govt. wages and salaries as % of GDP	Average central govt. wage as multiple of per capital GDP	Ratio of public to private sector wages
Africa	21	6.7	5.5	1.0
Asia	14	4.7	3.0	0.8
Europe and Central Asia	21	3.7	1.3	0.7
Latin America and the Caribbean	12	4.9	2.7	0.9
MENA	8	9.8	3.4	1.3
OECD	16	4.5	1.6	0.9
Overall	92	5.4	2.9	0.8

Source: World Bank 1997c.

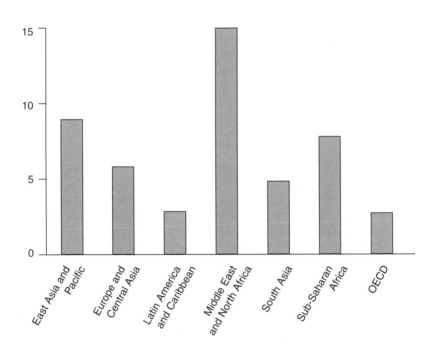

Figure 4.3 Unemployment rate by region, 1993 (%)

Note: * Algeria, Egypt, Iran, Jordan, Morocco, Syria, Tunisia and Yemen.
Source: World Bank 1995c.

Partly as a consequence of these labour market distortions, the MENA also has the highest recorded rates of unemployment internationally (Figure 4.3). While the unemployment problem is fundamentally a product of low economic growth rates and high population growth, governments are reluctant to exacerbate the problem by aggressive privatization of those public enterprises employing large numbers of workers. Fear of labour redundancies has slowed down privatization, particularly in the manufacturing sector, in Algeria, Egypt, Jordan, Kuwait, Tunisia and Yemen. The Egyptian case was particularly dramatic. In 1994 textile workers in Kafr-al-Dawar struck and engaged in mass demonstrations of more than 7,000 workers to protest privatizations proposed under an agreement with the International Monetary Fund.

Some governments in the region have attempted to deal with the political fallout from labour shedding by requiring that potential investors maintain existing employment levels. In Morocco, for example, informal agreements with new employers not to shed labour for five years from the date of purchase were used to insulate workers from large-scale layoffs. Tunisia sought similar agreement with potential purchasers. In Egypt many of the first companies slated for privatization were those where overstaffing was not a significant problem. In general this has reduced investor interest in the enterprises subject to employment constraints and lowered bid prices, sometimes to levels below the government's reservation price.

Financial incentives for voluntary redundancy such as severance pay, retraining or small business promotion grants have not been widely used due to fiscal constraints. While public sector wages declined in real terms in most MENA countries during the 1990s, the public sector remains the wage leader for unskilled and production labour in many, especially when the cash value of benefits is taken into account. Thus the costs of financial incentives for voluntary redundancy are substantial.

One study of the potential costs of providing redundancy payments to workers in Egypt's public sector (Assaad 1996) indicates that rents to public sector workers in Egypt remain substantial – especially for better educated women and older workers – despite the stagnation of public sector wages during the last ten years. He estimates that the average rent to a public sector worker is approximately equal to 100 times the monthly wage. His estimates of the total cost of providing acceptable voluntary redundancy packages to public sector workers, through combinations of one time buy-outs and early retirement, sufficient to achieve a 30 per cent reduction in the labour force, range from approximately US$1–2 billion, or about 1.5–3.0 per cent of GDP. Similar, although less careful, estimates of the costs of voluntary redundancy programmes in Morocco and Yemen yield results which are equal to or larger than the estimates for Egypt as a share of GDP.

Governments, thus, find themselves caught between the desire to increase privatization transactions to maintain the credibility of their privatization programme, to generate revenue, and to reduce the fiscal burden imposed by loss-making enterprises, and the need to minimize potential worker backlash arising from expected job losses. The key to resolving this conflict is accelerated growth. More rapid economic growth will result in tightening of the labour market, rising real wages and a decreasing premium to public sector employment. Increased tax revenues from rising income will permit greater fiscal space to governments to undertake more active labour redundancy policies.

The MENA, the global economy and growth

Growth in the MENA has been disappointing. The economies of the MENA were among the slowest growing in the world between 1985 and 1995. Notwithstanding an acceleration of growth rates across the region during the second half of the 1990s, the region's economies failed to generate sufficient growth to absorb new labour force entrants and to make moderate reductions in unemployment. Figure 4.4 contrasts the rate of growth needed to reduce unemployment with the historical growth rates for four MENA economies: Algeria, Egypt, Morocco and Tunisia.[2] With the exception of Egypt's historical performance and Tunisia's projected growth, none of the economies

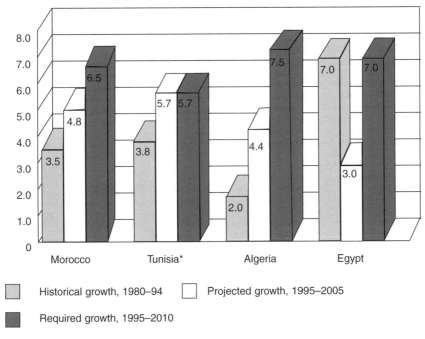

Figure 4.4 Rates of growth 'required' to reduce unemployment to natural rates (% per year)

Note: 'Required' output growth is that needed to absorb new labour force entrants as well as to reduce unemployment towards natural rates by 2010.
* Tunisia's projected growth is for 1995–2000 period only.
Source: World Bank estimates.

has achieved, nor is projected to achieve, the rate of growth needed to reduce unemployment through the first decade of the twenty-first century.

While the origins of the MENA region's prolonged economic stagnation are linked primarily to oil, lagging productivity change has been an important contributory factor.[3] Average total factor productivity (TFP) growth has been negative for the MENA since 1975 with the consequence that output has grown at a slower rate than would have been predicted on the basis of the region's record of factor accumulation.

The MENA region's prospects for a sustained recovery and acceleration of growth are linked to the global economy. The correlation between integration with the world economy and economic growth is dramatic (Figure 4.5). World-wide, economies with higher ratios of imports plus exports to GDP (real trade ratios) have higher GDP growth rates, higher rates of TFP growth and higher rates of foreign investment. Indeed, for the most part only fast integrating countries have had per capita income growth rates sufficiently high to close the income gap with the more advanced economies.

The MENA have lagged behind most other regions in the pace of trade integration. Together with Africa and South Asia, MENA's real trade to GDP ratios have stagnated since 1960 and are projected to grow only modestly during the next ten years (World Bank 1997b). Individual countries in the region show remarkable consistency with the regional trend. Only Jordan recorded a substantial increase in its real trade ratio between the first half of the 1980s and the first half of the 1990s; Iran, Morocco, Saudi Arabia and the UAE posted modest gains. The remainder of the region's economies had declining real trade ratios, with major declines in Egypt, Iraq, Oman and Yemen.

One of the key links between rapid integration and growth occurs through the

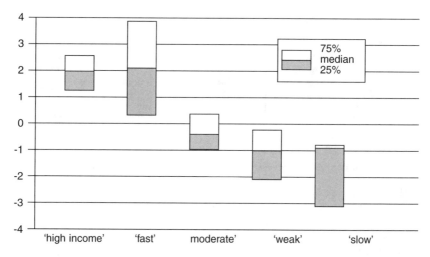

Figure 4.5 Median real per capita GDP growth and speed of integration, 1984–93

Source: World Bank 1995a, 1996.

Table 4.3 Required rates of export growth consistent with achieving 6% real growth per year, 1996–2010

	Required export growth	Projected export growth	Difference
Morocco	6.3	5.6	0.7
Tunisia	6.4	3.7	2.7
Algeria	8.8	4.4	4.4
Egypt	6.3	4.3	2.0
Jordan	7.5	5.2	2.3
Syria	3.8	2.5	1.3
Iran	5.6	3.9	1.7
Yemen	9.5	2.5	7.0

Note: growth rates are compound averages over 1996–2010.
Source: World Bank data and projections.

expansion of manufactured exports. Cross-country evidence shows that countries with high levels of manufactured exports have higher rates of TFP change (Pack and Page 1994). Because MENA's economies are small, export growth is also important as a source of aggregate demand. Table 4.3 summarizes the 'required' rates of export growth consistent with the goal of achieving 6 per cent real growth in the region's major economies. The implied rates of export expansion are feasible but ambitious in comparison with MENA's historical performance.

The MENA region's performance in manufactured export growth has been particularly disappointing. The region's share of manufactures in merchandise trade in the range of 20–25 per cent, similar to that of Latin America. Together with Africa and Latin America it has also experienced the lowest rate of growth in shares of manufactured exports over the past decade (World Bank 1997b). The MENA is one of only two regions in which export growth has lagged behind the rate of growth of imports in its major trading partners (Figure 4.6).

Thus, the MENA faces a critical challenge to accelerate the speed of trade integration. Rapid export expansion – and in particular the growth of manufactured, non-traditional exports – is central to achieving the economic growth rates needed to reduce unemployment. The region's governments have begun to respond to this challenge. Trade liberalization, involving both the removal of non-tariff barriers and the reduction and rationalization of tariffs, is taking place in virtually all of the developing countries of the MENA.[4] (The countries of the Gulf Cooperation Council have traditionally been quite open to international trade.) Jordan, Morocco and Tunisia have signed free trade agreements with the European Union (EU) which when fully implemented will open their home markets to European imports while providing access to the EU for manufactured exports. Egypt is in the final stages of negotiations with the EU for a similar agreement, and Lebanon and Syria have begun preliminary talks.

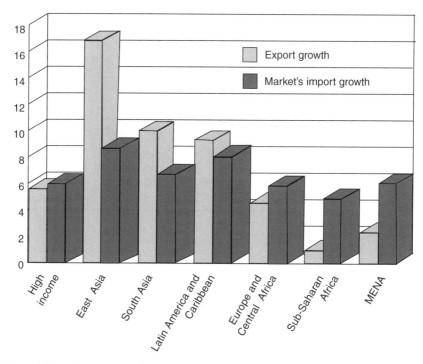

Figure 4.6 Real export growth and market's import growth, 1991–95 (annual average
    % change)
Source: World Bank 1997b.

Trade related infrastructure is critical to global success

While trade liberalization is a necessary first step in reducing anti-export bias
and increasing trade, it is not sufficient. Good transport and communications
systems have become critical to competitiveness in both service and
manufacturing industries. Global manufacturing and marketing systems have
become increasingly dependent on just-in-time processes, close contact with
customers, and flexible manufacturing systems. Just-in-time purchases have
doubled since 1987 and now account for nearly half of all purchases in the
textile industry and 35 per cent of all purchases in electronics in North
America and Europe. Adequate and reliable electric power is essential to
competitive manufacturing. Internationally, there is an association between
slow trade integration and inadequate infrastructure (World Bank 1996).
Several recent studies also indicate that quality of infrastructure is a key
determinant of the choice of location by foreign direct investors (Wheeler
and Mody 1992, Brunetti *et al.* 1998).

Transport and logistics play a vital role in manufactured goods trade.
Roads, seaports, and the related areas of stevedoring, warehousing and
customs management are critical for the competitiveness of manufactured and

processed agricultural exports. Airfreight plays an increasingly important role in the success of time sensitive manufactured exports such as high fashion clothing and footwear. Most high value agricultural exports, such as truck crops and cut flowers, are critically dependent on reliable low cost airfreight.

Communications improvements and the revolution in information technology have greatly expanded the range of services traded among economies. It is increasingly possible to unbundle the production and consumption of such information intensive service activities as: research and development, inventory management, personnel administration, secretarial and transcription services and advertising. Data entry, analysis of income statements, medical transcription, 'back office' operations for airlines and the development of computer software, financial products and chemical processes are all examples of activities which have become traded internationally (World Bank 1995b).

Trade in commercial services has grown more rapidly than merchandise trade over the past decade (Hoekman 1998). Average annual growth in commercial services between 1980 and 1993 was 7.7 per cent compared with 4.9 per cent for merchandise trade. Trade in 'other private services' the component of commercial services in which information intensive, long-distance services are concentrated, grew at 9.5 per cent over the same period.

Access to low cost, high quality telecommunications is an indispensable element of success in long-distance services. Gains in carrying capacity arising from optical fibre and satellite networks make the transfer of vast amounts of data possible, creating entirely new areas of comparative advantage such as computer software exports. The information hubs or teleports which make advanced communications links possible are expanding rapidly world-wide; nearly 100 are in operation or under construction (ITU, 1995). Average-per-minute costs of international phone calls have fallen at about 4 per cent per year in the developing countries and at about 2 per cent per year in the industrial countries. Not surprisingly, countries with the greatest success in information-intensive services are among the low cost providers of telecommunications (World Bank 1996).

MENA lags in trade related infrastructure

While there are substantial variations among countries, the MENA lags behind the more rapidly integrating developing economies in Asia, Europe and Latin America in providing most types of trade-related infrastructure. With the exception of the high-income countries of the GCC (and Israel), telecommunications density is low, service charges are high and quality is uncertain. The region performs better in the provision of electrical power, but a number of economies that are attempting to liberalize trade lag behind fast integrators internationally. Port services and trade logistics are relatively high-cost and suffer from quality problems, and state airfreight monopolies have kept air cargo prices high and have reduced service.

Telecommunications

Telecommunications density is normally measured by the number of lines per 1,000 residents. In high income economies telephone density typically ranges from 400 to 600 per thousand. The average for rapidly integrating developing economies is 120. In the MENA only the high income, sparsely populated countries of the GCC (plus Turkey and Israel) exceed or approach that level of density (Figure 4.7). It is particularly noteworthy that the four developing MENA economies which have signed agreements or are in advanced stages of negotiation with the European Union – Egypt, Jordan, Morocco, and Tunisia – all have substantial deficits in telephone density.

Telecommunications charges are high in the MENA relative to both advanced country providers and rapidly integrating developing economies. The cost of a three minute call from the US to Middle Eastern destinations is about US$2.00. Rapid integrators have charges that are about three times that level at US$6.24. In the MENA region call charges range from about US$3.50 (Israel) to more than US$14.00 (Syria) with the majority of countries exceeding the charge level for rapid integrators (Figure 4.8). Among the countries that have pursued more aggressive policies of trade liberalization Morocco and Jordan have particularly high telephone charges (exceeding US$9.00).

Telecommunications quality is more difficult to measure but also appears problematic. Prior to the introduction of cellular service, one measure of unserved demand was the waiting period for installation of a telephone line. Waiting periods in most of MENA substantially exceeded the developing country average of 1.5 years. In Jordan, Lebanon, and the West Bank and Gaza

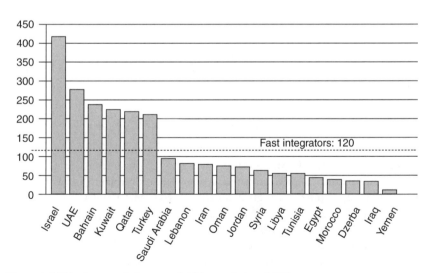

Figure 4.7 Telephone mainlines per 1,000 population, 1995
Source: Smith *et al.* 1997, ITU 1995.

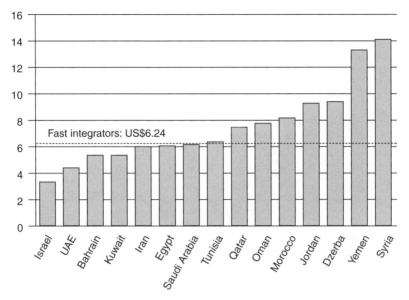

Figure 4.8 Average price of a three-minute call to the USA in 1995 (in US$)
Source: Smith *et al.* 1997, ITU 1995.

it could take nearly a decade to receive a new line. In 1995 the average wait time was 5.7 years in Egypt, and over 9.5 years in Algeria and Jordan. Only Morocco and Tunisia among the developing MENA economies had waiting periods of less than four years. Telephone faults (per 100 main lines) are relatively high in Tunisia, Morocco, Algeria and Jordan and exceed the average for lower middle income countries. In Jordan the call completion rate was only 45 per cent in 1994, while in Lebanon it was less than 30 per cent (Smith *et al.* 1997).

Electrical power

The developing countries of the MENA also lag behind rapidly integrating economies in the production of electricity (Figure 4.9). While the GCC economies and Israel are relatively well supplied with electrical power, the remaining countries in the region all fall short of the 1,585 kilowatt hours per person that fast integrating economies averaged in 1994. The shortfall is particularly acute in Tunisia, Algeria, Morocco and Yemen, all of which also trail comparator countries at their income levels. Electricity system losses on the other hand are below those expected on the basis of comparator country performance (Smith *et al.* 1997). Egypt, Tunisia and Algeria are particularly noteworthy for system losses that approach the levels of higher income comparators. Taken together these trends suggest that countries in the MENA region face a greater immediate challenge in expanding the capacity of the power grid than in its administration and maintenance.

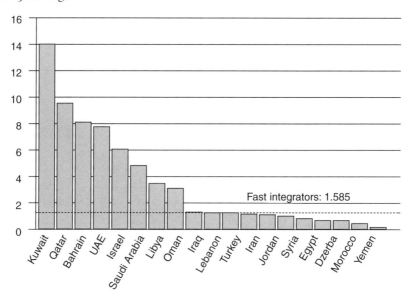

Figure 4.9 Electric power production: kilowatt hours per person, 1994
Source: Smith *et al.* 1997, ITU 1995.

Trade logistics

The MENA region's performance in providing infrastructure for trade logistics, including roads, ports, trade-related services and airfreight is mixed. Roads in general are adequate, although considerable maintenance deficits are present in many countries. Road safety and traffic flow are problems, however, because road capacity and design have failed to keep pace with growing traffic volumes (Smith *et al.* 1997).

Comprehensive data on port infrastructure and operations are lacking, but the evidence available suggests that outside of the GCC and Israel, the high cost and poor quality of service in the MENA's ports – operated as state monopolies – may act as a significant deterrent to expanded trade. In Egypt for example, seaport service charges for imports are triple those of Mediterranean competitors and raise the CIF cost for imports by more than a 10 per cent (Hoekman 1996). Housekeeping and maintenance are of low quality resulting in poor physical condition of the port. Vessel turn around times are slow and increase total chargeable times by more than 10 per cent. Export transactions costs are not as high – due to lower charges by the state monopoly on seaport services for exports – but still represent as much as 10–15 per cent of the export price, primarily due to cumbersome procedures, delays and housekeeping problems (World Bank 1997a).

Airfreight charges are high throughout the region, due to the monopoly position of national carriers and restrictive tariff regulation. In Egypt for example air cargo costs for exports to Europe are double those of Israel due to restrictions on the ability of Egypt Air (the state airline) to carry backhaul cargo. The pricing policy adds 40 per cent, for example, to the cost of grape exports to the European market (World Bank 1997a).

Toward a new strategy for privatization

It may be possible for MENA governments to accelerate the pace of privatization in the region while at the same time increasing popular support for the privatization process by shifting to a new strategy based on three key elements:[4]

1 Enterprises targeted for early privatization should be clearly linked to improving the competitive position of MENA economies in the global marketplace.
2 Privatizations of such enterprises should be explicitly and publicly linked to relieving investment or productivity constraints.
3 Employee ownership or mass privatization schemes should be included in all large scale privatizations.

To date MENA governments have offered little coherent, strategic justification for privatization beyond demonstrating a commitment to private sector development and relieving the fiscal burden imposed by public enterprises. For most MENA economies, however, fiscal adjustment has taken place and fiscal discipline has been reasonably good. Fiscal space is limited more by the size of the public administration than by the size of the public productive sector (IMF 1997). Moreover, private investors – both foreign and domestic – do not identify lack of privatization as a major deterrent to increased private investment in MENA economies. Surveys of potential foreign investors (Page and Underwood 1997) and domestic private investors (Brunetti, Kisunko and Weder 1998) rank infrastructure bottlenecks as the primary impediment to increased investment in the region. The high ranking accorded to infrastructure bottlenecks in MENA is unique among the six developing regions surveyed by the International Finance Corporation in 1997.

Thus, a strategy which focuses first on elements of trade related infrastructure – telecommunications, ports, electrical power, and transportation – may provide a more compelling rationale for privatization to investors and to the public at large than the present practice of privatizing 'targets of opportunity', often seemingly in response to pressures from aid donors or international financial institutions. The empirical links between greater trade integration – especially through the growth of manufactured exports – more rapid economic growth and increased employment provide a strong basis for defining private provision of trade related infrastructure as a key element of an employment-oriented growth strategy (Sachs and Warner 1995). This rationale should be particularly compelling in the case of those MENA economies which have signed or are negotiating free trade agreements with the European Union. Recent research shows that without the dynamic gains coming from increased foreign direct investment and improvements in the productivity of existing enterprises the association agreements offer very limited potential for increases in national income (Page and Underwood 1997).

Why private provision of trade-related infrastructure? First, outside of the countries of the GCC, most countries in the region have been unable to find the public resources to keep pace with expanding infrastructure needs. If the region continues to spend 3–4 per cent of GDP on infrastructure at projected rates of GDP growth in the 2.5–3.0 per cent range, about US$300 billion will be invested in all infrastructure during the next decade. This amount will be sufficient to replace old assets and to expand coverage in line with population growth, but not to close the service gaps outlined above. If the region's developing economies increase growth to about 6 per cent and raise the share of infrastructure investments in GDP to the 4–5 per cent range, characteristic of more integrated economies, an incremental US$100 billion will need to be found. Under reasonable assumptions concerning the capacity for domestic funding and the volume of lending from international financial institutions, about US$15 billion would need to come from private sources. Within the GCC there is also scope for private investment perhaps on the order of US$35 billion (Smith *et al.* 1997).

One characteristic of successful privatizations in Latin America has been the extent to which they have been used to break investment constraints. The 'capitalization' programme in Bolivia is the clearest example, because it was explicitly designed to require substantial incremental investment by the private purchasers as a condition of the transfer of existing assets and managerial control. This led to an expansion of services in telecommunications, electrical power generation and air transport as a direct outcome of the privatization programme (Pierce 1997). In Argentina, Chile and Mexico one outcome of the privatizations of telecommunications was a substantial increase in investment and an expansion of services (Edwards 1995). One careful study of the welfare effects of privatizations concluded that for the Latin American cases examined the largest welfare gains came as a consequence of breaking investment bottlenecks in infrastructure (Galal *et al.* 1994).

Table 4.4 summarizes the status of privatization efforts in trade-related infrastructure in the MENA region. Private provision of power, primarily via independent power production agreements (IPPs) is most advanced. In telecommunications several countries have permitted entry of private cellular service, and some ancillary services, but only Jordan has taken the initiative of putting up a substantial share of its core telecommunications capacity (40 per cent of assets) for private bid. Egypt has initiated the process of bidding out a *build-own-operate-transfer* (BOOT) private airport, and Morocco, Oman and Yemen have undertaken efforts to bring the private sector into expansions of port capacity.

In some key sectors, such as ports and air transport, increased capacity may be a less immediate need than improved efficiency. Under those circumstances, the key actions by government must be to eliminate public

Table 4.4 Highlights of recent trade-related progress on infrastructure

Country	Telecom	Electricity	Transport
Egypt			Closed the prequalification process for a private BOOT airport
Jordan	Launched the sale of 40% stake to private investors; one GSM mobile network was established two years ago		
Lebanon	Two GSM mobile networks have been set up		
Morocco		1,320 MW thirty-year BOOT power plant expansion contract is under way	Opened a preliminary round of bidding process for a US$300 million BOT port serving a 1,000 ha industrial zone near Tangier
Oman		90 MW thermal power facility was built on a BOOT agreement; announced plans to privatize water sectors	
Tunisia		Competition has begun for contract to build a 350–500 MW combined-cycle gas plant with an estimated cost of US$300 million; electricity concession concluded	
West Bank and Gaza	Private Pal-Tel was formed to rebuild and expand the network; they raised US$65 million via IPO and through institutional investors		

Notes: BOOT: build–own–operate–transfer; BOT: build–operate–transfer; IPO: initial public offering.
Source: Damji 1997.

monopolies and allow private competition. In ports, the efficiency gains from allowing private competition can be substantial. In 1991 Mexico began a process of port deregulation by allowing free entry of service firms, eliminating service segmentation, allowing free determination of service charges and subcontracting across firms. Union work rules were re-negotiated. These actions resulted in a 30 per cent reduction in costs and an increase in container volume of 47 per cent in the port of Veracruz (Edwards 1995). Argentina, Bolivia, Chile and Mexico have all successfully privatized their national flag air carriers, resulting in improvements in revenues and services. Bolivia successfully privatized operation of its three major airports through a concession agreement.

There are relatively few examples of deregulation of and private entry into ports and aviation in the MENA region. Tunisia has begun a process of legislative change to allow greater competition in the provision of port services. It also successfully offered a minority position in the national airline Tunis Air to domestic private investors through the stock market. Jordan has recently increased efforts to privatize Royal Jordanian Airlines. Yemen has contracted with the Port of Singapore authority for the running of the port of Aden.

Latin American governments widely used large scale employee ownership or mass privatization schemes as a complement to direct sales or placements through the capital market. Bolivia's capitalization programme included the provision that 50 per cent of all shares in 'capitalized' companies would pass to a collective capitalization fund which acts as a social insurance scheme. Employees were further entitled to buy shares equivalent to 10 per cent of the sale value of the firm. In Argentina employees were given the option to purchase 10 per cent of the firm's stock in most large transactions (Alexander and Corti 1993). In Mexico unions were given 'right of first refusal' on all transactions, allowing them to purchase any percentage of the shares offered subject to a minimum holding period. Unions from some of the larger companies – including TelMex, the telephone company and AeroMexico, the state airline – were sold large portions of shares at a discount, and formal agreements were put in place in a number of transactions to offer non-unionized employees the option to purchase up to 5 per cent of the public offering. In Chile which has the longest history of privatization in Latin America, deliberate actions to cast the privatization effort as 'popular capitalism' by broadening the ownership base of privatized companies through active use of pension funds and employee buy-outs have resulted in more than 60 per cent of the labour force becoming shareholders (Hachette and Luders 1993).

There are few similar examples in the MENA. Egypt has experimented with employee buy-outs in the construction industry and has allowed employee purchases of minority shareholdings. In Jordan, the government has proposed stock ownership schemes allowing employees to purchase shares at a discount to market prices. Tunisia's privatization programme includes provision for a 'public enterprise restructuring fund' (FREP) which is intended to support worker compensation packages, liabilities to the social security system associated with the privatization and technical assistance to firms for privatization transactions (Saghir 1993). Tunisian public enterprise assets, however, have been sold to a relatively small number of buyers, and employee stock ownership schemes have not been widely used. In general, in the MENA there has been little use of pension funds to diversify ownership of listed shares in public enterprises.

Conclusion

Privatization programmes in the MENA have not kept pace with those in other regions of the developing world. Neither has the pace of globalization. This chapter has argued that these two incomplete transformations of the MENA's economies are linked and provide a strong rationale for a new strategic approach to privatization in the region. Without faster integration into the world economy, the MENA cannot generate the rates of growth needed to absorb rapidly growing labour forces and to reduce unemployment. But without robust employment growth and rising real wages in the private sector, privatization faces an uphill battle; public sector workers will oppose attempts to make them redundant in the course of privatization. Faced with fiscal constraints, to employee compensation, governments in the MENA will continue to accede to worker demands, either by reducing the scope of their privatization programmes or by placing unacceptable constraints on the management of labour relations by potential private purchasers.

By shifting from generalized privatization programmes to a strategy of privatization based on improving the availability and efficiency of trade-related infrastructure, governments in the MENA can resolve their dilemma. The experience of privatization of trade related infrastructure – telecommunications, transport corridors, ports and trade related services – in Latin America indicates that these transactions tend to break investment constraints and to be either employment neutral or generating. Complemented by employee share ownership schemes, they have won broad popular support. Better infrastructure, coupled with the reforms already underway to reduce tariff protection and accelerate integration with the world economy should result in more rapid TFP and economic growth, and with them rising employment and real wages. At that time governments in the MENA can turn to privatizing the public industrial and services sectors.[5]

Notes

I am indebted to Sahila Damji for research assistance and to Jamal Saghir for helpful discussions. The findings, interpretations and conclusions expressed in this paper are entirely those of the author. They do not represent the views of the World Bank, its executive directors or the countries they represent.

1 Unless otherwise specified, in this chapter the MENA region is defined to include all Arab countries except Mauritania and Sudan, plus Iran.

2 The 'required' rate of growth is found by estimating the rate of aggregate economic growth needed to fully absorb the cohorts of first-time workers entering the labour force and to reduce the rate of unemployment in each country from existing levels to a rate of less than 5 per cent.

3 For an analysis of the sources of growth in the MENA see Page (1998).

4 For a further discussion see World Bank (1995b).

5 This chapter does not consider the privatization of the financial sector, which has also lagged behind in the MENA. Financial sector innovation and improvements in financial services are also critical for successful growth. These can only be achieved by a combination of liberalized entry – including entry of foreign banks – and privatization of state banks, which dominate the financial sectors of many MENA economies. The pace and sequencing of financial sector liberalization will require careful thought in light of recent experiences in East Asia, but is essential to a growth oriented strategy.

Bibliography

Alexander, M. and Corti, C. (1993) 'Argentina's privatization programme: experience, issues, and lessons,' discussion paper 103, Cofinancing and Financial Advisory Services, World Bank, Washington, D.C.

Assaad, R. (1996) 'An analysis of compensation programmes for redundant workers in Egyptian public enterprise', paper presented at the Conference on 'Public Sector Retrenchment and Efficient Compensation Schemes', World Bank, Washington, D.C., November.

Brunetti, A. Kisunko, G. and. Weder, B. (1998) 'How businesses see government: responses from private sector surveys in 69 countries', discussion paper 33, International Finance Corporation, World Bank, Washington, D.C.

Damji, S. (1997) 'Facts on privatization in Latin America and the Middle East: looking back and looking ahead', World Bank, Middle East and North Africa region, Social and Economic Development Group, mimeo, Washington, D.C.

Edwards, S. (1995) *Crisis and Reform in Latin America: From Despair to Hope*, published for the World Bank, New York: Oxford University Press.

El Erian, M., Helbling, T. and Page, J. (1998) 'Education, human capital development and growth in the Arab economies', prepared for the Annual Joint Arab Monetary Fund/Arab Fund for Economic and Social Development Seminar on 'Human resource development and economic growth', Abu Dhabi, United Arab Emirates.

Galal, A. Jones, L., Tandon, P. and Vogelsang, I. (1994) *Welfare Consequences of Selling Public Enterprises: An Empirical Analysis*, published for the World Bank, New York: Oxford University Press.

Gates, J. R. and Saghir, J. (1995) 'Employee stock ownership plans (ESOPs): objectives, design options and international experience.' discussion paper 112, Cofinancing and Financial Advisory Services, World Bank, Washington, D.C.

Gupta, V. (1997) 'Determinants of wage differentials in Morocco', mimeo, World Bank, Middle East and North Africa region, Washington, D.C.

Hachette, D. and Luders, R. (1993) 'Privatization in Chile: an economic appraisal', International Center for Economic Growth, San Francisco.

Hoekman, B. (1996) 'Trade and investment liberalization: issues and options for Egypt', mimeo, World Bank Development Research Group, Washington, D.C.

—— (1998) 'The World Trade Organization, the European Union, and the Arab world: trade policy priorities and pitfalls', in N. Shafik (ed.), *Prospects for Middle*

Eastern and North African Economies: From Boom to Bust and Back?, New York: St. Martin's Press, in association with Economic Research Forum for the Arab Countries, Iran and Turkey: 96–132.

International Monetary Fund (1997) *World Economic Outlook*, Washington, D.C.: IMF.

International Telecommunications Union (ITU) (1995) 'World telecommunications development report', Geneva: ITU.

Kikeri, S. (1998) 'Privatization and labour: what happens to workers when governments divest?', technical paper 396, World Bank, Washington, D.C.

Mody, A. (1996). 'Infrastructure delivery: private initiative and the public good', *Economic Development Institute Development Studies*, World Bank, Washington, D.C.

Oxford Analytica (1995) 'Egyptian Privatization', Oxford, UK: Oxford Analytica.

Pack, H. and Page, J. (1994) 'Accumulation, exports and growth in the high-performing Asian economies', *Carnegie Rochester Conference Series on Public Policy*, vol. 40, no. 0: 199–236.

Page, J. (1998) 'From boom to bust – and back? The crisis of growth in the Middle East and North Africa', in N. Shafik (ed.), *Prospects for Middle Eastern and North African Economies: From Boom to Bust and Back?*, New York: St. Martin's Press, in association with Economic Research Forum for the Arab Countries, Iran and Turkey: 133–58.

Page, J. and Underwood, J. (1997) 'Growth, the Maghreb and free trade with the European Union', in A. Galal and B. Hoekman (eds), *Regional Partners in Global Markets: Limits and Possibilities of the Euro-Med Agreements*, London: Centre for Economic Policy Research.

Pierce, M. H. (ed.) (1997) 'Capitalization: the Bolivian model of social and economic reform', papers commissioned by the Ministry of Capitalization for two conferences: 'Capitalization: A New Model for Latin America', at the North South Center, University of Miami, May, and 'Bolivia's Capitalization: Analysis and Perspective', at Woodrow Wilson Center for Current Studies on Latin America, May.

Privatization International Magazine (1996) December.

Sachs, J. D. and Warner, A. M. (1995) 'Economic reform and the process of global integration', *Brookings Papers on Economic Activity*, vol. 10, no. 1: 1–95.

Sader, F. (1995) 'Privatizing public enterprises and foreign investment in developing countries, 1988–93', Foreign Investment Advisory Service, Occasional Paper 5, World Bank, Washington, D.C.

Saghir, J. (1993) 'Privatization in Tunisia', Cofinancing and Financial Advisory Services., discussion paper 101, World Bank, Washington, D.C.

—— (1997) 'Infrastructure privatization in the Middle East and North Africa', World Bank, Middle East and North Africa Region, draft mimeo, Washington, D.C.

Smith, G. R., Shafik, N., Guislain, P. and Reichert, J. A. (1997) 'Getting connected: private participation in infrastructure in the Middle East and North Africa', World Bank, Middle East and North Africa Economic Studies, Washington, D.C.

Wheeler, D. and Mody A. (1992) 'International investment location decisions: the case of US firms', *Journal of International Economics*, August, vol. 33, nos 1–2: 57–76.

World Bank (1995a) 'Claiming the future: choosing prosperity in the Middle East and North Africa', Washington, D.C.: World Bank.

—— (1995b) 'Global economic prospects and the developing countries' Development Prospects Group, Washington, D.C.: World Bank.

—— (1995c) 'Will Arab workers prosper or be left out in the twenty-first century?', *Regional Perspectives on World Development Report 1995,* Washington, D.C.: World Bank.

—— (1996) 'Global economic prospects and the developing countries', Development Prospects Group, Washington, D.C.: World Bank.

—— (1997a) 'Arab Republic of Egypt country economic memorandum vol. II: promoting outward orientation through exports', Washington D.C.: World Bank.

—— (1997b) 'Global economic prospects and the developing countries', Development Prospects Group, Washington, D.C.: World Bank.

—— (1997c) 'Quality education for all: embracing change in the Middle East and North Africa', Washington, D.C.: World Bank.

—— (1998) 'Global economic prospects and the developing countries: short-term update 1998', Development Prospects Group, Washington, D.C.: World Bank.

5 Infrastructure privatization in the MENA region

Jamal Saghir

Introduction

The wave of infrastructure privatizations that swept Argentina, Chile, Mexico, New Zealand and the United Kingdom in the 1980s and early 1990s is now quickly sweeping the globe. Since 1984, around 600 infrastructure projects in some 100 countries have been privatized and over 700 greenfield projects have been completed or awarded with significant private participation in the core infrastructure sectors of natural gas, power, transport, telecommunications and water and wastewater. Another 2,700 projects are currently under active preparation or consideration.

The wave of reforms has also reached the Middle East and North Africa (MENA) region. No region in the world could benefit more from privatization than MENA, where the role of the public sector in the economy has been particularly strong. However, despite rapid change, the share of public enterprises remains higher in the MENA region than in other middle income countries (26–60 per cent of gross domestic product and gross investment).

The overwhelming majority of infrastructure service providers in the MENA region are either government departments, state-owned enterprises, or parastatals operating inefficiently under bureaucratic rules and without hard budget constraints. Box 5.1 shows a few examples of the shortfalls in the coverage and quality of the services they provide.

While a decade ago the agenda of reform in MENA countries rarely included privatization, the number and scale of privatizations is growing rapidly across the region as most countries reduce their role in competitive sectors and begin to experiment with private provision of public services. However, the region as a whole is still lagging behind regions such as Latin America, Eastern and Central Europe and the former Soviet Union countries and even East Asia, and progress has been slow, with the region accounting for only a tiny share (1 per cent) of the total value of infrastructure privatization and new private participation in infrastructure (PPI) projects undertaken around the world since 1984.

This chapter explores the status of privatization and PPI in MENA countries and their increasing momentum and draws a set of guidelines or principals that should be followed in order to accelerate infrastructure privatization.[1] The

---

Box 5.1 Shortfalls in coverage and quality of infrastructure services

The public sector in the region has done a poor job of managing infra-structure. Only the countries of the Gulf Cooperation Council (GCC) and Israel provide infrastructure services comparable in quality and coverage to those in countries with similar income levels. World Bank figures indicate that Egypt, Yemen, Lebanon and the West Bank and Gaza all lag behind comparators in provision of kilometers of paved roads per million population, that Syria and the West Bank and Gaza lag behind in terms of access to fresh water and sanitation, that Yemen, Jordan and Syria lag behind in terms of power-generating capacity per million population, and that Algeria, Tunisia, Morocco, Syria and the West Bank and Gaza fall short of comparable economies in terms of telephone lines per hundred population. Meanwhile, the waiting period for telephone service ranges from a low of nearly six years in Egypt and Yemen to eight years in Algeria to a high of over ten years in the West Bank and Gaza. Efficiency of service provision is also a problem, even in economies generally considered to be good performers. Thus, Lebanon, Morocco and Tunisia all have very high levels of faults per hundred telephone lines, and Jordan and the West Bank and Gaza have a staggeringly high proportion of unaccounted-for water: 55 per cent. With respect to electric power, coverage is lower than in many comparable countries. For example, in 1993 kilowatt hours of electricity produced per capita amounted to 0.73 in Tunisia, 0.66 in Algeria and 0.41 in Morocco, well below the 2.44 average for comparable countries. Distribution losses in the West Bank and Gaza amount to 20 per cent of output, and power losses in Egypt are about 12–15 per cent of output.

---

chapter discusses the need for infrastructure privatization, presents the potential benefits of infrastructure privatization, reviews the status and prospects for infra-structure privatization in the MENA and explores the specific features of the regional economic environment and how opportunities in the region are growing, all of which will affect the process of privatization. The final section presents a summary of emerging international lessons and explores some of the strategic principles.

The need for infrastructure privatization and PPI

Rapid and sustained economic growth in the region must be the primary order of the day in the MENA. In order for growth to be sustainable MENA countries must gear themselves up to become full partners in the interna-tionally competitive global economy. This will be accomplished through gradual integration of trade and finance, privatization of state-owned enter-prises and PPI and dramatic improvement in both the quantity and quality of infrastructure provision. The last point is vital because the unprecedented opportunities for economic growth offered by expansion of world trade and globalization of production are essentially infrastructure-driven (Sud 1996). The first two points are intrinsically linked to the last: privatization and quality of services. The following summarizes the main considerations that must be addressed.

Information technology development and greater participation in the global economy
From telecommunications links, without which the information revolution could not have become the driving force behind new production systems and the emerging internationalization of services, to container ports and reliable power supplies, on which modern world-class industry – with its multinational subcontracting and 'just-in-time' production systems – depends; advances in efficient infrastructure provision have been critical to success. One of the most fundamental challenges facing the region is to make a quantum leap forward in those infrastructure sectors that contribute most directly to internationally competitive private sector development – telecommunications, information technology and information systems, power and transportation (including ports and airports).

Greater investment in basic infrastructure services Rapid population growth (3 per cent per year) and explosive rates of urbanization in each country in the MENA region mean that substantial investments are needed to maintain existing and often unsatisfactory levels of 'essential needs' infrastructure sectors: water supply, sanitation and solid waste collection and disposal. However the shortfalls that the region already faces in the provision of these basic infrastructure needs are staggering. For example, up to 60 million people lack access to safe water and 80 million lack access to adequate sanitation. Hence, meeting the needs of the population for basic and essential services so that they are able to participate to their utmost ability is a vital ingredient for success.

Greater role for the private sector, greater coverage, better quality and a friendlier economic environment There is a recognition that in order to compete in the global market place, countries must raise the efficiency and quality of their infrastructure. Many surveys of international companies have indicated that the quality and cost of infrastructure is one of the primary considerations as to where to locate new investments. Satisfying power, telecommunications, transportation and water and sanitation requirements in the eight MENA countries now borrowing from the World Bank (Morocco, Algeria, Tunisia, Egypt, Lebanon, Jordan, Lebanon and Yemen) over the next decade will require an estimated US$60–100 billion in new investment. While governments and multilateral and bilateral donors can be expected to supply about US$15 billion, the remainder will need to be made up by the private sector. Consequently, meeting the challenge of attracting private funding for infrastructure on this order of magnitude will require intensive efforts to create an investor-friendly economic environment and to develop capital markets that can channel savings into productive new investment.

Potential benefits of infrastructure privatization

Private involvement can take a range of forms, from management contracts, leases and concessions to demonopolization or outright sale of existing enterprises. The potential benefits vary according to the form of private participation involved (Table 5.1. Additional information on each type is contained in Appendix 5.A).

In general, experience has shown that the benefits that have been realized from private participation include, *inter alia*, greater access to management expertise, incentives for private investors to maximize revenues through efficient billing and collection for utility services and a commitment to cost-covering tariffs, as well as access to much needed private investment funds for the expansion and improvement of infrastructure. However, the principal source of benefits from privatizing infrastructure is the establishment of an arm's-length relationship between the infrastructure provider and short-term political pressures. While commercialization and corporatization initiatives under public ownership promise that as well, in practice World Bank experience has shown that it is virtually impossible to keep politics at bay while the government is the owner, regulator and operator (Kerf and Smith 1996). Many specific benefits follow from this fundamental change in the institutional relationship.

Increased efficiency in investment management and operation Superior efficiency in investment management, and operation flows from several distinct but complementary factors, including commitment to cost-covering tariffs, improved incentives for operational efficiency and access to management expertise and technology.

Access to private finance When assured of predictable revenue flows and sound management, private firms are prepared to commit owner's equity and to borrow on their own account, without the need for full sovereign guarantees.

Table 5.1 Main forms and potential benefits of infrastructure privatization

	Management contract	Lease	Concession/ BOOT	De-monopolize/ BOO	Divestiture
Management expertise	x	x	x	x	x
Tariff discipline		x	x	x	x
Access to private capital			x	x	x
Capital market development			x	x	x
Potential capital revenues					x

Source: Kerf and Smith 1996.

Government revenues A corollary of access to private finance is reduced public expenditure and indebtedness. In addition, where privatization is accomplished through the divestiture of existing enterprises the revenues generated may be used to pay down public debt. For example, Argentina used its US$22 billion in privatization revenues, not as palliative to finance recurring fiscal deficits, but primarily to correct important structural balances such as retiring excessive internal indebtedness or restoring the integrity of the contractual savings system. When an infrastructure enterprise is operating efficiently, it may also be a source of ongoing taxation revenues, in contrast to being a drain on the public budget.

Opportunities for capital market development There are potentially important linkages between infrastructure privatization and the development of local capital markets: while local resource mobilization greatly facilitates infrastructure privatization, the latter can, in turn, enhance the development of local capital markets. For instance, the large scale and predictable cash flows associated with appropriately regulated infrastructure projects allow them to issue debt and equity instruments which are often highly valued by institutional investors. During the early phases of infrastructure privatization in Latin America, telecommunications privatization alone provided around two-thirds of the market capitalization on major stock exchanges. Infrastructure privatization can thus be used to deepen local capital markets and sometimes to induce the return of flight capital: this is of particular interest to MENA countries. The experience of Chile demonstrates the positive impact infrastructure privatization can have on the development of the capital market (see Box 5.2).

Boost for pension funds and insurance companies In many countries, such as Argentina and Chile, infrastructure privatization is providing a stable, high return on investment in domestic debt and equity. These yields mean better pensions for individuals or lower fiscal demands on the government.

Potential to stimulate foreign direct investment (FDI) Experience in reforming economies in Latin America and Eastern Europe confirms the potential of infrastructure privatization to catalyse large inflows of FDI. This is particularly critical in MENA countries, where direct investment has been very mixed across different countries.

Privatization in MENA: status and prospects

Economic environment: a region in transition

The MENA region today stands at a crossroads. After having notched up very rapid advances in the 1960s and 1970s, the region reached the limits of growth in the 1980s and entered an era of stagnation. The decline in oil prices was a major factor in this stagnation, affecting the non-oil economies as well as the oil producers.

Box 5.2 Infrastructure privatization and capital market development: the example of Chile

Most divestitures of companies operating in the electricity, telecommunications and air transport sector in Chile involved substantial sales of shares to employees and to private pension funds. Workers were offered the option of using and advance on their severance payments to acquire those shares, often in combination with other benefits. Pension funds were gradually allowed by their supervising authorities to purchase shares in privatized utilities as long as those shares fulfilled certain legal requirements. The table demonstrates how the financing of private infrastructure and the development of local capital markets occurred in parallel in Chile:

Development of capital markets and financing of private infrastructure

	1989	*1990*	*1991*	*1992*	*1993*
Stock market capitalization (US$ million)	9,587	13,545	27,984	29,644	44,622
Infrastructure stocks as a % of total capitalization	30	35	49	52	59

Source: Kerf and Smith 1996.

Between 1980 and 1995, the combination of very slow aggregate GDP growth and very rapid population growth – about 3 per cent a year, which well exceeds the 1.8 per cent population growth rate for all developing countries – meant that real per capita income actually fell by 2 per cent a year, the largest decline in any developing region.

The severe structural problems that have emerged in the last few years essentially reflect the legacy of a historically inward vision of economic management, one that has featured a highly protectionist trade regime and a large government presence in the economy marked by an omnipresent, cumbersome bureaucracy and regulatory regime, deteriorating productivity, the existence of a wide range of wholly or partly state-owned enterprises, underdeveloped financial markets and a generally less dynamic business sector insulated from the increasingly complex – but creative – winds of domestic and international competition that have helped spur dynamic, private-sector-based, export-led-growth elsewhere in the world (Sud 1996).

In a period when private financial flows have become the most dynamic component of investment world-wide, the MENA region as a whole has been left out, attracting in the period 1994–6 less than 2 per cent of total net foreign FDI to developing countries world-wide and less than 1 per cent of the region's GDP (World Bank 1997).[2] Domestic investment has also been constrained by a high level of capital flight from the region, driven at least in part by perceptions of political risk. The World Bank has estimated that stocks of MENA capital held abroad amount to about US: $350 billion (about half from the GCC countries), the highest level in relation to GDP for any region in the world. In MENA the ratio of flight capital stock to GDP was estimated to be 118 per cent in 1991, substantially higher than in Sub-Saharan Africa (81 per cent), Eastern Europe and Central Asia (40 per cent), Latin American and the Caribbean (35 per cent) and South East Asia (15 per cent) (Kant 1995, Claessens and Naudé 1993).

Changing circumstances: towards a new vision

In the last few years, restoring economic growth has become an urgent priority in the MENA region. It is beginning to transform itself into a more dynamic business-oriented area. Virtually every government in the region is coming to share a common vision regarding their economic future, namely:

- The private sector must become the engine of growth and job creation.
- Investment needs, particularly for infrastructure, are enormous and cannot be financed by government alone; the private sector must become a more active partner in financing, *inter alia*, power, telecommunications, water and sanitation, and transport projects.

Box 5.3 Highlights of MENA economic trends

- During the past decade, the MENA region has had the lowest rate of income growth of any region in the world.
- Its share of world trade is only about 3 per cent (1991–3).
- While the region's population is growing at around 3 per cent a year, the labour force is growing at a much faster rate of 3.3 per cent. Overall jobless rates in most of the World Bank's MENA active countries ranges from 10 to 20 per cent (the number of unemployed stands at 9 million), with unemployment of the young approaching three times this level in some countries. Jobs for 47 million new entrants into the labour force in the MENA countries will have to be found by 2010.
- Rising productivity in agriculture is likely to free up even more labour from rural areas to join the ranks of the unemployed or the urban informal sector.
- The region's share of net private capital flows to MENA countries is very low: only about US$ 7 billion in 1996 (3 per cent of all developing countries).
- Real wages remain stagnant at 1970 levels.
- Current projections for GDP growth indicate that the number of poor (those living on less that US$1 a day will rise to about 15 million by 2010 if effective reforms are not introduced.
- The reputation of the region as an attractive place to do business has not been very high. The role of state-owned enterprises is still very large in most countries of the region, and the private sector, with some exceptions, is not very active or aggressive.

- Privatization of existing state-owned enterprises is necessary to enhance overall efficiency in the economy.
- Foreign investment will be essential in meeting MENA countries' infrastructure financing needs in helping industries to modernize and become truly competitive in the global economy.

The World Bank estimates that potential infrastructure investments in the region could be US$300–350 billion over the period 1997–2006, including US$60–100 billion for the eight economies now borrowing from the World Bank, and US$200–250 billion for Gulf and other MENA countries (World Bank 1996). Given fiscal austerity in much of the region, of the US$100 billion needed by World Bank borrowers, governments may be able to finance about US$70 billion. International financial institutions like the World Bank will contribute, but their capital and exposure limits prevent them from lending more than $15 billion (15 per cent of the total). In the GCC countries and the rest of the region infrastructure needs will be less pressing, given the large stock built up during the oil boom. If, like the World Bank borrowers, these countries succeed in attracting private capital to finance about 15 per cent of their needs, their market for private infrastructure will be at least US$35 billion.

Thus, the potential market for private participation in the region could be more than US$50 billion over the next decade, more than three times the amount currently provided by international financial institutions. With the right policies and incentives, the market for PPI could be larger still. But raising private participation from its current low levels to 15–20 per cent of the total will require rapid implementation of the policy changes many governments in the region are now initiating.

A slow start

Until recently, privatization in the MENA region has lagged behind eastern Europe, Latin America and even east Asia. Globally, between 1988 and 1995 governments in developing countries sold state enterprises (tradeable and infrastructure sectors) worth about US$130 billion (World Bank 1987). In the MENA, the total was only $3.4 billion, or about 3 per cent (see Figure 5.1 and Table 5B.1 in Appendix 5B). Moreover, as of February 1997, only 4 per cent of all PPI projects in emerging countries are in the MENA region (see Figure 5.2).

As of early 1997, the World Bank has tracked more than 4,000 projects world-wide (infrastructure privatizations and new projects completed, construction underway, and under consideration). Around 115 infrastructure projects (3 per cent), including oil and gas investments, are in the MENA region, of which fifteen projects are completed, underway or awarded and around 100 projects announced. In terms of value, between 1984 and 1997 (February) there were US$322 billion in infrastructure privatizations world-wide and an additional US$327 billion in new infrastructure projects (see

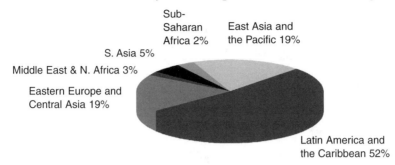

Figure 5.1 Percentage of privatization revenues by region, 1988–95
Source: See Table 5B.1.

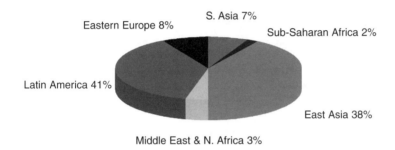

Figure 5.2 Percentage of PPI projects in emerging markets by region, January 1984–February 1997
Source: See Table 5B.1.

Appendix 5B, Tables 5B.2–5 for a breakdown of data per region). However, as Figure 5.3 demonstrates, the share of MENA countries in these projects is very low, around US$9 billion (1 per cent).

Why such slow progress?

Most MENA countries launched privatization programmes of some form or another in the late 1980s. Appendix 5C presents an overview of privatization in the region and Box 5.4 presents the highlights. In the Maghreb, Tunisia got off to an early start (1987), but the process has been uneven in recent years and the majority of public enterprises remain in the public sector. Morocco's programme, which is considered one of the region's most successful, has been steadier but has only recently gained momentum. Algeria, which has a huge state-owned sector, has been plagued by civil strife and therefore unable to mobilize the necessary support to embark strongly on privatization. Under considerable pressure from international organizations and donors, the first phase of Egypt's programme (1991–4) achieved its privatization targets through minority sales that relied on

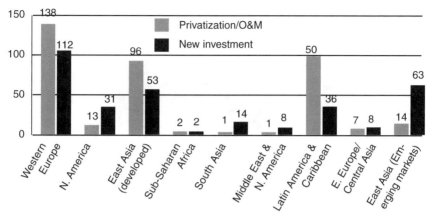

Figure 5.3 Estimated value of private infrastructure projects by region, January 1984–February 1997 (US$ billion)

Source: World Bank, Private Participation in Infrastructure Database.

Box 5.4 Highlights of privatization and private participation in infrastructure in the MENA region

Morocco

- The Privatization Law took effect in April 1990; all key institutions were in place by September 1991.
- The Privatization Law enables the transfer to the private sector of 114 listed entities (seventy-seven companies and thirty-seven hotels) before 13 December 1998. Over half the firms come from the industrial sector, but their great share of sectoral value added is in finance and oil refining.
- As of October 1996, twenty-seven companies and eighteen hotels have been transferred to the private sector, raising over US$1.2 billion.
- Morocco issued privatization bonds that gave bearers priority over buyers of privatization assets who paid in cash. The bonds have been very successful in:
  - gauging demand for privatized assets (which facilitates planning)
  - stimulating interest in the programme
  - reducing pressure to sell assets to cover shortfalls
  - creating indigenous pressure on government to bring assets to market.

Egypt

- At the end of 1996, Egypt had totally or partially privatized forty-six Law 203 companies, amounting to around US$ 2 billion of sale proceeds in a wide range of sectors through various methods of privatization. In addition, around US$1 billion of unutilized fixed assets, miscellaneous activities, local governorates' assets and joint venture companies have been privatized.

Box 5.4 (continued)

- The government has earmarked the majority of public enterprises for privatization. For 1997, the government plan is to privatize thirty-three companies through Anchor Investors and twelve companies through initial public offerings of shares.
- Plans have been announced for the construction of two new ports on a build-operate-transfer (BOT) basis, a container terminal at Adobiya (near Suez) and a facility for trans-shipment to be built further north in the eastern branch of the Suez Canal near the Mediterranean coastline.
- Initial steps are being taken toward introducing private sector participation in the power and telecommunications sectors.

Kuwait

- Between June 1994 and November 1996, the Kuwait Investment Authority sold its major stakes in seventeen companies for a total value of US$1.9 billion.
- The sale of shares in privatized companies has stimulated the development of mutual funds and the Kuwait Stock Exchange; the Kuwait Stock Exchange index climbed about 90 per cent from December 1994 to November 1996.
- A second phase of privatization includes the sale of state holdings in public services such as water, telecommunications and electricity.
- A unique aspect of Kuwaiti privatization has been that almost all revenues have come from sales arranged through the stock exchange by auctions, subscriptions and sales via brokers.

---

providing restricted shares to employees on concessional terms and liquidation. Jordan, Israel and Yemen have also been slow to sell state-owned enterprises, and in the GCC countries, there has been considerable discussion of privatization issues but very little action, except in Kuwait and Oman.

Politics, bureaucracy and various risks factors have been behind the slow progress. Many governments in the region were reluctant to give up the power and patronage opportunities that state-owned enterprises provide, despite growing evidence of the huge fiscal costs (Shafik 1996).

In the majority of MENA countries, the political will and commitment to privatization were also lacking, and as experience elsewhere (Latin America, East Asia) shows, there is a direct relationship between the degree of government commitment at the top and the clarity of its objectives and the success a country has in attracting private investment in infrastructure and privatization. The intellectuals and media in much of the region tend to be statist in their orientation and were critical of the social impact of privatization. Public sector employees and trade unions, which are important supporters of many MENA governments, were wary of potential layoffs and wage cuts. In the infrastructure sector in particular, where investment tends to be large and immobile and infrastructure prices tend to be politically sensitive, the risks are particularly acute. Infrastructure investments are especially vulnerable to political risks, including the risk of government reneging on its regulatory commitments on tariffs or other matters such as war and civil disturbance. The combination of these forces resulted in a very gradualist and cautious approach to privatization and PPI through the region.

Attitudes are rapidly changing and privatization is gaining momentum

Recently there have been important signs of changes across the region. Privatization of existing state-owned enterprises in sectors such as tourism, manufacturing, textiles, real estate and banking has accelerated. Around US$2 billion worth of assets were sold in 1996 (Table 5B.6 in Appendix 5B), accounting for 8 per cent of privatization in developing countries, Eastern Europe, and Commonwealth of Independent States (CIS) countries compared to US$600 million in 1994 (3 per cent). Egypt, Morocco, Kuwait and Tunisia were the main focus of privatization activity (Figure 5.4). Indicative compilations show that the countries of the MENA region, especially Morocco, Egypt, Yemen, Tunisia, Jordan and Algeria, will put up for sale in the next few years state-owned assets worth over US $2 billion (Privatization International 1996). Almost 600 enterprises in the tradeable and infrastructure sectors have been identified for sale in the next few years. These will include around 100 enterprises in Morocco, 250 enterprises in Algeria, up to sixty enterprises in Tunisia, up to 100 enterprises in Egypt, and up to seventy enterprises in Yemen. Foreigners will be allowed to become partial or majority shareholders in most of these countries.

Fiscal constraints have not only pushed governments to sell existing state-owned enterprises, they require that governments look to the private sector to finance the region's massive infrastructure investment requirements. Governments in the region are now inviting private participation in utilities in many countries. Contracts have been awarded to private operators for solid waste and mobile telecommunications in Lebanon, power and water in

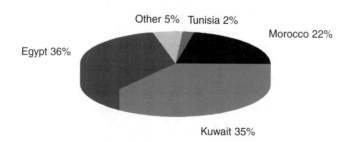

Figure 5.4 Total privatization revenues in MENA countries 1988–96
Source: See Table 5B.1.

Morocco, power, water and wastewater in Oman, a port terminal in Yemen, mobile telecommunications in Jordan and Lebanon and a water and wastewater management contract in Gaza (see Box 5.5). The list of projects under study or preparation is growing and includes private power generation in Morocco, Egypt, Tunisia and several countries of the GCC; privatization of the fixed telecommunications network in Jordan, Morocco, Oman and the West Bank and Gaza; performance-based management contracts for water and wastewater in Jordan, Egypt and Yemen; container ports in Oman and port services in Morocco and Tunisia; and concessions for toll roads in Jordan,

---

Box 5.5 Utilities reform in MENA countries: recent highlights

Telecommunications In early 1997, Jordan launched the sale of a 26 per cent stake in Jordan Telecommunications to private investors. One GSM mobile network was established two years ago. In Lebanon two GSM mobile networks have been set up: the first is two-thirds owned by France Telecom and the second is owned mainly by local interests. In May 1995, PALTEL, a new private telecommunications company, was formed to rebuild and expand the network in the West Bank and Gaza, and successfully raised US$65 million through a public offering of shares and from institutional investors.

Electricity In Oman a 90 megawatt thermal power facility was built on a build-own-operate-transfer (BOOT) arrangement. In Morocco, a 1,320 megawatt thirty-year rehabilitate-own-operate-transfer (ROOT) power plant expansion contract is under way (the Jorf Lasfar project). In Tunisia, ten firms are competing to build the country's first independent power generation plant, a 350–500 megawatt combined-cycle gas plant with an estimated cost of US$300 million. Both Oman and the United Arab Emirates have announced plans to privatize their electricity and water sectors, including distribution systems.

Gas The US$2.4 billion Ras Laffan liquefied natural gas (LNG) project, including construction of a gas pipeline and liquefaction plant, is being developed by a private sponsor in Qatar. In Jordan, a private developer has finalized negotiations on a US$300 million regasification plant supplying gas to the domestic market. A 500 megawatt plant using some of the gas has also been proposed.

Transport Morocco recently opened a pre-qualification process for a US$300 million port BOT serving a 1,000 hectare industrial zone near Tangier. Egypt has closed the pre-qualification of bidders for the construction and operation of a private airport at Mersa Alam on a BOOT basis. A similar tender for an airport near Al Alamein is also planned.

Water In September 1996 a private management contract operator started implementing a Service Improvement Programme in the Gaza Strip. A water and electricity concession for Casablanca was concluded in April 1997.

Lebanon, Morocco and Tunisia. Based on the projects under consideration, the estimated value of potential private infrastructure projects in the MENA region is US$45 billion, 3 per cent of global private infrastructure investments (Figure 5.5).

Policy issues and lessons of experience: some strategic principles

Attracting private sector participation in infrastructure requires a number of policy, legal and regulatory decisions on the part of the government. Some pre- and post-privatization lessons have emerged from recent experiences in the UK, Argentina, Chile and the newly industrializing economies of East Asia (Tilmes 1996) These lessons are first summarized below. This chapter will then explore how these lessons could be applied in MENA.

Pre-privatization lessons for infrastructure

1   Focus on upstream economic, structural and policy issues first, finance later:
    • Unbundle and vertically separate potentially competitive elements from natural monopolies prior to privatization (for example, power

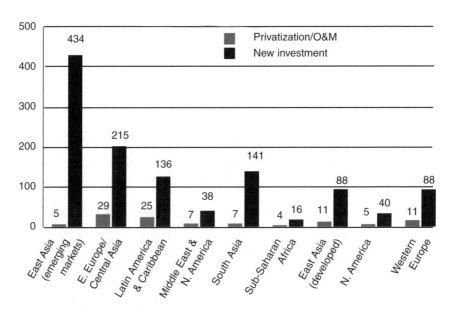

Figure 5.5 Estimated value of potential PPI projects by region, February 1997 (US$ billion)

Source: World Bank, Private Participation in Infrastructure Database.

generation, gas production and long distance telecom). Structural changes are much more difficult after privatization, when there are private shareholders with contractual rights.

- Maximizing revenue should not be the prime objective; economic efficiency should drive privatization and there should be a positive impact on consumers. This is especially true in telecommunications. For example, most Latin American countries privatized their telecommunication companies and allowed a monopoly period on basic services ranging from five to nine years. The transactions raised a significant amount of cash for the governments, but consumers and the economy would have benefited much more if competition had been introduced quickly.
- Deregulate wherever possible.

2   Address labour issues up-front; provide a safety net and retraining when necessary and build public support through share ownership. For example, Egypt's programme of employee shareholding allocates a percentage of shares (10 per cent) of enterprises to employees; and Peru splits sales between strategic investors and widespread share ownership, with discounts and installment payments for local citizens.

3   Establish a regulatory framework or mechanisms early on in order to build credibility with investors and consumers and avoid transferring state-owned enterprise and ministry staff to newly-formed regulatory agencies:

- Rely on competitive discipline, market forces and efficiency incentives. Even in a natural monopoly, it is preferable to establish pricing regimes that include incentives for efficiency and expansion, rather than rely solely on regulatory penalties and sanctions.
- Focus on a few key regulatory aspects that matter. For example, within telecommunications, the interconnection price that new long-distance operators and cellular providers will pay for fair access to the local network is very important. For electricity, decisions should be made carefully regarding the transmission price that generators and/or distributors will pay for use of the grid, and how costs of new transmission capacity will be allocated to generators and distributors.

4   Adjust tariffs to economic costs; establish clear adjustment mechanisms; and eliminate cross-subsidies and replace with targeted subsidies to the poor if necessary.

5   Ensure that the procurement process is flexible but transparent.

Post-privatization lessons for infrastructure

1   Distinguish between what is policy and what is regulation so that there is no confusion regarding the role of the sector ministry and that of the regulator.

2   Emphasize the need for both government and operators to honour contracts. At the same time, it is important to design contracts to accommodate modifications due to changing circumstances. The challenge is to

adapt/modify the contract in a transparent and credible manner. Regulators have a key role.

3   Regulators cannot ignore issues relating to the concurrent introduction of competition and privatization. Introducing competition and privatization creates new dynamics and regulatory issues, especially concerning interconnection/access pricing: the price that new entrants in the competitive segments pay to owners/operators of the natural monopoly network. Strong economic skills on the part of the regulator are needed to determine the rates long distance operators pay to local networks or that generators pay to transmission companies.

4   Do not neglect consumer education regarding the effects of privatization, in particular the level of service improvements and tariff changes.

Applying the lessons to the MENA region

Privatization of infrastructure in the MENA will necessitate:

i   unbundling services to promote competition
ii   restructuring tariffs to reflect costs and permit commercial operation
iii explicitly identifying any non-commercial requirements to be met by privatized entities or PPI projects
iv   developing appropriate sector policies, transparent and stable legal and regulatory frameworks, and environmental and consumer safeguards to capture efficiency gains associated with competition and private involvement
v   mobilizing domestic capital markets and attracting FDI,
vi   developing mechanisms to provide long-term debt (Saghir 1995).

Based on international results, there are at least six sets of guidelines that must be developed. Two main assumptions underlie all the guidelines:

i   infrastructure should be managed like a business, not a bureaucracy
ii   the provision of infrastructure needs to be conceived and run as a service industry that responds to customer demand (World Bank 1995b).

1   Set sound policy and establish an adequate legal, regulatory, and institutional framework:
    • As MENA governments move further in the direction of involving the private sector in infrastructure, they will have to formulate overall objectives, strategy and priorities, including a transparent and universally applicable set of policies and standards under which private infrastructure providers are expected to operate (World Bank 1996). These standards need to define, *inter alia*, pricing policies, scope of competition, performance criteria and monitoring arrangements and service quality expectations. The specifics will vary according to country and sectoral

circumstances; what is important, however, is that policies, regulations and standards are fair and reasonable for all parties involved, that they are clear and unambiguous, and that they are dependable and not subject to arbitrary change.

- Given that private participation in infrastructure is a relatively new area for most MENA countries, most countries still lack an overarching regulatory framework. Almost all of these private infrastructure projects have developed regulatory rules on a case-by-case basis. Instead, MENA governments will have to develop more systematic approaches to regulation. In particular, governments will have to:
    i define those sectors in which competition can carry much of the burden of regulation
    ii introduce regulatory mechanisms or create regulatory bodies that can monitor those sectors where competition is insufficient;
    iii develop procedures for awarding infrastructure concessions, and
    iv decide on a consistent policy for providing government support (guarantees, subsidies, revenue enhancements, and so on) to different types of projects.
- The procurement arrangements for attracting potential operators must be clear, credible and well designed. The bidding process should be fully transparent and the terms of privatization or the proposed concession build–operate–transfer (BOT) or management contract need to be organized so as to attract serious bidders. Competitive bidding is the most transparent approach but must be adapted to the complexity of project finance transactions and the desire to derive maximum benefit from the flexibility and innovation that private enterpreneurship can bring.
- Regulation will have to provide incentives for private suppliers of infrastructure services to cut costs and provide better services to customers. On the other hand, where infrastructure activities involve important external effects, for good or bad, or where market discipline is insufficient to ensure accountability to users and other affected groups, the government needs to address its concerns through other means. Users and other stakeholders should be represented in the planning and regulation of infrastructure services.
- Governments will have to deepen reforms of the judiciary systems to enable the private sector to finance infrastructure projects. Given the long-term nature of infrastructure projects, the private sector needs assurances of property rights protection, easy transferability of foreign exchange, and expeditious dispute resolution mechanisms, including international arbitration. Without these supporting reforms, private infrastructure providers will demand higher returns to compensate for higher risks – which will be translated into higher prices for consumers.

2 Competition should be introduced where feasible:
- Competition should be introduced directly, if feasible, or indirectly if not. Competition gives consumers choices for better meeting their

demands and puts pressure on suppliers to be efficient and to respond to customer demand.

- Foreign capital and expertise are much needed in the region, even in the high-income GCC economies. Thus, allowing foreigners to participate in privatization and infrastructure financing is important. Political fears of foreign control over strategic sectors can be mitigated through the use of 'golden shares' or 'special rights shares' or though effective regulation.

3   Risks have to be addressed:

- Government guarantees are almost certainly needed in order to reduce perceptions of risk. Infrastructure provision does not take place in isolation; the success of a project depends on a wide variety of factors outside the control of potential investors or operators, ranging from government macroeconomic or sectoral policies to the reliability of purchasers of the service to be provided. Given the uncertainties involved, effective guarantees are a powerful factor in encouraging private participation.

- The basic approach to risk management should be based on the principle that the party best able to manage a risk at least cost should mitigate it. It may be necessary to unbundle the various risks so as to determine which participant is best placed to manage which risks at the lowest cost and how the cost of risk mitigation can be shared equitably

- Non-commercial, exogenous risks may be particularly acute in the infrastructure sector. For example, revenues from most infrastructure services are denominated in local currency while obligations to suppliers, lenders, and shareholders are often in hard currency. In some MENA countries there may be risk associated with war or civil strife. The findings summarized in Box 5.6 show that perceived political risks remain relatively high in the MENA region as a whole. However, the picture that emerges is far from uniform across MENA countries.

4   Deal openly with employees and the public:

- Fears of layoffs have thwarted privatization and PPI in many MENA countries, including Algeria, Egypt, Jordan, Kuwait, Tunisia and Yemen. The solution is not to postpone privatization or to force private investors to maintain employment levels. The solution is to deal fairly with unnecessary workers by giving them a choice of generous severance payments, retraining, relocation grants and/or small business promotion (Saghir 1993). Putting such programmes in place alongside privatization is essential for minimizing potential adverse social consequences.

- Popular participation in privatization and PPI is an important means of overcoming public resistance: public offering of shares, employee share ownership and voucher schemes are all mechanisms for encouraging participation and gaining political support (Gates and Saghir 1995).

5   Mobilize finance and accelerate capital market development:

- Lack of appropriate term financing is widely considered a binding constraint. In most countries in the MENA, there is no medium or long-

Box 5.6 Political risk in the Middle East and North Africa: how do countries compare?

Euromoney compiles rankings of political risk based on a poll of risk analysts, risk insurance brokers and bank credit officers, each of whom is asked to rank countries from 0 to 25. A score of 25 indicates no risk of non-payment; zero indicates that there is no chance of payment being made. The risk was defined as the risk of non-payment for goods or services, loans, trade-related finance and dividends, and the non-repatriation of capital. Findings of the March 1997 survey of MENA are summarized in this table:

Euromoney survey of risk of non-payment

Country	Rating
United Arab Emirates	17.50
Kuwait	16.22
Saudi Arabia	16.17
Oman	15.96
Qatar	16.05
Tunisia	14.92
Bahrain	14.98
Morocco	13.24
Egypt	12.21
Jordan	11.30
Lebanon	9.52
Libya	9.43
Iran	8.20
Syria	7.52
Algeria	6.43
Yemen	3.89
Iraq	0.97

term debt, limited benchmark prices for term debt and limited skills or experience in debt financing. Because of the nature of their assets, most infrastructure projects require long-term maturity – fifteen to twenty years – debt financing. Governments and/or the private sector need to establish arrangements to promote long-term financing of infrastructure projects. Guarantees can play an important role, but specific new instruments – infrastructure funds or arrangements to attract private equity funds and to permit pension and insurance funds to participate in infrastructure invest-ments – will also be important for mobilizing additional finance.

- Government financial support can take many forms, including equity guarantee, debt guarantee, exchange rate guarantee, grant, subordi-nated loan, minimum revenue or physical output throughout guarantee (such as in a power purchase agreement), guarantee of performance of

public enterprises or other public entities, revenue enhancements (such as income from duty-free shops at an airport) and concession extension. These mechanisms have varying abilities to facilitate private financing, resulting in varying government financial exposure. Guarantees from organizations like the World Bank can further enhance the creditworthiness of projects.
  • Investment funds or debt funds could reduce transaction costs and increase the overall flow of long-term debt financing. However, such private funds are likely to be efficient only in countries with potential for a significant number of private projects.
6   Redefine government role: going from player to referee:
  • Privatization and the introduction of public-private partnerships will profoundly change the role of governments in enterprises and infrastructure operations. Instead of being direct providers, players or sponsors – via state-owned enterprises – of services, government will need to develop two new roles: that of 'government as promoter' and that of 'government as referee' (Dervis 1996).
  • Government as promoter needs first and foremost to foster an economic environment that is attractive to private investment generally. This involves the whole panoply of private-sector-oriented measures, ranging from maintaining national macroeconomic stability to ensuring fiscal, capital market, legal, administrative and regulatory regimes are investor-friendly – effective without being burdensome.
  • The second role of government – 'government as referee' – also raises complex issues, and there is bound to be some tension between this role and that of 'government as promoter'. The referee function involves setting the rules of the game, ensuring a level playing field, and regulating the activities of providers so as to ensure that services are comprehensive in coverage, high quality, safe, fairly priced and generally responsive to consumers needs (World Bank 1996).

Conclusion

This chapter has drawn four main conclusions. First, there has been a shift in privatization and PIP in recent years in MENA countries. A decade ago privatization was almost 'untouchable': not included on the reform agenda. Foreign investment was not attracted or interested. Privatization has now taken root in many countries including in Egypt, Jordan, Kuwait, Morocco, Oman and Tunisia. MENA countries are setting their sights firmly on the objective of restoring economic growth based on private-sector-led participation in the global economy. Second, to successfully compete in the global economy, countries must address the challenge of upgrading the coverage, quality and efficiency of the infrastructure services essential for dynamic private sector development. Third, privatization of infrastructure in the MENA will necessitate:

i   unbundling services to promote competition

ii   restructuring tariffs to reflect costs and permit commercial operation
iii explicitly identifying any non-commercial requirements to be met by privatized entities or PPI projects
iv   developing appropriate sector policies, transparent and stable legal and regulatory framework, and environmental and consumer safeguards to capture efficiency gains associated with competition and private involvement
v   mobilizing domestic capital markets and attracting FDI, and
vi   developing mechanisms to provide long-term debt.

Fourth, as MENA governments move further in the direction of involving the private sector in infrastructure, they will have to:

i   define those sectors in which competition can carry much of the burden of regulation
ii   create regulatory bodies or introduce regulatory mechanisms that can monitor those sectors where competition is insufficient
iii develop procedures for awarding infrastructure concessions, and
iv   decide on a consistent policy for providing government support (guarantees, subsidies, revenue enhancements and so on) to different types of projects.

Notes

Special thanks to Ebru Engin for her research assistance in compiling information and data on privatization in MENA countries, to Omer Karasapan and Albert Amos for providing information on infrastructure privatization and private participation in infrastructure world-wide and in MENA countries, to Elisabeth Sherwood for providing editorial comments and to Sonia Wheeler for production assistance. The data on privatization and private participation in infrastructure contained in the World Bank Private Participation in Infrastructure Data Base is based upon secondary sources from reports and open press, which could affect the reliability and exhaustiveness of the information presented. The findings, interpretations and conclusions expressed herein are entirely those of the author, and should not be attributed in any manner to the World Bank, its affiliated organizations, its officers, or to the Board of Executive Directors or the countries they represent.

1   The geographical coverage includes the World Bank's MENA region: Algeria Iran, Libya, Malta, Morocco, Tunisia, Bahrain, Egypt, Iraq, Jordan, Kuwait, Lebanon, Oman, Qatar, Saudi Arabia, Syria, United Arab Emirates, West Bank and Gaza and Yemen. We have also briefly reviewed privatization programmes in Israel and Turkey. However, relevant aggregated statistical data were not included in the various tables. For a review of guidelines related to privatization of enterprises in the tradeable sector see Saghir 1995.
2   In 1996, FDI flows into the MENA region increased to an estimated US$2.5 billion, a 19 per cent gain over 1995. However, investment was highly concentrated: 80 per cent of the region's net FDI went to Egypt, Morocco and Tunisia. In Morocco for example, FDI rose from US$165 million in 1990 to US$818 million in 1995. In Tunisia the jump was fourfold, rising from US$76 million in 1990 to US$330 million in 1995. Preliminary estimates for Egypt indicate foreign investment could amount to US$2.1 billion in 1996: up 254 per cent from the previous year. However, FDI remains disappointing in Algeria, Iran, Iraq, Jordan, Lebanon, Libya, Syria, Yemen and much of the GCC (Shafik 1997).

Appendix 5A: Options for private sector participation

Concession contract

- Long-term (twenty to thirty years) contract with a private company:
- Private company finances the investment costs of the system, including replacement costs and the working capital required for its operation and maintenance.
- Selection of the private company is based on charging the lowest tariff while committing to meet service levels and performance targets:
- Concessionaire's compensation is based on tariffs, which are determined according to agreement set out in the concession contract. The tariff revenue should be sufficient to cover the operational expenses as well as debt services and depreciation on the concession's investment. Tariffs are usually reassessed every few years (say five) based on an updated investment plan and estimates of expenditures. An inflation index formula would be agreed upon in the contract.
- Concessionaire provides both expertise and capital.
- Concession contract and procurement require detailed preparation.

Affermage (lease) contract

- Medium-term (eight to fifteen years) contract.
- Private company is responsible for operation and maintenance (O&M) and for financing working capital and replacement of short-lived assets. Private company bears full commercial risks.
- Customers are clients of the private company, which usually collects the tariff revenue directly and returns an agreed portion to an SOE as a rental or license fee. The profit for the contractor is the difference between the gross revenues collected and the sum of operating costs and this fee.
- Investments are done by the public sector, which remains responsible for debt servicing.
- Tariffs are set by government.
- Selection of the private company by percentage of net income and part of tariffs reserved to lease;
- Affermage requires fairly detailed preparation and staff reduction. Lessee has no control over bulk water.
- Need to define service targets and what investments the government will finance.

Management contract

- Short-term (three years) contract.
- Private company is responsible for O&M (full managerial responsibility).
- Private company could also manage the investment programme (procurement, supervision of preparation and implementation).
- Investments are done by the public sector but could be managed by the management contractor on implementation fee.

- Bills are collected by the private company.
- Tariffs and levels of service are decided by government.
- Selection of the private company is by fee (reimbursement of cost plus performance bonus).
- Compensation is based on fixed fees (to cover cost of the management contractor) and performance bonus based on the results and/or achievement of specific service and performance targets/criteria defined in the management contract.

Divestiture

- Infrastructure owned by an incorporated entity.
- Incorporated entity may operate the infrastructure under a license of limited duration (for example, twenty-five years).
- All or part of this entity are sold to private interests.
- Unlike concession, divestiture transfers ownership of assets to the private sector;
- Investments and working capital are financed by incorporated entity, which in turn may access capital markets.
- Requires a highly sophisticated independent regulatory structure, with an elaborate formula for setting tariffs.
- Whereas other solutions typically involve periodic rebidding, this solution envisages periodic renegotiation with the regulator. Hence, there is a danger of diminished competition or regulatory capture.

Appendix 5B: Infrastructure privatizations and new investments

Table 5B.1 Privatization revenues by region, 1988–95 (US$ million)

	1988	1989	1990	1991	1992	1993	1994	1995	Total
East Asia/ Pacific	21	196	376	835	5,161	7,155	5,507	5,447	24,698
L. America/ Caribbean	2,530	1,436	7,279	17,989	15,797	10,646	7,818	4,623	68,136
E. Europe/ C. Asia	27	685	1,304	2,783	4,341	4,151	2,879	8,937	25,107
M. East/ N. Africa	7	14	2	17	70	627	626	1,999	3,362
South Asia	—	3	29	996	1,557	974	2,666	159	6,384
Sub-Saharan Africa	10	683	74	60	191	648	792	544	3,002
Total	2,595	3,017	9,082	22,680	27,117	24,201	20,288	21,709	130,689
% MENA region	0.27	0.46	0.02	0.07	0.26	2.59	3.09	9.21	2.57

Note/sources: see overleaf.

Note and sources for Table 5B.1

Note: Table 5B.1 includes privatization of state-owned companies in the tradable and non-tradable sectors. Sales of miscellaneous activities or unutilized assets of enterprises (lands, shops, etc.) are excluded.

Sources: World Bank Privatization Database (International Economics Department), *Global Development Finance* 1997, *Privatization International, Privatization Yearbook, IBTCI* 1997.

Table 5B.2 Number of actual projects (infrastructure privatizations and new investments) by region and sector, January 1984–October 1995

	Gas	Power	Telecom	Transport	Waste	Water	Total
Sub-Saharan Africa	2	8	24	5	1	4	44
East Asia	7	83	51	60	13	13	227
Western Europe	24	87	52	32	65	33	284
Eastern Europe/CIS	6	12	33	9	4	3	67
Latin America & the Caribbean	11	88	31	90	11	8	239
Middle East & North Africa	7	0	6	0	0	1	14
North America	19	84	128	21	57	11	320
South Asia	0	7	13	3	0	0	23
Total	76	369	338	320	142	73	1,218

Notes: The information contained in the Private Participation in Infrastructure Database is based on secondary sources, which affects the reliability and exhaustiveness of the information presented. As a result the database does not represent an official World Bank inventory. Infrastructure privatization O&M: includes completed asset sales to private investors and awarded operation and maintenance contracts (O&M), management contracts, operating licences and concessions. Infrastructure new investments: includes investments in which financial closure has been reached and construction is under way. Project classifications under this category include: build–operate–transfer (BOT); build–own–operate–transfer (BOOT); build–transfer–operate (BTO); build–lease–transfer (BLT); build–own–operate (BOO); rehabilitate–own–transfer (ROT). Actual project: project completed or awarded.

Sources: World Bank Private Participation in Infrastructure Database, *Public Works Financing, Project Finance International, Euromoney, Privatization International, Middle East Economic Digest, Infrastructure Finance, International Financing Review, Financial Times, Project Finance in Latin America,* government documents, World Bank publications and company annual reports.

Table 5B.3 Number of actual projects and estimated total value by region and sector, February 1997 (infrastructure privatizations)

	Gas		Power		Telecom		Transport		Waste		Water		Total	
	No.	(US$M)	No.	(US$M)	No.	(US$M)	No.	(US$M)	No.	(US$M)	No.	(US$M)	No.	(US$M)
Sub-Saharan Africa	0	0	10	810	10	518	22	396	1	0	10	119	53	1,843
East Asia (emerging markets)	2	894	8	5,831	9	78,883	6	9,930	2	137	0	0	27	95,675
East Asia (developed)	1	502	23	7,830	9	3,751	17	1,809	1	192	0	0	51	14,084
Western Europe	3	17,305	42	39,429	25	53,797	26	7,160	17	10,333	22	10,334	135	138,359
Eastern Europe/CIS	4	386	15	2,135	7	3,914	2	32	6	422	5	362	39	7,251
Latin America/Caribbean	13	6,339	65	8,621	23	23,042	37	5,893	7	3,229	6	3,179	151	50,303
Middle East and North Africa	2	47	0	0	2	600	0	0	0	0	1	0	5	637
North America	6	1,091	6	1,156	116	8,443	3	826	24	648	11	448	166	12,612
South Asia	0	0	2	390	1	898	1	80	0	0	0	0	4	1,368
Total	31	26,564	171	66,202	202	173,846	114	26,126	58	14,961	55	14,443	631	322,132

Notes: The information contained in the Private Participation in Infrastructure Database is based on secondary sources, which affects the reliability and exhaustiveness of the information presented. As a result the database does not represent an official World Bank inventory. Infrastructure privatization O&M: includes completed asset sales to private investors and awarded operation and maintenance contracts (O&M), management contracts, operating licences and concessions. Actual project: project completed or awarded.

Sources: World Bank Private Participation in Infrastructure Database, *Public Works Financing, Project Finance International, Euromoney, Privatization International, Middle East Economic Digest, Infrastructure Finance, International Financing Review, Financial Times, Project Finance in Latin America*, government documents, World Bank publications and company annual reports.

Table 5B.4 Number of actual projects and estimated total value by region and sector, February 1997 (new investments)

	Gas		Power		Telecom		Transport		Waste		Water		Total	
	No.	(US$M)	No.	(US$M)	No.	(US$M)	No.	(US$M)	No.	(US$M)	No	(US$M)	No.	(US$M)
Sub-Saharan Africa	3	1,253	3	271	4	52	1	300	2	15	2	16	15	1,907
East Asia (emerging markets)	0	0	8	2,681	17	3,240	14	46,414	4	226	4	255	47	52,816
East Asia (developed)	1	1,600	69	27,795	13	8,020	39	21,577	3	2,647	7	1,706	132	63,345
Western Europe	24	22,271	53	22,363	41	17,470	18	49,122	9	809	1	240	146	112,275
Eastern Europe/CIS	3	20	9	5,087	11	364	7	1,202	2	81	3	1,681	35	8,435
Latin America/Caribbean	2	909	36	9,863	6	2,492	75	13,209	10	4,376	3	4,670	132	35,519
Middle East and North Africa	5	4,697	1	1,700	4	1,720	0	0	0	0	0	0	10	8,117
North America	17	3,271	95	19,967	15	1,207	16	3,422	28	2,947	1	12	172	30,826
South Asia	0	0	16	9,635	14	4,019	3	202	0	0	0	0	33	13,856
Total	55	34,021	290	99,362	125	38,585	173	135,448	58	11,101	21	8,579	722	327,095

Notes: The information contained in the Private Participation in Infrastructure Database is based on secondary sources, which affects the reliability and exhaustiveness of the information presented. As a result the database does not represent an official World Bank inventory. Infrastructure new investments: includes investments in which financial closure has been reached and construction is under way. Project classifications under this category include: Build-Operate-Transfer (BOT); Build-Own-Operate-Transfer (BOOT); Build-Transfer-Operate (BTO); Build-Lease-Transfer (BLT); Build-Own-Operate (BOO); Rehabilitate-Own-Transfer (ROT). Actual project: project completed or awarded.

Sources: World Bank Private Participation in Infrastructure Database, *Public Works Financing, Project Finance International, Euromoney, Privatization International, Middle East Economic Digest, Infrastructure Finance, International Financing Review, Financial Times, Project Finance in Latin America,* government documents, World Bank publications and company annual reports.

Table 5B.5 Number of actual projects and estimated total value by region and sector, February 1997 (infrastructure privatization and new investments)

	Gas		Power		Telecom		Transport		Waste		Water		Total	
	No.	(US$M)	No.	(US$M)	No.	(US$M)	No.	(US$M)	No.	(US$M)	No.	(US$M)	No.	(US$M)
Sub-Saharan Africa	3	1,253	13	1,081	14	570	23	696	3	15	121	135	68	3,750
East Asia (emerging markets)	2	894	16	8,512	26	82,123	20	56,344	6	363	4	255	74	148,491
East Asia (developed)	2	2,102	92	35,625	22	11,771	56	23,386	4	2,839	7	1,706	183	77,429
Western Europe	27	39,576	95	61,791	66	71,268	44	56,282	26	11,142	23	10,574	281	250,634
Eastern Europe/CIS	7	405	24	7,222	18	4,278	9	1,234	8	503	8	2,043	74	15,685
Latin America/Caribbean	15	7,248	101	18,484	29	25,534	112	19,102	17	7,605	9	7,849	283	85,822
Middle East and North Africa	7	4,744	1	1,700	6	2,320	0	0	0	0	1	0	15	8,754
North America	23	4,362	101	21,123	131	9,650	19	4,248	52	3,595	12	460	338	43,438
South Asia	0	0	18	10,025	15	4,917	4	282	0	0	0	0	37	15,224
Total	86	60,585	461	165,563	327	212,431	287	161,574	116	26,062	76	23,022	1,353	649,237

Notes: The information contained in the Private Participation in Infrastructure Database is based on secondary sources, which affects the reliability and exhaustiveness of the information presented. As a result the database does not represent an official World Bank inventory. Infrastructure/privatization/ O&M includes completed asset sales to private investors and awarded operation and maintenance contracts (O&M), management contracts, operating licences and concessions. Infrastructure new investments: includes investments in which financial closure has been reached and construction is under way. Project classifications under this category include: build–operate–transfer (BOT); build–own–operate–transfer (BOOT); build–transfer–operate (BTO); build–lease–transfer (BLT); build–own–operate (BOO); rehabilitate–own–transfer (ROT). Actual project: project completed or awarded.

Sources: World Bank Private Participation in Infrastructure Database, Public Works Financing, Project Finance International, Euromoney, Privatization International, Middle East Economic Digest, Infrastructure Finance, International Financing Review, Financial Times, Project Finance in Latin America, government documents, World Bank publications and company annual reports.

Table 5B.6 Privatization revenues in MENA, 1988–96 (US$ million)

	1988	1989	1990	1991	1992	1993	1994	1995	1996	Total
Egypt	–	–	–	–	–	328	203	590	858	1,979
Kuwait	–	–	–	–	–	–	34	925	968	1,927
Morocco	–	–	–	–	–	273	347	240	356	1,216
Tunisia	7	14	2	17	60	–	–	32	–	132
Other	–	–	–	–	9	26	42	2112	–	289
Total	7	14	2	17	69	627	626	1,999	2,182	5,543

Note: This table includes privatization of state-owned enterprises in the tradable and non-tradable (infrastructure) sectors. Sales of miscellaneous activities or unutilized assets (land, shops, etc.) are excluded. (–): not available.
Sources: World Bank Privatization Database (International Economics Department), *Global Development Finance* 1997, *Privatization International* 17 January 1997, *Privatization Yearbook* 1996, Kuwait Investment Authority, IBTC 1997.

Appendix 5C: Overview of privatization in MENA

Privatization in the MENA region has taken different approaches in different countries:

- Some countries are still in the design process (most of the GCC countries).
- Some countries are focusing privatization on state-owned enterprises operating in the commercially-oriented sector (Egypt and Tunisia, Yemen).
- Some countries are privatizing or intend to privatize state-owned enterprises operating in the tradeable and non-tradeable sectors (for example Algeria, Jordan, Morocco, Oman, Turkey and Israel).
- Other countries are complementing increasing private sector participation in infrastructure activities and mainly new projects (for example Lebanon and some GCC countries).

The varied privatization and PPI experience of different countries is as follows.

Morocco There are 800 state-owned enterprises (SOEs) and participations in Morocco accounting for 12 per cent of GDP; 12 per cent of wages and salaries and 6 per cent of the urban, formal-sector labour force. Unlike many other MENA countries, Morocco's privatization programme has benefited from high-level political support and a substantial indigenous private sector interested in buying privatized assets or shares. The parliament enabled privatization in December 1989, and the law took effect in April 1990. All key institutions were put in place by September 1991. The privatization programme complements other liberal measures taken during the 1980s to open up Morocco's economic and industrial structure. The Privatization Law enabled the transfer to the private sector of 114 listed entities (seventy-seven companies and thirty-seven hotels) before 13 December, 1998. Over half the firms come from the industrial sector but their greatest share of sectoral value added is in finance and oil refining. As of October 1996 a total of twenty-seven of the seventy-seven companies and eighteen of the thirty-seven hotels have been transferred to the private sector, raising over US$1.2 billion.

The government has also solicited private participation in the power sector (1,300 mega watt Jorf Lasfar project) and in water and electricity concession (Casablanca) and is preparing privatization of telecommunications. An important innovation introduced by Morocco was the issuance of privatization bonds that gave bearers priority over buyers of privatization assets who paid in cash. The bonds have been very successful in:

i   gauging demand for privatized assets (in order to facilitate planning)
ii   stimulating interest in the programme
iii   reducing pressure to sell assets to cover fiscal shortfalls, and
iv   creating indigenous pressure on government to bring assets to market.

Two offerings of privatization bonds raised around US$314 million. These bonds pay a compound annual interest of 8 per cent upon conversion or 8.5 per cent at redemption in December 1998. Bond holders have absolute priority over buyers who pay cash.

Morocco's privatization programme welcomes foreign investment and, in general, no restrictions exist on foreign ownership. Of the twenty-seven companies and eighteen hotels privatized ten and four, respectively, were sold in whole or in part to foreign buyers. Industrial operators and financial investors have provided 27 per cent of privatization revenue so far.

Algeria   Algeria has developed an ambitious privatization programme. At least three methods of privatization have been adopted: share transfers, management buy-outs and complete sale to outside investors. Since early 1996, twenty-six sales have occurred, in which seven share transfers brought to the treasury more than US $18 million. Recent announcements indicate government willingness to accelerate and deepen privatization and to consider large schemes, including a voucher programme. In January 1997, the Algerian government announced plans to privatize the loss-making airline Air Algeria, as well as shipping firms and ports. The Algerian government is due to produce a list of around 250 companies to be privatized.

Tunisia   The SOE sector in Tunisia dates from independence in 1956. It was established to enable Tunisia to gain control over key sectors of the economy (banking, utilities and so on); to exploit the country's natural resources (phosphates, petroleum and gas); to develop the agriculture sector; to open new sectors (tourism, textiles and motor cars); to encourage regional industrial development; to undertake capital intensive projects (cements, oil and refining); and to pursue various socioeconomic objectives. From inception to the 1960s, the public sector continued to grow, accounting for 55 to 60 per cent of all investment in Tunisia. In the 1970s, development of the private sector was encouraged through a series of incentives and exemptions, but proliferation of SOEs through the creation of affiliates and the establishment of a small number of new SOEs continued to take place. In 1985, SOEs, in which the state held 34 per cent or more of the capital, accounted for 31 per cent of GDP, 26.5 per cent of value added and 40 per cent of total investment in the economy. These SOEs employed about 156,000 people, accounting for some 13 per cent of the total employment in the country. Tunisia first embarked on a privatization programme in 1986, as part of a structural adjustment programme. However, the programme was launched in 1989 with the promulgation of Law no. 89–9, which set the general framework for public enterprise restructuring and privatization. Approximately seventy companies, with an estimated total worth of about US$133 million, have been totally or partially privatized since 1986. Most of the enterprises privatized in the early phases of the programme had been relatively profitable and small and were sold directly to private parties rather than to the public via the Tunis Bourse.

Tunisia planned to speed up the privatization programme in 1997, with sixty enterprises with total net assets of US$1.5 billion identified for sale in the next few years. However, the government is still very cautious: it has not published a list of state-owned enterprises to be privatized so as to minimize resistance from the enterprises, it has imposed on buyers tight restrictions on firing workers and has moved slowly on involving the private sector in infrastructure projects.

Egypt   is at a turning point. After decades of reliance upon the public sector as an engine of growth and employment generation, by the late 1980s the Egyptian economy had become dominated by SOEs, operating under different legal regimes in nearly all sectors of the economy. The public sector includes four major groups; central and local government administration; service authorities (institutions of higher education, the High Dam Authority and the sanitary, sewerage department); economic authorities; and the public enterprises (PEs) sector, which includes financial and non-financial PEs. It accounts for about 40 per cent of aggregate employment and about half of total GDP and two-thirds of non-agricultural GDP. In industry and mining (including petroleum and electricity), the public sector share of GDP is over 60 per cent. The PEs sector comprises some 399 financial and non-financial PEs which were formed during the socialist era, either through the merger of nationalized firms or the establishment of new PEs. This group employs about one million workers and operates in all of the tradeable and competitive sectors of activity, with a major concentration in manufacturing, followed by construction, trade and transport. In 1991, the government reorganized (Law 203 of 1991) the twenty-seven Public Sector Authorities and 314 non-financial PEs that existed under Law no. 97/1983 into seventeen managerial-autonomous profit-driven holding companies (HCs), each with diversified portfolios and affiliated companies (ACs). The 314 non-financial PEs comprise roughly 70 per cent of the country's public sector. The economic authorities (EAs) encompass 50 entities, which are semi-autonomous corporations operating mainly in the area of public utilities, the two rent-earning monopolies (the Suez Canal and petroleum), the social and health insurance as well as the General Authority for Supply Commodities. The total employment of the EAs is around 455,000, the largest employers being the railways, telecommunications, bus transport, electricity, post office and social insurance.

The Public Enterprise Office (PEO) was established in 1991 to serve as a liaison between the government and new holding companies. The Egyptian privatization programme was officially announced in 1991. As of the end of 1996, Egypt had totally or partially privatized forty-six Law 203 companies, amounting to around US$2 billion of sale proceeds in a wide range of sectors through various methods of privatization (initial public offering, anchor investors, Employee Shareholders Association and liquidation). In addition, around US$1 billion of unutilized fixed assets, miscellaneous activities, local governorates' assets and joint venture companies have been sold (see Table 5C.1). With a new government in place in January 1996, guarded optimism and very strong political signals were given regarding the commitment of the Egyptian government to accelerating the pace of privatization. In 1996 assets worth over US $800 million were privatized. The government earmarked the majority of public enterprises for privatization.

Despite a generally slow start, the attitude of the public has gradually changed from negative to mildly supportive, and phenomenal learning has taken place on the part of all parties involved. For 1997, the government plans to privatize thirty-three companies through anchor investors sales and twelve companies through initial public offerings (IPOs). In the first quarter of 1997, four companies were privatized through IPOs and no companies were sold through anchor investors. Their share value amounted to US$117 million.

As Egypt's privatization process escalates, plans have been announced for the construction of two new ports on a BOT basis, a container terminal at Adobiya

Table 5C.1 Egypt: total sale proceeds by method as of March 1997

Method	Value (LE million)	% of total
Majority IPOs	2,355	22.72
Minority IPOs	2,377	22.93
Liquidation	625	6.03
Anchor investors	1,301	12.55
ESAs	245	2.36
ESOPs	3	0.03
Local governorates	300	2.89
Sale of unutilized assets	3,033	29.23
Joint venture companies	128	1.23
Total	10,367 (US$ 3,058)	100.00

Source: IBTC, Public Enterprise Office.

(near Suez) and a facility for trans-shipment to be built further north in the eastern branch of the Suez Canal near the Mediterranean coastline. Initial steps toward introducing private sector participation in the telecommunications and power sectors have been initiated. The state-owned Egyptian telecommunications company announced in April 1997 that it was inviting interested companies to purchase pre-tender qualification documents for two licenses for public phone systems to be installed throughout the country in partnership.

Turkey   The privatization programme in Turkey is over ten years old. Since 1986, 113 companies were privatized either via sale of shares or asset sale and the government has raised around US$3 billion. Earlier efforts to speed up privatization were hampered by court annulments, political turmoil and frequent reshuffles at the Privatization Administration Office, the agency responsible for privatization. Current plans are to speed up the process and accelerate build-own-operate projects in the infrastructure sectors. There are four methods of private participation being used in Turkey in the power generation sector-

- Build–operate–transfer (BOT), in which the power producing companies finance and build a plant and sell their output to the Turkish Electricity Distribution Company (TEDAS). There are four ongoing BOT projects in the energy sector. Three are gas-powered electricity-generation projects, all near Istanbul, with a combined capacity of 1,136 megawatts.
- Build–own–operate (BOO), a scheme introduced by the government in an effort to circumvent the constitutional court's objections to BOT. Under a BOO scheme, project sponsors become owners and can sell electricity to the private sector as well as to TEDAS. Although there are also some legal problems over implementation of the BOO model, the government has opened tenders and received bids for one coal-fired and five gas-fired projects.
- Auto power generation, in which Turkish manufacturers are allowed to generate their own power. Excess capacity may be sold to the national grid. This is the only scheme that is free of legal entanglements, but there are problems that could be equally daunting: the shortage of gas and TEDAS's refusal to pay market prices for producers' excess capacity. These projects are small enough to allow Turkish financial institutions to take an active part in their financing.
- Electricity distribution privatization. Electricity distribution in twenty-five regions will be handed over to the private sector by TEDAS. Nearly 200 bids have been submitted.

Lebanon   During the seventeen years of civil war, due to the lack of basic services provided by the government, the people responded by turning increasingly toward private sector solutions, such as self-contained private telecommunications systems or diesel generators. Building on these initiatives, the government decided to increase the role of the private sector in infrastructure financing, management and operation. However, due to legal impediments and other social and political constraints, the government is still reluctant to transfer majority ownership of utility services to the private sector.

There are around twenty public enterprises in Lebanon representing a small percentage of GDP. Privatization of commercially oriented public enterprises such as airline and tobacco companies is not on the government agenda in the short term. In the case of infrastructure activity, the government has opted for rehabilitation, phased corporatization and private sector participation in major infrastructure sectors, beginning with private provision of certain services. Its approach has been, so far, to introduce private participation in infrastructure through three main avenues.

- BOT Concessions. Lebanon has already awarded the first two BOTs for the delivery of a mobile telephone network and has an ambitious programme of BOT projects worth around US$2 billion, including a toll highway (Beirut–Masnaa), postal services, and the Awali–Beirut Water Conveyor.
- Contracting Out. This method does not affect ownership of existing assets but allows the private sector to operate and manage existing governmental or municipal facilities. Lebanon has adopted such an approach in at least three projects: collection of garbage in the Greater Beirut area, operation and management at the Amrousiyhe incinerator, and management and operation of the compost plant in the Karantina area of Beirut.
- Twinning and Technical Assistance. This method involves the assistance of an external operator to support the day-to-day running of the sector or company through the presence of on-site experts. This type of operation is currently used in the electricity and telecommunication sectors. Electricité de France is assisting Electricité du Liban and Cable & Wireless is supporting the Ministry of Post and Telecommunications.

Jordan   There are thirty-five public corporations. Many of these public corporations are not effective in providing services, and are not operated at high levels of efficiency due to political interference, rigid bureaucratic procedures, uncompetitive pay scales and poor incentive structure. Estimates show about a 55 per cent public-sector share in employment and 35 per cent in investment, dominance in infrastructure, tourism and mining sectors and a varying (mostly 10 per cent) share in 60 per cent of the companies listed on the stock market. In 1996, the government embarked on an ambitious privatization programme, encompassing various sectors of the economy. As part of this programme, several privatization activities have been launched with the initiative of the concerned ministries. To strengthen its institutional and technical capacity to implement such a programme, the government has established a separate unit, the Executive Privatization Unit.

The first candidates for privatization include the national telecommunications company, the public railway company, the public bus company and some of the shareholdings of the Jordan Investment Company, such as the Maan Spa

Complex and Jordan Cement Factories. In addition to these transactions, work has also been initiated to involve the private sector in the operations and management of the Water Authority of Jordan (WAJ) and in power generation activities of the Jordan Electricity Authority.

Israel   State companies play a significant role in the Israeli economy. The Israeli government currently owns approximately 119 state companies, fifty-seven of which are commercially-oriented. The remainder of the state-owned companies are non-commercial institutes such as funds established as vehicles for employee savings. state-owned enterprises are divided into two categories: state companies and mixed companies. State companies are companies in which more than 50 per cent of the control rights are owned by the government. They are subject to the provisions of the Israeli Government Companies Law (GCL), as well as to the directives of the Companies Authority.

Mixed companies are companies in which the state owns less than a controlling interest. Under the GCL, mixed companies are not subject to the same degree of regulation as government companies. In 1994, government companies accounted for 17.5 per cent of total exports and about 15.5 per cent of the GNP, although they employed only 3.6 per cent of all Israeli employees.

The government has initiated a number of regulatory arrangements regarding the major state companies which are designed to increase competition in the markets in which those state companies participate and thus prepare such companies for privatization in the future. The government has established a ministerial privatization committee to speed up the privatization programme.

Yemen   There are about 140 SOEs registered, but many in the south are not operative. The work force in SOEs is estimated at 76,000 people, of which about 30,000 receive salaries directly from the Ministry of Finance and not from the concerned SOEs, because their workplaces are either closed or financially bankrupt. In January 1995, the government announced that it would privatize (or liquidate) a group of seventy PEs and other entities accounting for about 70 per cent of the public enterprise sector in employment terms. The enterprises to be privatized would cover a broad range of sectors: industry, tourism, agriculture, fishing, transportation, construction, trade, electricity and financial institutions. So far, the bulk of enterprises in the tourism sector have been privatized. Other industrial, transport and agriculture enterprises are being prepared for privatization in the next few months. Also, a number of large projects (the Aden free zone, grain silos and floor mills in Hodeida, a refinery in Aden and a 60 megawatt gas-fired BOT power generation plant) have been agreed in principle with investors.

The Gulf   In the Gulf Cooperation Countries (GCC), privatization has tended to occur on a case-by-case basis without an overall policy or legal, procedural and regulatory framework. Oman is the exception, with a more proactive government policy to promote privatization of both tradeable and non-tradeable sectors. With a few notable exceptions, the initial skepticism about privatization and PPI has given way to enthusiasm and cautious optimism. While the legal and regulatory framework may not yet be in place, economic need is driving the GCC states into a new era of private investor participation in a variety of businesses and projects.

A prime candidate for privatization in the Gulf is infrastructure, in particular power generation, water desalination and telecommunication networks. Following closely behind are established state-owned businesses operating in aviation, hotels and downstream oil and gas, as well as joint ventures involving high-profile foreign technical partners. The opportunities are numerous and diverse although, for the moment, completed transactions remain thin on the ground. Nevertheless recent years have seen some interesting developments in the various GCC states. A brief summary of these is set out next.

Bahrain In 1994, the government sold a 20 per cent stake in one of the country's largest food companies (the General Trading and Food Processing Company) on the Bahrain stock exchange for US$10.3 million. Prior to the Gulf crisis, 20 per cent of the Bahrain Aluminum Extrusion Company (Balexco) was privatized. The government appears now to be going ahead with its programme to privatize the state-owned hotels and tourism companies and this may be followed by privatization of the public utilities, power and water and desalination plants. However, for the time being, there is no structured privatization policy. Bahrain's stock market will assist in providing a good medium through which privatization can take place, and the opportunities for foreign investor participation will serve to stimulate interest in any new development in the market.

Kuwait After the Iraqi occupation, the budget deficit resulting from costs of restructuring has meant that Kuwait had to explore privatization. This has been encouraged by an unpublished internal World Bank report, which recommended the privatization of over seventy local companies.

As with many Gulf countries, Kuwait has been wary of privatization due to reduced employment opportunities in the restructured, privatized companies. Since 1994, in its first phase of privatization, the Kuwait Investment Authority has sold over US$1.9 billion of stakes in seventeen listed and unlisted companies. The sale of shares has stimulated the Kuwait Stock Exchange (KSE). A second stage of the plan involves the passage of a privatization law and the sale of state holdings in public services such as water, telecommunications and electricity. Privatization has helped create a resurgence in capital markets. The KSE index climbed about 90 per cent from December 1994 to November 1996. Valuing of trading increased from KD584 million in 1994 to over KD5.3 billion for the first eleven months of 1996.

Oman Oman has seen a considerable expansion of private sector industrial development. Encouragement of export-oriented industry has complemented the country's privatization strategy. In recent years, the government has sold its share in a number of companies (for example, the Oman Cement Company, the

Oman National Insurance Company and Oman Gulf Hotels), as well as in the National Insurance Company and Oman Gulf Hotels). Moreover the private sector already participates in the operation and management of electricity and will participate in new power stations and wastewater projects. Oman has been one of the first Middle East states to adopt PPI on a broad basis and cites the 90 mega watt Al Manah Project as an example to the rest of the region of how private investors can be attracted to ambitious infrastructure projects. The power station will be operated privately for twenty-two years before being returned to the state.

A variety of factors, including a broad range of investment initiatives, adequate local financing, political stability, an established legal and regulatory framework, an effective stock exchange and a state policy of financial caution have combined to present an attractive offer to foreign as well as national investors.

The privatization programme planned for the near future includes the offering of shares in government-owned hotels, such as the Holiday Inn in Salalah and the Novotel and Intercontinental in Muscat. Other possible offerings include power projects at Barqa and privatization of the electricity system in the country, as well as the Salalah and Muscat BOOT wastewater schemes which are now awaiting financial closure.

Qatar   The change of leadership in June 1995 brought with it greater economic liberalization. Privatization has become more appealing to the government since capital spending has been constrained by the drop in oil prices. The government is also seeking international finance for its gas projects, including a second liquefied natural gas (LNG) venture and numerous other industrial proposals based on North Field Gas feed stock. In addition, it is reported that the government is considering privatizing the sewerage network.

Saudi Arabia   In 1994, the kingdom's public sector, which comprises both oil and non-oil activities, accounted for 63 per cent of GDP. The non-governmental sector accounted for 27 per cent of GDP and 12 per cent of employment. Many SOEs receive budgetary support from the government to sustain their operations. These fiscal subventions to the state enterprises totalled SR15.5 billion in 1995. The industry sector is dominated by SABIC, the holding company for the country's petrochemical complex, which is 70 per cent state-owned. SABIC currently owns shares ranging from 20–100 per cent in nineteen industrial projects. Petromin, which is the state-owned petroleum products refining and distribution organization, straddles the oil and non-oil sectors. In 1996, Petromin was absorbed by Aramco, the country's oil company. The state enterprises in the infrastructure sector include power, rail, ports, telecommunications, the national airline and airports. The legal form of these enterprises varies, the telecommunications utility is a government department with the minister as the head. The power utilities are corporatized with shares owned partly by the private sector and traded on the stock exchange. Others, such as the railways and ports, are agencies with a budget approved by the government. The financial institutions sector consists of twelve commercial banks (SR 382 billion total assets), in four of which the government has shareholdings, and the state-owned specialized financial institutions (SR 220 billion).

In 1994 King Fahd made a commitment to release government ownership of productive and profitable state-owned entities, which is beginning to bring results. Development of privatization programmes for different sectors, including electricity, have begun..

The existence of qualified and experienced management, a developed commercial banking system, adequate lending facilities, a large capital market and a population with a high savings ratio are all factors which are likely to lead to developments in the kingdom very soon. In addition, the extensive Saudi funds invested or deposited abroad will provide adequate liquidity for many years to come.

United Arab Emirates   Privatization in the United Emirates has been developing in the past few years, although there is no official government policy on privatization. Nearly 40 per cent of the government interest in the Emirates Telecommunications Corporation have been privatized. In Abu Dhabi, the most recent privatization project involved the establishment of Abu Dhabi Ship Building (ADSB) involving an IPO of 41.5 per cent of the company's shares to local investors. Abu Dhabi's General Industry Corporation is planning to sell shares in a number of profitable state-owned enterprises and expectations are high. The twenty-five year BOOT wastewater concession currently under negotiation for the entire emirate of Ajman is a major milestone in the UAE.

It is expected that privatization in the UAE will gain momentum. Two water and wastewater privatization concessions are planned in UAE. This is reflected by the involvement of the UAE Offsets Group in the programme and the establishment of the National Investor, a local, privately-owned corporate finance and investment house that acted as lead manager on the ADSB IPO.

In summary, there is no overall policy of privatization in the GCC countries, and generally privatization has often happened without the assistance of a clear legal and procedural framework. Only Oman and to a certain extent Kuwait have made an effort to pave the way for its privatization programme with the wholesale review of its legal and financial infrastructure. Stock markets in the Gulf countries have yet to develop significantly and market capitalization is still half that of developed countries.

Notes

1   This synopsis (prepared in 1997/8) provides a brief and by no means an exhaustive review of privatization programmes in selected MENA countries. It is based on a compilation of information from several sources including internal World Bank data-

bases, *Privatization International* (1996a, 1996b); *Privatization in Middle East and North Africa* (1996), *Middle East Economic Digest* and privatization agencies.
2 *Privatization International*, March 1997.
3 *Privatization International*, January 1997 and *Financial Times*, 25 March 1997.

Bibliography

Al Bader (1996) 'Kuwait Investment Authority's experience in implementing the privatization programme', paper presented at seminar on 'Privatization Programme: Review and Prospects', Kuwait.
Claessens, S. and Naudé, D. (1993) 'Recent estimates of capital flight', Policy Research Working Paper no. 1186, Washington, D.C.: World Bank.
Committee for Economic and Commercial Cooperation (1996) proceedings of workshop on 'Privatization in the Islamic Countries', October.
Dervis, K. (1996) 'Growth and public–private investment in infrastructure in the Middle East and North Africa', speech delivered at conference on 'Public–Private Partnerships in Infrastructure', Istanbul, 15–17 October.
Economist Intelligence Unit (1997) published by the *Economist* 14 April.
El-Erian, M. and Kumar M., (1995) 'Equity markets in Middle Eastern Countries', IMF Staff Paper 42, no. 2, Washington, D.C.: IMF.
Euromoney (1996) September, London.
Gates, J. and Saghir J. (1995) 'Employee stock ownership plans (ESOP): objectives, design options and international experience', CFS Discussion Paper Series no. 112, Washington, D.C.: World Bank.
Guislain, P. (1997) 'The privatization challenge: a strategic, legal and institutional analysis of international experience', Washington, D.C.: World Bank.
International Finance Corporation (1996) *Monthly Review of Emerging Stock Markets* World Bank, Washington D.C., December.
International Business and Technical Consultants (IBTC) (1997) *Quarterly Report Review of Egypt Privatization Programme*, USAID Privatization Project Evaluation Service Contract, Cairo, Egypt.
Kant (1994) 'Foreign direct investment and capital flight', Washington, D.C.: International Finance Corporation.
Kerf, M. and Smith, W. (1996) 'Privatizing Africa's infrastructure', World Bank Technical Paper no. 337, *Africa Region Series,* Washington, D.C.: World Bank.
Middle East Economic Digest, various issues.
Page, J., Saba J., and Shafik, N. (1997) 'From player to referee: the changing role of competition policies and regulation in the Middle East and North Africa', paper presented at seminar on 'The Role of the State in a Changing Arab Economic Environment' Kuwait, 4–5 March.
Privatization International (1996a) *Privatization Yearbook–1996,* London.
—— (1996b) *Privatization Monthly,* London, various issues.
—— (1997) *Privatization Monthly* London, various issues.
—— (1997) http://www.pmena.com
Privatization Middle East and North Africa (1996) 30 December.
Saghir, J. (1993) 'Privatization in Tunisia', CFS Discussion Paper Series no. 101, World Bank, Washington, D.C.: CFSPS.
—— (1995) 'World Bank experience in privatization and overall review in the Arab World', in A. T. Al Sadek, M. Ali al-Jarhi and N. A. W. Loutalfa (eds), *Efforts and*

Impediments of Privatization in the Arab Countries Abu Dhabi, UAE: Arab Monetary
Fund.

—— (1996) 'The challenge of privatization and infrastructure development in the
Middle East and North Africa', presentation at the 12th Session of the Standing
Committee for Economic and Commercial Cooperation of the Organization of the
Islamic Conference, Istanbul, Turkey, November.

—— (1997a) 'Private sector participation in infrastructure financing in Middle East and
North Africa Region', presentation at the European Investment Bank, Luxemburg, 17
February.

—— (1997b) 'Opening the doors: privatization in the Middle East', presentation at
conference organized by the Center for Near East Studies, UCLA, Los Angeles World
Affairs Council and American University of Cairo, Los Angeles, 30 April.

Shafik, N. (1996) 'Selling privatization politically', *International Journal of the Economics
of Business*, November, vol. 3, no. 3.

—— (1997) 'Public policy and private initiative: towards new partnerships in the Middle
East and North Africa', paper presented at the conference on 'Globalization and the
Middle East and North Africa' organized by the Institut du Monde Arabe and the
World Bank, 14 March.

Sud, I. (1996) 'The challenge of infrastructure in MENA', Middle East Economic Digest
Conference, Bahrain.

Tilmes, K. (1996) 'International trends in liberalization of utility services and regulatory
systems', presentation at CRI conference on 'Public Confidence and Regulated
Network Industries: An International Review'.

World Bank (1994) 'Infrastructure for development', *World Development Report*, New
York: Oxford University Press for the World Bank.

—— (1995a) 'Claiming the future: choosing prosperity in the Middle East and North
Africa', Washington, D.C.: World Bank.

—— (1995b) 'Bureaucrats in business', Washington, D.C.: World Bank.

—— (1996) 'Getting connected: private participation in infrastructure in the Middle
East and North Africa', Washington, D.C.: World Bank.

—— (1997) 'Global development finance', Washington, D.C.: World Bank.

6   Savings and privatization

Ahmed Galal

Introduction

At the most basic level, the transfer of ownership from the government to the private sector should leave savings unaffected. After all, privatization is merely a transfer of the same assets from one actor to another, involving no sacrifice of consumption today for consumption tomorrow. This view, however, is too simplistic. Privatization could increase savings, in part because the transfer of ownership to the private sector is associated with higher productivity (Galal *et al.* 1994, World Bank 1995). Higher productivity, in turn, generates more resources, which can either be consumed or saved. In addition, privatization could attract savings from abroad, which may not otherwise be possible without privatization. This typically happens when specialized multinational firms buy such enterprises as telecommunications. Beyond these first-round effects, privatization could stimulate savings indirectly. For example, if the sale proceeds are used to retire public debt, this could lead to a reduction in the size of government through lower taxation, with favourable effects on public savings (Sachs 1996).[1] Another example relates to the favourable effect of privatization on the competitiveness of other industries if it lowers the cost of producing intermediate goods and services (for instance, power and telecommunications services). Finally, privatization could contribute to savings indirectly by boosting capital market development, which has been shown to contribute positively to growth (Levine and Renelt 1992).

The view argued here is that there is a positive link between privatization and savings. This view differs from, but does not negate, the view that the causal relationship runs from growth to savings, stressed, for example, by Angus Deaton (Deaton 1995). If the view argued here holds, it has important implications for countries that are keen to grow fast but cannot wait for savings to accumulate from economic growth. To such countries, privatization, along with other reforms (for example, of pension funds), can help jump-start the growth process, thereby creating a virtuous circle of higher savings, investment and growth. An important question in this context is: what is the magnitude of the potential addition to savings from privatization? Another is: what does it take to attain the gains? These two fundamental questions are addressed in this chapter, using Egyptian public enterprise (PE) sector data. The chapter follows a modified version of the applied welfare methodology adopted by Galal *et al.* (1994) to evaluate the welfare effects of privatization. The methodology is based in comparing the savings from the PE sector under continued public ownership and its savings under the counterfactual scenario of privatization and commercialization.[2] Because the potential gains in savings depend on the initial conditions of the PE sector (including its level of efficiency and size), the chapter also measures the performance of the PE sector in Egypt over time and explores the roots of the problem.

The rest of the chapter is organized as follows. The next section documents the level and trend of the PE savings–investment (S–I) gap, as well as productivity and returns to capital over the period 1986/7–93/4; this is followed by a discussion of the root causes of the problem. The chapter then estimates the potential savings from PE reforms and concludes.

The PE savings–investment gap and its roots

Starting with the historical performance of the PE sector, the main questions addressed in this section are: how much savings did PEs in Egypt generate in comparison with their capital expenditures? If they did not save enough to meet their needs for expansion, how did they fill the gap? And, what are the root causes of the gap?

Lack of availability of consolidated accounts for the entire PE sector in Egypt limited the analysis below to 356 enterprises.[3] These enterprises operate in almost all branches of the industrial sector, but the few missing PEs, known as the 'economic authorities' in Egypt, are relatively important ones, and include such large entities as the Suez Canal, telecommunications, power and the railway. The bias in the sample favours PEs, given that a previous analysis has shown that the 'economic authorities' tend to perform less well than other PEs on average (World Bank 1987).

The PE savings–investment gap

The PEs' savings–investment (S–I) gap is defined as the difference between the PEs' current surplus, before transfers to or from the government, and their net fixed capital formation. Current surplus is defined as operating revenues minus operating expenditures (including depreciation), plus net non-operating income before taxes and dividends. For the sample analysed, the net S–I gap for the PE sector in Egypt averaged 2 per cent of gross domestic product (GDP) over the period 1987/8–93/4.[4] This gap is to be contrasted with the surplus on average of 0.4 per cent for forty-six developing countries (Figure 6.1), but the Egyptian PEs did better over time. The S–I gap that was 5.2 per cent of GDP in 1987/8 turned into surplus in 1991/2. In other words, starting in 1991/2, the PEs in Egypt became self-sufficient, generating the resources they needed for operation and expansion.

Of course, whatever gap Egypt's PEs accumulated in the past had to come from elsewhere in the economy: the government budget, domestic savings,

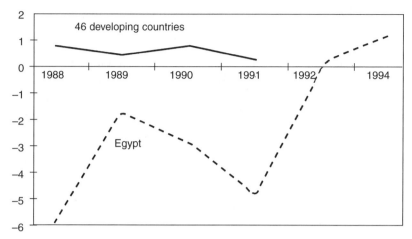

Figure 6.1 Net savings–investment gap, 1987–93 (% of GDP)

Sources: developing countries: World Bank 1995; Egypt: calculated from CAPMAS data; *Financial and Economic Statistics of Developing Countries,* various issues.

foreign borrowing or a mix of all three. As can be seen from Figure 6.2, the government clearly carried the bulk of the burden, although the budget's contribution fell dramatically in recent years. The banks were the second major contributor to PEs, and this contribution increased in recent years to partially offset the reduction in budgetary transfers dictated by tighter fiscal policies. The shift of financing from the government budget to the banking sector is problematic, given that banks are also publicly-owned, which means that commercial criteria may not have been followed in allocating these funds.

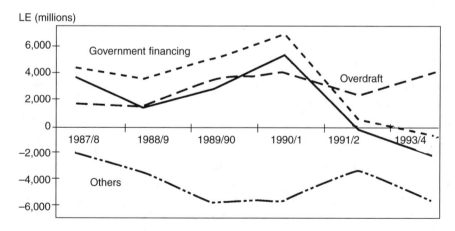

Figure 6.2 Net savings–investment gap of Egypt's public enterprise sector and its sources of finance, 1987/8–93/4

Sources: calculated from CAPMAS data; *Financial and Economic Statistics of Developing Countries,* various issues.

While a smaller PE S–I gap is desirable because it frees resources for the more productive private sector, the way this gap is reduced matters. Unfortunately, the improvement in the S–I gap of the PE sector in Egypt came primarily from a reduction in capital expenditures, rather than from an increase in savings (see Figure 6.3). Capital expenditures were cut sharply twice (in 1988/9 and 1991/2), and have never recovered. At the same time, savings as a percentage of GDP have deteriorated between the beginning and end of the period. The reduction in investment, especially in infrastructure activities, could adversely affect the growth of private sector investment, and thus economic growth (Easterly and Rebelo 1993).

The reasons for the deterioration in savings are low rates of return on capital and low productivity. Egyptian PEs were not net losers on average, but they made only modest rates of return on capital (Figure 6.4).[5] Between 1986/7 and 1993/4, their operating surplus relative to capital employed was 11.9 per cent, which is relatively low, given that the surplus represents returns to both owners and lenders. Profits net of taxes and subsidies to net worth average below the deposit rate over the last few years. Finally, the rates of return on revalued capital only averaged close to 5.5 per cent during the period.

Productivity is difficult to measure for the entire PE sector, in part because no meaningful composite price indices exist for outputs and inputs. However, a comparison between real per unit variable cost and operating surplus to sales of the PE sector in Egypt and a sample of eight countries (Figures 6.5a and 6.5b) indicates that Egypt's PE sector is an average performer. Moreover, the performance of the sector lags significantly behind such successful reformers as Korea, Chile and Mexico.

Roots of the gap

The roots of the modest performance of PEs in general are relatively well known. Governments often engage in activities unsuited for public ownership.

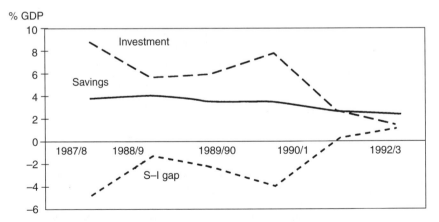

Figure 6.3 Net savings–investment gap of public enterprises in Egypt, 1987/8–93/4
Sources: calculated from CAPMAS data; *Financial and Economic Statistics of Developing Countries*, various issues.

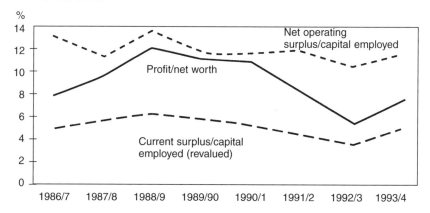

Figure 6.4 Financial performance of public enterprises in Egypt, 1986/7–93/4

Sources: calculated from CAPMAS data; *Financial and Economic Statistics of Developing Countries*, various issues.

Moreover, they do not provide PE managers with the policy and institutional environment necessary to ensure that they have sufficient incentives to behave efficiently. In Egypt, the government clearly extended its domain in the past to activities less suited for public ownership. The size of the PE sector in Egypt was about 30 per cent of GDP, compared with the world average for developing countries of 11 per cent (World Bank 1995). The PEs in Egypt operate not only in utilities and heavy industries, where market failure may justify government intervention, but also in food processing activities, retail distribution, ready-made garments, etc. These activities require decentralized decision-making in response to changes in tastes and market conditions, which the private sector is more able to handle. Moreover, despite progress on improving the policy and

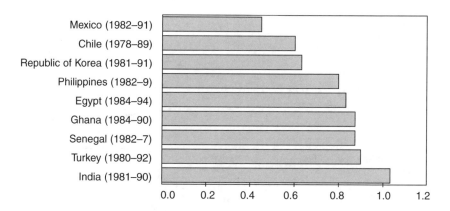

Figure 6.5a Real variable cost per unit (annual average), selected countries, 1978–94

Source: all countries except Egypt and India: World Bank 1995; Egypt, calculated from CAPMAS data; *Financial and Economic Statistics of Developing Countries*, various issues; India: Torres 1996.

institutional environment facing PE managers (elaborated later), some deficiencies remain.

To be sure, the government has attempted to address the two causes of the problem of PEs in Egypt. With respect to privatization, a process was initiated a few years ago, and picked up more steam in 1996. Not only have the proceeds from sales increased in the first nine months of 1996, but the nature of privatization has changed in favour of the sale of majority stake, in some cases to anchor investors. By mid-1997 the government had sold thirty-nine companies, of which the private sector acquired a majority of the shares in eighteen (forty-four acquired by anchor investors and the remaining fourteen sold on the stock market). In addition, the government has sold a majority of the shares in eleven companies to employees, along with the partial sale of twenty-one enterprises on the stock market. The total proceeds from sales to date are just below US$1 billion.[6]

As for commercialization, the government has also made substantial progress. It eliminated price controls on tradable goods, and revised the prices of non-tradeable goods to approximate market values. Budget transfers to PEs have been reduced, and the banking sector is being encouraged to lend to PEs on commercial grounds. Competition has been enhanced by opening up the economy and allowing the private sector to participate in many sectors previously reserved for PEs. Finally, seventeen holding companies were formed with a view to giving managers more autonomy in decision-making.

Notwithstanding the progress on privatization and commercialization, success in reducing the relative size of the sector to restore a healthy balance between the public and private sectors in the economy remains to be seen. On the commercialization front, some PEs still receive subsidies. The hard budget

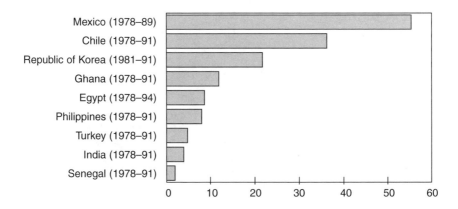

Figure 6.5b Net operating surplus as a percentage of sales revenues, selected countries, 1978–94

Source: all countries except Egypt and India: World Bank 1995; Egypt, calculated from CAPMAS data; *Financial and Economic Statistics of Developing Countries*, various issues; India: Torres 1996.

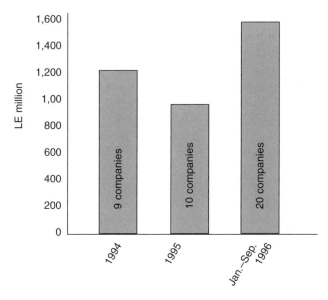

Figure 6.6 Proceeds from privatization of Law 203 companies in Egypt, 1994–September
1996
Source: Public Enterprise Office.

constraint was imposed by cutting investment, with limited progress on
measures to improve savings. Banks have not been prudent in lending to PEs.
The holding companies are proving to be less than keen on privatization, as it
diminishes their power. In short, despite the improvement in the PE S–I gap in
recent years, the sharp cut in investment and the relatively low rates of return on
capital suggest that there is some room for squeezing more savings from
reforming the PE sector.

Potential gains in savings from reforms: a simulation

The question addressed in this section is: assuming that the government
undertakes the necessary reforms to improve the performance of the PE
sector, how much additional savings will such reforms bring about?

In answering this question, the emphasis is centred on the addition to
savings as a result of privatization, rather than on the budgetary impact of
privatization. This means that what matters is whether or not privatization
and commercialization generate additional resources which could be
consumed or saved by the public or the private sector.[7] As argued at the
outset, these additional savings could come from behavioural changes at the
firm level, such as improved productivity and increased investment. The next
section elaborates the methodology followed to estimate the addition to
savings.

Methodology

The potential gains in savings from privatization and commercialization of the PE sector in Egypt are obtained by subtracting the net present value (NPV) of profits before taxes under continued public ownership (or the counterfactual scenario). Profits before taxes are net of depreciation and exclude other transfers to or from the government. To this end, three scenarios are first constructed:

- The No Reform Scenario, in which the current performance of the sector is projected into the future by extrapolating the sector's revenues, costs and investment according to their historical trends over the period 1986/7–1993/4. The projections are made for all items in the income statement and balance sheet. Profits before taxes are then discounted at 10 per cent to obtain the NPV under the No Reform Scenario.
- The Privatization Scenario, in which the performance of the sector is also projected into the future, but under the assumption that productivity of capital, labour and intermediate inputs will improve annually by 1.5 per cent, and net fixed assets will increase annually by 220 per cent rather than 14 per cent under the No Reform Scenario. (The rationale for these assumptions is discussed below.) The same procedure with respect to discounting is then applied as in the No Reform Scenario. The result is another NPV of the sector, representing one extreme counterfactual scenario (100 per cent privatization).
- The Commercialization Scenario, in which the performance of the sector is projected into the future assuming that commercialization will lead to an improvement in productivity of 1 per cent per annum, accompanied by no change in investment behaviour. (the rationale for these assumptions is also elaborated below.) The result is a third NPV of the sector, representing another extreme counterfactual scenario (100 per cent commercialization).

From these three NPVs, the addition to savings is estimated by making the realistic assumption that the government will sell only half the sector and commercialize the operation of the rest. In all instances, the NPVs are calculated by discounting the stream of benefits and costs over the firm's useful lifetime.[8] The benefits can be seen as the sum of the returns to the buyers and sellers. The costs are the resources used to generate the benefits, including the cost of labour, capital and intermediate inputs. Because the assumptions are key to the results, their rationale is elaborated next.[9]

Rationale of key assumptions

In view of available evidence on the impact of privatization and commercialization on performance, the productivity and investment differentials assumed under he counterfactual scenarios are on the conservative side. For example, the assumption that privatization will improve productivity by 1.5 per cent per annum is in fact relatively modest, compared with the experience in several cases. In Chile, the privatization of the electricity company CHILGENER and of the telephone company CTC led to an improvement in total factor productivity of 1.5 and 3.5 per cent per annum, respectively (Galal *et al.* 1994). In China, the growth of productivity in the non-state sector in the 1980s was 1.5 to 2.5 times the productivity of the state sector: the latter was 2–3 per cent per annum (Jefferson, Rawski and Zheng 1992). In Mexico, the privatization of AeroMexico led to a 92 per cent improvement in labour productivity between 1981 and 1991 (Galal *et al.* 1994). In most cases, the improvement in productivity came from better management of existing resources, higher capacity utilization, development of new products and penetration of new markets.

As for investment, the evidence also shows that privatized companies tended to relax the resource constraint faced by PEs, leading to a significant expansion in the post-divestiture period. The magnitude of the increase in investment varied from case to case, depending on the initial conditions of excess demand, the severity of the fiscal constraint impose on PEs prior to privatization, and the commitments governments demanded from privatized firms to expand. To cite only a few examples, the privatization of CTC in Chile led to a doubling of capacity in just five years, compared with an annual growth rate of 4 per cent per year in the pre-divestiture period. The same thing happened in Argentina, where the new owners of the divested telecommunications companies made a commitment to invest about US$7 billion. A similar observation was seen in Malaysia, where the Malaysian airline increased its real operating assets by four times the rate of increase in the period prior to divestiture.

What about commercialization? In particular, why is it assumed that commercialization will improve productivity by only 1 per cent (compared with 1.5 per cent for privatization), while leaving investment behaviour unchanged? That commercialization improves productivity to a lesser degree than privatization is evident from the observed improvement in productivity of the best commercialized PEs, most notably in Chile, the UK and South Korea (Galal 1994, World Bank 1995).[10] (See Box 6.1 for a detailed description of PE reforms results in Chile.) Commercialization is assumed to leave investment behaviour unchanged because PEs continue to face the same resource constraints they faced before reform. In

Table 6.1 Estimated increases in savings from reforming public enterprises: total

	NVP of profits before taxes LE million (1994/5)	Total increase in savings	Annual increase in savings (% of 1994/5 GDP)
Base case: no reform	89,879		
50% privatization	132,095	42,216	2.1
50% privatization and 50% commercialization	140,032	50,153	2.4

Source: calculated from CAPMAS data; *Financial and Economic Statistics of Developing Countries*, various issues.

Box 6.1 Chile's public enterprise reform

The commercialization process in Chile began when CORFO (the holding company) instructed its enterprises to pursue 'goals and procedures similar to those of a private company'. Managers were notified that their company would be expected to finance their operating costs and debt service. They were instructed to get rid of any unnecessary assets and stocks, improve their billing procedures, search for new sources of financing and reduce personnel. Public utilities were ordered to apply to public sector entities the same rules of service suspension for unpaid bills as were applied to the private sector. Transfers to PEs became the exception rather than the rule. Other favourable treatments of PEs, such as tax and import duty exceptions, were also eliminated. In addition, since CORFO enterprises had always been joint stock corporations, they were subject to the same regulations and information disclosure rules as applied to private corporations in the same category.

Self-financing would not have been possible, however, if pricing policies had not been changed. Thus, the government increased the prices of PEs, which had eroded in the period 1970–3. It then freed the prices of tradeables and established the basis for setting tariffs for non-tradeables (regulatory framework for electricity and telecommunications in 1982 and water and sewage in 1989).

In parallel, PEs increasingly faced intense competition. As quantitative restrictions on imports were eliminated and import tariffs reduced, firms producing tradeable goods had to compete internationally. In the monopoly sectors, the government eliminated entry barriers, and divided a number of large PEs into independent companies; for instance the electricity holding company CHILECTRA was divided into two electricity distribution companies and one generation company in 1981.

As a result of these reforms, the operating performance of most PEs improved. Revenues as well as taxes and transfers to the government increased substantially in relation to GDP after 1973, while expenditures fell. The PE savings-investment gap practically vanished.

Source: Galal *et al.* 1994.

particular, they remain subject to the fiscal constraint imposed by governments, as well as the credit ceiling imposed on the public sector in general. While commercialized PEs become relatively more profitable and efficient, governments are likely to demand more dividends from them, as seen in Chile and the UK. This will leave them with little retained earnings to expand beyond the historical trend.

Results

Based on the above assumptions, privatization and commercialization of the sample of PEs analysed are expected to bring about additional savings to Egypt with a magnitude of 2.4 per cent of 1994/5 GDP (Table 6.1).[11] For reasons explained above, the gains from privatization (2.1 per cent of GDP)

Table 6.2 Estimated increases in savings from reforming public enterprises: by government and private sector

	Total increase in savings LE millions (1994/5)			Annual increase in savings % of 1994/5 GDP		
	Govt	*Private*	*Total*	*Govt*	*Private*	*Total*
50% privatization	−17,751	59,967	42,216	−0.9	2.9	2.1
50% commercialization	7,937	0	7,937	0.4	0.0	0.4
50% privatization and 50% commercialization	−9,814	59,967	50,153	−0.5	2.9	2.4

Source: calculated from CAPMAS data; *Financial and Economic Statistics of Developing Countries,* various issues.

are much more substantial than from commercialization (0.4 per cent of GDP). More significantly perhaps, given that the PE sample analysed only represents about a third of the PE sector in Egypt, the addition to savings could be much more. Indeed, short of diminishing returns to the gains in savings, these gains could be as high as 7 per cent of GDP, which is close to what Egypt needs to increase its investment ratio to GDP to match the fast-growing economies.

The gains in savings from privatization and commercialization will be made both by the government and the private sector. Table 6.2 shows the distribution of these gains between the two of them, without taking into account the price to be paid by the private sector to the government for the

Table 6.3 Estimated increases in savings from reforming public enterprises: origin of the change

	Total increase in savings LE millions (1994/5)			
	Productivity improvement	*Additional investment*	*Synergies*	*Total*
50% privatization	11,966	23,300	6,950	42,216
50% commercialization	7,937	0	0	7,937
50% privatization and 50% commercialization	19,903	23,300	6,950	50,153
	Annual increase in savings % of 1994/5 GDP			
	Productivity improvement	*Additional investment*	*Synergies*	*Total*
50% privatization	0.6	1.1	0.3	2.1
50% commercialization	0.4	0.0	0.0	0.4
50% privatization and 50% commercialization	1.0	1.1	0.3	2.4

Source: calculated from CAPMAS data; *Financial and Economic Statistics of Developing Countries,* various issues.

purchase of 50 per cent of PEs in the sample. As long as this price is higher than LE17.75 billion, the budgetary impact will be positive.[12] Conversely, if the price to be paid by the private sector is less than LE17.75 billion, privatization will impact negatively on the treasury in the long run. Either way, the ultimate effect on savings is positive.

Finally, Table 6.3 shows the gains in savings from privatization and commercialization by origin. The gains are split almost evenly between investment and productivity. More interestingly, however, the gains to the country are greater when both behavioural differences are present because of synergies, or the interaction between productivity and investment. When both are present, a larger stock of resources is used more efficiently, and there is a compounded effect on performance and thus on savings.

Sensitivity analysis

Given that the results depend on the assumptions made, it is useful to separate the effect of each assumption from the effect of the other, and to explore the sensitivity of the results to these assumptions. The separation of the impact of each assumption has already been done, and can be used by the reader to accept or reject any of the assumptions and still obtain useful results. The remaining issue is to explore the sensitivity of the results to the key assumptions. This is done here, and presented in Table 6.4. The table shows the results under two extreme scenarios: full privatization of the sample of PEs analysed and full commercialization. For each of these scenarios, the results are shown for various discount rates (8, 10 and 12 per cent), various productivity differentials (1, 1.5 and 2 per cent for privatization, and 0.5, 1and 1.5 for commercialization), and various investment possibilities (15, 20 and 25 per cent of net fixed assets).

Two broad conclusions can be drawn from Table 6.4. First, reforms of the sample of PEs investigated here can produce gains in savings of 1.2 per cent of

Table 6.4 Sensitivity analysis (annual increase in savings as percentage of GDP)[a]

	Discount rate			Productivity[b]			Investment[c]		
	8	10	12	1	1.5	2	15	20	25
100% privatization	4.40	4.10	3.90	3.5	4.1	4.7	1.7	4.1	7.7
100% commercialization	0.80	0.77	0.75	0.4	0.8	1.2	0.8	0.8	0.8
50% privatization and 50% commercialization	2.60	2.40	2.30	1.9	2.4	3.0	1.2	2.4	4.3

Notes:
a Increases in savings include the interaction of changes in productivity and changes in investment.
b Annual growth rates of productivity under privatization. (The corresponding rates under commercialization are 0.5% 1% and 1.5% respectively.)
c Per cent of net fixed assets.
Source: calculated from CAPMAS data; *Financial and Economic Statistics of Developing Countries*, various issues.

GDP at a minimum, but the gains can be as high as 4.3 per cent of GDP. Second, the results are least sensitive to variations in the discount rate. They are moderately sensitive to variations in productivity and most sensitive to variations in investment. This not only suggests that the gains from investment in the course of privatization are significant, but also that care must be taken to ensure that investment will be forthcoming. Care must be given to ensure that the design of privatization transactions commits the new owners to an investment programme, where appropriate, to maximize the gains to society.

Conclusion

Although the assumptions adopted in the chapter are conservative, the results are impressive. Egypt could generate 2.4 per cent of GDP in additional savings from reforming one-third of its PE sector, by selling 50 per cent of this sample and commercializing the operation of the other 50 per cent. If the reforms are extended to the rest of the PE sector, the gains in savings could be much greater. Accordingly, PE reform is critical for future economic growth in Egypt: especially since national saving is only 18 per cent of GDP, compared with a minimum of 25 per cent in the fast-growing economies.

How may these gains be attained? The government has already begun a process of privatizing and commercializing the operation of PEs. Both types of reform should be speeded up and deepened. On the privatization front, the process is gaining momentum, and is being conducted in a relatively transparent fashion. Further, the sale of shares on the stock market is now being supported by direct sale of the majority of shares to anchor investors, to ensure a change of behaviour within the enterprises once sold. However, for privatization to contribute to savings in a significant way, the pace of transferring ownership to the private sector has to be much faster. Only when a large fraction of the enterprises are sold will the effect of privatization on savings be felt. To speed up the process, it may be necessary to find institutional mechanisms – other than relying primarily on the holding companies – to carry out the sale of enterprises, especially as the holding companies have a stake in slowing down the process. Second, it should be recognized that the simple act of selling firms to the private sector is no guarantee that privatization will produce the gains expected from it. More attention should be given to the environment into which the firms are being privatized. This issue will become more important as larger and monopolistic PEs are put up for sale. With large enterprises, it will be necessary to split them into smaller units, in part to increase competition, and in part to make their sale more feasible. In the case of firms operating as natural monopolies, it would be necessary to set up an appropriate regulatory framework, not only to protect the consumers, but also to assure the private sector a fair rate of return on investment. In all cases, the gains from privatization will be maximized where the new owners are committed to invest to meet excess demand, where it exists.

As for commercialization, it is clear that past reform attempts in Egypt have not been as successful as those in countries such as Chile and South Korea.

Perhaps the reason for the limited success in Egypt is that reforms have been piecemeal. At one point, it was thought that the reorganization of the sector under holding companies would do the trick. At another, the emphasis shifted to reducing distortions and increasing competition. Recently, the focus has been on privatization. To ensure success, it is essential that Egypt make the most of all reform components simultaneously, privatization, competition, hard budget constraints, financial sector reforms, and manager incentives. Like a chain with several links, reforms only work when all the pieces are connected.

To conclude, it is often thought that countries like Egypt are unable to compete in a more globalized world because they are saddled by large and inefficient PE sectors. The irony is that the same countries can be said to have an opportunity to turn their situation around by privatizing and commercializing the operation of their PEs. The fact that the gains from reforms, especially in terms of savings, can be substantial suggests that some countries have a real opportunity to break the vicious circle, and begin a process of catching up with the fast-growing economies. Egypt is one of those countries.

Notes

This chapter was prepared for the World Bank's Country Economic Memorandum for Egypt. Special thanks go to Merih Celasun and Arvind Subramanian for helpful comments, Amal Rifaat for excellent research assistance, Clemencia Torres for help with modelling and other computations and Hala El Khamissi for research support. Patti Lord provided copy editing, and Maha Philip provided valuable secretarial support. The views expressed in this chapter are those of the author, and should not be attributed to the Egyptian Center for Economic Studies or its board of directors.

1   From a welfare perspective, it has been argued that $1 in the hands of government is worth less than $1 in the hands of the private sector, because raising US $1 by government through taxation is distortionary. For further discussions of this point see Jones, Tandon and Vogelsang (1990).

2   Privatization refers to the transfer of ownership and/or control to the private sector. Commercialization refers to a package of reforms: increased competition, hard budget constraints, regulation of monopolies, financial market reforms and incentives to managers to perform efficiently.

3   The number of PEs in the sample declined from 364 in 1991/2 to 356 in 1992/3, which CAPMAS attributes to liquidation and privatization.

4   Gross S–I is provided in Table 6A.3 in the statistical appendix, and presented here in net terms to maintain comparability with the data for developing countries.

5   Returns to capital are measured using three indicators: first, the ratio of net operating surplus to capital employed, which measures the returns to all contributors (the government as equity holder, recipient of taxes, and creditors), second, the ratio of profit after taxes and before other transfers to or from government to net worth, which reflects the returns to the government, as if it were a private owner, and third, the ratio of net current surplus to revalued capital employed, which measures the returns to capital if it were purchased at market prices today. (See statistical appendix for more details).

6   Unutilized assets sold add another LE3 billion to the sales proceeds.

7   Where the budgetary impact of privatization is the main concern, it is important that all flows to and from and to the treasury are taken into account. In particular, two

flows of funds have to be compared: first, the flow of funds from the private sector to the government (in the form of sale price and taxes from privatized firms, minus the cost of privatizing), and second, the flow of funds the government gives up by privatizing (profits before taxes).

8 Firms are assumed to continue indefinitely into the future. However, flows are projected only for ten years, and assumed to remain constant thereafter.

9 No attempt is made to take into account any of the second-round effects of privatization and commercialization referred to in the introduction. However, these can only reinforce the positive results presented below.

10 To be sure, commercialization did not achieve these results in other cases, for example, in India and Turkey. Where it did succeed, governments followed a comprehensive reform strategy; making the most out of divestiture, competition, financial sector reform, and managerial incentives.

11 The magnitude of the gains relative to GDP will be lower over time given that these gains remain constant while GDP will grow. Moreover, the gains from reform will also be lower to the extent that higher investment in privatized firms is drawn from the rest of the economy and to the extent that a fraction of profits is consumed rather than saved and invested.

12 The reason why the budgetary impact will be positive if the sale price is higher than LE17.75 billion is that this value will allow the treasury to break-even compared with the no reform scenario. Under the no reform scenario, the government gets a discounted stream of profits before taxes equal to LE89.88 billion. Under the scenario of 50 per cent privatization, the government gets taxes from the privatized firms (50 per cent of PEs) and a discounted stream of profits before taxes from the firms remaining under its ownership (the other 50 per cent of PEs).

Appendix: statistics

Sample and sources of data

The data used cover the public enterprises operating under Law 203 (1991) and Law 97 (1983), for the period 1986/7–93/4. The sample analysed consists of 356 enterprises, but does not include financial institutions or economic authorities. It represents about one-third of the value added of the entire PE sector in Egypt. The sources of the PE data are: *Financial and Economic Statistics of Public Companies* (various issues), CAPMAS; and the national parameters (GDP, inflation, CPI, WPI) taken from *International Financial Statistics*, (IMF) (various issues).

Definitions

- Net operating surplus to capital employed. Net operating surplus is defined as operating revenues (excluding subsidies) minus operating expenses (wages, intermediate inputs, depreciation and other costs of operation). Capital employed is the sum of net fixed assets and inventories. This indicator measures the return to owners and creditors.
- Profits after taxes to net worth. Profits after taxes are defined as net operating surplus plus non-operating revenue minus non-operating expenses. Net worth is measured by the sum of equity, reserves and provisions other than for depreciation. This indicator measures government's returns on its investment as if it were a private owner.
- Current surplus (profits before taxes) to revalued capital employed. Revalued capital employed is calculated using the perpetual inventory technique. According to this technique:

Table 6A.1 Consolidated balance sheet of public enterprises, 1986/7–93/4 (LE million)

	1986/7	1987/8	1988/9	1989/90	1990/1	1991/2	1992/3	1993/4
Liabilities								
Net worth								
Equity	7,227	7,465	8,483	8,895	11,274	11,967	11,646*	13,060
Reserves	4,355	5,124	5,991	7,766	8,368	9,477	10,179	11,182
Deficit carried forward	−1,636	−1,791	−1,950	−2,148	−2,912	−4,259	−6,632	−8,781
Other provisions	2,923	3,481	4,118	4,751	5,479	6,142	6,670	7,587
Debt								
Long-term loans	8,472	10,944	12,077	14,302	18,059	18,43`	16,932	16,470
Overdraft	5,527	6,928	8,054	11,036	14,500	16,535	19,298	22,682
Creditors and credit accounts	14,454	17,955	20,671	23,300	27,224	31,118	34,129	38,248
Assets								
Fixed assets								
Net fixed assets	10,907	13,988	15,156	17,238	21,243	24,058	22,107*	22,392
Work in progress	5,314	5,403	6,676	7,934	8,820	7,660	7,516	8,597
Financial assets								
Financial investment	1,152	1,253	1,503	1,649	1,797	1,890	1,939	2,040
Long-term loans	308	505	465	523	570	584	563	659
Current assets								
Inventories	9,330	11,539	13,269	15,538	19,156	20,798	21,865	22,553
Accounts receivable	10,607	12,773	14,972	18,294	23,063	26,352	29,950	34,750
Cash	3,703	4,645	5,404	6,726	7,345	8,068	8,283	9,458
Total net assets = total liabilities	41,341	50,106	57,445	67,901	81,994	89,411	92,222	100,049

Note: * CAPMAS attributed the drop in equity and fixed assets between 1991/2 and 1992/3 to a decline in GFA and paid-up capital of a number of public companies, liquidation of some companies, and privatization.
Source: Calculated from CAPMAS data; *Financial and Economic Statistics of Developing Countries*, various issues.

Revalued capital in year (t) = net fixed assets (t − 1) * (1 + inflation rate (t) * (1 − depreciation rate) + investment (t)

The value of net fixed assets in 1979 was used as a starting point in the revaluation process.

- Real variable unit costs. Real variable costs are estimated as the ratio of total real variable costs (the cost of labour and intermediate inputs) to real output. Wages are deflated by the CPI and the remaining variables by the WPI.
- Savings–investment gap. Savings are defined as the difference between operating and non-operating revenues (excluding all transfers to and from the government, such as subsidies) and all operating and non-operating expenses (excluding depreciation and dividends). The savings–investment gap is the difference between savings and capital expenditures (the sum of fixed investment and change in inventories).

Table 6A.2 Consolidated income statement of public companies, 1986/7–93/4 (LE million)

	1986/7	1987/8	1988/9	1989/90	1990/1	1991/2	1992/3	1993/4
1 Operating revenues								
Operating revenues	25,341	31,589	37,210	43,921	55,099	62,188	62,656	65,174
Changes in inventories	116	34	113	314	55	104	430	–22
Subsidies	278	496	327	363	283	272	141	231
2 Operating expenditure								
Wages	3,268	3,838	4,406	4,969	5,614	5,979	6,275	6,694
Intermediaries	18,092	23,107	27,142	33,244	42,499	47,959	49,364	50,419
Depreciation	1,407	1,704	1,901	2,078	2,299	2,931	2,737	2,807
Rent	46	54	68	98	99	121	91	76
3 Operating surplus (1 – 2)	2,921	3,418	4,134	4,209	4,927	5,574	4,761	5,387
4 Non-operating revenues								
Return on financial securities	37	51	66	97	149	154	176	256
Net capital gains	23	28	19	7	65	139	257	240
Others (net of imputed interest)	1,033	1,309	1,457	1,874	2,650	2,672	3,232	3,947
5 Non-operating expenditure								
Interest payments	1,007	1,342	1,651	2,049	2,608	3,865	4,565	5,115
Income taxes	449	624	748	828	1,049	1,192	1,315	1,451
Others (net of imputed interest)	1,101	778	705	556	1,107	896	750	552
6 Net non-operating income (4 – 5)	–1,464	–1,356	–1,563	–1,455	–1,899	–2,978	–2,965	–2,676
7 Profit after taxes (3 + 6)	1,457	2,062	2,572	2,754	3,028	2,596	1,796	2,711
8 Total revenues = total expenditure	26,828	33,508	39,192	46,576	58,302	65,530	66,893	69,826

Source: calculated from CAPMAS data; *Financial and Economic Statistics of Developing Countries*, various issues.

Bibliography

Central Agency for Public Mobilization and Statistics (CAPMAPS) *Financial and Economic Statistics of Public Companies*, various issues.

Deaton, A. (1995) 'Growth and savings: what do we know, what do we need to know, and what might we learn?', manuscript, Princeton University.

Easterly, W. and Rebelo, S. (1993) 'Fiscal policy and economic growth: an empirical investigation', *Journal of Monetary Economics*, vol. 32, no. 3: 417–58.

Galal, A. Jones, L., Tandon, P. and Vogelsang, I. (1994) *Welfare Consequences of Selling*

Table 6A.3 Savings–investment gap and its sources of financing, 1978/9–93/4 (LE million)

	1987/8	1988/9	1989/90	1990/1	1991/2	1993/4[a]
Gross savings	3,893	4,894	5,297	6,092	6,448	6,739
Gross investment	6,698	5,698	7,255	10,456	5,543	3,987
Savings–investment gap	−2,804	−804	−1,958	−4,364	905	2,751
Financing of the gap:						
Government financing[b]	3,755	3,075	4,380	5,939	568	−497
Bank overdraft	1,401	1,127	2,982	3,464	2,034	3,384
Depreciation	1,319	1,526	1,647	1,947	2,245	1,933
Others[c]	−3,670	−4,924	−7,051	−6,986	−5,753	−7,571

Notes:
a Excluding 1992/3 because the reported drop in fixed assets in that year distorted the calculations of investment.
b Net financial flow from government.
c A residual item that includes changes in financial assets, cash and accounts receivable.
Sources: calculated from CAPMAS data; *Financial and Economic Statistics of Developing Countries*, various issues.

Public Enterprises: An Empirical Analysis, New York: Oxford University Press.

International Monetary Fund (IMF) *International Financial Statistics*, various issues.

Jefferson, G., Rawski, T. and Zheng, Y. (1992) 'Growth, efficiency, and convergence in China's state and collective industry', *Economic Development and Cultural Changes*, vol. 40, no. 2: 239–66.

Jones, L. P., Tandon, P. and Vogelsang, I. (1990) *Selling Public Enterprises: A Cost-Benefit Methodology*, Cambridge, Mass.: MIT Press.

Levine, R. and Renelt, D. (1992) 'A sensitivity analysis of cross country growth regressions', *American Economic Review*, September, vol. 82, no. 4: 942–63.

Sachs, J. (1996) 'Achieving rapid growth: the road ahead for Egypt', Distinguished Lecture Series, Egyptian Center for Economic Studies. Cairo, Egypt.

Torres, C. (1996) 'How and how much can public enterprises in India contribute to national savings?', mimeo, World Bank.

World Bank (1987) 'Egypt: review of the finances of the decentralized public sector', Report no. 6421.

—— (1995) *Bureaucrats in Business: The Economics and Politics of Government Ownership*. New York: Oxford University Press.

Part II
Country studies

7   An analysis of compensation programmes for redundant workers in Egyptian public enterprises

Ragui Assaad

Introduction

The purpose of this chapter is to analyse alternative designs of severance programmes to reduce labour redundancy in Egyptian public enterprise slated for privatization, restructuring or liquidation. Given Egypt's existing labour code, which makes involuntary layoffs impossible, compensation programmes must be able to exit the desired number of workers while remaining voluntary in nature. An efficient voluntary severance programme must be targeted in such a way so as to compensate workers for the individual-specific losses. Like other public policies that require targeting under conditions of incomplete information about workers, labour compensation schemes face agency costs. An efficient design would attempt to minimize these costs.

A voluntary severance scheme acknowledges that workers have some kind of property rights to their public sector jobs and aims to compensate them for the loss of these rights. It must therefore compensate workers for the rent they received by being in the public sector. Since different workers will, in general, have different rents, a uniform severance offer that is acceptable to high-rent workers will result in overpayments to low-rent workers. These overpayments can be reduced somewhat by indexing severance payment to observable worker characteristics, but they cannot be entirely eliminated when worker attributes are not fully observable. Further reductions in agency costs can be achieved through a judicious design of the severance programme that takes advantage of self-selection to reveal unobservable differences in rent.[1]

This chapter will focus on reducing agency costs through indexation on observable characteristics. Conventional indexation formulas, which index compensation on the worker's wage, match the severance payment to the individual-specific losses of displaced workers. Since there is no previous experience with large-scale layoffs or voluntary exits from the public enterprise sector in Egypt, there are no follow-up surveys of displaced public sector workers that could be used to directly estimate displacement losses and relate them to observable worker characteristics. I must instead pursue an indirect approach that relies on selectivity-corrected sectoral earnings equation estimates to determine potential earnings in the private sector and, from those, the rents that public sector workers stand to lose if they leave the sector. The advantage of such an indirect method of estimating worker losses is that it only makes use of standard labour force survey data, which are much more readily available than the expensive, customized, follow-up surveys used in other studies of worker retrenchment.[2]

Assuming that transitional unemployment can be minimized because of the voluntary nature of the severance programmes under consideration, worker losses would be approximately equal to the rent they would have received if they stayed in the public sector. This rent is equal to the discounted difference in the expected stream of total compensation in the public and private sectors up to the age of mandatory retirement.

The main challenge in estimating worker rents in this way is to come up with a reasonable estimate for the non-monetary component of compensation in each sector. Much of the attraction of public sector jobs lies in the value workers place on the non-wage aspects of the job, such as job security, retirement and health benefits and low expectations of effort, among others. Since it is virtually impossible to directly evaluate what these job characteristics are worth to workers, I pursue an indirect estimation strategy here as well. By assuming that at least some workers dissipate their lifetime rent by queuing for public sector jobs, I am able to estimate the magnitude of non-wage benefits for a marginal group of workers. This is then generalized to all workers under plausible assumptions of how non-wage benefits relate to wages.

Once worker-specific rent estimates are available, it is possible to simulate the fiscal cost and compositional implications of compensation programmes using different indexation formulas. In each case, I fix the desired exit rate and vary the parameters of the indexation formula to obtain the desired number of exits at the lowest cost. Two extreme cases serve as useful benchmarks:

1   a flat payment scheme, where no indexation is used, and
2   a scheme where workers are paid exactly their estimated rent, which I refer to as the full indexation scheme.

While the latter is not a practical alternative because of the complexity of the formula it is based on, it serves as a useful benchmark of the lowest cost programme achievable by indexation alone. To allow for comparison, each indexation scheme is calibrated in such a way as to achieve the desired number of exits at the minimum fiscal cost.

Although the analysis assumes that a balance is desired in the distribution of the remaining workers among three broad educational categories, it does not attempt to set any other *ex ante* controls on the composition of exiting workers in terms of age, sex, occupation or worker quality. However, the proportion of exiters in each age, sex and occupational categories are compared across the various severance programmes *ex post*.

The determination of the rate of redundancy or the identification of specific types of redundant workers is beyond the scope of this study. This generally requires detailed firm by firm information, which is not available to us. Instead, the purpose is to develop a method that takes that kind of information as given and to simulate the operation of a severance programme that attempts to exit the redundant workers voluntarily. For the purpose of this exercise, I assume a 30 per cent redundancy rate that applies equally to workers in three broad educational categories. Thus, the objective will be to exit 30 per cent of each educational group. Within each category workers who opt to accept each package will self-select based on their rents. The methodology developed in the chapter can be applied equally well, however, if there are multiple redundancy rates across various identifiable groups of workers.[3]

The first section of the chapter describes the general features of Egypt's public enterprise reform programme and provides a brief assessment of the labour redundancy problem. The chapter then develops and implements a methodology for estimating worker-specific rents and continues with a simulation of the alternative indexation schemes and an analysis of the simulation results.

The setting

The public enterprise reform program

The public sector retrenchment and compensation scheme is intended to support the public enterprise reform component of Egypt's Economic Reform and Structural Adjustment Programme (ERSAP), which began in 1991. As part of this programme, the government is committed to carrying out the privatization, restructuring and liquidation of a number of public enterprises in several stages. With the passage of the Public Investment Law (Law 203 of 1991), all Egyptian public enterprises were reorganized into seventeen diversified companies, which were granted considerable managerial and financial autonomy. These holding companies were cut off from the fiscal budget and no longer receive public investment allocations or public credit guarantees.

ERSAP includes a timetable for privatizing, restructuring, or liquidating a significant proportion of public enterprise. According to the plan, a first batch of seven companies with a total work force of 25,000 were to be fully or wholly privatized in 1991/2. A second batch of thirteen companies with a total labour force of 33,000 were to be privatized in 1992/3. A third batch of forty companies with a labour force of 133,000 were to be privatized in 1993/4.[4] In addition, thirty companies with a labour force of 166,000 workers were candidates for restructuring in 1992/3 and seven companies with a labour force of 8,000 were to be liquidated. The sixty companies identified in all three categories make up about a fifth of the total number of public enterprises in Egypt and employ a total of 366,000 workers, about 30 per cent of the total public enterprise labour force.[5]

The implementation of the public enterprise reform programme described above faced significant obstacles and delays. Some of these delays were due to problems with the heavy indebtedness and cross arrears of some enterprises, legal and assets title problems and procedural obstacles, but the main hindrance has clearly been concern and uncertainty about what to do with the labour redundancy problem (Integrated Development Consultants 1993). While the privatization programme guidelines issued by the Public Enterprise Office in 1993 recognize the right of the new owners to 'set the optimal size and composition of their labour force', it does not spell out how this could be done (ibid.: 3).

The legal context

The existing labour law in Egypt (Law 137 of 1981) makes it very difficult, if not virtually impossible, for either public or private firms to adjust the size and composition of their work force to adjust to changes in technology or demand conditions. Employers wishing to stop operations completely or partially, or to change the size of their enterprise or its activity, can only do so with an authorization from a 'stoppage committee' appointed by the prime minister. This usually involves a lengthy appeals process that involves a high-level inter-ministerial committee at the deputy-minister level, and a review of the decision by the minister of manpower and training. A recent report states: 'there is no memory among labour experts and lawyers of any such approvals being granted on grounds of efficiency, financial difficulty, or even bankruptcy' (ibid.: 3).

A draft labour law, currently being discussed in parliament contains significant changes to labour regulations that provide employers with greater flexibility in adjusting the size and composition of their work force. However, as currently worded, the provisions of the existing law would continue to apply to contracts enacted prior to the passage of the new law (Article 7).[6] The draft labour law makes several significant changes in the job security regulations. First, it allows for fixed duration contracts to be extended an indefinite number of times in contrast to the existing law which stipulates that such contracts turn into indefinite duration contracts once renewed (Article 106). Second, it allows for either party to end an indefinite duration contract, for cause, after a notification period of two months for workers with ten years or less in tenure and three months for workers with more than ten years of tenure (Article 111). Unlike the current law, which specifies an exhaustive list of the grave errors that can lead to a worker's dismissal, the draft law simply states that there should be a 'valid and sufficient justification related to a worker's failure to perform one of his essential obligations' for an employer to terminate an indefinite period contract (Article 110).[7] In contrast to the existing law, which simply forces the reinstatement of the worker, with full back pay, in case of termination without cause, the draft law specifies a compensation amount at no less than one month of pay per year of service, if the worker is entitled to a pension, and one-and-a-half months per year of service otherwise (Article 122).

Like the current law, the draft law stipulates that firms wishing to stop or curtail their activities must obtain authorization from a stoppage committee appointed by the prime minister (Article 199). However, in contrast to the current law, the draft law explicitly states the rights of firms to undertake full or partial closure for economic reasons (Article 198) and allows for the termination of indefinite duration contracts in such circumstances. It also allows employers who receive such authorization to temporarily alter the conditions of employment, including the reassignment of a worker's responsibilities and a reduction of the wage down to the legally stipulated minimum wage (Article 203). While the ease with which such authorizations can be obtained will not be known until the executive decisions accompanying the new law are published, the draft law appears to be considerably more permissive with regard to economically motivated layoffs and alterations in employment conditions.

Since rights obtained under existing labour contracts would continue to be protected under the draft law (Article 7), only new contracts would be covered by the new rules. As a result, the changes regarding job security and layoffs have limited direct relevance to the privatization and restructuring of existing public enterprise. The new law, if confirmed by parliament, would, however, open up some design options for compensation programmes that would not be available otherwise. Public enterprise workers can be compensated for voluntarily terminating their existing contracts and can then be re-hired under the new rules. In that way, the adjustment to more flexible arrangements can be undertaken prior to privatization while leaving the final say as to which workers stay and which workers leave to the new buyers, who would have better information about the labour needs of the privatized firms.

Determining the extent of redundancy

One of the issues that comes up in the literature on public sector retrenchment is the difficulty in determining the extent of redundancy (Svejnar and Terrell 1991, Fiszbein 1992). Svejnar and Terrell (1991) define redundant labour as labour whose marginal product falls short of the shadow wage rate. Operationally, this means that redundant workers in each skill group are those whose marginal productivity in the firm is lower than elsewhere in the economy (ibid.: 7). Because data are often lacking to make such a determination, it is common practice to use what is referred to as the technical or engineering approach. This approach compares average measures such as output-labour, capital-labour or labour cost-total cost ratios to experts' assessments of optimal targets (ibid.: 31, Fiszbein 1992: 5).

While figuring the extent of labour redundancy in this way is essential when examining a particular firm or group of firms, for our purposes its suffices to have a rough estimate of the rate of redundancy in the public enterprise sector as a whole. There are no precise estimates of labour redundancy in public enterprise in Egypt, but, based on pilot studies and expert opinion, a figure of 30 per cent seems to come up on a regular basis (Integrated Development Consultants 1993: 10, 1994). El-Khawaga (1993) used an analysis of detailed occupational categories as reported by the 1986 census to identify redundant workers. She estimates the rate of redundancy to be 46 per cent in government administration, 16 per cent in the service authorities, 15 per cent in the economic authorities and 21 per cent in public enterprise (ibid.: 210–11). Given the uncertainty involved in inferring redundancy from occupational labels, these figures should be taken as merely indicative.

Since determining a precise rate of redundancy is beyond the scope of this study, I use the 30 per cent rate and assume that it applies equally across three categories of workers grouped according to three broad educational levels: below secondary (Level 1), secondary and technical institute (Level 2), and university and above (Level 3).

Estimating the cost of job loss for public enterprise workers

An opportunity cost approach to compensation

In designing voluntary redundancy compensation programmes, an opportunity cost approach can be used to determine the minimum compensation a worker must receive to voluntarily leave the enterprise (Fiszbein 1992). Workers will voluntarily accept a severance package only if its value is at least equal to losses they incur by leaving their public enterprise jobs and accepting the next best alternative in the private sector. These losses are equal to the discounted value of the rents they would lose by leaving the public sector as well as any transitional costs of job dislocation.

The most important of these transitional costs is likely to be income loss associated with the job search unemployment that follows exit from the public sector. The design of the compensation programme can minimize these costs, however, by allowing workers to select the time of their departure within a fairly wide window, so that most of the job search will occur while still on the job. Moreover, workers who experience transitional unemployment would be eligible to receive unemployment insurance under current law.[8] These payments would, in theory, compensate them for the short-term losses associated with job loss. The compensation package would therefore need to compensate them only for long-term losses.

The separate issue of higher expected unemployment and greater job instability in the private sector, once a job has been found, is accounted for in two ways in this analysis. First, it is taken care of by excluding compensating differentials attributable to intermittent employment and work outside fixed establishment from the earnings displaced workers can expect to achieve in the private sector wage equation.[9] Thus, I would be comparing public sector wage schedules with those of relatively stable jobs in the private sector. Second, any hardship resulting from the increased risk of unemployment and job instability in the private sector is implicitly taken into account in the adjustment of the public sector wage schedule for differences in the non-wage job attributes.

Thus, the main loss that a severance programme would have to compensate workers for is the loss of rents that are associated with public sector jobs. To estimate the value of these rents, it is necessary to determine the expected total remuneration in public enterprise and in alternative employment in the private sector.[10] In theory, there could be downward shifts in the private sector wage schedule resulting from the increased labour supply generated by large-scale exits from public enterprise. I neglect such supply effects in this analysis for several reasons. First, exits are likely to take place over a fairly long period of time so that the impact on the private sector will be limited. Second, given the rapid rate of labour force growth in Egypt, the total number of public enterprise workers to be retrenched under the 30 per cent redundancy assumption (about 400,000) is roughly equal to a single year's increment to the labour force. It is therefore unlikely to be a major additional disturbance to the labour market. Finally, any wage impact on the private sector is likely to be short-lived.

Since I only have individual-level earnings data from a single round of the Egyptian Labor Force Survey (the October 1988 round), I rely on cross-sectional estimates of earnings functions to derive public and private sector earnings profiles. I partially correct for unobservables by taking into account revealed preferences as manifested in self-selection into the government, public enterprise, and private sectors.

A worker's public sector rent is assumed to equal the difference between the present value of future earnings in the public sector and the present value of earnings in alternative employment in the private sector.[11] The estimation of these rents is complicated by the presence of more desirable non-wage job attributes in the public sector and the absence of reliable measures for the value of these attributes. These attributes include lower effort expectations, retirement and other social insurance benefits, paid leaves, and medical benefits, among others. Much of the subsequent analysis hinges on the estimation of the compensating differentials required to equalize for these differences in job attributes, which I refer to as non-wage benefits.[12]

Model description and assumptions

Upon entry into the labour market, a worker faces a choice between queuing for a lifetime employment contract in the public sector or searching for private sector employment.[13] If both wage and non-wage aspects of employment in the public and private sectors are taken into account, public sector workers undoubtedly receive some rent over the duration of the contract, but these rents are likely to be dissipated by the queuing process at the margin.[14] For the marginal worker, whose lifetime rent is fully dissipated, the present value of total lifetime compensation across the two career paths are equalized. This equality can be used to indirectly estimate the present value of the marginal worker's non-wage benefits in the public sector over his or her entire career.[15] With some assumptions about how non-wage benefits vary across workers, these estimates can be extended to all public sector workers.

The most important non-wage aspects of public sector jobs are the higher probability of receiving a retirement pension and paid vacations, and the lower effort required relative to private sector jobs. The benefits derived from these non-wage job attributes are either directly related to monetary remuneration, or depend on the value of a worker's time, which relates them indirectly to wages. It is therefore, reasonable to assume that non-wage benefits in the public sector are proportional to monetary earnings. Some non-wage benefits, such as health insurance, are admittedly independent of wages. Others, such as the opportunity to engage in moonlighting, are related to wages, but may vary systematically across workers who reside in different locations or who have different levels of educational attainment.

The maintained assumption in this analysis is that non-wage benefits in the public sector are proportional to monetary earnings and the constant of proportionality is invariant across workers. The latter assumption is necessary because I make use of worker heterogeneity along observable characteristics to identify the 'marginal worker' and then apply the constant of proportionality determined for that worker to all others.[16] I must further assume that the constant of proportionality between non-wage benefits and earnings is the same for civil service and public enterprise workers. Since state-owned enterprises were removed from the Ministry of Manpower's centralized allocation scheme in 1978, the queuing process for public enterprise jobs is not well defined. It is therefore not clear whether lifetime rents are in fact dissipated for any public enterprise workers. Thus I use a 'marginal worker' for the public sector broadly defined to estimate the ratio of non-wage benefits of both public enterprise and civil service workers. Finally, I assume that the discount rate is constant across workers.

To identify the 'marginal worker', I sort public sector workers into a twelve-cell classification by sex (male and female), educational level (Levels 1, 2 and 3), and subsector (government and public enterprise).[17] The cell with the largest difference in monetary earnings in favour of the private sector is assumed to contain the workers that are most likely to have dissipated their lifetime rents in the public sector and thus to be the cell that describes the 'marginal worker'. Because there were multiple shocks to wage schedules and many changes in the operation of the queue over time, I restrict the estimation to recent entrants to the public sector by limiting it to workers under 35 years of age.

In calculating the earnings stream in each career path, I take into account the time spent in the public sector job queue. Under the employment guarantee, vocational secondary, technical institute (equivalent to two-year colleges) and university graduates are entitled to a government job after a certain waiting period. As of 1988, the date of the survey, the last cohort of graduates to be offered government appointments under the employment guarantee was the 1982 cohort for university graduates and the 1981 cohort for secondary and technical institute graduates, implying waiting periods of six and seven years, respectively. An assumption that queuing is costly does not mean that applicants have to remain unemployed while queuing, but that they simply earn less than workers who are not queuing. Since workers with less than secondary education are not guaranteed public sector jobs, I assume that they do not engage in costly queuing for such jobs.[18]

Armed with the estimate of the value of non-wage benefits, I am now in a position to estimate the rents of civil service and public enterprise workers at different points in their career. Following the opportunity cost approach, the rent is equal to the difference in the discounted stream of total compensation in the public and private sectors from their current age to the age of retirement. Differences in retirement benefits after that point need not be taken into account explicitly since they are already included in the estimated non-wage benefits. Figure 7.1 shows the estimated earnings profile of a male secondary school graduate in a white collar occupation in a civil service, public enterprise or private sector career path. The figure is based on actual parameter estimates from earnings equations but assumes that the worker spends seven years in a queue for a public sector job, where he is able to earn 50 per cent of his potential private sector wage. The figure also shows total compensation in the civil service and public enterprise sector under the assumption that non-wage benefits are proportional to wages. The losses for which a public sector worker should be compensated in a voluntary severance scheme are equal to his remaining public sector rents. The latter are equal to the area between the adjusted public sector curve and the private sector curve from his current level of experience to his retirement, taking discounting into account.

In estimating sector-specific wage equations, I assume that wages are determined by marketable and non-marketable individual attributes. Marketable attributes include sex, occupation, education and, to a lesser extent, experience. Non-marketable attributes include tenure with a particular employer. Tenure is particularly important in the public sector where seniority is an important factor in wage determination. Tenure can be transferred from one job to another within the public sector, but cannot be carried across to the private sector. Thus

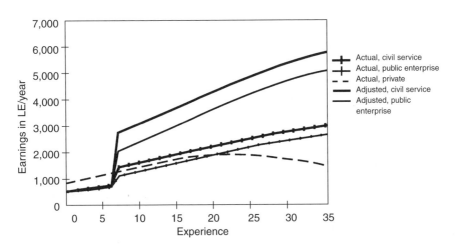

Figure 7.1 Civil service, public enterprise and private sector earnings profiles for male white collar workers with secondary education

Note: the adjusted earnings profiles include an estimate of non-wage benefits obtained by assuming that non-wage benefits are proportional to wages.

the private sector wage schedule shown in Figure 7.1 excludes any returns to public sector tenure, but assumes that other worker attributes are fully transferable to the private sector.[19]

Finally, it should be kept in mind that all the estimates in this chapter are based on 1988 data and are therefore expressed in 1988 prices. I also assume that the wage structure in the economy has not changed significantly since then.

The model

For any experience level T and tenure N, the predicted log earnings of a government (or public enterprise) worker is given by:[20]

$$\ln \hat{E}_{iG}(T) = \hat{\beta}_G X_i + \hat{\alpha}_{1G} T - \hat{\alpha}_{2G} T^2 + \hat{\alpha}_{3G} N + \hat{\theta}_G \hat{\lambda}_{iG} \tag{1}$$

where X_i is a vector of observed characteristics, $\hat{\lambda}_{iG}$ is the inverse Mill's ratio from the multinational logit selection model into the government, public enterprise and private sectors, and $\hat{\beta}_G$, $\hat{\alpha}_G = [\hat{\alpha}_{1G}, \hat{\alpha}_{2G}, \hat{\alpha}_{3G}]$ and $\hat{\theta}_G$ are the parameter estimates of the selectivity-corrected earnings equation in the government or public enterprise sectors.[20] Accounting for the fact that the premium for tenure is not transferable to the private sector, the same workers predicted log earnings in the private sector are given by:

$$\ln \hat{E}_{iR}(T) = \hat{\beta}_R X_i + \hat{\alpha}_{1R} T - \hat{\alpha}_{2R} T^2 + \hat{\alpha}_{3R} N + \hat{\theta}_R \hat{\lambda}_{iG} \tag{2}$$

where $\hat{\beta}_R$, $\hat{\alpha}_R = [\hat{\alpha}_{1R}, \hat{\alpha}_{2R}, \hat{\alpha}_{3R}]$ and $\hat{\theta}_R$ are the equivalent parameter estimates from the private sector earnings equation.[21]

To estimate the value of non-wage benefits, we need an expression for lifetime rents, which are given by the difference in discounted earnings streams in the two career paths at entry. The net present value of the discounted estimated earnings over the life of the contract in the public and private sector paths are given by:

$$L_{iG} = \int_0^{\tau_r} E_{iu} \exp(-\rho T) dT + \int_{\tau_u}^{\tau_r} \tilde{E}_{iG} \exp(-\rho T) dT \tag{3}$$

$$L_{iR} = \int_0^{\tau_r} \hat{E}_{iR} \exp(-\rho T) dT \tag{4}$$

where Δ is the discount rate and τ_u, τ_r are the time in the queue and the time of retirement, both measured from the date of entry into the labour market. E_{iu} represents the worker's earnings while waiting in the public sector queue and is given by $E_{iu}(T) = \rho \hat{E}_{iR}(T)$, where $0 \geq \rho < 1$. $\tilde{E}_{iG}$ is the total annual compensation in the public sector, which is assumed to be some multiple η of public sector earnings as follows: $\tilde{E}_{iG}(T) = \eta \hat{E}_{iG}(T)$ where $\eta > 1$. The marginal group of workers, indexed by m, has zero lifetime rents, implying that the present values of total lifetime compensation in the two career paths are equal: $L_{mG} = L_{mR}$. All other workers are assumed to have positive rents.

Let 0_j be the ratio of total compensation to monetary compensation that will equalize lifetime compensations in the two career paths for workers in group j.

$$\eta_j = \frac{L_{jR} - \int_0^{\tau_{uj}} \hat{E}_{ju}\exp(-\rho T)dT}{\int_{\tau_{vj}}^{\tau_r} \hat{E}_{jG}\exp(-\rho T)dT} \tag{5}$$

Thus, η_m the ratio that equalizes the compensation streams for the marginal group of workers is given by:

$$\eta_m = \max(\eta_j) \tag{6}$$

assuming that the ratio of total compensation to monetary compensation is independent of worker characteristics $\eta = \eta_m$ for all public sector workers. The rent of a public sector worker with experience ϑ, is therefore given by:

$$R_{iG} = \eta \int_\tau^{tr} \hat{E}_{iG}\exp(-\rho T)dT - \int_\tau^{tr} \hat{E}_{iR}\exp(-\rho T)dT \tag{7}$$

The closed form expression for the integrals as a function of the earnings equation parameters is shown in equation (8) on page 160.

Earnings equation estimates

The earnings equation estimates are reduced-form equations based on a standard Mincerian model with limited modifications to account for non-random sectoral selection, institutional wage setting practices and compensating differentials for employment instability and working conditions. I correct for selectivity using a standard Heckman-type two-stage model with a multinomial logit selection rule that predicts the probability of selection into the government, public enterprise and private sectors.[22] The selection equation estimates are shown in Appendix Table A7.1.

In the earnings equations, a tenure variable is included to account for seniority-based pay. Tenure is calculated as the time since joining the public sector for public sector workers, and the time since the last job change for private sector workers.[23] Experience is calculated as the time since entry into the labour market and may therefore include a period of unemployment at entry. Two dummy variables indicating intermittent employment and work outside fixed establishments are included in the private sector wage equation to account for compensating differentials. These variables are set to zero when predicting the opportunity wage of public sector employees to allow for comparison between fairly similar employment conditions in the two sectors. Because of the way in

Equation 8 closed form expression for the integrals as a function of the earnings equation parameters

$$\int_{\tau}^{\tau_r} \hat{E}_{iG}\exp(-\rho T)dT = \hat{E}_{iG}^0 \sqrt{\frac{B}{\hat{\alpha}_{2G}}}\, \exp\left[\frac{(\rho - \hat{\alpha}_{1G} - \hat{\alpha}_{3G})^2}{4\hat{\alpha}_{2G}}\right]\left[\Phi\left(\frac{[\rho - \hat{\alpha}_{1G} - \hat{\alpha}_{3G}] + 2\hat{\alpha}_{2G}\tau_r}{\sqrt{2\hat{\alpha}_{2G}}}\right) - \Phi\left(\frac{[\rho - \hat{\alpha}_{1G} - \hat{\alpha}_{3G}] + 2\hat{\alpha}_{2G}\tau}{\sqrt{2\hat{\nabla}_{2G}}}\right)\right]$$

$$\int_{\tau}^{\tau_r} \hat{E}_{iR}\exp(-\rho T)dT = \hat{E}_{iR}^0 \sqrt{\frac{\pi}{\hat{\alpha}_{2R}}}\, \exp[-\hat{\alpha}_{2R}\tau]\exp\left[\frac{(\rho - \hat{\alpha}_{1R} - \hat{\alpha}_{3R})^2}{4\hat{\alpha}_{2R}}\right]\left[\Phi\left(\frac{[\rho - \hat{\alpha}_{1R} - \hat{\alpha}_{3R}\vartheta_r] + 2\hat{\alpha}_{2R}\tau_r}{\sqrt{2\hat{\alpha}_{2R}}}\right) - \Phi\left(\frac{[\rho - \hat{\alpha}_{1R} - \hat{\alpha}_{3R}] + 2\hat{\alpha}_{2P}\tau}{\sqrt{2\hat{\alpha}_{2R}}}\right)\right]$$

where $\hat{E}_{iG}^0 \equiv \hat{\beta}_G X_i + \theta_G\hat{\lambda}_{iG}$, $\hat{E}_{iR}^0 \equiv \hat{\beta}_R' X_i + \hat{\theta}_R\hat{\lambda}_G$, and Φ is the cumulative normal distribution function.

which data are collected, education is specified as the attainment of specific educational credentials rather than years of schooling. Occupation is not taken into account explicitly, but a rough division between blue collar and white collar employment is implied by the education variables. In Egypt, individuals educated up to and including the preparatory level can be assumed to be engaged in blue collar occupations. Those educated at the technical institute and university levels can be assumed to be white collar workers. The same is true for those with general secondary education. Since vocational secondary education can lead to either blue or white collar occupations, I use information on occupation to classify vocational school graduates into blue and white collar workers. Finally, regional dummy variables take into account regional differences in cost of living and institutional wage setting rules.

The data are obtained from the October 1988 round of the Egyptian Labor Force Sample Survey, which was a special round designed to collect much more detailed information than the standard survey. In particular, it includes special modules on earnings and labour mobility, which are being relied on extensively here.[24] While the overall survey was administered to a stratified random sample of 10,000 households, the mobility module was only administered to a randomly selected subsample of 5,000 households. The data used here is limited to that subsample. The wage equation estimates are also limited to non-agricultural wage workers between the ages of 18 and 59, the age groups that are likely to have regular employment in the government and public enterprise sectors.

The earnings module was used to collect data on earnings net of payroll taxes and deductions. An attempt was made to get data on earnings in kind, but the quality of that data is poor. I therefore use net monetary earnings per year as the dependent variable. Descriptive statistics on the variables used in the earnings equations are provided in Table 7.1.

The earnings equation estimates for males and females in each sector are shown in Table 7.2. While the earnings-experience profile has the usual concave shape in all three sectors, the profile has significantly more curvature in the private sector. As expected, tenure is a significant determinant of earnings in the government and public enterprise sectors, but not in the private sector. The returns to education are similar in the government and public enterprise sectors but significantly higher than they are in the private sector.[25] The compensating differential term on work outside fixed establishments has the expected sign, showing that such workers earn a substantial wage premium to compensate them for these undesirable working conditions. The negative coefficient on the irregular employment dummy is due to the fact that irregular workers works fewer hours per year even though they have higher wages per hour. It should also be noted that while wages in the public sector are roughly equal for males and females, there is a large gender wage gap in the private sector. Female public sector workers are therefore likely to have significantly higher rents than their male counterparts.

An examination of the selection terms reveals that there is negative selection into the government sector for both males and females. This is consistent with

Table 7.1 Descriptive statistics for variables in earnings equations, non-agricultural wage workers (standard deviations are in parentheses)

Variables	Males				Females			
	Govern ment	Public ent'prise	Private	All	Govern- ment	Public ent'prise	Private	All
Log annual	7.09	7.41	8.89	7.08	6.81	7.00	6.32	6.73
earnings	(0.675)	(0.592)	(1.005)	(0.828)	(0.722)	(0.954)	(1.149)	(0.895)
Experience	18.9	20.6	13.7	17.2	9.89	11.9	6.88	9.48
	(11.6)	(11.0)	(10.2)	(11.3)	(8.31)	(8.74)	(8.21)	(8.48)
Tenure	13.8	14.7	4.80	10.5	9.17	11.0	3.84	8.17
	(10.7)	(10.3)	(7.39)	(10.5)	(8.18)	(8.38)	(7.01)	(8.33)
Educational attainment								
Illiterate (reference)	0.124	0.185	0.302	0.206	0.031	0.075	0.308	0.099
	(0.330)	(0.388)	(0.459)	(0.404)	(0.172)	(0.263)	(0.462)	(0.298)
Read and write	0.146	0.236	0.195	0.184	0.010	0.037	0.055	0.023
	(0.353)	(0.425)	(0.397)	(0.388)	(0.097)	(0.191)	(0.229)	(0.151)
Primary	0.064	0.092	0.084	0.078	0.006	0.075	0.049	0.025
	(0.245)	(0.289)	(0.277)	(0.268)	(0.076)	(0.264)	(0.217)	(0.155)
Preparatory	0.040	0.074	0.101	0.071	0.017	0.047	0.077	0.035
	(0.197)	(0.262)	(0.301)	(0.257)	(0.130)	(0.212)	(0.267)	(0.183)
General secondary	0.033	0.028	0.048	0.038	0.017	0.056	0.038	0.027
	(0.179)	(0.166)	(0.213)	(0.190)	(0.130)	(0.231)	(0.193)	(0.163)
Vocational	0.232	0.197	0.170	0.201	0.469	0.467	0.264	0.423
secondary, all	(0.422)	(0.398)	(0.376)	(0.401)	(0.499)	(0.499)	(0.441)	(0.494)
Vocational sec'ry,	0.016	0.062	0.113	0.063	0.004	0.093	0.077	0.032
blue collar	(0.124)	(0.241)	(0.317)	(0.243)	(0.062)	(0.292)	(0.267)	(0.176)
Vocational sec'ry,	0.217	0.136	0.057	0.138	0.466	0.374	0.187	0.391
white collar	(0.412)	(0.343)	(0.232)	(0.345)	(0.499)	(0.486)	(0.391)	(0.488)
Technical institute	0.077	0.030	0.024	0.047	0.134	0.037	0.033	0.099
	(0.267)	(0.171)	(0.153)	(0.211)	(0.341)	(0.191)	(0.179)	(0.298)
University and	0.283	0.158	0.076	0.177	0.316	0.206	0.178	0.270
above	(0.451)	(0.365)	(0.265)	(0.381)	(0.465)	(0.406)	(0.382)	(0.444)
Region of residence								
Greater Cairo	0.231	0.387	0.376	0.320	0.307	0.533	0.544	0.390
(reference)	(0.422)	(0.487)	(0.484)	(0.467)	(0.461)	(0.499)	(0.498)	(0.488)
Alexandria and	0.085	0.197	0.125	0.124	0.151	0.215	0.159	0.162
Suez Canal	(0.280)	(0.398)	(0.331)	(0.330)	(0.359)	(0.413)	(0.367)	(0.368)
Urban lower	0.145	0.137	0.148	0.144	0.224	0.150	0.110	0.189
Egypt	(0.352)	(0.344)	(0.355)	(0.352)	(0.417)	(0.358)	(0.314)	(0.391)
Urban upper	0.171	0.046	0.086	0.112	0.151	0.019	0.049	0.111
Egypt	(0.377)	(0.209)	(0.280)	(0.315)	(0.359)	(0.136)	(0.217)	(0.314)
Rural lower	0.216	0.165	0.176	0.190	0.138	0.047	0.099	0.117
Egypt	(0.412)	(0.372)	(0.381)	(0.392)	(0.345)	(0.212)	(0.299)	(0.322)
Rural upper	0.152	0.067	0.090	0.110	0.029	0.037	0.038	0.032
Egypt	(0.359)	(0.250)	(0.286)	(0.313)	(0.167)	(0.191)	(0.193)	(0.176)

Table 7.1 (continued)

Variables	Males				Females			
	Govern-ment	Public ent'prise	Private	All	Govern-ment	Public ent'prise	Private	All
Job-related variable								
Intermittent			0.373				0.148	
employment			(0.484)				(0.356)	
Work outside			0.386				0.187	
establishments			(0.487)				(0.391)	
Selection term (1)	0.701	1.231	0.670	0.800	0.389	1.382	0.839	0.621
	(0.420)	(0.334)	(0.481)	(0.484)	(0.335)	(0.422)	(0.576)	(0.540)
Number in sample	1,089	568	1,050	2,707	522	107	182	811
Number in population in 1,000s	1,897	1,018	1,904	4,820	866	193	366	1,395

Source: author's calculations.

the operation of the queue, which results in adverse selection into the government sector. In contrast there is positive selection into the private sector, consistent with the operation of a more competitive labour market there. There is no significant selectivity into the public enterprise sector.

Estimation of non-wage benefits in the public sector

As described above, non-wage benefits are estimated indirectly by calculating the ratio of total compensation to monetary compensation (η) that sets lifetime rents to zero for a marginal group of public sector workers, but yields positive rents for all workers. I find η, which is assumed to be constant across different types of workers and the two segments of the public sector, by determining the maximum hj that equalizes total lifetime compensation cross relatively homogeneous groups of workers (equations 5 and 6). The groups are based on a twelve-cell classification of public sector workers on the basis of sex, educational level, and civil service or public enterprise affiliation.[26] The estimation is subject to several assumptions and methodological considerations listed above. These include the following:

- constant discount rate ($\rho=0.05$)
- the length of the queuing process (τ_u) is seven years for Level 2 workers and six years for Level 3 workers
- Level 1 workers do not queue
- queuing involves a loss of private sector earnings while queuing (p=0.5 for males and p=0 for females[27]
- the ratio between non-wage benefits and wages is constant across workers and over the two subsectors of the public sector
- the age cutoff used to identify the marginal group of workers is 35

Table 7.2 Selectivity-corrected earnings equation estimates (dependent variable: log annual earnings (t-ratios in parentheses))

Variables	Males			Females		
	Govern ment	Public ent'prise	Private	Govern– ment	Public ent'prise	Private
Constant	6.477† (38.48)	6.528† (37.11)	6.314† (55.35)	6.079† (26.12)	5.713† (10.08)	5.770† (25.99)
Experience	0.047† (8.83)	0.039† (5.28)	0.083† (8.60)	0.039† (2.99)	0.131† (3.25)	0.077† (2.84)
Experience 2/100	−0.081† (−7.79)	−0.057† (−3.91)	−0.192† (−9.39)	−0.116† (−3.91)	−0.232† (−2.41)	−0.259† (−2.88)
Tenure	0.021† (8.77)	0.013† (4.47)	0.017† (4.18)	0.043† (4.22)	—0.001 (−0.03)	0.034* (1.81)
Educational attainment[a]						
Read and write	0.072 (1.24)	0.165† (2.69)	0.042 (0.55)	0.414 (1.58)	−0.339 (−0.75)	0.333 (0.96)
Primary	0.084 (1.10)	0.168† (2.16)	0.155 (1.09)	0.128 (0.40)	−0.041 (−0.10)	0.257 (0.68)
Preparatory	0.222‡ (2.52)	0.284† (3.29)	−0.122 (−1.12)	0.110 (0.51)	0.492 (1.16)	−0.334 (−1.02)
General secondary	0.215‡ (2.15)	0.671† (5.47)	−0.237* (−1.70)	0.432‡ (2.10)	0.849‡ (2.09)	0.228 (0.52)
Vocational sec'ry, blue collar	0.536† (3.94)	0.631† (6.64)	0.072 (0.58)	−0.799* (−1.89)	0.963† (2.64)	−0.057 (−0.16)
Vocational sec'ry, white collar	0.324† (4.33)	0.532† (7.13)	0.099 (0.66)	0.262 (1.63)	0.693‡ (2.30)	−0.332 (−1.03)
Technical institute	0.298† (3.00)	0.615† (5.05)	−0.133 (−0.64)	0.133 (0.73)	0.081 (0.19)	−0.481 (−0.97)
University and above	0.586† (6.50)	1.062† (14.73)	0.529† (3.28)	0.591† (3.56)	0.720† (2.34)	0.796‡ (2.58)
Region of residence[b]						
Alexandria and Suez Canal	−0.071 (−1.18)	−0.201† (−3.68)	0.070 (0.84)	0.027 (0.37)	0.094 (0.53)	−0.076 (−0.37)
Urban lower Egypt	−0.278† (−5.13)	−0.149‡ (−2.43)	−0.266† (−3.34)	—0.085 (−1–14)	0.041 (0.20)	−0.563‡ (−2.29)
Urban upper Egypt	−0.332† (−5.13)	−0.072 (−0.65)	−0.502† (−4.92)	−0.051 (−0.53)	−0.315 (−0.53)	−0.347 (−0.94)
Rural lower Egypt	−0.434† (−7.61)	−0.140‡ (−2.27)	−0.199† (−2.58)	−0.241† (−2.65)	0.012 (0.03)	0.127 (0.50)
Rural upper Egypt	−0.454† (−6.59)	0.075 (0.84)	−0.140 (−1.38)	−0.195 (−1.34)	−0.175 (−0.48)	−0.478 (−1.17)
Job-related variable						
Intermittent employment			−0.685† (−10.5)			−0.473* (−1.67)

Table 7.2 (continued)

Variables	Males			Females		
	Govern ment	*Public ent'prise*	*Private*	*Govern– ment*	*Public ent'prise*	*Private*
Work outside establishments			0.209† (3.24)			0.105 (0.38)
Selection term (1)	−0.227† (−3.06)	−0.087 (−0.92)	0.246‡ (2.45)	−0.342† (−2.82)	−0.234 (−0.91)	0.330 (1.68)
R2	0.471	0.439	0.362	0.457	0.502	0.317
N	1,089	568	1,050	522	107	182

Notes:

a Illiterate is the reference category.

b Greater Cairo is the reference category.

Significance levels at the 1 per cent level (†) 5 per cent level (‡) and 10 per cent level (*) are indicated. Standard errors are adjusted for the inclusion of the predicted selection term.

- the level of disaggregation used in the classification scheme.

To the extent possible, the consequences of these assumptions on the estimates obtained will be assessed in the sequel.

Based on the maintained assumptions, the marginal group of workers (that is, the workers with the lowest lifetime rents in the public sector) turns out to be female public enterprise workers with Level 3 (university) education ($\eta_j = 2.15$) followed closely by male civil service workers with Level 1 (less than secondary) education ($\eta_j = 2.02$). The first group engages in costly queuing, but the second does not.[28]

Government wages and benefits are therefore just sufficient to attract these two categories of workers to public sector employment. Given the relative imprecision of these estimates and the sparse number of observations in the first group, I will use $\eta = 2$ as the baseline ratio of total compensation to monetary compensation in the public sector.

Because the ratio of non-wage benefits is an important parameter in the subsequent analysis, it is worth doing a sensitivity analysis to determine its robustness to the various assumptions. First we test the extent to which the rankings of the various groups and the estimate of η changes when the age cutoff is increased or decreased. At an age cutoff of 30, the same two groups of workers emerge as the lowest lifetime rent workers, with $\eta_j = 2.32$ for male civil service workers with Level 1 education (thirty-eight observations) and $\eta_j = 2.26$ for female public enterprise workers with Level 3 education (five observations). At an age cutoff of 40, the ranking remains the same, with $\eta_j = 1.87$ for male civil service workers with Level 1 education and $\eta_j = 2.01$ for female public enterprise workers with Level 3 education. Thus the estimate of h ranges from 1.9 to 2.3 depending on the choice of age cutoff.[29]

Second, I test for robustness relating to queuing. Shorter queuing time and less costly queuing raises the lifetime rent of Level 2 and Level 3 workers, but does not affect the rent of Level 1 workers who do not queue. Since shorter and less costly queuing will not displace male civil service workers with Level 1 education as the lowest rent workers, we need only to test the robustness of the estimate to longer and more costly queuing. To increase the cost of queuing to a maximum I set p the fraction of private sector earnings that can be earned while queuing to zero and τ_u, the length of the queue, to ten years for Level 2 workers and nine years for Level 3 workers. Despite these changes, the two groups with the lowest lifetime rents (highest η_j) remain the same. Increasing the queuing time to nine and ten years raises the η_j of female public enterprise workers with Level 3 education to 2.38 at an age cutoff of 35.

Sensitivity analysis on the discount rate shows that the marginal groups of workers remains the same for a range of discounts rates from 0.03 to 0.07 and that η ranges from 1.95 to 2.29.

The assumption that the ratio of non-wage benefits is invariant across the two segments of the public sector turns out not be important since we found a group of marginal workers in each of the two subsectors and both gave us similar estimates for η.

These various sensitivity tests suggest that the identification of marginal group of workers and the estimate of η are fairly robust to changes in the assumptions. We use $\eta = 2.0$ as our baseline estimate, but also discuss results for a low estimate of $\eta = 1.9$ and a high estimate of $\eta = 2.3$.

Estimation of public sector rents

Once the ratio of total compensation to monetary compensation (η) is obtained, the estimation of worker-specific rents is fairly straightforward using equations (7) and (8). The average estimated rents for civil service and public enterprise workers by educational level and sex are shown in Table 7.3, where they are expressed in absolute terms and as multiples of monthly salaries. The average rent for public enterprise workers is estimate at about LE16,000.[30] This is equivalent to 108 months of salary. This figure is in line with severance payments being currently paid out to elicit voluntary exits from public enterprise in Egypt.[31]

The overall average reported here masks considerable variation by type of worker, however. Workers with less than intermediate education (Level 1) have average rents that are less than a third of those with the next higher level of education. The difference in rent between workers with intermediate and those with university education is fairly small however. The highest rent workers are male public enterprise workers with university-level education and female public enterprise workers with intermediate levels of education. Both of these groups have significantly higher wages in the public sector than in the private sector. The rents of female workers at intermediate levels of education are particularly high when expressed as multiples of their monthly salary in both the civil service

Table 7.3 Estimated rents for civil service and public enterprise workers[a]

	Civil service				Public enterprise			
	Level 1[b]	Level 2	Level 3	All	Level 1	Level 2	Level 3	All
Males:								
Percent of public sector work force	18.6	16.0	13.1	47.7	14.6	6.5	4.5	25.6
Average tenure in years	17	11	11	13	16	12	12	14
Average monthly salary in LE	92	98	148	109	120	158	251	152
Average rent in LE	4,139	12,872	15,151	10,088	7,061	21,050	30,079	14,660
Average rent in monthly salaries	45	132	103	92	59	134	120	96
Females:								
Percent of public sector work force	1.4	13.5	6.9	21.8	1.0	2.8	1.0	4.9
Average tenure in years	12	9	8	9	11	10	15	11
Average monthly salary in LE	61	85	113	92	84	134	218	141
Average rent in LE	6,955	20,584	22,597	20,361	11,816	32,423	15,799	24,618
Average rent in monthly salaries	114	242	200	220	141	243	73	174
All:								
Percent of public sector work force	20.0	29.6	20.0	69.5	15.6	9.3	5.6	30.5
Average tenure in years	17	10	10	12	16	11	13	14
Average monthly salary in LE	90	92	136	104	117	150	244	151
Average rent in LE	4,332	16,403	17,717	13,308	7,365	24,501	27,404	16,248
Average rent in monthly salaries	48	179	131	128	63	163	112	108

Notes:
a Based on the assumption that non-wage benefits are proportional to earnings.
b Level 1 refers to workers with less than a secondary certificate; Level 2 refers to workers with secondary and technical institute certificates; Level 3 refes to workers with university and graduate certificates.

and public enterprise. This reflects the very poor prospects women with secondary education face in the private labour market in Egypt.[32] With one exception, women at all education levels have significantly higher rents than men, which is a reflection of their generally poorer prospects in the private sector.[33]

Because of their lower public sector wages, civil service workers have lower rents than their public enterprise counterparts. Although the difference is significant at each level of education, the difference in the overall average between the two sectors is small because the civil service workforce has a higher proportion of the educated workers.

The estimated rent profiles for public enterprise and civil service workers by educational level and sex are shown in Figures 7.2a and 7.2b. Since rents are equal to the area between the public and private sector earning profiles up to retirement age, they vanish at retirement. Because of discounting, there could first be an increase in rent and then the decline sets in. It is clear from these profiles that the common practice of indexing severance pay on tenure in the job are fiscally inefficient because they pay the highest compensation to the workers with the lowest rents. The most efficient schemes will be ones that trace the rent-tenure profile as closely as possible. The next section evaluates various indexation schemes on the basis of how well they do in matching compensation payments to worker rents.

The significant difference in rent between workers at different education levels has important implications for the design of severance pay programmes. If the same package of benefits is offered to all workers to achieve a certain rate of exit, the likely outcome is that all the low-rent Level 1 workers, who are mostly blue collar workers, will exit first, leading to a highly distorted occupational structure. Some control can be achieved over the composition of the exiting workers by setting up separate programmes for each level of education. This is the approach pursued below.

Since there is some uncertainty over the estimate of non-wage benefits in the

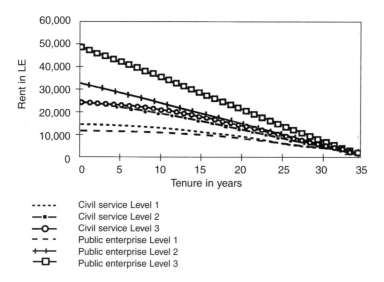

Figure 7.2a Estimated rents versus job tenure for male public enterprise and civil service workers by educational level

Note: for the purposes of this figure, all worker types are assumed to have a total of thirty-six years of tenure from entry to retirement.

public sector, I calculated rents based on the high and low values of η obtained in the sensitivity analysis above. For η varying from 1.9 to 2.3, the average rent for all public enterprise workers varies from LE14,900 to LE20,300, a range of 8 per cent below to 26 per cent above the baseline estimate. In the low non-wage benefits scenario ($\eta = 1.9$) the maximum difference in the rent estimates with the baseline scenario for any cell in Table 7.3 is 10.6 per cent. For the high non-wage benefits scenario ($\eta = 2.3$), the maximum difference compared to the baseline scenario in any cell is 32 per cent. The basic ranking of the various cells is not altered as η changes. This sensitivity analysis suggests that while the magnitude of the rents may increase, the ordinal ranking of workers of different groups of workers in the public sector is not sensitive to fairly significant changes in η.

Simulation of severance pay schemes based on alternative indexation formulas

In the presence of heterogeneous workers, indexing the severance payment to observed differences in characteristics should reduce the cost of the programme for given exit rate targets. A uniform compensation package will be fiscally costly because it must be set at a level that compensates the worker with the largest rent

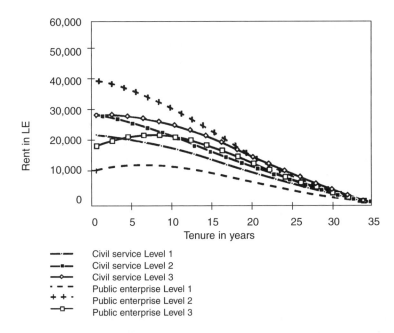

Figure 7.2b Estimated rents versus job tenure for female public enterprise and civil service workers by educational level

Note: for the purposes of this figure, all worker types are assumed to have a total of thirty-six years of tenure from entry to retirement.

among those who exit. As a result, it would end up over-compensating most workers who accept the package, who would be receiving 'information rents'. Indexing the package on observed worker characteristics is one way to reduce these information rents. However, a uniform compensation package might be cheaper than programmes that rely on the wrong formula to index wages. In this section, I evaluate how well commonly used indexation formulas perform compared to this fixed payment benchmark.

The method I used to estimate worker rents makes full use of observed worker attributes and revealed preferences to estimate individual-specific rents. Hence, matching the severance payments exactly to these estimated rents would provide the greatest fiscal savings possible from indexation. Given the lack of transparency of the method and the complexity of the formulas used, it would be quite difficult to implement it in practice. However, the rents obtained in this way serve as another useful benchmark of the maximum savings that are possible through indexation.

In what follows, I carry out simulations with alternative indexation formulas to determine the average cost per worker and the total cost of the programme relative to the two benchmarks discussed above. The effect of each programme on the composition of the exiting and remaining work forces is also determined. Since it may be desirable to maintain the skill composition of the workers that remain in the public sector, I allow for separate programmes for workers at each educational level. It is possible in practice to set different exit rates at each level if information is available about the rates of redundancy at each level. In the absence of such information, however, I set the target exit rate at 30 per cent for each of the three levels for the purposes of this analysis.

I start with indexation schemes that apply to all workers within each of the three educational categories and then consider schemes that offer an early retirement option for workers aged 50 years and older and a regular severance package for workers below that age. In all cases, the payment amount is calculated as if it were a lump sum payment, but this does not preclude various payments methods, including annuities, combinations of annuities and lumps sums and pension payments.

A description of the alternative schemes

Schemes without provisions for early retirement

The following alternative indexation formulas were considered:

1   Fixed payment (no indexation): $C = C_1$. This is the simplest possible scheme and serves as the high-cost benchmark. Since separate programmes are being considered at the three levels of education, this would in fact imply that the payment is indexed only on education. Any programme that results in higher total costs is probably not worth considering. The fixed payment would be fixed at the level that would just compensate workers

whose rent is equal to the 30th percentile of the rent distribution at each educational level.

2   Fixed payment plus a given amount per year of denied service: $C = C_2 + c_2$ $(60 - Age)$. In this scheme, the compensation amount is declining with tenure, and thus captures some of the negatively sloped portion of the rent profile shown in Figures 7.2a and 7.2b.

3   Fixed payment plus given amount per year of tenure: $C = C_3 + c_3N$. Positive indexation by tenure is a common feature of severance programmes. This is the simplest such scheme. It is clear that this scheme would do a poor job in matching the declining rents with tenure of older workers and will therefore end up over-compensating these workers.[34]

4   Fixed payment plus given number of monthly wages: $C = C_4 + c_4\hat{W}_G$. Linking compensation payments to monthly wages is also quite common. This formula explores that linkage independent of the role of tenure or years of denied service. Here again, the most senior workers receive the highest compensation, even though they have the lowest rents.

5   Fixed payment plus given number of monthly wages per year of denied service: $C = C_5 + c_5\hat{W}_G$ $(60 - Age)$. This scheme attempts to mimic the curvature in the rent curve by linking compensation positively to wages, which are an increasing function of tenure, and to years of denied service, which are a decreasing function of tenure.

6   Fixed payment + constant * monthly wages * years of tenure * years of denied service: $C = C_6 + c_6\hat{W}_G N (60 - Age)$. This is the most complex among the indexation formulas being considered. It indexes on tenure, monthly wage, and years of denied service. A variant of this formula was used in the Bulmulla package in Sri Lanka (Fiszbein 1991).

All the indexation schemes described above are compared to the full indexation benchmark, which pays each exiting worker exactly his or her estimated rent, achieving the desired number of exits at the lowest possible fiscal costs.

A worker is assumed to exit if the compensation he or she receives under any of the programmes equals or exceeds his or her estimated rent. For any given level of the fixed payment C_j, c_j is at the minimum level that achieves the desired number of exits, which is set at 30 per cent of the workers at each educational level. The value of the fixed payment C_j is optimized by electing the value that minimizes average cost per exiting worker under the jth formula. Since different programmes are implemented at each of the education levels, different parameters are computed at each level for each indexation formula.

Schemes with early retirement provisions

To take advantage of the declining rents of older workers, the early retirement scheme offers two separate severance packages for workers of 50 and above and for those below 50. Under Egyptian social security regulations, workers who are 50 or above can still receive a retirement pension if they retire early, but their pensions are reduced significantly compared to what they would be if they retired at the age of 60.[35] Assuming that workers of 50 and older would voluntarily retire early if offered full retirement benefits, one approach would be to offer them a compensation package equal to the present value of the lost benefits they and their survivors would incur for as long as they receive pension benefits.[36] However, this assumption is not necessarily justified. Retirement, even at full benefits, may not be more desirable than continuing to work, so workers may not opt to choose that option. In fact that is why retirement at the age of 60 is mandatory rather than voluntary. Moreover, it may be very difficult to calculate the value of lost benefits. The calculation would require detailed actuarial information of the expected life span of the retirees and their spouses to calculate the duration over which loses are incurred.

Rather than rely on an approach that substitutes for lost benefits, I use the opportunity cost approach, which implies matching the compensation to the individual specific rents. The main difference in the early retirement plan is that it uses an indexation formula that pays workers aged 50 and above a lump sum payment plus a multiple of their monthly wage until retirement.[37] Both the lump sum and the multiple of the monthly wage (C_7 and c_7) are optimized to achieve the exit target of people of 50 and over at the lowest cost.

Workers under 50 are offered a separate severance package based on one of the indexation formulas described above. The parameters of that formula and the choice of the formula itself are optimized to exit at the lowest cost the appropriate number of people to achieve the overall 30 per cent exit target.

Simulation results on programme costs

Schemes without early retirement provisions

Figures 7.3 to 7.5 show the average cost per worker versus the fixed component of the compensation for the various indexation formulas. Each point on any given curve is the result of an optimization process that sets the coefficient of the relevant index to the minimum required to exit the target number of workers. The point at the extreme right side of the figure, where all the lines meet, is the point for which the entire compensation is fixed. This is therefore the payment level under formula 1. As shown in Figure 7.3, for example, some commonly used indexation formulas are almost always more costly than the fixed payment benchmark. These include formula 3, which indexes on tenure, and formula 4, which indexes on wage.[38] Formula 6, which indexes on years of denied services, as well as on tenure and wages, reduces the costs somewhat for Level 1 workers but performs poorly for Level 2 and Level 3 workers. Therefore the use of these formulas will result in higher programme costs for any value of the parameters than a fixed payment to all workers.

It is also worth noting that purely variable compensation payments (that is, where the parameter C_j is set to zero) perform significantly worse that the fixed

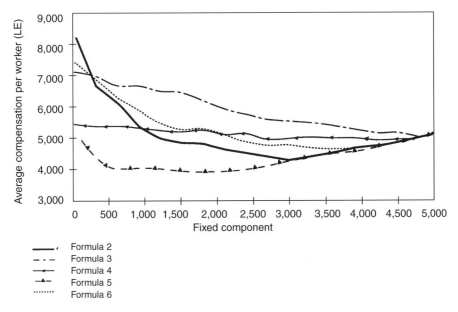

Figure 7.3 Average compensation per worker versus fixed component under various indexation formulas, Level 1 public enterprise employees (30% exit target)

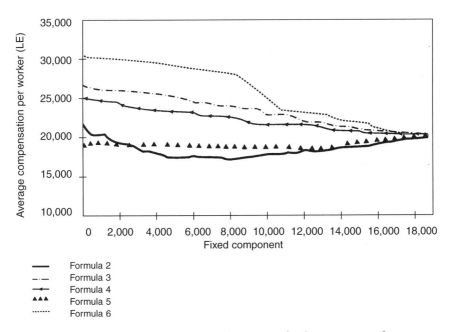

Figure 7.4 Average compensation per worker versus fixed component of severance payment under various indexation formulas, Level 2 public enterprise employees (30% exit target)

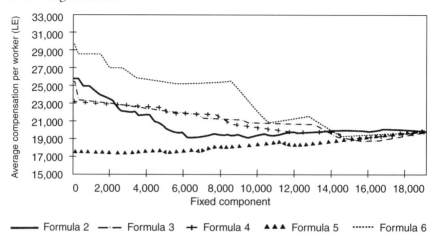

Figure 7.5 Average compensation per worker versus fixed component of severance payment under various indexation formulas, Level 3 public enterprise employees (30% exit target)

payment benchmark. Compensation costs rise sharply as the fixed portion of the compensation package goes to zero.

The best performing formulas are those that index on years of denied service alone (formula 2) and years of denied service and monthly wage (formula 5). Formula 5 is optimal for Level 1 and Level 3 workers and formula 2 is optimal for Level 2 workers.

Table 7.4 compares the average cost per worker and the total cost of the programme at the optimum (lowest cost) point for the various indexation formulas to the full indexation and the fixed payment benchmarks. All of the indexation schemes fall well short of the savings that are possible with full indexation. If full indexation were possible, the average cost of the programme would be LE7,225 per worker and the total cost LE2.6 billion, a saving of about 40 per cent over the fixed payment benchmark. The best performing indexation formula (formula 5) can only bring down the cost to LE10,415 per worker, a savings of LE1,573, or 13 per cent, over the fixed payment benchmark. The savings are greatest in relative terms for Level 1 workers (22 per cent) and smallest for Level 2 workers (10 per cent).[39] For these savings to be achieved, however, the parameters of the indexation formulas must be optimized. The results indicate that one-third to one-half of the payment needs to be fixed, with the remainder varying by worker characteristics.

Schemes with early retirement provisions

As described above, I explored whether further savings could be achieved by offering workers of 50 and over early retirement with a lump sum compensation plus some fixed multiple of their current wage. The lump sum and the multiple

Table 7.4 Cost of compensation programme under alternative indexation formulas, 30% exit target

Formula no.	Expression	Cost per retrenched worker in LE				Total cost of programme in LE million			
		Level 1	Level 2	Level 3	All	Level 1	Level 2	Level 3	All
0	C=Ri	2,505	11,898	12,705	7,255	458	1,270	836	2,564
1	C=C1	4,967	19,351	19,220	11,987	937	2,152	1,307	4,396
2	C=C2+c2 (60-age)	4,244	16,107	18,722	10,540	791	1,787	1,248	3,826
3	C=C3+c3N	4,977	19,370	18,718	11,904	930	2,154	1,256	4,340
4	C=C4+c4WG	4,847	19,380	18,394	11,795	912	2,155	1,234	4,301
5	C=C5+c5WG (60-age)	3,871	17,359	17,025	10,415	721	1,924	1,152	3,797
6	C=C6+c6NWG (60-age)	4,587	19,349	18,175	11,598	855	2,184	1,219	4,258
	Number of exiters (1,000s)	186	111	68	365	186	111	68	365

Notes: level 1 refers to workers with less than secondary educational certificates; level 2 refers to workers with secondary and 2-year higher-education certificates; level 3 refers to workers with bachelor and graduate degrees. The parameters C_j and c_j for each alternative j are given in Appendix Table 7A.2.

Table 7.5 Average compensation for public enterprise workers with early retirement plans, 30% exit target

Exit rate / Alternative no.	Age group	(%)	Cost per retrenched worker in LE				Total cost of programme in LE million			
			Level 1[b]	Level 2[c]	Level 3[d]	All[e]	Level 1[b]	Level 2[c]	Level 3[d]	All[3]
1	Older than 50[a]	72	2,486	5,868	12,164	6,053	260	114	209	583
	Younger than 50	22	5,398	17,984	18,561	8,730	444	1,694	945	3,083
	All	30	3,766	15,933	16,946	9,949	704	1,808	1,154	3,666
2	Older than 50[a]	83	2,826	6,391	12,770	6,736	340	140	254	734
	Younger than 50	19	5,072	17,891	17,985	8,388	344	1,632	885	2,861
	All	31	3,633	15,700	16,515	9,721	684	1,772	1,139	3,595
3	Older than 50[a]	92	3,261	6,637	13,001	7,323	444	152	276	872
	Younger than 50	19	4,620	17,703	17,936	7,848	243	1,571	868	2,682
	All	31	3,639	15,475	16,433	9,618	687	1,723	1,144	3,554
4	Older than 50[a]	100	3,888	6,980	13,140	7,902	579	174	291	1,044
	Younger than 50	17	4,102	17,529	17,606	7,340	156	1,506	780	2,442
	All	30	3,932	15,189	16,117	9,583	735	1,680	1,071	3,486
Number of workers (1,000s)	Older than 50		148.8	25.0	22.1	195.9	148.8	25.0	22.1	196
	Younger than 50		472.2	344.2	199.2	1,015.6	472.2	344.2	199.2	1,016
	All		621.0	369.2	221.3	1,211.5	621.0	369.2	221.3	1,212

Notes: level 1 refers to workers with less than secondary educational certificates; level 2 refers to workers with secondary and 2-year higher-educational certificates; level 3 refers to workers with bachelor and graduate degrees. The parameters Cj and cj for each alternative are given in Appendix Table 7A.3.
a Indexation formula 7 was used for workers aged 50 and above.
b Indexation formula 4 was optional for level 1 workers.
c Indexation formula 2 was optional for level 2 workers.
d Indexation formula 5 was optimal for level 3 workers.
e Based on the 'All' category for the three levels.
f Refers to total number of workers not exiters.
The number of exiters varies under each option.

are computed using the opportunity cost method as before. I explore several scenarios where the exit rate of workers of 50 and over varies from 70 to 100 per cent, keeping the overall exit rate to 30 per cent at each level of education. Workers younger than 50 are offered the plan that achieves the remaining number of voluntary exits needed to reach the 30 per cent overall target at the least cost.

Table 7.5 summarizes the results for the various early retirement scenarios considered. Since workers of 50 and over typically have lower rents than those under 50, cost minimization means that the exit target for the older worker may be up to 100 per cent. Because this may be impractical for operational reasons, I examine alternative scenarios where the early retirement exit target ranges from 50 to 90 per cent. The lowest cost plan is in fact the one that exits 100 per cent of workers of 50 and above. The average cost per worker under this plan is LE 9,583, 8 per cent lower than the best performing scheme without early retirement discussed above. Further savings can be obtained by setting exit targets somewhere between 80 and 90 per cent for Level 1 workers who are 50 and over. An exit target of 70 per cent for all workers 50 and above, would raise the cost of the programme to LE9,950, which is still below the best alternative without early retirement provisions.

Unlike younger workers for whom compensations payments are roughly comparable for Level 2 and Level 3 workers, there is a big gap between these two levels for workers of 50 and above. Compensation amounts for these older workers double between Level 1 and Level 2 and then double again between Level 2 and Level 3. This implies that it would be more cost effective to exit as many older Level 1 workers as possible, before attempting to exit Level 2 and Level 3 workers. Such an approach would also make sense from a managerial perspective since the senior managers that the sector would not want to lose are likely to be Level 3 workers. As a general rule, it makes sense from a fiscal perspective to maximize the exit rate among workers with low levels of education until managerial and operational consideration preclude any further reductions.

Although the optimal indexation formulas for Level 2 and 3 workers under 50 are the same as the schemes without early retirement (formulas 2 and 5, respectively), the optimal formula for Level 1 workers is now formula 4, which indexes on wage only. Once the older workers were removed from consideration, indexation on years of denied service no longer achieves any further savings for these workers.

Because the compensation is based on individual-specific rents, which includes non-wage benefits, the multiple of the current wage paid to early retirees until the mandatory age of retirement is generally larger than 1. As shown in Appendix Table A7.3, the multiple ranges from 1.17 multiples of the monetary wage for Level 1 workers in the 70 per cent exit scenario to 1.85 in the 100 per cent exit scenario for workers 50 and over. It may seem surprising that these workers will be told not to report to work and receive more in compensation every month that they are currently receiving in money wages. It should be kept in mind, however, that out of these payments, they have to make both the employers and employee contributions to the social security fund if they wish to receive full benefits when they reach the age of 60. These payments alone amount to approximately 40 per cent of the monthly wage.

Simulation results on work force composition

As mentioned earlier in the chapter, the main compositional variable over which I attempted to maintain some control was the proportion of exiters in each of three broad educational categories, which was kept at 30 per cent. In the early retirement plans I also fixed the target exit rate for workers aged 50 and older. In practice, it may be necessary to control the composition of the remaining labour force along several other dimensions, such as the proportion of managerial or production workers, the proportion of males and females, and so forth. This can be easily achieved by offering each of the categories for which a separate target needs to be achieved, its own severance programme and tailoring the parameters of the indexation formulas to achieve the desired exits.

Since exit rates were not set *ex ante* for specific age, sex, region or occupational groups, it is interesting to see what they turned out to be under the various indexation formulas that proved cost-effective. Table 7.6 shows the *ex post* exit rate produced by the simulation for different categories of workers. The full indexation plan is not shown because it exits exactly the same people as the fixed payment plan. I also do not show the exit rate by educational category since it is set at the 30 per cent target.

First, in terms of age composition, it is interesting to note that most of the options without special provisions for early retirement exit workers aged 50 and above at close to the 90 per cent rate. The main exceptions are the fixed payment scheme (and consequently the full indexation scheme) and the suboptimal formulas 3 and 4, which exit these workers at a rate of 93 per cent. Since the full indexation scheme is the most efficient, 93 per cent is likely to be the optimal target rate for the early retirement scheme as well. Workers under 35 exit at very low rates, ranging from 8 to 16 per cent. The highest rates for that group are obtained for formula 2, which places a relatively high weight on years of denied service. The different early retirement schemes, labelled by a preset target for workers of 50 and over, have a relatively constant exit rate for workers under 35, but as the proportion of workers of 50 and over increases, the proportion of workers in the intermediate age category decreases.

With respect to the other observable characteristics of workers, the simulation reveals that the composition of workers does not vary significantly across the various indexation schemes, including the early retirement schemes. As expected, females exit at lower rates than males because they have higher rents. However, the difference between males and females is not large, especially for formula 2. The Alexandria/Suez Canal region and to a lesser extent the rural Lower Egypt region, have disproportionately high exit rates. Conversely, Upper Egypt, a region with poor private sector prospects, has disproportionately low exit rates.

Table 7.6 Simulated exit rates for various categories of workers under selected indexation schemes (%)

	Fixed payment	Indexation scheme					Early retirement			
		indexation formula no.					70%	80%	90%	100%
		2	3	4	5	6				
Age category										
Age below 35	9	16	9	8	10	8	13	12	11	11
Age between 35 and 49	27	21	27	27	27	28	31	29	26	22
Age equal to or above 50	93	89	93	93	90	91	72	83	92	100
Sex										
Male	31	30	31	31	31	31	31	32	32	31
Female	26	30	25	25	27	28	26	25	24	24
Region										
Greater Cairo	28	25	27	28	28	27	25	27	28	28
Alexandria and Suez Canal	48	50	48	48	47	48	52	50	47	46
Urban lower Egypt	29	28	29	29	29	30	27	29	29	29
Rural lower Egypt	39	31	39	39	36	39	35	35	35	35
Urban upper Egypt	25	28	25	24	25	24	30	26	27	26
Rural upper Egypt	17	19	17	17	19	20	18	18	18	16
Occupational category										
Professional/ technical	22	24	22	22	23	22	25	24	23	22
Managerial	78	68	77	77	78	77	74	78	80	77
Production	27	27	27	27	26	27	29	28	27	26
Clerical	29	26	29	29	28	30	29	30	30	30
Services	37	41	37	37	39	36	30	29	35	36

On the occupational front, the most noteworthy result is the very high exit rates among managerial occupations, with over 77 per cent of that category of workers exiting under most schemes. Because managerial employees tend to have higher than expected wages, their exit rate drops when a relatively high weight is placed on tenure and a lower weight on wage in determining the compensation, as in formula 2. The disproportionate exit of managers may be welcome if the private owners want to hire their own managerial staffs. However, if the retention of more managers is deemed necessary, they could be offered a separate severance package that sets their exit targets *ex ante*. The other occupational group that exits disproportionately is service workers. These workers are generally considered fairly unproductive. Again, if that exit rate is deemed insufficient, they could be offered a more generous severance package that would exit more of them.

Conclusion

This chapter had two major objectives: first, to estimate the rents that public enterprise workers would lose if they left their jobs and, second, to simulate various voluntary severance schemes to determine their relative efficiency in achieving the target exit rates at the lowest fiscal cost. The most challenging aspect of estimating the rents was to come up with a reliable estimate for the value of the non-wage aspects of public sector jobs. By identifying a marginal group of workers that receives no lifetime rents in the public sector, I was able to place the value of non-wage benefits at about double the monetary wage. This estimate is conditional on a number of assumptions, however, and would need to be confirmed through further research.

Once an acceptable estimate for non-wage benefits was obtained, it was quite straightforward to estimate workers rents by comparing their public sector compensation stream with what they would get from alternative employment in the private sector. I estimate the average rent of a public enterprise worker at LE16,250 or 108 average monthly wages in 1988 prices. There is considerable variation by sex and across educational levels. Because of their poorer job prospects in the private sector, rents for female workers are about 68 per cent higher than those of males. Similarly, because returns to secondary education are significantly higher in the public than in the private sector, there is over a threefold jump in rents between workers with less than secondary education (Level 1) and those with secondary or technical institute degrees (Level 2). There is much smaller additional increment in rent for university educated workers (Level 3).

The second objective of the chapter was to simulate the operation of compensation schemes based on alternative indexation formulas to determine which one can achieve the exit target at the lowest cost. The target is to exit 30 per cent of the labour force in each of the three broad educational levels. In 1988, this represented 356,000 workers distributed as follows: 52 per cent in Level 1, 29 per cent in Level 2 and 19 per cent in Level 3.

If there were no indexation, meaning that all workers in each of the three educational categories were paid a fixed amount high enough to exit the desired number of workers, the required compensation would be LE4,967 per worker for Level 1 workers, LE19,350 for Level 2 workers and LE19,220 for Level 3 workers, or LE11,990 on average, all in 1988 prices. The cost of the programme under such a fixed payment would be approximately LE4.4 billion (8 per cent of gross domestic product (GDP)).[40] If, on the other hand, compensation payment could be matched exactly to the individual-specific estimated rents, the average compensation could be reduced to LE7,250 and the cost of the programme to LE2.6 billion (4.8 per cent of GDP), a 40 per cent reduction.

Since it may not be practical to use an indexation formula as complicated as the one used to estimate the rents, I investigated how indexation formulas commonly used in severance programmes fare in reducing fiscal costs relative to this formula. Two types of programmes were investigated. The first applies the same formula to workers of all ages and the second offers workers aged 50 and over an early retirement scheme and one of the standard indexation formulas for workers below 50.

First, it should be noted that compensation formulas made up of a purely variable payment based on wages, years of tenure or years of denied service generally performed worse than a purely fixed payment. To get additional savings, the relative size of the variable and fixed components must be optimized.

Second, some of the commonly-used indexation formulas, such as those that index on years of tenure or seniority, perform worse for almost all parameter values than the simple fixed payment programmes. They tend to pay the highest compensations to the lowest rents workers. The formulas that perform the best are those than index on years of denied service and wages.

The optimal formula for Level 1 and Level 3 workers indexes on wages and years of denied service (formula 5) and the optimal one for Level 2 workers indexes on years of denied service only (formula 2). For instance, Level 1 workers would be offered LE2,100 plus 1.56 monthly wages per year of denied service, which yields an average compensation of LE3,871. Level 2 workers would be offered LE8,100 plus LE418 per year of denied service, yielding an average compensation of LE16,107 (see Appendix Table A7.2 for the optimal parameters of the indexation formulas). If the same formula were to be used for all three categories of workers, the lowest cost programme would use formula 5 and would cost LE10,415 per worker or LE3.8 billion overall (6.9 per cent of GDP), a 14 per cent savings over the fixed payment option. formula 2 would be a close second.

Analysis of the early retirement options revealed that the most efficient strategy would be to set the exit target for workers of 50 and over at the highest level that can be justified by administrative considerations. Given a certain overall exit target, the higher the exit rate among older workers, and especially among those with lower levels of education, the lower the overall cost of the program. The highest exit rate I considered for the three educational levels was 100 per cent, which yielded an average compensation cost pre worker of LE9,583, which is well below the best programme without early retirement provisions. The total cost of the programme under that option is LE3.5 billion (6.4 per cent of GDP), a saving of 21 per cent over the fixed payment option.

Besides producing estimates of the relative costs of various programmes, the simulation can also determine the composition of exiters and stayers in terms of the various observable characteristics. The most noteworthy result is that the various severance programmes tend exit workers in managerial occupations in disproportionate numbers, with over 80 per cent of them exiting under some schemes. This may be desirable if the new private owners want to select their own managers. If this is not the case, a special programme that offers them a less generous severance package might have to be devised for these workers.

This chapter has not dealt with several important issues relating to voluntary severance schemes. These include adverse selection problems, the form in which the compensation is provided, whether a menu of choices should be provided, and issues relating to the timing and speed of the retrenchment program. Adverse selection can occur if some worker attributes affect a worker's productivity in similar ways in both the public and private sectors. High productivity workers will tend to have low rents and will leave the public sector disproportionately. If these attributes can be observed, however, as in the case of occupation or education, adverse selection can be reduced or eliminated by designing special severance programmes along these observable characteristics or by using exit vetoes. With partial observability of the characteristics that determine public sector productivity, the adverse selection problem is more difficult to address but can be reduced through the use of randomization (see Diwan 1993a).

The form that the compensation takes is another crucial issues in the design of severance programmes, which has not been dealt with here, except in the context of early retirement. Compensation packages can take the form of lump sum payments, annuities, retraining assistance, wage subsidies for private sector employers and early retirement pensions. Providing a menu of choices for workers to choose from may allow for a further reduction in costs through better targeting as workers self-select according to their unobservable characteristics.

Notes

1 See Diwan (1993a and 1993b) for an in-depth discussion of these issues.
2 Studies which rely on follow-up surveys of displaced workers include Orazem, Vodopivec and Wu (1995) on Slovenia; Mills and Sahn (1995) on Guinea; and O'Leary (1995) on Hungary.
3 For example, if information were available to indicate that the redundancy rate was significantly higher among workers with intermediate levels of education than for workers with low levels of education, then the exit ratio for the first category of workers could be set higher than for the second, say 60 per cent and 20 per cent. The same logic applies to any categorization of workers for which different rates of redundancy might apply.
4 Privatization Unit, Public Enterprise Office 1993, and Integrated Development Consultants (1993).
5 In 1988, the year when the data used for this study was collected, the public enterprise labour force was estimated at 1.21 million, which was about 13 per cent of the non-agricultural employment (source: Public Enterprise Information Centre, Employment and Wages Database). The May 1995 round of the Labour Force Sample Survey puts the figure at 1.37 million.
6 This and subsequent references to the draft law refer to the version published in the *Al-Ahali* newspaper on 30 November 1994.
7 Examples of failures of a worker to fulfil essential obligations are listed in Article 69, but the list is not meant to be exhaustive.
8 Under Egypt's Social Insurance Law (Law 79 of 1975), workers who lose their jobs are eligible for 60 per cent of their last wage for a period of sixteen weeks, extendible to twenty-eight weeks for workers with more than two years of social insurance contribution (Assaad 1996).
9 Because the allocation of workers to jobs tends to match the worker's risk averseness with the characteristics of the job, observed compensating differential in the private sector may understate the necessary compensation needed for public sector workers

to accept the same level of risk, because they are likely to be more risk averse on average than private sector workers. If this is the case, my rent estimates are likely to be somewhat understated.

10   I do not distinguish, however, between a formal and an informal private sector wage schedule. Exiting public sector workers are therefore assumed to enter into these two subsectors in the same proportion as existing private sector workers.

11   Female workers may be comparing the public sector wage schedule with their reservation wage for market work, which may be higher than their private sector wage. Rents based on wage comparisons from the two sectors may therefore overstate the compensation needed for voluntary exit of females.

12   An attempt was made to estimate these non-wage benefits from data on labour mobility between 1981 and 1988 available from the same survey. The basic idea behind the method was that if workers are observed to have moved from the public to the private sector, their private sector earnings must be compensating them for the loss of public sector non-wage benefits, thus allowing for an indirect estimate of these benefits. Private sector earnings for these workers are available from the survey and their public sector earnings could in theory be estimated from the public sector wage schedule. Before a comparison of earnings can be made, however, it is necessary to correct earnings estimates for selectivity because public sector workers who move to the private sector cannot be assumed to be randomly selected from among all public sector workers. The small number of public to private movers in the sample (fifty-four out of a total public sector sample of 1,837 workers in 1981) made it impractical to implement this method.

13   Although I do not distinguish between the civil service and public enterprise in developing the model, I do so in the empirical analysis.

14   Rents will be dissipated only if queuing is costly. A requirement to leave the queue upon accepting a private sector job offer would make queuing costly by forcing workers to forgo private sector income while queuing. While such a requirement is not enforced in Egypt, there is ample evidence of significantly higher unemployment rates among groups covered by the public sector employment guarantee, indicating that queuing is costly (Assaad 1997).

15   Since the aim of the exercise is to determine the difference between public and private sector total compensation, all we need to do is estimate the difference in non-wage benefits between the two sectors.

16   Actually, the 'marginal worker' is really a group of workers who share the same observable characteristics.

17   The three educational categories are Level 1 for those with less than secondary education, Level 2 for those with secondary or technical institute degrees, and Level 3 for those with bachelor or graduate degrees.

18   See Assaad (1997) for a more detailed discussion of the workings of the public sector queue.

19   It should be noted, however, that once workers transfer to the private sector, they begin to accumulate private sector seniority.

20   The subscript G refers to government, but the same equations would also apply to public enterprise workers.

21   In estimating the private sector wage equation, we include two variables indicating intermittent employment and work outside fixed establishments, job characteristics for which private sector workers may earn compensating differentials. These variables are not included in X_i however, so we are in effect comparing employment in the public sector with stable employment inside fixed establishments in the private sector. This goes some of the way in equalizing non-wage aspects of employment in the two sectors.

22   The standard errors of the wage equations are adjusted for the inclusion of the predicted sample selection terms. See Lee (1983) for more details on the multinomial logit selection model.

23   This takes into account that public sector workers can transport their seniority level across public sector jobs.

24   The earnings module was designed by Mohaya Zaytoun and the mobility module by Hayam El-Biblawi. Overall technical direction for the special round was provided by Nader Fergany.

25   For further discussion of this issue see Assaad (1997).

26   I could have used a finer classification that also classifies workers by region or urban–rural status, but that would have given cells with a very sparse number of observations for which estimates would be unreliable.

27   Fergany (1991: 134) attributes the higher proportion of new entrants among unemployed females to the fact that males are more likely to engage in marginal or occasional economic activities while waiting for government employment.

28   Among workers of 25 and under, there are only eight observations in the sample in the first group and eighty-four observations in the second group. The group with the next lowest lifetime rents is male civil service workers with university-level education ($\eta_j = 1.46$).

29   Younger age cutoffs yield very sparse cells and therefore increasingly unreliable estimates. Older age cutoffs may include workers who entered the public sector facing significantly different wage schedules.

30   In 1988, US$1.00 was equivalent to LE3.3.

31   According to an interview with the official responsible for the employment and retraining program, which is financing such severance schemes, current severance payments range from LE20,000 to 30,000. Interview with Mr. Omar El-Farouk, 16 October 1997.

32   Besides having the highest relative gap in wages in favour of the public sector, they also have by far the highest unemployment rates, an indication of queuing for public sector jobs. See Assaad (1997) for further discussion of this issue.

33   The exception is among university-educated public enterprise workers, for whom the estimates must be considered tentative because of their small number in the sample (twenty-two observations).

34   A more common variant of this formula is to index on wage and tenure by paying a certain number of monthly wages per year of tenure. An example of such a programme is the Leather Corporation package in Sri Lanka discussed in Fiszbein (1991). I tried this variant, but it produced results that were clearly inferior to this formulation from a cost point of view.

35   The amount of reduction is determined by a complicated formula that distinguishes between a basic and variable component of the wage. The rules are described in some detail in Assaad (1996). Based on a detailed analysis of workers in the Delta Spinning and Weaving Company, a report by Integrated Development Consultants estimates that the loss of benefits amounts to 66 per cent of full benefits at the age of 50, 57 per cent at the age of 53, and 40 per cent at the age of 57 (IDC 1994, Table B.5).

36   This approach is pursued in IDC (1994). However it appears that the IDC reports did not take into account in their calculations the losses incurred due to lost benefits after retirement.

37   Formula 7, the formula for this option, is given by $C = C_7 + c_8 I$, where I is the present value of the current annual earnings until retirement.

$$I = \int_{\tau}^{tr} \hat{E}_G(\tau) e^{-\rho t} dt = 12 \hat{W}_G(\tau) \; \frac{e^{-\rho \tau} - e^{-\rho \vartheta r}}{\rho}$$

38   The results from a formula that indexes on both monthly wages and tenure are not shown but behave very much in the same way.

Appendix

Table 7A.1 Selection equation estimates, multinomial logit model (dependent variable: y=0 for government[a], y=1 for public enterprise, y=2 for private sector (t-ratios are in parentheses))

Variable	Males		Females	
	Public enterpise	Private	Public enterpise	Private
Constant	1.824†	10.89‡	4.347†	11.330‡
	(1.94)	(12.87)	(2.19)	(6.05)
Age	−0.041	−0.350‡	−0.215*	−0.454‡
	(−0.81)	(−7.61)	(−1.88)	(−4.19)
Age 2/100	0.024	0.306‡	0.253	0.500‡
	(0.40)	(5.38)	(1.62)	(3.35)
Educational attainment[b]				
Read and write	−0.078	−0.683‡	0.455	−1.084
	(−0.42)	(−3.93)	(0.51)	(−1.40)
Primary	−0.451*	−1.390‡	0.847	−1.258
	(−18.9)	(−5.84)	(1.00)	(−1.49)
Preparatory	−0.115	−1.290‡	−0.230	−1.238*
	(−0.43)	(−4.91)	(−0.29)	(−1.79)
General secondary	−0.709†	−1.539‡	0.002	−1.331*
	(−2.05)	(−4.62)	(0.00)	(−1.83)
Vocational secondary	−0.880‡	−2.678‡	−1.459‡	−3.900‡
	(−4.51)	(−14.00)	(−2.71)	(−8.48)
Technical institute	−1.935‡	−3.546‡	−2.697‡	−4.739‡
	(−6.03)	(−11.67)	(−3.71)	(−7.44)
University or above	−2.164‡	−4.027‡	−2.792‡	−3.794‡
	(−8.58)	(−14.35)	(−4.22)	(−7.40)
Bachelor of engineering	1.553‡	1.791‡	2.308‡	0.446
	(4.14)	(4.24)	(2.59)	(0.38)
Bachelor of science	1.724‡	1.075*		
	(3.03)	(1.68)		
Bachelor of commerce	1.222‡	1.533‡	1.846‡	0.699
	(4.02)	(4.48)	(3.45)	(1.34)
Region of residence[c]				
Alexandria and Suez Canal	0.301*	−0.219	−0.169	−0.527*
	(1.68)	(−1.12)	(−0.55)	(−1.60)
Urban lower Egypt	−0.619‡	−0.732‡	−1.012‡	−1.359‡
	(−3.50)	(−4.07)	(−2.96)	(−3.89)
Urban upper Egypt	−1.934‡	−1.454‡	−2.531‡	1.870‡
	(−8.17)	(−7.34)	(−3.34)	(−3.71)
Rural lower Egypt	−1.000‡	−1.131‡	−1.382‡	−0.917‡
	(−5.75)	(−6.54)	(−2.56)	(−1.98)
Rural upper Egypt	−1.572‡	−1.554‡	−0.296	−0.046
	(−7.19)	(−7.60)	(−0.44)	(−0.07)
Parents' characteristics				
Father farmer/agricultural worker	−0.255*	−0.604‡	−0.668	0.284
	(−1.87)	(−4.40)	(−1.32)	(0.71)
Father educated	0.209	0.083	0.573†	0.922‡
	(1.21)	(0.46)	(2.05)	(3.06)

Table 7A.1 (continued)

Variable	Males		Females	
	Public enterpise	Private	Public enterprise	Private
Parents' characteristics (con't)				
Mother educated	−0.645‡	−0.134	−0.613	0.154
	(−1.98)	(−0.47)	(−1.43)	(0.42)
Household–level variables				
Currently married	0.125	−0.331*	0.216	−0.487
	(0.64)	(−1.90)	(0.66)	(−1.59)
No. of children under 2			−0.474*	−0.529†
No. of children 3 to 6			−0.064	0.028
			(−0.37)	(0.15)
No. of children 7 to 11			0.303*	0.321†
Other private non–agricultural wage workers			−0.171	0.443*
			(−0.52)	(1.65)
Other public wage workers			−0.079	−0.471‡
			(−0.47)	(−2.77)
Log likelihood	−2,171.1		−501.8	
No. of observations	2,707		811	

Notes:
a The parameters of the government equation are normalized to zero.
b Illiterate is the reference category.
c Greater Cairo is the reference category.
Significance levels at the 1 per cent level (‡) 5 per cent level (†) and 10 per cent level (*) are indicated.

39 Since formula 2 rather than 5 is optimal for Level 2 workers, savings of 17 per cent could be achieved for these workers if formula 3 were used.
40 In comparison, the share of the public enterprise in GDP in 1987 was 27.1 per cent (World Bank 1995).

Table 7A.2 Optimal parameters of indexation formulas, 30% exit target

Formula	Level 1		Level 2		Level 3	
Formula expression	C_j	c_j	C_j	c_j	C_j	c_j
1 C=C1	4,967	0	19,352	0	19,220	0
2 C=C2+c2* (60 − Age)	3,000	104.0	8,100	418.0	9,600	572.0
3 C=C3+c3N	4,800	7.9	19,200	8.4	14,400	196.4
4 C=C4+c4WG	4,200	5.2	19,200	0.9	15,000	11.0
5 C=C5+c5WG (60 − Age)	2,100	1.56	11,100	2.06	5,100	3.16
6 C=C6+c6WG (60 − Age)	3,600	0.032	18,600	0.011	15,600	0.028

Notes:
Level 1 refers to workers with less than secondary education certificates.
Level 2 refers to workers with secondaary and two-year-higher-education certificates.
Level 3 refers to workers with with batchelor and graduate degrees.

Table 7A.3 Optimal parameters of indexation formulas under the early retirement scenarios

30% exit target			Level 1[b]		Level 2[c]		Level 3[d]	
Alterna- tive no	Age group	Exit rate (%)	C_j	c_j	C_j	c_j	C_j	c_j
1	Older than 50[a]	70	900	1.17	1,500	1.47	3,000	1.20
	Younger than 50		4,200	11.2	8,100	429.0	9,300	2.35
2	Older than 50[a]	80	900	1.31	1,200	1.60	3,900	2.35
	Younger than 50		2,700	21.0	8,400	417.0	6,900	2.80
3	Older than 50[a]	90	1,200	1.33	900	1.73	900	1.58
	Younger than 50		2,700	18.0	8,700	402.0	5,700	3.05
4	Older than 50[a]	100	900	1.85	600	1.86	1,200	1.55
	Younger than 50		3,000	12.3	8,100	420.0	6,900	2.75

Notes:
Level 1 refers to workers with less than secondary education certificates; Level 2 refers to workers with secondaary and two-year-higher-education certificates; Level 3 refers to workers with with batchelor and graduate degrees.
a Indexation formula 7 was used for workers aged 50 and above.
b Indexation formula 4 was optimal for Level 1 workers.
c Indexation formula 2 was optimal for Level 2 workers.
d Indexation formula 5 was optimal for Level 3 workers.

Bibliography

Assaad, R. (1996) 'Structural adjustment and labor market reform in Egypt', in H. Hopfinger (ed.), *Privatization and Economic Liberalization in the Socialist Countries of the Arab World*, Stuttgart: Klett/Perthes.
—— (1997) 'The effects of public sector hiring and compensation policies on the Egyptian labor market', *World Bank Economic Review*, vol. 11, no. 1: 85–118.
El-Khawaga, L. (1993) 'Underemployment in the public sector: the case of Egypt', *Proceedings of the Expert Conference on Unemployment in the ESCWA Countries*, Amman, Jordan, 26–9 July 1993. In Arabic.
Integrated Development Consultants (IDC) (1993) 'Labor policy issues in privatization', Final Report to Bechtel/PID, November.
—— (1994) 'El Delta Spinning and Weaving Company: organizational structure and human resources', Final Report to Bechtel/PID, February.
Diwan, I. (1993a) 'Public Sector Retrenchment and Efficient Severance Pay Schemes', mimeo, Washington, D.C.: World Bank.
—— (1993b) 'Public sector retrenchment and severance pay: nine propositions', mimeo, Washington, D.C.: World Bank.
Fergany, N. (1991) 'Overview and general features of employment in the domestic economy', Final report, CAPMAS, Labor Information System Project, Cairo, Egypt.
Fiszbein, A. (1992) 'Labor retrenchment and redundancy compensation in state-owned enterprises: the case of Sri Lanka', Internal Discussion Paper, South Asia Region, Washington, D.C.: World Bank.
Lee, L. F. (1983) 'Generalized econometric models with selectivity', *Econometrica*, vol. 51: 507–12.

Mills, B. and Sahn, D. E. (1995) 'Reducing the size of the public sector workforce: institutional constraints and human consequences in Guinea', *Journal of Development Studies*, vol. 31, no. 4: 505–28.

O'Leary, C. (1995) 'An impact analysis of labor market programmes in Hungary', Upjohn Institute Staff Working Paper no. 95–029.

Orazem, P., Vodopivec, M. and Wu, R. (1995) 'Worker displacement during the transition: experience from Slovenia', mimeo, Washington, D.C.: World Bank.

Svejnar, J. and Terrell, K. (1991) 'Reducing labor redundancy in state-owned enterprises', Policy Research and External Affairs Working Paper no. WPS 792, Washington, D.C.: World Bank.

World Bank (1995) *Bureaucrats in Business: The Economics and Politics of Government Ownership*, Oxford: Oxford University Press.

8 State-owned enterprise in Jordan
Strategy for reform

Taher H. Kanaan

Introduction

This chapter contributes a review of the status of state-owned enterprises (SOEs) in Jordan (as of mid-1996) together with an assessment and critique of recent 'reform' policies and measures that are under active consideration or implementation for changing that status.

The presentation is organized as follows: the first section provides a taxonomy of SOEs and a review of recent developments affecting publicly-owned productive assets. The taxonomy distinguishes the sectors where private enterprise dominates, namely, manufacturing, agriculture and most non-governmental services. It further reviews public corporations totally owned by the government as well as government equity ownership in shareholding companies. This is followed by an evaluation of the performance of SOEs in each of the categories outlined earlier.

The chapter then reviews government reform policies towards SOEs consisting of slow if not hesitant steps towards commercialization of public utilities mainly in the telecommunications and power sector, together with partial divestiture of limited amounts of government equity in shareholding companies. The following section summarizes the reform strategy recently firmed up by the government in consultation with the World Bank, entailing further measures to privatize SOEs.

The study concludes with a critique of the current reform strategy and recommends more precise terms of reference to rearrange reform priorities. It proposes that policy analysis should avoid preoccupation with the issue of public versus private ownership, and concentrate instead on policies that emanate from understanding the relevant markets, their mode of operation, their accessibility and the degree of competition that can be made to prevail in them. Policies and measures to change ownership patterns or to effect divestiture of state property should be considered only if and when such policies and measures are expected to lead to liberalization of the markets in question or to meaningful reduction of their imperfections. A high priority is to complete the liberalization and reform of the financial market. Market forces and the interaction of supply and demand can also be imaginatively applied to the reform of certain government services even if they are not of standard market-oriented nature.

Taxonomy and recent developments

The state-owned enterprise sector in Jordan, defined to consist of publicly-owned productive assets other than those providing standard government services, accounted for about 14 per cent of aggregate value added (gross domestic product (GDP)) in 1992.

Sectors where state enterprise dominates

In standard sectoral classifications of GDP, aside from government services, public ownership and control, value added in state-controlled establishments, measured in 1992, has been significant only in mining and quarrying (89 per cent), electricity and water (76 per cent), and transport and communications (58 per cent). The pattern is familiar since activities in these sectors include the conventional public utilities and the natural resource-based monopolies.

Mining and quarrying

In the mining and quarrying sector, the state is the major shareholder in the Jordan Phosphates Company (41.5 per cent), in the Arab Potash Company (55.4 per cent) and the General Mining Company (51.3 per cent); the three being public shareholding companies listed in the Amman Financial Market.

Recently, the state was instrumental in the creation of yet another natural resource-based company, namely the Jordan Company for Dead Sea Industries where 61 per cent of the equity is publicly-owned and controlled directly through the Jordan Investment Corporation (10 per cent), and indirectly through the Arab Potash Company (51 per cent).

In a development in the opposite direction, and as part of the efforts to experiment with commercialization as a first stage in privatization, the government decided in 1994 to carve out all its petroleum and natural gas exploration and extraction activities from the public administration of the Natural Resources Authority, and turn them over to a private shareholding company (unlisted), almost totally owned by the Jordan Investment Corporation (JIC).

Power

In the electricity sector, the state has totally owned and controlled power generation through the Jordan Electricity Authority (JEA). It also owned and controlled power distribution all over the country with the exception of the governorates of Amman, Zarka, and Irbid, where electricity distribution was conceded to two public shareholding companies (PSCs), namely Jordan Electric Power Company (JEPCO) and Irbid District Electricity Company (IDICO). Ownership of JEPCO is shared between the public sector (through JEA) and the private sector in the ratio of 33 per cent to 77 per cent. In contrast, 89 per cent of IDICO is owned by the government and the municipalities, leaving only 11 per cent in private hands.

Water

In the water sector, the state owns and controls the water supply for domestic and industrial uses through the Water Supply Authority, and water for irrigation through the Jordan Valley Authority.

Transport

In the transport sector, the state owns and controls the national airline (Royal Jordanian) the Aqaba Port Corporation, two minor railway companies (Hijaz–Jordan Railway and Aqaba Railway Corporation) as well as a number of public transport bus lines through the Public Transport Corporation. The rest of surface transport has been in private free enterprise domain with the exception of tourist transport which until very recently (1994) was a private monopoly in the form of a concession granted by law to Jordan Express Tourist Transport Company (JET) being a PSC owned up to 92.7 per cent by the private sector and 8.3 per cent by the government.

Telecommunications

In the telecommunications sector, until very recently telecommunication services were publicly-owned and controlled by the Telecommunications Corporation (TCC). The Commercialization of the TCC, pending since 1988, was by May 1996 nearing completion, as discussed in the section on the reform process.

Sectors where private enterprise dominates

Private enterprise has been dominant in agriculture (100 per cent), construction (100 per cent), manufacturing (94 per cent), and non-government services – financial, business community and personal services – (95 per cent).

Manufacturing

State ownership and control of enterprise in the manufacturing sector and non-government services sectors consist principally of equity participation in commercially-run enterprises by two state investment vehicles, namely the Jordan Investment Corporation (JIC) and the Social Security Corporation (SSC). However, the concept of investment differs somewhat between the two.

The SSC, like any portfolio investor, is supposed to place funds in profitable investments, in order to maximize return on its assets originating in contributions by private sector employers and employees towards their old age security and/or end of service benefits.

The JIC was established early in 1970s under the name of the Pension Fund. It started with an initial capital of JD 5 million financed from a capital gain made by the central bank as a result of revaluation of its gold reserves. The original objective of the Pension Fund was to invest money in growth assets, the future income of which was to assist the government in meeting its mounting obligations towards civil service pensions. In practice, it was given the mandate to act as public entrepreneur and investment leader to break new grounds in industrial and other production where private enterprise appeared too timid to venture. It gradually became an investment arm of the public sector engaging in investment promotion activities, identifying investment opportunities, conducting feasibility studies of projects and inviting the private sector to join its investments. In 1989 it was decided to revise the law of the Pension Fund, bringing it under closer control of the Ministry of Finance and changing its name to the Jordan Investment Corporation consistent with its *de facto* functions.

At the end of 1994, a large part of the JIC holdings were in the form of equity in forty-three public shareholding companies (PSCs) listed in the Amman Financial Market (AFM) and which constituted 18 per cent of AFM's capitalization. Another part of JIC investments was in twenty-eight unlisted companies. Of the former, the JIC has had management control over at least seven PSCs where its share exceeded 50 per cent of equity, and varying influence over seventeen others where it held between 10 per cent and 50 per cent of equity. Of the unlisted companies, the JIC had 50 per cent control share in six companies, and significant share (10–50 per cent) in eleven others.

Equity investments of the Social Security Corporation at the end of 1994 were in sixty-six listed and twenty-four unlisted companies. In only three of these companies, the SSC had greater than 30 per cent share of equity, entitling it to management board membership.

The trend in recent years, however, has been that of relative decline in the proportion of enterprise ownership by the public sector. Thus, between 1987 and 1992 the total number of registered private companies increased by 118 per cent, from 1,990 to 4,349 companies. In contrast, the number of PSCs in which the public sector held equity declined from 115 to 112.

Public corporations

In addition to equity participation in commercial enterprises through JIC and SSC, the state has direct financial interest and varying degrees of leverage and control of management in a large number of financial and other infrastructure service establishments that have official or public status but that enjoy administrative and financial independence. Table 8.1 gives a list of such establishments.

Performance of state-owned enterprise in Jordan

No rigorous comprehensive studies have been made on the relative performance of SOEs in Jordan. Nevertheless, anecdotal evidence and consumers' experience with all the public utilities have resulted in an almost general consensus that public corporations and establishments in Jordan operate at low efficiency levels, and that their

Table 8.1 Establishments with official or public status but administrative and financial independence

Official financial institutions	*Official service institutions*
The Central Bank	Jordan Public Universities
Amman Financial Market	Institute of Public Administration
Social Security Corporation	Vocational Training Corporation
Jordan Investment Corporation	Jordan Academy of Arabic
Agricultural Credit Corporation	Royal Geographic Centre
Industrial Development Bank	Radio and TV Corporation
Housing Bank	Special Communications Commission
Cities and Villages Bank	Industrial Estates Corporation
Development and Employment Fund	Free Zones Corporation
National Aid Fund	Exports Development Corporation
Zakat Fund	Housing and Urban Development
Orphans Fund Corporation	Corporation
Military Service Consumers Corporation	Agricultural Marketing Corporation
Economic and Social Organization for	Civil Service Consumers Corporation
Retired Servicemen	

performance suffers from bureaucratic procedures, non-competitive pay scales, a poor incentive structure, and excessive labour redundancy. Furthermore, and without comparable research on the incidence of investment failures in the private sector, the general public took special notice of spectacular failures of a few large state investment ventures, such as the Jordan Wood Company, the Jordan Glass Company, the Jordan Pre-Cast Concrete Company, the Cinemagraphic and Television Production Company and the Jordan Publishing Company. The total initial capitalization of these ventures, which were established during the 1970s, amounted to about JD 35 million.

Observers' judgement came across on some of the already mentioned SOEs as follows and are quoted verbatim:

Power

The enterprises in the power sector all suffer from a weak financial condition due in part to pricing policies that do not cover costs. The regulatory framework has not worked satisfactorily: JEA is the *de facto* regulator, and the two power distribution companies have not been able to operate with a degree of independence that would allow them to pursue efficiency enhancing measures. The Natural Resources Authority suffers from lack of commercial focus, and functions as both a regulator and an operator.

Telecommunications

TCC has not been able to meet the growing demand of an economy that is increasingly becoming information intensive. Demand satisfaction is low (connected lines were forecast to be only 55 per cent of demand by 1997), and the quality of service is unsatisfactory (calls completion rate is 40 per cent compared to 65–75 per cent in developed countries. The existing institutional structure impedes private participation and competition. As a public enterprise subject to political influence, TCC has not achieved a level of efficiency and responsiveness that would support the development of an efficient private sector.

Transport

Royal Jordanian Airlines has been suffering significant losses; it is currently insolvent.[1]

State portfolio in commercial enterprises

As already mentioned, there is significant state ownership of equity shares in public shareholding companies (PSCs listed in the Amman Financial Market) as well as in private (unlisted) shareholding companies. The effect of such ownership on the performance of those enterprises becomes an issue only in cases where the state shares in a company constitute a high enough percentage of equity to give the state a controlling influence on the management of the company.

The evidence points to very little constructive influence of the presence of public officials on the boards of corporations. Quite to the contrary, a comparative study of the performance of government-controlled PSCs (defined as those in which government equity exceeds 15 per cent of a company's stock) versus the corresponding performance of companies with no, or negligible public interest, indicates a positive correlation between government ownership or control and inferior financial performance.

The study was initiated at the office of the Prime Minister by Safwan Bataineh, and has been utilized in a recent report by the World Bank (World Bank 1994). The study concludes that companies in which the government has invested heavily appear to have experienced lower growth in sales, lower average annual pre-tax return on investment and significantly lower productivity gains. These trends are evident cross-sectorally, in declining industries (for example steel) as well as in emergent ones (for example, telecommunications), indicating that either ownership or control or both, and not some other variable, is responsible.

The evidence is that companies in which the government had no ownership interest grew faster, invested more, earned higher returns, achieved larger productivity gains and generated more employment for each dinar worth of investment than in the case of either public enterprises or public shareholding companies with sizable government equity.

A more recent study by Jordanian academic economists Khalid Al-Wazani and Ghalib Salih utilized a more sharply defined analysis of PSCs listed in the directory of the Amman Financial Market. Two groups were selected, one consisting of companies where the government owns 50 per cent of more of equity, representing companies influenced by government management; the other, where government equity was either nil or not exceeding two per cent, representing companies under private sector management. Furthermore, the companies selected had to have financial data covering the whole decade 1984–94. As a result, six companies turned up in each group. The findings were that companies under private sector influence showed more favourable results in terms of two sets of indicators used in the study, one set included indicators of profitability, and the other set included indicators of capital adequacy and indebtedness (Al-Wazani and Salih 1996).

While the broad conclusions of both studies about the inferior efficiency in government-associated enterprises appear plausible, it is still an open question whether the blame should essentially fall on the ownership as such or on the control and management pattern associated with it. It may be true in theory that representation of the government on companies' boards tends to open the way for non-commercial considerations to influence corporate policies. In practice, however, this is not the main or the most important drawback of that representation. The main drawback appears to be that government representatives are generally the less concerned and the less active members of boards of directors, being as they often are civil servants whose appointment to board membership is meant primarily to reward them for services rendered elsewhere, rather than to contribute dynamic managerial skills to the companies to which they are deputized. However, this does not necessarily lead to the conclusion that private sector board members of PSCs are the more skillful or the more dynamic. This writer's experience has shown that the motives and attitudes of private sector representatives could be as remote from the objective interests of the company as those of the least competent of government representatives. More seriously, the incidence of abusive behaviour pertaining to conflict of interest tends to be more rampant among private sector board members than among government representatives.

The reform process

Acknowledgment of the generally poor performance of SOEs has induced the government to deliberate SOE privatization policies and measures as far back as the mid-1980s. However, practical steps were slow and disorderly. Important reasons for the slow progress in reform are the inertia, resistance to change and vested interest in the government machinery. Decision-making with regard to privatization is to a large extent delegated to the governing bodies in charge of the corporations and enterprises that are candidates for privatization. These bodies are not keen to liquidate themselves or reduce their control domain. The government at large is also highly sensitive to the adverse politics of laying off large numbers of staff and employees that will inevitably result from privatizing the highly over-staffed corporations. A large number of members of parliament are sensitive to this issue as well as to the very idea of giving up public control over the so-called 'strategic' industries. It is of relevance that most of the present generation of politicians and civil servants have come of age amidst the ideological precepts of the 1950s and 1960s.

Over the last several years considerable momentum has been gathering to implement reform. The following are among the more important measures already taken.

Power

By 2 April 1996 the General Law of Electricity had completed the legislative circuit and was issued as Law no. 10 of 1996 which terminates in principle the state monopoly of power generation by allowing the licensing of other companies, including major industrial companies that desire their own power plants. It provides for the organization of electric energy generation and for its transmission, distribution and consumption as follows:

- Electricity generation, including the construction of power plants for public purposes, will be provided by the 'National Electricity Public Shareholding Company' (NEPSC), as well as by other public shareholding companies that are licensed for this purpose.
- Companies undertaking major industrial projects may be licensed to have their own power generation facilities to meet their own needs and to exchange electric power with other similarly licensed companies.
- The NEPSC will be responsible for the transmission of electric power, the construction of transmission lines and the management of the transmission network. It shall also allow other companies licensed to generate power to use the transmission network.
- The NNEPSC is initially totally owned by the government and in accordance with the General Law of Electricity it is exempted from all provisions of the current Companies Law that might conflict with this singular ownership. However, all such exemptions from the Companies Law will be annulled once the NEPSC offers its shares for public subscription.
- As far as the electric power is concerned, the functions of the Ministry of Energy and Natural Resources are therefore redefined to focus on policy-making, supervision and quality control, planning and regulation.

The law, however, does not deal with the monopolistic concessions of the two electricity distribution companies in the Amman and Irbid governorates. The draft that preceded its enactment provides for further similar concessions for distribution companies in other parts of Jordan, originally supplied by the Jordan Electricity Authority. The subject, presumably, is still under deliberation.

Telecommunications

Efforts towards privatizing the telecommunications sector started as early as 1987. The Ministry of Planning sought World Bank assistance to draw up plans and terms of reference for turning the TCC into a company operating on sound commercial principles. Although the decision was to keep it for the time being within state ownership, the policy was to open up space for private enterprise to provide ancillary services in telecommunications, other than the conventional telephone network which the TCC did not provide but which were by law within its exclusive monopoly. The measures for commercialization reached the stage of an international tender to select world class management consultants to undertake the restructuring of the TCC on modern management principles. The process was interrupted in the wake of the economic crisis of 1989, but was revived with fresh momentum in 1994. In the meantime, and as an interim measure, the law of telecommunications was reinterpreted to allow the government to license private sector producers to provide ancillary services. The first to benefit from this amendment was the Jordan Paging Radio Company.

Subsequently, a new law of telecommunications (Law no. 13 of 1995) was enacted which limits the duties of the Ministry of Post and Telecommunications to policy-making and regulatory functions. This law establishes a legally and financially independent entity named the Organization for Regulating the Telecommunications Sector (ORTS) which has the power to recommend to the Council of Ministers 'granting licenses (to private parties) for the construction and operation of public telecommunications networks and the provision of telecommunications services to beneficiaries on fair competitive basis'.

Accordingly, licenses have been granted since then to a cellular telephone service with participation by Motorola (Jordan Mobile Telecommunications Services), to two local electronic mail services with patch access to international electronic mail (NETS and ACCESS), and lately to SPRINT for on-line access to the international internet.

State portfolio in commercial enterprise

Recent measures taken by the Jordan Investment Corporation (JIC), where the minister of finance is the chair of the board, reflect the current official drive towards commercialization and privatization of SOEs but without JIC giving up on its role in promoting new investment ventures. Thus, in the course of 1994–5, JIC unloaded to the private sector about JD 17.3 million (about US$ 25 million) worth of its shares in PSCs, reducing in one case its share from a majority of 87 per cent to a (still significant) minority of 31 per cent (Table 8.2). At the same time, the JIC has been a main player and participant in the capitalization of public corporations that have been converted from SOEs into PSCs. It has been also instrumental in promoting and capitalizing no less than six new important investment ventures in the course of 1994–5.

Strategy of future reform

The strategy of economic reform in Jordan is the subject of active discussion between the government and the staff of the World Bank and the IMF. The general public is also involved through the debate in parliament, in the media, in academic and professional seminars and public lectures and, most recently, across the infant local networks of electronic mail.

With regard to SOEs, the strategy currently under consideration by the government, as suggested by the draft of an action plan drafted in consultations with the World Bank, include the following components:

Table 8.2 Jordan Investment Corporation (JIC): main disinvestments in 1994 and
1995

Company name	Company's capital (JD million)	JIC share in capital before disinvestiture (%)	JIC share in capital after disinvestiture (%)	Value of sales (JD '000)
1994				
Jordan Tobacco and Cigarettes	1.5	16.7	13.3	205.0
Arab Investment Bank	10.0	<1.0	0.0	216.0
Arab International hotels	7.24	34.7	32.6	420.0
Middle East and Commodore hotels	5.1	<1.0	0.0	228.2
Miscellaneous				23.2
1995				
Paper and cardboard	3.0	27.4	19.7	951.8
Hotels and tourism	3.668	87.7	31.2	15,300.0
Total 1994 and 1995				17,344.1

Source: Jordan Investment Corporation (unpublished).

- Complete the registration of the public utilities in the power and telecommunications sectors as public shareholding companies under the existing companies law. Financial advisers should then be recruited to assist with their privatization and, finally, shares should be sold to strategic partners.
- Complete divestiture of the district electricity distribution companies IDECO and JEPCO.
- Privatize the Aqaba Railway Company by tendering a concession for the operation of the company.
- Proceed with plans to privatize selected SOEs in which the state has large equity (>40 per cent) by selling its stake to strategic partners. A first case in point is the Jordan Cement Company.
- Sell or lease out to private sector loss-making enterprises in the portfolio of the Jordan Investment Corporation.
- For the JIC, consolidate its minority holdings in a mutual fund, with technical assistance by an experienced and reputable bank. Once the mutual fund is ready, its shares will be floated on the Amman Financial Market.

Concluding remarks on the reform strategy

This writer supports the efforts to restructure SOEs into shareholding companies with modern management systems. However, there is a serious problem with a strategy based on the proposition that disposing of state shares to the private sector is an unqualified blessing in all circumstances. There are three cases to consider when we examine the validity of this proposition.

1 The case of PSCs that operate in competitive markets and in which the state has a share, which does not give it control over management. Examples for this case are the Arab International Hotel Company, owner of the Amman Marriott Hotel, and the Jordan Hotels and Tourism Company owner of the Jordan Inter-Continental Hotel. The state owns about 32 per cent of equity in each, but control is clearly in the hands of private sector partners and the hotels are professionally managed by world-class hotel management firms. In this case, the basis for the JIC decision to keep or sell the state's shares is purely on a profit maximization basis as practiced by a normal portfolio investor that weighs the trade-off between capital gain in the short run and a steady stream of income over the long run. An additional consideration for the JIC in its capacity as investment promoter is whether the proceeds of the sale are needed to take advantage of imminent investment opportunities. There should be no doctrinaire attitude in this case one way or the other as the performance and efficiency of the enterprise are not affected by the decision.

2 The case of PSCs that operate in competitive markets and in which the state has a control share which gives it virtual control over management. An example of this case is that of Jordan Hotels and Tourism Company at the time when the state owned 87 per cent of its equity. Here there is a good reason to divest the larger part of the state's equity in order to hand over control to the private sector which is in principle more responsive to market considerations and more protective of the enterprise's business interests against political and other non-business considerations.

3 The case of PSCs that operate in a non-competitive market in accordance with the state's concession. Examples of this case are the legal monopolies such as the Jordan Phosphate Mines Company, the Arab Potash Company, the Jordan Cement Company, the Jordan Petroleum Refinery Company and the Jordan Leather Tanning Company.

Regardless of the state's share in these so-called 'concession companies', and regardless of the original reasons for according them the concessions, these companies by and large, are no less than full-fledged state monopolies, and are likely to be models of inefficiency. The inefficiency is perhaps less obvious in the phosphates and the potash companies because they have to complete in the export markets, but the fact that they are natural resource-based enterprises that generate considerable rent value helps to conceal the inefficiency. Therefore, serious thought should be given to terminating their concessions and opening up their markets for competing producers. Divestiture of the state's shares in these companies should take place together with the termination of the concessions. Otherwise we would be substituting the state monopolies with private sector monopolies.

A meaningful strategy to deal with SOEs in particular, and with privatization and economic liberalization policy in general, should have as its starting point and general course of analysis, not the relative public versus private ownership, but the nature of the relevant markets and the degree of competition and accessibility of those markets. Changes of ownership patterns and divestiture of state property should be considered only if and when they can help liberalize markets or reduce their imperfections, and/or contribute significantly to the improvement in the efficiency of enterprise management.

Since the span of management in government is limited, and since reform of markets in which enterprises operate have precedence over the issue of enterprise ownership, it is suggested that the order of priorities of the strategy for the future should be drawn up accordingly.

A high priority in my view is to complete the liberalization and reform of the financial market. While the market is highly competitive for the most part, distortion is still introduced by the so-called specialized lending institutions, namely the Housing Bank, the Industrial Development Bank and the Agricultural Credit Corporation. These institutions are granted various privileges which are not only costly to the taxpayer but distortive of the market for term lending. Term lending for housing and investment projects should involve all banks, and should be further encouraged by speeding up the creation of the proposed Secondary Mortgage Facility.

Market forces and the interaction of supply and demand can also be imaginatively applied to the reform of certain government services even if they are not of standard market-oriented nature. A good example is what this writer had proposed to the Board of High Education as an approach for overcoming the chronic financial crises of the official (government-run) universities. The approach consists of reforming the financial management of the official universities so that they are run on a cost effective basis, charging students the full cost of a quality education service, while any subsidies to higher education are managed independently by a competent government agency through a system of scholarships reflecting social and economic priorities (see Appendix).

Note

1   Unpublished draft report of a World Bank mission in 1995 made available to the author by courtesy of the Ministry of Planning.

Appendix: a proposal for the financial viability of Jordanian official universities

The government universities are in the business of providing a service (higher education) which is highly valued both by the individual users/consumers (the students and their parents) as well as by the state, which considers expenditure on higher education as investment in social overhead capital. Both sides express their appreciation by willingness to pay a price for this service in the form of university fees paid by the private users and budget subsidies paid by the government.

Unfortunately, however, a severe dichotomy exists between the cost of producing the service and the sum of revenue received from university fees and government subsidies, with the latter (revenue) being far from adequate to cover the costs incurred in providing the service even at the current below standard levels of quality.

That the total price paid by the private and the public sector is below the minimum required for a viable service is shown by the fact that the rate of growth of the number of students admitted to each of the official universities is much higher than the rate of increase of university revenues, and that the ratios of students per classroom and per teacher are continuously rising. The result is continuous deterioration in the quality of education, and the mushrooming of private sector universities which command much higher fees from the students, and are able to pay higher salaries for their teachers, thus successfully competing with the official universities for the better teachers.

Furthermore, with the dichotomy between revenues and costs, the system of accountability is blurred, and there is no way to discover genuine cases of waste and inefficiency. The quality of education is also largely concealed by the supply-determined value of education in the form of the issued university degrees, since these degrees are being marketed in the public sector and in much of the private at their nominal value on par with world standard degrees from the best universities.

A market-supportive reform which is also sensitive to socially desired objectives, will deal with the problem along the following lines:

- Establish university fees per student on the basis of minimum actual costs of delivery of the required educational service at the pre-specified quality. The university management will be accountable for efficient performance through auditing this direct link between costs and revenues. In addition to such quantitative and financial efficiency controls, qualitative controls can be established by the gradual deflation of the nominal value of university degrees through generalizing the practice of competitive examinations for applicants to appointments/employment vacancies in the public as well as in the private sector.
- At the same time the government departments concerned, independent from the management of the universities, should put in place a system of partial and complete scholarships to subsidize the university fees of various well defined categories of students in accordance with equally well-defined social and political criteria which the state deems appropriate and consistent with the financial allocation it is willing to budget for the investment. It could readily be seen that this arrangement would bring to transparency all hidden subsidies, and so improve public accountability and general efficiency of governance.

Bibliography

Al-Wazani, K. W. and Salih, G. (1996) 'Privatization: towards an alternative to enhance effectiveness and efficiency. A comparative study', paper submitted to the Second Conference on Public Administration in Jordan, Yarmouk University, September.

World Bank (1994) 'Consolidating economic adjustment and establishing the base for sustainable growth, country department II', report no. 12645 Ho. 24, chapter v, August, Jordan.

9 Privatization of public enterprises in Sudan

Prospects and problems

El-Khider Ali Musa

Evolution of public enterprises

The emergence in developing countries (DCs) of government-owned (51 per cent or more) and government-controlled entities which were supposed to earn most of their revenues from the sale of goods or services coincided with the initial stages of industrialization and modern economic development. The drive towards industrialization emerged as a policy, given the belief that industrialization would lead to a more rapid rate of economic growth than would otherwise be possible.

Another historical factor which led to the growth of public enterprises (PEs) in DCs, besides ideological conviction in some countries, was that the PEs represented the beginnings of national development efforts following independence (Ramanadham 1984). Although state entrepreneurship on this scale can be found in all countries with mixed economies, according to an international statistical study, their role in the industrialized OECD countries is more limited than in the DCs (Luke 1988). The international statistical study also suggests that the PE sector in the Africa region is larger in terms of the share of weighted gross domestic product (GDP) and weighted gross fixed capital formation than in other regions. While African PEs have remained important in the traditional public utility, transport and communication sectors, they are becoming increasingly prominent in the manufacturing sector (ibid.). The PE sector in Africa is strategically placed in African economies and consequently its performance in each country has important implications for the performance and reform of the national economy.

The evolution of PEs in Sudan is a typical example of the role of PEs in the planned development of DCs (Musa 1990, 1991b). At the time of independence in January 1956 there was virtually no modern private sector. The few private enterprises that existed were owned by foreigners, engaged in retailing and small scale. During the Ten-Year Plan of 1960–70, the onus to achieve economic and social development was placed on PEs. However, the majority of PEs in Sudan, especially those in the manufacturing sector, were established during the Five-Year Plan of 1970–5 and the Six-Year Plan of 1977–83. All PEs established during these economic and social development plans were required to pursue and to achieve the following development roles:

- To create jobs on a large scale to stop emigration from rural to urban areas.
- To obtain balanced development within and between regions within a framework of regional specialization and complementarity to ensure that development of programmes and projects would reflect the potentialities and needs of every region.
- To ensure a balanced distribution of investment over the different regions of the country, so as to eliminate the sense of humiliation and backwardness felt in some Sudanese regions.
- To develop industry as a complement to agriculture giving priority to agro-based and import-substitution industries.
- To achieve self-sufficiency in major consumer goods.

Alongside this role in regional and rural development, PEs in Sudan provided social services to their employees and to citizens of the rural areas. They were seen as necessary to achieve the government's economic and social development goals.

The smooth flow of foreign aid, grants and loans from Arab and international financial agencies and from other friendly countries during the period 1960–80 facilitated the growth of PEs in Sudan. Manufacturing investment in these enterprises grew from 7.5 per cent of total gross investment during the period 1960–70 to 13.2 per cent in 1970–5 and 21.3 per cent by 1983. By the end of 1990, this stood at little more than 25 per cent (Musa 1991b). As a result, the scope of the public enterprise sector grew rapidly and has extended to manufacturing, transport and communications, hotels and tourism, commerce, insurance and agriculture. To date, the size of PEs in Sudan is still significant and their role is important, privatization notwithstanding (Galal 1996).

The financial performance of PEs, however, has been very poor and unsatisfactory for many years (Musa 1987, 1990, 1994a). The aggregate statistics in Table 9.1 illustrate the poor financial performance of seven manufacturing industries: sugar and distillery, textile, food, cement, leather, mining and building materials. Although there is no breakdown for losses per manufacturing industry, the message is clear: generally rising losses from 1971/2 until 1979/80.

These financial losses are attributable to a host of factors, some of which arise because of public (government) ownership and others due to macroeconomic problems. Some of the factors are:

- PEs are required to start or to run activities of a kind or in a location which on strict commercial grounds would not be undertaken.
- PEs may conduct their development role inefficiently and with overmanning for the tasks to be undertaken.
- Compensation for any development role undertaken, including the social role in constructing roads, schools, hospitals and so on, is inadequate to cover the extra costs.
- PEs have overstaffing (disguised unemployment) because of their employment creating role.

Table 9.1 Financial performance of public enterprises in the manufacturing sector (Sudanese
£ million)

Years	Profit(loss)
1971–2	(0.4)
1972–3	(0.3)
1973–4	(1.4)
1974–5	(0.9)
1975–6	(1.6)
1976–7	(2.0)
1977–8	(9.7)
1978–9	(18.2)
1979–80	(17.7)
1980–1	(4.2)
1981–2	(3.8)
1982–3	(0.8)
1983–4	(0.3)

Source: Kappalu 1986.

- There is a chronic shortage of the basic production inputs (e.g. raw materials, spare parts and energy supplies such as fuel and electricity).
- The price of goods considered strategic in Sudan, such as sugar, is held down for economic and social reasons in an attempt to stem inflation and to benefit the poorer sections of the community (Musa 1994b).
- PEs design their accounting and budgeting systems according to the provisions of the government's detailed financial regulations, which do not suit commercial operations (Musa 1987).
- PEs are also required to adhere to the purchases and sales status of the government. These are very bureaucratic and do not facilitate commercial operation.

For more than three decades, therefore, PEs have been a major institution and a vehicle for economic development in Sudan. By the early 1980s, however, a host of exogenous and endogenous factors emerged to constrain the previous subsidization by the exchequer. The huge financial losses made by PEs are now perceived as a burden on the public treasury. Consequently, various governments have shown a willingness to make fundamental reforms, basically privatization, as part of their structural adjustment programmes (Musa 1994b).

The privatization debate world-wide

The term privatization was first used in Britain when the Conservative Government assumed power in 1979. Despite the fact that the term is widespread world-wide, it has no strict definition in the *Oxford English Dictionary* or other dictionaries (Hastings and Levie 1983). According to Hastings and Levie (1983), the term privatization covers a multitude of practices designed to alter the status of business or industry from public to private ownership or control. These include the selling of PEs to management, workforce or private share-holders, public issues of a minority or a majority of shares on the stock exchange, placement of shares with institutional investors, sales of publicly-owned physical assets, allowing private competition where a public corporation previously had monopoly rights and encouraging private contractors to tender to provide social services previously provided within the public sector.

Thus, a privatization policy was first adopted by Britain in the early 1980s. By mid-1989, barely one third of the UK's state enterprises which had existed a decade earlier remained in public ownership, and those which did remain were being prepared for privatization. The government, whose programme for selling off public corporations was almost complete, was increasingly directing its attention to privatization of local authority and health services (Wright, Thompson and Robie 1989). The privatization debate soon spread over the developing and developed countries and has become one of the dominant themes of public policy throughout the world (Heald 1985). Indeed, privati-zation has become the political creed of the 1990s. Governments of every stripe from Moscow to Mexico City are selling their state-owned enterprises as fast as they can (*Economist* 1995). Some scholars urge DCs to emulate Britain and privatize (Young 1986), while others maintain that privatization is the only cure for the ills of the economies of the DCs (Boghilal 1985). Young (1986), suggests that advice and financial support by Britain and western countries for privatization promotion in DCs would do more to accelerate economic devel-opment than unconditional grants.

Political and ideological reasons aside, the privatization of PEs in developed and developing countries, despite the fact that the two may not be twin sisters (van der Well 1992), has been triggered by the claim that PEs are less efficient than their counterparts in the private sector (Pryke 1982, Boghilal 1985, Heald 1985, Young 1986, Kay and Thompson 1986, Iyer 1988, Nellis and Kikeri 1989). Moreover, it has been argued that privatization by itself is likely to lead to some gains in the efficiency of what are now PEs. The underlying idea of privatization is to improve efficiency through encouraging competition by allowing free entry to the market. Proponents of the free market model argue that privatization can address and solve the sources of inefficiencies of PEs which emerged as a consequence of bureaucratic control within the government domain. In addition to these reasons, the privatization literature attributes the spread of the privatization debate to the developing countries to the huge financial losses made by PEs, external pressures from international aid donors and financial agencies like the International Monetary Fund (IMF) and the World Bank, reduction of government's subsidies for PEs and generation of funds to finance new development projects (Heald 1985, Young 1986).

The poor financial performance of most African PEs and the drain on the scarce resources which this represented was the basis of the skepticism that emerged about their role in economic development (Rasheed, Beyene and Otobe 1994). As African governments became increasingly besieged by economic difficulties, it became clear that dissipation of resources through PEs could not be sustained (Economic Commission for Africa (ECA) 1992). Therefore, it is in the course of reacting to the deteriorating economic situation in the continent that the development policies and strategies pursued by many African governments have come under attack. In particular, the use of PEs as opposed to the market has been blamed for the economic woes of the continent (Oyugi 1990). It is this concern that has given birth to what is generally referred to today as privatization.

By the mid-1980s, most African governments had some programme of PE reforms, including privatization, typically in conjunction with effort at economic adjustment and restructuring. Kenya, Nigeria, Senegal, Sierra Leone, Tanzania, Sudan, Egypt, Ghana, Zimbabwe, to mention only a few, are among the African countries implementing wide-ranging reforms and the divestment and/or liquidation of a number of PEs as part of structural adjustment loan agreements with the World Bank (Luke 1988, Adam, Cavendish and Mistry 1992, Zayyad 1992, Agera 1994, Danquah 1994, Ott 1992, Musa 1991a). Thus, privatization is expected to remain high on the agenda for development in Africa for the rest of the 1990s (ECA 1993a). A conference on the subject organized by ECA in Khartoum, Sudan in 1992 had recommended a number of options under privatization, including:

- public offer of shares
- private placement of shares
- management buy-out
- debt–equity swap
- deferred public offer
- liquidation of the PE via the break-up and/or sale of its assets.

The details and an evaluation of the privatization programme in Sudan follow in the next two sections.

The privatization debate and measures in Sudan

The privatization debate in Sudan has been fuelled by the same factors as in other DCs. The major issue which triggered the privatization debate, however, was the poor financial performance of PEs and the negative impact on the public purse. Thus, the most critical policy issue over the ten-year period 1975–85 was the breakdown of fiscal discipline which was first observed in the middle and late 1970s and has remained uncorrected until the present. Government expenditure was stepped up continuously in the second half of the 1970s, from about 20 per cent of gross domestic product (GDP) to a peak of 29 per cent in 1980. As expenditure rose sharply in the late 1970s, revenue followed a gradual downward trend, falling from about 16 per cent of GDP to about 14 per cent. To finance the deficits the government borrowed heavily at home and abroad. The primary source of domestic borrowing was the Bank of Sudan. Credit extended to the government and PEs raised the monetary base twelvefold in just ten years, from 1975 to 1984. Money supply rose at a compound rate of about 30 per cent per year. Inflation rose to an average of 20 per cent per year over the decade between 1975 and 1984 (World Bank 1987).

External public debt rose from US$ 1.2 billion to US$ 8.3 billion over the same period. Debt servicing became a real problem and limited the country's access to additional capital. This change upset both the internal and external balance of the economy. Little progress was made in the real economy. In fact, between 1981 and 1985 the real GDP fell by more than 10 per cent. In spite of the resources devoted to industrialization, the share of manufacturing in GDP was well below 10 per cent.

In view of this situation, the government was urged to adopt a series of adjustment programmes with the IMF and the World Bank. The IMF diagnosed the problem as one of fundamental disequilibrium. Among the factors it listed as causes were:

- distortion in the allocation of resources between sectors, resulting from a distorted cost/price structure
- pervasive public sector inefficiency
- over-involvement of the state sector and the suppression of private initiatives.

The Sudanese Government followed the strategy recommended by the IMF and the World Bank very closely during the period 1978–85. The credit ceiling was extended and expenditure on all social services was cut to the bone to curtail the budget deficit.

None the less, the Sudanese economy continued to deteriorate rapidly throughout the 1985–9 period. The protracted drought, the outbreak of the civil war in the south and political instability were among the factors that aggravated the situation. As a result the cumulative real growth of GDP over the period was hardly positive. The real growth rate calculated over the period was negative by 3 per cent. In 1989, Sudan's total debt amounted to US$ 13 billion and the inflation rate was nearly 80 per cent. The situation was further aggravated by the IMF's declaration of Sudan as a non-cooperative country. Rationing of foreign exchange was extensive. This in turn augmented the shortage of spare parts, imported raw material, infrastructure and energy supplies (electricity and fuel) for the local manufacturing industry.

It was against this background of an acute public finance crisis that the government started privatizing PEs in the early 1980s. The basic object at that time was to ease the state budget deficit through savings from subsidies which otherwise would have been allocated to the loss-making PEs, and by generating other sources of public finance out of the transfer revenues. Thus, in 1983, the government privatized three vegetable oil processing enterprises by selling off 51 per cent of shares to a private investment authority retaining 49 per cent of the share capital. At the same time the government offered two confectionery factories for sale, though these were only sold in 1992. Under pressure from the IMF and the World Bank, the national government planned to privatize more PEs in the second half of the decade. This plan, however, was slowed down by a host of problems.

It is obvious that during the 1980s the national government approached the privatization issue on an *ad hoc* basis. There was no well articulated privatization policy and strategy. Moreover, no institutional and legal framework had been established to prepare and implement privatization of PEs. The decision to privatize any given PE was a purely political one, and was taken by the head of state or the parent minister in charge of the PE. Also, there was neither a clear criterion for the selection of the target enterprises nor identification of the privatizable candidates.

A privatization policy continued in the 1990s under the present government, which took over in June 1989. Ironically, this time the privatization policy was adopted within the so-called 'Sudan's Structural Adjustment Program', which was prepared without pressure from or coordination with international financial institutions. The privatization policy was a major feature of the Three-Year Economic Salvation Programme (1990–3) and the Ten-Year National Comprehensive Strategy (1992–2002). The major objective of the programme was to attach high importance to the role of the private sector, foreign or domestic, as an 'engine of growth'. This represents a major turnaround in the economic development policies of the Sudan which had previously emphasized the role of PEs as vehicles of social and economic development. The following sections provide more details and a critical evaluation of the privatization programme of the 1990s.

Has the privatization programme been effective?

The privatization process in the Sudan has been underway for over a decade. It is high time, therefore, to take stock of its successes and failures and to draw the appropriate lessons and policy implications to date. Two indicators will be used for this purpose: the number of privatization operations carried out so far compared to the number of PEs earmarked for privatization and the microeconomic impact of the privatization operations. To this effect, an analytical framework has been developed. It borrows heavily from a framework developed in a similar study carried out in 1992 by the International Development Research Centre (IDRC) and also a World Bank study (Galal 1990). Following are the components of the framework used for the privatization evaluations. This, however, does not amount to a fully-fledged evaluation of privatization operations. More detailed evaluation should take into account the gains obtained and losses incurred at the macro and micro economic levels. These should include growth of the economy, improvement of the financial performance and productivity of the privatized firms and the costs of privatization such as the loss of jobs and consumers' dissatisfaction.

Diagnosis

Tables 9.2 to 9.6 list the PEs that have been privatized in Sudan to date. With the exception of the vegetable oil mills, which were privatized in 1983, all the other PEs were privatized in the 1990s. Although the privatized PEs represented a number of activities, it is obvious that most of them were in the manufacturing and hotel industries. Also, all the privatized PEs were 100 per cent government-owned and were subject to tight government control, as evidenced by their organizational structure. This was characterized by the multiplicity of authority levels involved in the decision-making process. At the topmost level came the supervising (parent) ministry, which varied from one sector to another. For instance the Ministry of Industry assumed the supervisory role over the manufacturing sector. It was at this ministerial level that all the key decisions, such as pricing, investment and appointment of key management positions were made. Other central ministries also shared the supervisory role in specific decision areas. The Ministry of Finance, for instance, issued government financial laws and regulations to tighten government financial controls, whereas the Ministry of Public Service and Administrative Reform issued regulations related to salaries and wages and other conditions of work. The various sectoral corporations came second in this hierarchy. These corporations coordinated the operations of the individual PEs and initiated the major decisions. Individual PEs came at the bottom of this organizational structure. They were organized as subsidiaries or production units subordinated to the sectoral corporations. All the strategic and operational decisions related to the individual PEs were made either at the ministerial or corporation levels.

Table 9.2 Public enterprises privatized through full sale

Privatized public enterprise	Privatization date
Three vegetable oil mills	1983
Abu Nemiamd sacks factory	March 1992
White Nile tannery	April 1992
Blue Nile packing company	November 1993
Sata company	November 1993
Rea confectionery factory	May 1991
Krikab confectionery factory	May 1991
Port Sudan spinning factory	March 1993
Khartoum tannery	November 1994
Rabak ginnery	December 1994
Koko dairy project	September 1994
Sudanese Mining Corporation	September 1993
Sudan Hotel	January 1993
Red Sea Hotel	January 1993
Atbara Rest Hotel	January 1993
Atbara Rest House	January 1993
Kosti Rest House	June 1992
Sudan Commercial Bank	April 1992
Sudan Cotton Company	December 1994

Source: HCDPSU, Khartoum, Sudan, May 1996.

Except for the telecommunications sector, all the privatized PEs have been working in a competitive environment in line with the liberalization policies of the government. By virtue of these policies, restrictions on imports were lifted and only confined to a few commodities banned for religious, security or health reasons. All other items which were previously banned for protection are now freely permitted. Moreover, price controls in the production, factory and wholesale areas, were eliminated and market forces set free to determine the price levels for all sectors.

Finally, it is worth mentioning at this juncture that most of the privatized PEs in the banking, telecommunications and hotel sectors are profit-making. In the manufacturing sector, however, most of the privatized PEs are either loss making or have not even started operations since installed. As we argued earlier, this is partly attributable to problems related to government ownership. Most important are macroeconomic problems, which are also applicable to the private sector, basically the shortage of production inputs (raw materials, spare parts, fuel and electricity supplies). These bottlenecks are so chronic that some public and private factories have been forced either to go out of business or to operate at a lower capacity. It is this set of problems that privatization *per se* is highly unlikely to solve. Unfortunately these problems will also reduce the possible benefits of privatization.

Strategy

As already mentioned, different governments have adopted a multi-track policy to reform PEs in Sudan since the beginning of the 1980s. One reform alternative which was tried in the sugar sector and in a few other utilities considered

Table 9.3 Public enterprises privatized through partial sale (partnership)

Privatized public enterprise	Privatization date
Gezira tannery	March 1993
Friendship Palace Hotel	March 1993
Telecommunications Corporation (Sudatel)	1993

Source: HCDPSU, Khartoum, Sudan, May 1996.

Table 9.4 Public enterprises privatized by lease

Privatized public enterprise	Privatization date
Grand Hotel	April 1996
Arroust Tourist village	August 1993
Some projects of the White Nile Agriculture Corporation	1993
Some projects of the Blue Nile Agriculture Corporation	1993

Source: HCDPSU, Khartoum, Sudan, May 1996.

as strategic, was commercialization. This reform option centred on the financial and physical rehabilitation of PEs, allowing them greater managerial autonomy, within the government domain, to facilitate commercial operations. This policy paid off in the sugar sector, where PEs have shown a sustainable improvement in their financial and production performance since the beginning of the World Bank-backed rehabilitation project (Musa 1994c).

The bulk of the reform strategies, however, focused on privatization, which was a key feature of the Three-Year Economic Salvation Programme (TYSP) (1990–3) and the Ten-Year National Comprehensive Strategy (1992–2002). As mentioned earlier, the major objective of the TYSP was to emphasize the role of the private sector as an engine of growth in the country. To promote the private sector, the TYSP identified two methods. First, to allow the private sector to invest in the various sectors of the economy which were previously a monopoly for the public sector. To this end, the investment acts were revised with a view to give potential investors, foreign or domestic, the necessary guarantees and privileges as a means to promote competition.

The second method used to facilitate greater involvement of the private sector in the economy was the launching of a sizeable privatization programme. It is worth

Table 9.5 Gratis transfers of public enterprises to state and organizations

Sector	Transferred public enterprise	Transfer date
Agriculture	Delta Tokar Agricultural Corporation	1993
	Delta El Gash Agricultural Corporation	1993
	Northern Agricultural Corporation, North Gezira dairy project	1994
Tourism	Juba Hotel	1992
Miscellaneous	Brick factory	1993
	Sudanese Construction and Building Company	1993
	Sudan Oil Seeds Company	February 1993
	National Cinema Company	August 1992
	Rainbow Paints Factory	1993
	Wafra Chemicals Company	October 1992
	National Distillery Company	January 1993

Source: HCDPSU, Khartoum, Sudan, May 1996.

Table 9.6 Liquidated public enterprises

Public enterprise	Remarks
Nuba Mountains Agricultural Corporation	Liquidated
White Nile Agricultural Corporation	Under gradual liquidation
Blue Nile Agricultural Corporation	Under gradual liquidation
Farm Implements Corporation (S. Kordofan)	Liquidated
Mechanized Agricultural Corporation	Liquidated

Source: HCDPSU, Khartoum, Sudan, May 1996.

mentioning that donors and the international financial institutions had no role in defining the privatization strategy. This was because since the mid-1980s Sudan had been declared a non-cooperative country by the IMF. However, it is obvious that the privatization path was pursued partly to appease the IMF and restore confidence in the Sudan Structural Adjustment Programme, which was not different from the traditional structural adjustment programmes (SAPs) normally prescribed by the IMF. Besides, the privatization programme was also meant to reduce the pressure on the public treasury by reducing subsidies and generating revenues.

The TYSP then outlined the sectors of the economy that would be privatized. These included the agricultural, manufacturing, hotel and tourism, transportation and communication, trading and marketing, banking and energy sectors. All in all, about 124 PEs were earmarked for privatization during the period 1990–3 (*Sudan el-Hadieth* 1992). Out of these only twenty-seven have actually been privatized (Tables 9.2–9.6). The privatization modalities (approaches) used included direct sale of PEs (full or partial) to the private sector (domestic or foreign), sale of physical assets (such as buildings), liquidation and lease. Some economic liberalization policies, such as scrapping import restrictions and price controls, have also accompanied the privatization measures.

A quick and a critical glance at the privatization strategy reveals some problems. First, judged by the number of PEs which have actually been privatized *vis-à-vis* the ones identified for privatization, it is quite obvious that implementation of the privatization programme has not been very successful. Thus, given the political and social constraints facing privatization in Sudan, this privatization programme was too ambitious to be achieved over a three-year time span. In this sense, and to use Bouin's (1991) concept and indicator of effectiveness of privatization operations, the programme has been ineffective.

Second, some of the economic liberalization policies accompanying the privatization strategy have not been implemented consistently. For instance, the Telecommunications Corporation still enjoys natural monopoly after privatization. Also, the trading in gum is still a public monopoly by virtue of the government policies which ban private entry in this business area. Third, while the government has launched the privatization programme to emphasize the leading role of the private sector in the economy, it continued to create PEs, unnecessarily, in the insurance and construction industries in which the private sector is well-established. Fourth, the government has transferred the ownership of some PEs to the state (regional) governments, which strictly speaking, cannot be regarded as privatization. To conclude, one can argue that implementation of the privatization strategy has not been coherent in many aspects. This despite the fact that the government has created the necessary institutional and legal frameworks for the privatization programme as discussed below.

Implementation

This part of the chapter will describe in some detail the privatization mechanism adopted to implement the privatization strategy. In contrast to its policies in the

1980s, the government took a more systematic and pragmatic approach in the privatization of the 1990s. Thus, to implement this programme, the government created the necessary legal and institutional frameworks. To start with, the National Salvation Revolution Command Council, then the highest authority in the country, issued the Disposal (Privatization) of the Public Sector's Utilities (Enterprises) Act in August 1990. The act specifies the establishment and constitution of the High Committee for the Disposal of the Public Sector's Utilities (HCDPSU). Accordingly, the HCDPSU was constituted as follows:

- the Minister of Finance and Economic Planning: chair
- the Minister of Justice and Attorney General: member
- the parent Minister (of privatized PE): member
- the Auditor General: member
- the chair of the Public Investment Corporation: member and rapporteur.

According to the act, the HCDPSU shall have the following powers and functions:

1 Take the decision of disposal (privatization) of the public sector's utilities (enterprises) through any of the following means, namely by:
   - seeking the participation of parties from outside the country in any form of privatization
   - selling to parties other than the government
   - final liquidation.
2 Specifying any of the public sector's utilities for disposal (privatization) and it may, following the identification decision, decide to assign the supervision of the identified utility to the Public Investment Corporation, pending disposal.
3 Concluding contracts of disposal of public utilities on behalf of the state.
4 In case of disposal by participation or sale contracts, restricting the contract by any of the following conditions:
   - by rehabilitation and operation of the utility in accordance with a specified programme
   - by the body into which the utility shall vest, to be transformed into a public company, or by introducing employees as shareholders in the utility
   - by the value of the utility, or part of it, which shall be calculated by capitalizing part of the debts due from government
   - by payment by installments of the value of the sold utility or prompt payment.
5 In case of disposal, by final liquidation, ordering legal procedures and transfer of the liquidated utility's assets to any government body or sell the same.
6 Exercising any legal power to end the service of the employees of the utility specified for privatization, without any prejudice to any post-service benefits.

7   The High Committee, upon breach by any contractor of the terms of the contract of disposal of the utility, after handing the same over to him, may reappropriate the utility, and adopt procedures with respect to the same, in accordance with provisions of this act.

To enable it to execute its functions and exercise its powers, the HCDPSU established the Technical Committee (TC) in which the government, the employees and the private sector were represented. The act then specified the functions and powers of the TC as follows:

1   specify assets and property of the privatizable utility (PE) and evaluate the same technically and financially
2   prepare introductory and publicity circulars for the utilities identified for privatization and submit them to the HCDPSU
3   specify debts and all legal obligations concerning the utility specified for disposal
4   specify the employees of the utility identified for disposal and assess their rights and the manner of dealing with matters thereof
5   specify the financial, technical and administrative systems for supervising the utility during the disposal period
6   specify systems of notification of those desirous of purchasing of, or participation in, the utility specified for disposal, and specify the systems of enabling them to collect information thereabout, and systems of handing the same to them upon completion of the disposal procedure
7   call for tenders from those desirous of purchasing the utility identified for disposal, or participation therein, as to such conditions and manner as may be specified by the HCDPSU
8   receive, analyse and evaluate tenders
9   submit recommendations to the HCDPSU concerning any of the above business or perform any work assigned to it by the HCDPSU or its rapporteur.

Following the establishment of the legal and institutional frameworks, the chairman of the HCDPSU commissioned a review study to make detailed recommendations on the appropriate reform option for the various PEs within the various industries. The review commission then compiled a fifteen-page report. It is this report which guided the privatization operations carried out by the HCDPSU (1990).

Despite the fact that the government has taken a programmatic and systematic approach to solve the many problems associated with the privatization process, serious limitations have been experienced in the implementation phase. First of all, using Bouin's (1991) criterion, implementation of the programme has not been effective. This can be explained by a host of political, economic and social constraints. Second, the HCDPSU failed to carryout some of its functions and exercise its powers according to the act

Table 9.7 Estimated value and actual sales proceeds of some privatized public enterprises

Privatized public enterprise	Estimated value in Sudanese pounds (S£) US dollars ($) and Sterling pounds (£)	Actual sales proceeds (S£, US$)
Abu Neiama sacks factory	S£432,749,347 + $9,251, 349 + £20,000	S£750,000,000
White Nile tannery	S£101,800,000 + $8,600,00	S£120,000,000 + $4,000,000
Sudanese Mining Corporation	S£457,456,799	S£50,106,768
Red Sea Hotel	S£158,553,250	S£110,000,000
Friendship Palace Hotel	$32,214,080	$20,000,000

Source: TNA 1995.

regarding the call for tenders inviting potential buyers. It is widely believed that some PEs have been privatized without publicity in the media (Transitional National Assembly 1995). Another constraint to implement the privatization programme properly in line with the provisions of the act is the HCDPSU's failure to evaluate the assets of the privatized PEs accurately. At times the HCDPSU chose to ignore the evaluations made by the technical government bodies such as the Industrial Research and Consultancy Centre of the Ministry of Industry. Table 9.7 shows the estimated value and the actual sale price of some privatized PEs.

Some believe that under-valuation of assets is deliberate to favour some potential buyers. While this might be true, this is essential to attract the private sector, given the various constraints impeding privatization in Sudan.

The HCDPSU was also very lenient with some private buyers who defaulted (payment of instalments) and did not exercise its powers of re-appropriation in line with the provisions of the act. Consequently, the public treasury lost billions of Sudanese pounds as a result of under-valuation of PEs assets and failure to pay installments on time (Auditor General 1993). These failures have created another political constraint: lack of transparency and popular support for the privatization programme. Instead, the public has become very suspicious about the real objectives of the privatization programme. Privatization has become one of the most controversial issues in the country. It has been hotly debated in the Transitional National Assembly (TNA) and the media.

Economic impact

Generally speaking, there are few empirical studies on the economic impact of the privatization operations at the macroeconomic and microeconomic

Table 9.8 Commercial profitability in three privatized public enterprises

Ownership status	Financial year	ROI
Public (before privatization)	1975–6	(5)
	1976–7	(17)
	1977–8	(8)
	1978–9	(7)
	1979–80	(4)
	1980–1	(7)
	1981–2	(2)
Private (after privatization)	1983	(11)
	1984	11
	1985	(8)
	1986	(0.007)
	1987	(2)
	1988	2
	1989	0.002
	1990	12

Note: Figures in parentheses indicate negative ROI (return on interest).
Source: Musa 1994c.

levels. A study has been carried out by the author in the three vegetable oil enterprises, which were privatized early in 1983 (Musa 1994c). The study compared the operational efficiency of the three PEs, measured in terms of total factor productivity (TFP) and financial ratios, seven years before privatization and seven years after. As Table 9.8 indicates, the study confirms a significant improvement in the financial performance of the privatized PEs in terms of return on investment (ROI), after privatization.

Thus, this improvement in the financial performance is partly attributable to 'going private'. This is because if the company had not gone private, management could not have enjoyed greater managerial autonomy, which enabled it to ease the problem of shortage of production inputs. Moreover, this improvement could also be attributable to declaring massive optional redundancies. Furthermore, a new professional management replaced the government bureaucrats and the fiscal accounting and budgeting systems were scrapped and replaced by sophisticated management information systems such as cost accounting and commercial budgeting. It is worth mentioning, however, that the financial performance of the three PEs show significant fluctuations over the period 1983/1990 following privatization. These range from negative ROI in three financial years 1983, 1986 and 1987 to positive ROI in the other five years 1984, 1985, 1988, 1989 and 1990. This sharp fluctuation is closely associated with the degree of severity of the economic environment of the country, that is, the availability or shortage of the production inputs. None the less, the gains from the privatization operations cannot be judged without considering their macroeconomic (fiscal) impact and the associated social costs.

Political, economic and social constraints

For many reasons, the prospects for widespread privatization in the developing countries are limited (Cook and Kirkpatrick 1988, Adam *et al.* 1992, Bouin and Michalet 1991, Bouin 1991). In this respect Sudan is no exception and a host of political, economic and social constraints have slowed down the privatization process. This is evidenced by the fact that only twenty-seven of the 124 PEs earmarked for privatization, have actually been privatized to date. The following are some of the obstacles experienced in the privatization programme in Sudan:

- Lack of efficient capital markets makes privatization by means of conventional equity sales fairly difficult. Defaults are a good case in point. A recommendation was made to use the Khartoum stock exchange to facilitate the privatization process. The stock exchange, however, is too young to carry out this ambitious programme over a short period.
- In pursuit of the developmental role some PEs were located in rural areas with no or poor infrastructure (transport, communication and electricity supply). This makes them less attractive.
- Since most PEs are experiencing huge financial losses, they are less attractive to potential investors who are profit-motivated.
- Lack of transparency as discussed earlier. This made the privatization strategy unpopular and a sensitive and controversial political issue. It is widely seen as a strategy of transferring PEs to few individuals rather than a new strategy for economic development.
- Despite a reasonably developed entrepreneurship in the private sector, privatization is unlikely to bring optimum gains. This is because of the macroeconomic bottlenecks, that is, the shortage of production inputs (raw materials, spare parts and so on).
- Privatization has brought about negative social consequences (Musa 1995). This is because the divestiture of the Public Enterprises Act 1990 authorized the HCDPSU to create redundancies to facilitate the privatization process. Though there are no statistics on the exact number of layoffs, it is certain that thousands of workers have been retrenched. In Sudatel, in which the government still owns 60 per cent, 6,000 workers out of the total workforce of 8,000 have been made redundant. There is neither a re-deployment programme nor training for the redundant workers. Though the government is committed to the payment of the end of service benefits, at times lack of resources makes these payments 'too little too late'.
- Sudan is trying to implement the privatization programme against all odds: civil war in the south, the public finance crisis, occasional droughts, UN sanctions and above all the lack of support of the World Bank and the IMF. In addition to the other factors, the latter certainly make the programme less feasible since it deprives the HCDPSU of badly-needed technical assistance (for example, foreign expertise) and the resources needed to mitigate the social consequences of privatization such as training of

redundant workers. In this respect Sudan seems to be a unique case if compared to other MENA countries.

- Implementation of the privatization strategy has not been coherent and consistent with the established policies. Examples of the inconsistencies are the invitation and selection of buyers, valuation of assets and creation of new PEs.

The future of the privatization strategy and related agenda for research

It is now more than a decade since the privatization strategy was first used as a reform option. It is essential, therefore, to take stock of the successes and failures of this reform alternative and to draw the necessary conclusions and policy implications. This is vital since privatization will still be high on the agenda of many African countries, as well as in the MENA region. In Sudan, privatization evaluations are badly needed, as privatization is pursued in the Ten-Year National Comprehensive Strategy (1992–2002).

In view of my earlier discussions in the chapter, one can draw the following policy implications, which in my opinion, are useful for effective privatization. Whatever reform option is pursued, the need for urgent PE reform cannot be over-emphasized. As PEs still dominate the economy, their poor financial performance is partly responsible for Sudan's economic malaise. Hence, reform of PEs is a prerequisite and should be part and parcel of an effective economic reform in the country.

- To date privatization has been a useful reform strategy. Besides improving the financial performance of the privatized PEs, it sends a strong wake-up call to all managers of PEs, urging them to improve their financial performance or face the consequences. However, because of the obstacles to privatization discussed earlier, privatization can only be pursued as a long-term programme. The three-year time span initially envisaged is impractical. Various steps have to be taken before offering PEs for sale. In addition to addressing the other problems that contributed to the poor financial performance of PEs, some of them have to be relocated in areas with relatively good infrastructure. The importance of profitable and efficient PEs is widely recognized in this context. Aylen maintains that:

  > A program of privatization in a developing country is really a program for reform. State enterprises that are closely integrated into government bureaucracy need to be separated off. An independent board, financial autonomy and operating freedom are first steps towards improved efficiency and ultimate private ownership.
  >
  > (Aylen 1987)

- Although the government has created the necessary legal and institutional frameworks to avoid problems associated with the privatization process

(Adam *et al.* 1992), serious limitations were experienced in the implementation phase. Strict adherence to the provisions of the 1990 Act regarding invitation of potential buyers and evaluation of assets will restore public confidence and popular support for the privatization strategy.

- In addition, failure to implement the accompanying macroeconomic (liberalization) policies of the TYSP (1990–3) will render the privatization strategy incoherent. Strict adherence to the policies promoting private initiative and restricting state involvement in business, promoting competition and creating a conducive macroeconomic environment (for example, availability of production inputs) is vital.

- Although privatization is still a programme for PE reform, it should not be pursued as the sole reform option. This is particularly true given the various obstacles discussed above. Thus, while using privatization as a long-term reform strategy, alternative reform options have to be seriously considered. One of these is commercialization of PEs (Ndongko 1991). Evaluation of the World Bank-backed rehabilitation project in the sugar industry seems to suggest that, given political commitment, improvement of the financial PEs within public ownership is still possible (Musa 1994c). This is because commercialization will help address many of the problems that originally contributed to poor financial performance. Moreover, the experience of other African countries in using performance contracts to control and improve financial performance of PEs seems to be promising (ECA 1993b). It is worth mentioning, however, that the use of commercialization policies and performance contracts to improve the financial performance of PEs are not easy reform alternatives either. Their feasibility depends largely, among other things, on the credibility and commitment of the government.

- Privatization of PEs is a strategy for reform rather than disposition. Privatization evaluations, therefore, are vital to draw the appropriate policy implications. It is essential to follow up the privatization process with empirical studies to investigate whether privatization has had any impact at the macroeconomic and microeconomic (enterprise) levels and the social consequences thereof.

Despite the fact that many privatization programmes have been based on the argument that privatization improves the efficiency of PEs, there is little empirical evidence to support or refute this argument. A World Bank research project on the effects of privatization was launched in a sample of sixteen PEs in some developed and developing countries (Galal 1990) and there is a research network working on the assessment of PE reforms, including privatization, in some selected West African countries (IDRC 1992). Specifically speaking, the following questions should be put high on the agenda for future research:

1   Has privatization improved the financial performance of PEs?
2   Why has privatization improved or failed to improve the financial performance of PEs?

3   What is the impact of privatization operations on the macroeconomic level (state budget, economic efficiency and productivity)?
4   What are the social consequences (costs) of the privatization operations?

Moreover, a research network to address these questions across the MENA region will have meaningful and comparative policy implications for the decision-makers.

Bibliography

Auditor General (1993) 'Section on privatization of public enterprise', *Auditor General Chamber Report on Fiscal Year 1992–3*, Khartoum.

Adam. C., Cavendish, W. and Mistry, P. S. (1992) *Adjusting Privatization: Case Studies from Developing Countries*, London: James Currey.

Agera, S. T. (1994) 'The civil service and public enterprise reforms: the experience of Zimbabwe', senior policy workshop on 'Assessment of the impact of public sector management reforms in Africa', 5–9 December, Addis Ababa, Ethiopia.

Aylen, J. (1987) 'Privatization in developing countries', *Lloyds Bank Review*, 15–30 January.

Boghilal, P. (1985) 'Privatization of business', *Journal of the Indian Merchant Chamber*, May–June, vol. 97, no. 51: 3–4.

Bouin, O. (1991) 'Privatization in developing countries: reflections on a panacea', Policy Brief no. 3, Paris: OECD Development Centre

Bouin, O. and Michalet, C. A. (1991) 'Re-balancing the public and private sectors: developing country experience', Paris: Development Studies Centre.

Cook, P. and Kirkpatrick, C. (1988) *Privatization in Less Developed Countries: An Overview*, London: Harvester Wheatsheaf.

Danquah, Y. B. (1994) 'Public enterprise reforms and privatization: the experience of Ghana', senior policy workshop on 'Assessment of the impact of public sector management reforms in Africa', Addis Ababa, Ethiopia, 5–9 December.

Economic Commission for Africa (ECA) (1992) *Final Report*, Sudan Academy for Administrative Science and African Training and Research Centre in Administration and Development, seminar on 'Privatization in Africa', Khartoum, Sudan, 24–28 October.

—— (1993a) *Strategic Agenda for Development Management in Africa in the 1990s*, Addis Ababa, Ethiopia.

—— (1993b) *Performance Indicators for African Public Enterprises*, Addis Ababa, Ethiopia.

Economist Weekly (1995) 'How to privatize', 11 March, pp. 15–16.

Galal, A. (1990) 'Does privatization matter? a framework for learning from country experience', Country Economics Department, Washington, D.C.: World Bank.

—— (1996) 'Worldwide trends in size and performance of SOEs', workshop on 'The changing size and role of SOE', Economic Research Forum and World Bank, Amman, Jordan, May.

Hastings, S. and Levie, H. (1983) 'Privatization?' London: Spokesman Bertrand Russell House.

Heald, D. (1985) 'Privatization policies, methods and procedures', paper presented at Conference on 'Privatization Policies, Methods and Procedures', Manila, Philippines,

13 January–1 February.

High Committee for Disposal of Public Sector Utilities (HCDPSU) (1990) *Report of Review Commission on PEs*, November, Khartoum: HCDPSU.

International Development Research Centre (IDRC) (1992) *Analytical Framework for a Research Network on Parastatal Sector Reform in West Africa*, Dakar, Senegal.

Iyer, R. R. (1988) 'The privatization argument', *Journal of Economic and Political Review Weekly*, March: 554–6.

Kappalu, S. A. (1986) 'The public industrial sector', paper presented at the National Conference for the Industrial Sector, Khartoum, Sudan, February.

Kay, J. A. and Thompson, D. H. (1986) 'Privatization: a policy in search of rationale', *Economic Journal*, pp. 18–32, March.

Luke, D. F. (1988) 'The economic and financial crisis facing African public enterprises', *Public Enterprise*, vol. 8, no. 4: 165–75. Yugoslavia: ICPE.

Ministry of Finance *The Ten-year Plan 1960–70*, Khartoum, Sudan.

—— *The Five-year Plan 1970–75*, Khartoum, Sudan.

—— *The Six-year Plan 1977–83*, Khartoum, Sudan.

—— *The Three-year Economic Salvation Programme 1990–93*, Khartoum, Sudan.

Ministry of Planning *The National Comprehensive Strategy 1992–2002*, Khartoum, Sudan.

Musa, E. A. (1987) 'The role of management accounting and accountants in the management of selected Sudanese public and private enterprises', unpublished Ph.D. thesis, University of Bath School of Management.

—— (1990) 'Public enterprise and planned development in Sudan', in J. Health (ed.), *Public Enterprise at the Crossroads*, London: Routledge, pp. 220–7.

—— (1991a) 'Public enterprise and planned development in Africa: the case of Sudan', *Journal of Public Enterprise*, Yugoslavia: ICPE: 289–301.

—— (1991b) 'Privatization in the less developed countries: the case of Sudan', *Journal of African Administrative Studies*, no. 36: 63–9, Tangier, Morocco: CAFRAD.

—— (1994a) 'Comparative performance of the public and private sector companies in the sugar industry in Sudan, East Africa', *Social Science Research Review*, January, vol. 1x, no. 1: 39–58.

—— (1994b) 'Privatization of public enterprises in the less developed countries', in T. Clarke (ed.), *International Privatization: Strategies and Practices*, Berlin: Walter de Gruyter.

—— (1994c) 'Reform of public enterprises in Sudan: is it easy within the government public domain?' *Journal of Public Enterprise*, September–December, vol. 14, nos. 3–4: 404–17.

—— (1995) 'Privatization, worker participation and social consequences in Africa: the case of Sudan', paper presented at international conference on 'Privatization, participation and social Consequences in the East and the West', International Sociological Association, Chemnitz, Germany. 26–28 September.

Ndongko, W. A. (1991) 'Commercialization as an alternative to privatization: prospects and problems', *Africa Development*, vol. 16, nos. 3–4: 101–15.

Nellis, J. and Kikeri, S. (1989) 'Public enterprise reform: privatization and the World Bank', *World Development*, vol. 17, no. 5: 659–72.

Ott, A. (1992) 'Privatization in Egypt: reassuring the role and size of the public sector', in A. F. Ott and K. Hartley (eds), *Privatization and Economic Efficiency*, Aldershot, UK: Edward Elgar: 184–221.

Oyugi, W. O. (1990) 'Privatization in Africa: premises and prospects', in E. Chole, W. Mlay and W. Oyugi (eds), *The Crisis of Development Strategies in Eastern Africa*, Addis

Ababa, Ethiopia: OSSREA, pp. 175–92.

Pryke, R. (1982) 'The comparative performance of public and private enterprise', *Fiscal Studies*, vol. 3: 82–102.

Ramanadham, V. V. (1984) 'Public enterprise in developing countries: the development context', in V. V. Ramanadham (ed.), *Public Enterprise and the Developing World*. London: Routledge and Kegan Paul.

Rasheed, S., Beyene, A. and Otobe, E. (1994) 'Public enterprise performance in Africa', Ljubljana, Slovenia: ECA and ICPE.

Sudan El-Hadieth (1992) Khartoum, 2 April.

Transitional National Assembly (TNA) (1995) *Report of the Financial and National Economy Commission*, Session 21, Khartoum, pp. 1–66.

Van der Well, P. (1992) 'Twin sisters or step sisters? Privatization in the First and the Third World', unpublished paper, The Hague, Netherlands: Institute of Social Studies.

World Bank (1987) *Report on Sudan*, Washington, D.C.: World Bank.

Wright, M. S., Thompson, S. and Robie, K. (1989) 'Employee buy-outs and privatization: analysis and UK evidence', *Annals of Public and Cooperative Economy*.

Young, P. (1986) *Aiding Development*, London: Adam Smith Institute.

Zayyad, H. R. (1992) 'Privatization of PEs: the Nigerian experience', ECA seminar on 'Privatization in Africa', Khartoum, Sudan, 24–28 October.

10 State-owned enterprises and privatization in Turkey

Policy, performance and reform experience, 1985–95

Merih Celasun and Ismail Arslan

Introduction

In the post-1980 era, Turkey's economic policy stance has featured a sustained emphasis on openness in trade and finance, but has lacked a strong commitment to internal adjustment and public sector reforms. The trade policy regime has been liberalized in a gradual but credible manner that facilitated Turkey's accession in 1995 to the Customs Union with the European Union. From 1980 to 1989, the trade reforms were effectively supported by realistic real exchange rates, which yielded an impressive export performance and enhanced Turkey's international creditworthiness. In the post-1989 period, however, the capital account liberalization coincided with the revival of macroeconomic populism in an increasingly contestable political environment, thereby producing unsustainable fiscal and trade deficits. The mismanagement of the macroeconomy eventually led to a major currency crisis in early 1994, to which the government responded with a stabilization programme, entailing considerable social costs in the adjustment period.

As the recent Turkish experience shows, the openness in trade and finance restricts the range of policy instruments available for economic management. This is especially true when currency substitution becomes intensified, and heavy government borrowing distorts flows of funds in favour of the public sector within a shallow financial system. With the reduced government autonomy over trade, monetary and exchange rate policies, an efficient system of public finance gains crucial importance in the pursuit of public policy objectives. To derive greater benefits from market liberalization and increased international integration, structural weaknesses of the public sector also need to be removed, and the institutional basis of private sector development should be strengthened.

In this broad spirit, Turkey's official development plan (1996–2000) envisages a series of structural reforms to bolster the institutional framework of the market system, rationalize the public sector, and promote more vigorous human resources development. Although its ownership is not well-established in Turkey's unstable political environment, the economy-wide medium-term plan nevertheless represents a serious official effort to redefine the role of the state in social and economic development. It calls for the withdrawal of the state from commercial commodity production, more effective handling of the state's regulatory and oversight functions, greater emphasis on social sectors and urban development and broader participation of the private sector in infrastructure investments (State Planning Organization (SPO) 1995a).

At a more operational level, fiscal adjustment is viewed as the centrepiece of the post-1994 adjustment process, which attaches high priority to lowering public deficits and short-term debt stock. The mainstream consensus is that the measures for budget correction (mainly expenditure cuts) need to be complemented by public sector reforms in order to reduce the budgetary burden of public institutions outside the general government, and mobilize new revenues (read privatization) as far as possible. Hence the reform measures for state-owned enterprises and social security system are perceived as key structural components of the ongoing stabilization process.[1]

While the rapid worsening of social security finances is a relatively new phenomenon on the Turkish scene, the financial burden of state-owned enterprises (SOEs) has been a matter of policy concern since the adoption of formal state planning in the early 1960s. Following the post-1980 switch toward a market-oriented economy, the SOE role in manufacturing expansion has been de-emphasized contrary to the prevalent academic opinion favourable to the process of state-led industrialization.[2] In the 1980s, the SOE deficits were contained within financeable limits mainly due to a restrictive policy stance on income distribution. From 1989 to 1993, the SOE deficits quickly widened, however, with the pursuit of populist wage and incomes policies in conjunction with the rising interest burden associated with the new practice of borrowing at market rates. In the wake of the 1994 crisis, SOE borrowing was sharply reduced by deep cuts in wages and investment expenditure (in critical sectors such as energy and telecommunications). Despite the ample rhetoric, the process of privatization has been slow, yielding US$ 2.6 billion in total sales revenue from 1986 to 1995. On the basis of more solid and consistent legal arrangements, the privatization drive is likely to accelerate in the remainder of the 1990s, not so much on the basis of efficiency arguments but 'in response/reaction to the fiscal crisis of the State' as aptly pointed out by Ayubi (1995: 4) in his retrospective on privatization in developing countries.

Against the backdrop of major policy trends, the present chapter provides an evaluation of the aggregate SOE performance and privatization in Turkey during the decade from 1985 to 1995. The essential thrust of our analysis is to construct a consistent basis for the aggregate SOE financial balances, and trace and interpret the observed shifts in performance against the background of the economic policy cycle identified in the 1985–95 period. The present analysis brings out the sensitivity of overall SOE operating surpluses, budgetary transfers and borrowing requirements to changes in major policy characteristics at the macro level. The interpretation of findings is further extended by the consideration of available estimates of public–private productivity differentials and factor shares. Following the evaluation of observed SOE performance, we present a retrospective on Turkey's privatization experience, discuss strategy, methods and legal setbacks, and provide documentation on revenues, expenditures and major asset sales.

The remainder of the chapter is organized in two parts. The first provides background discussions on institutional framework, and outlines the major policy characteristics of successive episodes from 1985 to 1995. In the second section, the chapter first examines the SOE aggregate performance, and then presents an overview of Turkey's privatization experience, ending with the recapitulation of key points.

INSTITUTIONAL BACKGROUND AND POLICY SETTING: THE STATE-OWNED ENTERPRISE SECTOR IN THE TURKISH ECONOMY

Historical background

In the wake of the establishment of the republican regime in the mid-1920s, Turkey quickly discovered the potential role of the state as an owner and producer in industry and services. Although the initial legislation on industrial promotion and state enterprises stressed the eventual transfer of state assets to private industry, subsequent developments in the 1930s and 1940s (connected with foreign exchange shortages) reinforced the use of state enterprises as a vehicle of national development. The ruling elite widely embraced the ideology of statism (an eclectic mixture of capitalism and socialism) in the absence of private entrepreneurship, capital and skills. Notwithstanding the proclaimed economic liberalism of the ruling political party in the 1950s, the state enterprise sector continued to expand in conjunction with the promotion of private industry under heavy protection. The severe payments crisis in the late 1950s was followed by a political regime change (1960), adoption of a new and socially more progressive constitution (1961) and the introduction of formal development planning with the State Planning Organization (SPO) serving as the coordinating agency for planned development.

In contrast to the haphazard policy practice of the 1950s, the post-1961 formal planning approach exercised greater caution in macroeconomic management, attached importance to capital accumulation in industry and benefited considerably from foreign financial assistance The organizing framework was the loosely defined 'mixed-economy system', which allowed the coexistence of public sector and private sector with non-unified rules of the game in their own spheres. The state enterprises were used as direct tools for sectoral and regional development. In turn, private sector development was shaped by restricted trade regimes and financial repression, and encouraged by tax and credit incentives.[3] The early 1970s saw a brief episode of price corrections and export orientation, and a surge in workers' remittances. The response to the 1973 oil shock was reserve decumulation and heavy foreign borrowing, which produced a domestic-demand-led boom, ending with a deep debt crisis in 1978–80. From 1980 onward, Turkey switched to an outward-oriented and market-based economic strategy, which has been researched extensively in the recent literature (Aricanli and Rodrik 1990, Celasun and Rodrik 1989).

In the 1960s and 1970s, the state enterprises proliferated in mining, manufacturing, energy, transport and communications, and banking sectors. Their participation in private joint-stock firms also increased and diversified in an effort to provide additional capital resources to local entrepreneurs. In agro-industries, state enterprises served as institutional devices to support agricultural incomes and influence choices of product mix. The planners' primary motive in expanding this sector was to attain the planned output growth in key industrial sectors to secure the grounds for outward-orientation in later stages. Although not explicitly stressed in the actual planning process, it may also be asserted that state enterprises provided 'regulation by participation in an imperfectly competitive environment in order to prevent the monopolization of the market or exploitation of the consumer' (Adaman and Sertel 1995).

In the pre-1980 era of active development planning, the state enterprises were largely governed within the legal framework of Law 440, which emphasized their commercial nature, but provided large scope for government intervention and limited scope for managerial autonomy. They eventually became burdened by non-commercial objectives, political interference and redundant labour under the umbrella of strong unions.[4] During the foreign financed boom of 1975–7, the non-financial state enterprise borrowing requirement was 70 per cent of the total public sector borrowing requirement (PSBR), which averaged around eight per cent of GNP (in old national income series).

During 1975–7, the total PSBR was financed mainly by central bank credit expansion, which was greatly offset by falling net foreign assets (or rising foreign debt), producing moderate growth of base money and domestic price level. With the sudden termination of foreign lending, a smaller increase in central bank credits had a larger effect on base money and inflation during the episode of the 1978–80 debt crisis (Celasun and Rodrik 1989: 658). Besides a maxi-devaluation, the post-1980 adjustment process therefore entailed steep hikes in state enterprise prices to contain public deficits within financeable proportions, leading to a sharp worsening in income distribution. The latter historical episode justifies policy concerns with state enterprise financial performance, which we analyse further below for the 1985–95 period.

The SOE sector: definition, scope and position in the Turkish economy

For state enterprises, a new institutional framework was introduced by a decree with the force of law (Decree Law 233) in mid-1984. This arrangement contained a clause that allows the government to transfer state enterprises and assets to an extra-budgetary agency for divestiture. In 1986, Law 3291 was legislated to provide a formal legal framework for privatization, which has been revised in later periods as discussed further below.

Decree Law 233 (still in force in 1996) introduced two basic institutional forms: first, state economic enterprises operating on the basis of commercial principles and, second, public economic organizations with monopolistic characteristics, producing basic goods and services (subject to price controls), both of which are totally owned by the state. For both cases, Decree Law differentiates three layers of organization: 'enterprise' (*tesebbus*), 'company' (*muessese*) and 'affiliated partnership'(*bagli ortaklik*). Affiliated partnerships are undertakings with majority shares belonging to an enterprise (Kilci 1994, World Bank 1993). At the end of 1993, the number of so-called enterprises, companies and affiliated partnerships were 34, 120 and 71, respectively, including those in the privatization portfolio.

For the purposes of the present chapter, we refer to the total collection of enterprises, companies and affiliated partnerships defined by Decree Law 233 as state-owned enterprises (SOEs, corresponding to *KIT* in Turkish). It should be emphasized that this coverage excludes SOE participation with minority shares (15 per cent at the minimum) in other enterprises subject to private law. The sales of such minority shares have constituted a notable portion of privatization revenues documented in the last section of this chapter.

A proper review of the SOE sector also requires a distinction between financial and non-financial SOEs. The financial SOEs include major state banks for agriculture, housing and small enterprises, among other smaller units. In the remainder of the present chapter, all our data presentations and evaluations pertain to the non-financial SOEs (*Isletmeci KIT*), unless otherwise noted. For brevity, we shall hereafter refer to the non-financial state-owned enterprises simply as SOEs.

Table 10.1 shows selected indicators to bring out the relative aggregate position of SOEs in the Turkish economy in the post-1985 period. The available estimates show the downward trend in the SOE shares in gross domestic product (GDP) and fixed investment. The employment decline is also notable from 1990 onward. In absolute terms, the total number of SOE personnel were 635,000, 643,000 and 599,000 (including civil servants, contractual employees and workers) in 1985, 1991 and 1993, respectively.

In conjunction with the fall of the SOE share in total fixed investment, it is also observed that the SOE capital formation shifted toward energy, transport and communications at the expense of the manufacturing sector. This shift is definitely a sign of the government's policy bias against public-sector-led industrialization, which has been sharply criticized by a number of researchers (Boratav and Turkcan 1993). Given the budgetary constraints on public investment, it is also important to note, however, the growing importance of highly capital-intensive infrastructure services, which provide complementarities to fixed investments in tradables. In the mid-1990s, Turkey is in fact seeking

Table 10.1 Major indicators of state-owned enterprises in the Turkish economy

A. Share of SOEs in: (%)	1985	1990	1993
GDP[a]	8.5	7.0	6.5
Total employment	3.7[b]	3.6	3.1
Non-agricultural employment	6.8[b]	6.8	5.4
Total fixed investment	24.0	11.2	7.6
Public fixed investment	52.7	36.2	26.5

B. Sectoral structure (%)	SOE value added		SOE fixed investment	
	1985	1990	1985	1990
Agriculture	0.5	0.7	0.4	3.0
Industry				
Mining	16.5	11.2	16.5	7.3
Manufacturing	35.9	35.3	24.9	12.2
Electricity	15.8	13.4	28.1	42.8
Transport and communications	24.9	30.1	29.9	34.5
Trade and services	6.4	9.4	0.1	0.1
Total	100.0	100.0	100.0	100.0

Notes:
a based on 'new' national income series.
b 1988 employment data.
Sources: SPO 1996 for A, and Kilci 1994 for B.

private and foreign resources for energy and transport sectors to prevent infra-structural bottlenecks, which may emerge in the near future.

Finally, the review of aggregate SOE indicators would be incomplete without referring to SOE deficits, which we examine later. In 1993, the SOE borrowing requirement, before and after budgetary transfers was 5.2 and 3.6 per cent of GNP (market prices), respectively. The financing requirements of such proportions contrast sharply with the SOE share in GDP (factor cost), which was about 6.5 per cent in 1993 (SPO 1996: 71–2). At the economy-wide level, these figures point to a serious misallocation of resources, and more so if the high real cost of government borrowing is taken into account.

SOE reform efforts outside the privatization process

Following the initiation of the economic liberalization process in the early 1980s, policy measures taken to reform the SOEs may be viewed in three essential parts: first, price deregulation and reduction of monopoly powers; second, institutional restructuring through the passage of Decree Law 233 (in 1984) and its subsequent amendments and extensions; and third, divestiture process. The reform efforts have not involved the exercise of an intermediate option of involving private sector participation in management (rather than ownership). Although a formal framework for privatization was put in place in 1986, the pace was slow in the initial phases, but gradually gained some strength in the 1990s as discussed further in the last section.

The pricing policy issue is important for the SOE financial performance. Until 1984, SOE prices were subject to ministerial control, but were adjusted frequently in 1980–4 to achieve the financial targets set by the stabilization programme. Decree Law 233 provided the legal scope for price deregulation in the 'state economic enterprise' subsector of the SOEs, but limited the pricing autonomy of 'public economic organizations' with monopoly power in their respective spheres (mainly railways, electricity, communications, airlines, airports, tobacco and alcohol). The same legislation also contained a provision, however, for government-specified restrictions on 'state economic enterprise' prices whenever necessary. In a similar vein, the central government was allowed to impose other duties on the SOEs to pursue non-commercial objectives. For both cases of public policy interventions, the central government was obliged to compensate the SOEs (through budgetary transfers) for the loss of foregone profit (officially termed as 'duty loss') calculated in a way that guarantees a 10 per cent profit margin.

In the initial stages, the required budgetary compensation of the SOEs for duty losses was helpful in restraining government interventions in the price-setting process. In the mid-1980s, this particular policy measure was complemented by the removal of legal state monopolies in sugar, tea, cigarettes, some alcoholic beverages and fertilizer distribution. However, with the intensified political contestation in the late 1980s, the political interference in SOE pricing decisions (and their timing) increased without full reflection on duty losses, which were compensated with time lags and without interest in an inflationary environment.[5] Furthermore, the SOE losses connected with the pursuit of non-commercial objectives (such as regional development, maintenance of redundant employment and income support in various forms) have not been subject to explicit assessment and compensation.

With the passage of time, other weaknesses of the SOE institutional framework have also become apparent. They relate mainly to the rigid personnel regime and lack of managerial autonomy, accountability, performance-based incentive systems and – above all – hard-budget constraints. More critically, the SOEs have remained outside the main features of the normal commercial code from 1984 to 1994 until the enactment of Law 4011, which lifted the ban on the attachment and liquidation of the SOE assets due to non-payment of commercial and tax obligations (Tan 1996, OECD 1995). As part of the policy response to the 1994 crisis, the commercialization of the SOEs remaining outside the privatization process presents new possibilities for improved performance in this sector.

Macroeconomic background, 1985–95

Policy mix over time

The aggregate performance of the SOE sector should be evaluated not only against the background of its institutional framework, but also in relation to the economic policy mix and performance at the macro level. In the earlier inward-oriented policy era, a variety of techniques such as financial repression, forced saving, high tariff walls and concessional foreign lending provided a suitable setting for capital formation in the SOE sector, which in turn contributed strongly to output expansion at the aggregate level. In developing countries such episodes often ended, however, with severe payments crisis, requiring large external and internal adjustment and greater reliance on the price system.

As indicated earlier, Turkey has de-emphasized the role of SOEs in manufacturing development, and shifted public investments toward infrastructure sectors in the post-1980 liberalization period. From 1980 to 1989, the policy stance on income distribution was restrained, and real wages were depressed at historically very low levels through labour market repression (Boratav 1990). These arrangements became politically unsustainable from 1989 onward, and subsequent policy shifts had an adverse impact on public finance (Arslan and Celasun 1995).

Concurrent with the reversal of income distribution policies, the capital account was fully opened up in 1989 to complete the process of external financial liberalization initiated in 1984 with the introduction of foreign exchange (FX) deposit system. This policy move (decided by Turgut Ozal at the presidential level) caught all economic agents by surprise, including official planners, who just completed their work on the Sixth Development Plan (1990–4), which projected steadily rising current account surpluses to reduce foreign debt stock. Evidently, the deregulation of capital account aimed at the unification of domestic and world financial markets as a further step toward integration with the international economy in general and the European Union in particular. In our view, another important motive was to encourage and facilitate capital inflows to relax the financial constraint on surging public expenditures.

In unanticipated ways, the capital account liberalization turned out to be a major change in policy regime, involving floating exchange rates, interest-rate arbitrage and reduced effectiveness of monetary policy. The real exchange rate steeply appreciated in 1989–90 with an unfavourable impact on export expansion. Under the new policy regime, an opportunity was created to finance fiscal deficits by domestic borrowing from the banking system on the basis of rapidly increased short-term foreign liabilities of the banks. As correctly pointed out by Ekinci (1996), the short-term nature of capital flows had to be matched by shorter maturities of government bonds. In the presence of high inflation and risk premium, the budgetary burden of interest payments reached unprecedented levels from 1992 onward. Despite the moderated central bank financing of government deficits (until mid-1993), reserve accumulation induced a rapid expansion of base money and thereby fueled domestic inflation.

During 1992–3, the rise in capital account surplus was matched by the deterioration of the current account balance. The domestic counterpart of this process was the sharp fall in public sector saving. In late 1993, the treasury made a series of attempts to lower domestic borrowing rates by greater recourse to central bank advances and cancellation of bond auctions, when PSBR was rising at unprecedented rates. With the eventual collapse of confidence in government policies, financial markets were destabilized, triggering a currency crisis and sharp nominal depreciation (nearly 100 per cent) in early 1994.

On 5 April 1994, the government announced a stabilization programme, which attached high priority to fiscal adjustment and structural reforms in the pubic sector, including privatization and downsizing in the SOE sector. With the support of the IMF stand-by arrangement, the programme's short-term fiscal adjustment targets were largely realized in 1994 and early 1995. The emerging political instability, however, disrupted the implementation of the programme in late 1995.

For our purposes (that is, to trace the impact of economic policies on SOE financial performance), it seems useful to differentiate the following policy episodes over the 1985–95 period:

- 1985–9, trade and financial liberalization and restrained stance on income distribution
- 1990–1, wage boom and capital account liberalization
- 1992–3, foreign financed boom, greater income support to agriculture and interest shock on public finance
- 1994–5, crisis and incomplete adjustment.

Table 10.2 shows the changing configuration of policy characteristics in successive policy phases in a format used in previous research (Celasun 1994). The description of policy mixes is admittedly crude, but captures the salient shifts over time.

Economic performance

Table 10.3 shows the main indicators of Turkey's aggregate economic performance over the policy episodes identified in the preceding discussion. As a cautionary note, we stress that economic performance cannot solely be explained on the basis of policy premises alone, because it also depends on exogenous factors and changes in economic behaviour. Lacking an empirically tested model with a sufficient coverage, we confine our interpretations to a limited number of points that seem to be suggestive. These are the following:

- The aggregate growth in 1985–9 required minimal net foreign saving and benefited from high public saving and realistic real exchange rates. Nonetheless, the domestic inflation remained high. From 1991 onward, the aggregate growth became associated with widened trade imbalances, reflecting larger import penetration and lower export propensity (not shown explicitly in Table 10.3). The rising foreign saving (= current account deficit) in 1990–3 suggests domestic-demand-led expansion in this interval, which was strengthened by real appreciation. The fall and rise in real GNP in 1994 and 1995, respectively, also underline the strong linkage between growth and trade balance. This pattern points to the importance of demand management, while not ignoring the impact of exchange rates and tariff changes on external balance.

- In the historical period, the movements in real exchange rates and real wages seem to be highly correlated with the implication that real depreciations have been validated (in the general equilibrium system) by real wage reductions, which pose a difficult implementation problem. To maintain the price competitiveness of exports, a greater reliance of

Table 10.2 Post-1985 ecconomic policy cycle in Turkey

Policy characteristics	1985–89	1990–1	1992–3	1994	1995
1 Trade policy					
a Removal of QRs	X				
b *Ad hoc* use of import levies and export subsidies	X				
c Reductions in nominal protection and subsidies		X	X	X	X
2 Domestic finance					
Substantial liberalization	X	X	X	X	X
3 Capital acount					
a Reduced regulation	X				
b Liberalized		X	X	X	X
4 Exchange rate					
a Crawling peg	X				
b Partly managed float		X	X	X[a]	X
5 Demand management[b]					
a Contractionary				X	
b Moderately expansionary	X				X
c Highly expansionary		X[c]	X		
6 Real wages					
a Downward flexibility	X			X	X
b Real wage boom		X	X		
7 Transfers to agricultural producers[d]					
a Low	X				
b Moderately high		X	X		
8 IMF stand-by arrangement				X	X[e]

Notes:
a Currency crisis in early 1994; public announcement of exchange targets from mid-1994 to mid-1995.
b The stance on demand management is based on the comparison of the observed growth rates of domestic demand and GDP over the policy phases.
c Applicable mainly in 1990.
d Based on the estimated of producer-subsidy-equivalent reported by OECD 1994, which provides no data beyond 1993.
e Suspended in late 1995.
Source: author classification of policy characteristics.

Table 10.3 Selected indicators of economic performance, 1989–95

		Annual average				
		1985–9	*1990–1*	*1992–3*	*1994*	*1995[a]*
1	Annual change (%)					
	Real GNP	4.7	4.8	7.2	−6.1	8.1
	GNP deflator	52.5	58.4	65.4	107.3	84.0
2	Index (1985=100)					
	Real exchange rate[b]	92.0	111.0	105.0	85.0	98.0
	Real labour cost[c]					
	Public	106.0	196.0	240.0	222.0	189.0
	Private	96.0	141.0	146.0	117.0	121.0
3	External balance (US$ billion)					
	Trade balance	−3.1	−8.4	−11.2	−4.2	−13.2
	Current account	−0.2	−1.2	−3.7	2.6	−2.3
	Capital account	1.0	0.8	6.3	−4.2	5.0
4	Share in GNP (%)[d]					
	Saving[e]					
	Public	6.0	2.0	−1.9	−1.8	−1.0
	Private	18.4	19.6	23.2	24.8	22.0
	Investment[e]					
	Public	8.7	8.1	6.8	3.7	4.0
	Private	16.0	16.2	18.0	17.8	20.5
	Total public revenue	21.3	19.0	18.5	20.7	19.7
	Primary deficit[f]	1.7	5.2	6.7	0.4	−0.8
	PSBR (total)	4.7	8.8	11.4	8.1	6.5
	of which:					
	SOEs	2.5	4.0	4.0	1.9	0.9
	Central goverment	3.0	4.1	5.5	3.9	4.0
	Other public sector	−0.8	0.7	1.9	2.3	1.6
	Money					
	Reserve money	7.6	5.9	7.0	4.8	4.5
	Broad money (M2)	22.6	18.3	20.5	16.2	16.6
	FX deposits	5.9	6.9	13.1	15.4	17.7

Notes:
a Provisional estimates as of mid-1996.
b Appreciation up.
c In manufacturing.
d Based on 'new' national income series in current prices.
e Saving and investment data in the first column pertain to the 1987–9 period.
f The primary deficit is officially measured as total PSBR minus interest payments in the central goverment budget.
Source: SPO 1995b, 1996. The labour cost estimates for 1994 and 1995 are provisional data.

productivity growth seems to be essential as supported by econometric evidence provided by Arslan and Celasun (1995).
• The growth of real labour costs was indeed massive in 1990–1. This factor accounts for the large drop in public saving and rise in PSBR in this policy episode (see also Arslan and Celasun 1995). The comparison of primary deficit and PSBR values (as per cent of GNP) shows that the interest burden on public finance started to rise from 1992 onward in

response to high-cost short-term domestic borrowing, which was in fact the domestic currency counterpart of short-term external borrowing by the banking system. This is supported by data showing the large magnitude of capital account surplus in 1992–3.

• In terms of primary-deficit reduction, the 1994 fiscal adjustment was stronger than predicted, but the budgetary burden of interest payments (as per cent of GNP) reached a higher plateau. While public revenue showed some increase in 1994, the fiscal correction was engineered mainly through cuts in public-sector investment and real wages.

• Finally, the policy sequence and performance observed in 1985–95 suggest that the financial position of the SOE sector may have strong links with wage policy, trade and financial liberalization, income support policies and government-determined fixed investment expenditures. The next section explores such linkages on the basis of available data.

SOE FINANCIAL PERFORMANCE AND PRIVATIZATION EXPERIENCE

SOE financial performance, 1985–95

Determinants of SOE financial performance over time

In order to bring out and quantify the linkages between government policies and SOE aggregate financial performance, we have processed available data in a form that matches the periodization of policy experience reviewed in the previous section. The relevant indicators are expressed as annual averages over the policy episodes and measured as per cent of GNP, complemented by other measures to establish points of emphasis.

The aggregate financial performance of the SOE sector (as defined on page 228) is examined in two stages. In the first stage, the determinants of operating performance are identified, and their change over time is traced. In the second stage, the sources of SOE borrowing requirement, including factors other than operating results, are reviewed. The government policy effects can be differentiated in this two-stage analysis.

Table 10.4 shows the indicators of operating financial performance, including measures on revenues and main components of operating expenses. The key points emerging from the observed performance measures are highlighted as follows:

• In terms of operating surplus generation (measured either in per centage points of GNP or in relation to sales revenue), the performance was positive if not impressive in 1985–90. However, the operating balance turned sharply negative in the post-1990 period. The deterioration is caused partly by revenue decline and to a greater extent by increases in operating expenses. From 1985–9 to 1992–3, the fall in total SOE

Table 10.4 State-owned enterprise operational surpluses (% of GNP)

	1985–9	1990–1	1992–3	1994	1995
1 Revenues	25.06	21.85	21.46	23.77	20.08
of which:					
Sales	23.49	20.69	20.20	22.29	19.10
2 Operating expenses	23.76	24.23	25.09	26.42	20.79
of which:					
a Wages	2.80	4.65	5.10	4.02	3.12
b Interest payments	1.25	1.47	2.03	2.29	1.28
c Depr. and provisions	2.27	2.61	2.32	3.15	1.69
d Other expenses	17.44	15.51	15.65	16.95	14.69
3 Operating surplus/loss (=1–2)	1.30	–2.39	–3.64	–2.65	–0.71
4 Other income/expenditure	–0.82	–0.34	–0.36	–0.42	–0.70
5 Internally generated resources for investment financing (=2c+3+4)	2.75	–0.12	–1.67	0.09	0.28
Memo items:					
Duty losses accrued on goods sold	0.51	0.59	0.99	0.48	0.31
Operating surplus/loss adjusted for duty losses	1.82	–1.79	–2.65	–2.17	–0.40
Wages/sales (%)	11.90	22.50	25.20	18.10	16.30
Interest payments/sales (%)	5.30	7.10	10.00	10.30	6.70

Source: author calculations based on SPO 1995b, 1996.

operating surplus was nearly 5 percentage points of GNP, which is more than the size of annual public spending on education.

- If the ratio of total operating expenses to total revenues remained constant, the decline in SOE operating surplus (from 1985–9 to 1992–3) would have been 0.2 rather than nearly 5 percentage points, given the observed proportional decline in revenues. These figures underline the negative contributions of the sharp rise in factor costs in the early 1990s, stemming from changes in the institutional and policy environment. From 1985–9 to 1992–3, as expressed in terms of shares in sales revenue, wage costs increased from 12 to 25 per cent, and interest payments from 5 to 10 per cent, while 'other expenses' (mainly covering costs of intermediate inputs) remained proportionally unchanged.
- The post-1990 wage shock stemmed from the reversal of the government's policy stance on income distribution (Onis and Webb 1992, Senses 1992). The rise in interest payments also originated from the change in the government's policy, which shifted borrowing strategy from foreign sources to domestic debt in market terms. The SOE deficits induced by the wage shock were increasingly financed by high-cost domestic bank lending, leading to a rapid build-up of short-term debt in some SOEs. The debt consolidation exercise in 1992 was helpful in curbing further rise in interest payments.
- The declining trend in SOE revenues has a number of causal underpin-

nings such as more rapid real growth of the non-SOE sectors, policy interventions restricting market-responsive SOE price adjustments (some of which are measured by duty losses accrued), impact of trade liberalization on import-competing SOEs and some sales revenue drop due to the exit of a number of cement plants privatized in the early 1990s. The rise and fall in duty losses reflect mainly the policy stance on agricultural income support.

• In the context of adjustment to the 1994 crisis, the SOE operating losses have been reduced in a notable fashion. The reversal in the policy stance on income distribution resulted in lower wage costs and duty losses. The upward price adjustments are reflected in SOE sales revenues in 1994, but it seems that the price correction effort was weakened in 1995. The adjustment at the operational level, discussed later, was supported by investment cuts.

The evaluation of financial performance at the operational level needs to be extended further to crystallize other factors affecting the SOE borrowing requirement (shortly SOE's PSBR), which is measured by the difference between gross investment outlays and available resources as shown in Table 10.5. The SOE gross investment outlays comprise fixed investment and change in stocks, including the inflationary adjustment on stock levels. Resources include internally generated funds (defined on Table 10.4) and budgetary transfers (from the central government budget as well as extra-budgetary funds, also covering the privatization account). Budgetary transfers consist of capital injections, duty loss compensation and aid to the SOE sector.

As indicated earlier, SOEs became an institutional vehicle of the government's drive to develop infrastructure systems in the latter half of the 1980s. As shown in Table 10.5, SOE investment expenditure was high in

Table 10.5 State-owned enterprise borrowing requirement (% of GNP)

	1985–9	1990–1	1992–3	1994	1995
1 SOE gross investment	5.82	5.13	3.51	2.61	1.91
Fixed investment	4.23	2.41	1.99	1.36	1.10
Changes in stocks	1.59	2.72	1.53	1.25	0.81
2 Resources for SOE					
gross investment	3.34	1.17	−0.45	0.72	0.98
of which:					
Internal resources	2.75	−0.12	−1.67	0.09	0.28
Budgetary transfers	0.59	1.29	1.22	0.64	0.70
3 SOE borrowing requirement					
(SOE PSBR) (=1–2)	2.48	3.96	3.97	1.89	0.92
Memo item:					
SOE PSBR before budgetary					
transfers:	3.08	5.25	5.18	2.53	1.63

Source: author calculations based on SPO 1995b, 1996.

Table 10.6 Major loss-making state-owned enterprises and their PSBR, 1992–4

	1992	1993	1994
Share in SOE PSBR (%)			
major loss–making SOEs	7.15	65.9	73.2
of which:			
Soil Products Office (TMO)[a]	16.9	12.5	23.0
Sugar Corporation (TSFAS)	11.8	9.4	3.8
Monopoly Administration (TEKEL)[b]	14.2	21.1	10.0
Hard Coal Mining (TTK)	4.2	4.0	6.4
Electricity Board (TEK)	7.1	0.3	–1.6
Iron and Steel (TDCI)	13.3	10.0	16.6
Railways (TCDD)	4.0	8.6	15.0
Other SOEs	28.5	34.1	26.8
Total SOE PSBR	100.0	100.0	100.0
(borrowing requirement)			
Memo item: share of 7 loss-making SOEs			
in total SOE wage bill:	51.0	53.0	47.0

Notes:
a   Mainly engaged in state purchase of cereals.
b   Tobacco monopoly, also producing alcoholic beverages.
Source: SPO 1995 Annual Programme.

1985–9. It was financed to a considerable extent by internal funds, received mild support from the budget and thereby led to deficits which could be financed by foreign borrowing. In 1990–1, internal resources vanished (as shown in Table 10.4), fixed investment declined, but government's support policies for agriculture resulted in large stock accumulation (mainly, wheat and tobacco purchased above world prices), yielding large PSBR, despite more generous budgetary transfers. In 1992–3, additional investment cuts could not reverse the trend in borrowing requirement, because operating losses increased further (all changes viewed in per centage points of GNP). The SOE's PSBR was eventually lowered in 1994–5 by enhanced operating balances (via real wage cuts) and sharp reductions in fixed and inventory investments (involving deep cuts in infrastructure projects).[6]

The evaluation of aggregate SOE performance brings out strong connections with the government's investment programme, wage and agricultural income support policies, and financial liberalization. Our broad evaluation would be incomplete without a brief reference to the distribution of borrowing requirement within the SOE sector. Table 10.6 shows the largest loss-making SOEs and their shares in sectoral PSBR during 1992–4. The seven largest loss-makers account for about 70 per cent of SOE's PSBR and 50 per cent of the total SOE wage bill. The first three SOEs shown on Table 10.6 are agents of the government's agriculture support policies; and their aggregate deficit was more than 40 per cent of the total SOE borrowing requirement in 1992–3. It is instructive to note that 'the producer subsidy equivalent', which is a measure of the transfers to agricultural producers from consumers or tax payers due to agricultural policies, increased from 28 per cent in 1988–9 to 41 per cent in 1991 and about 38 per cent in 1992–3 as estimated by OECD for all agricultural commodities in Turkey (OECD 1994: 102).

Complementary indicators of SOE performance

The preceding evaluation of aggregate SOE financial performance may be extended by the consideration of additional indicators estimated elsewhere. Table 10.7 gives data on factor shares of public and private enterprises included in the 500 largest industrial firms regularly analysed by the Istanbul Chamber of Industry. The estimates for factor shares are annual averages for the historical policy episodes identified in the present chapter. These estimates further highlight the vast impact of the post-1989 wage boom on public-sector firms in contrast to the moderate impact on private firms. From 1990 to 1993, the annual average share of labour in (net) value added exceeded 100 per cent in public firms, exhibiting a drastic rise from 43 per

Table 10.7 Factor shares in the 500 largest industrial firms, 1985–94[a]

	Annual average			
	1985–9	*1990–1*	*1992–3*	*1994*
A Factor shares in net value added (%)[b]				
Public firms				
Wages	43.2	103.2	111.4	91.4
Interest payments	35.3	53.4	61.0	53.6
Rents	0.2	0.4	0.3	0.3
Profits	21.3	–57.0	–72.7	–45.3
Total	100.0	100.0	100.0	100.0
Private firms				
Wages	34.5	52.1	49.2	42.2
Interest payments	37.1	27.8	25.1	28.1
Rents	0.6	0.8	0.8	1.0
Profits	27.8	19.3	24.9	28.7
Total	100.0	100.0	100.0	100.0
B Private/public productivity differentials				
Ratio of labour productivities (LP)[c]				
Private LP/public LP	1.5	2.0	2.1[c]	
Ratio of capital productivities (KP)				
Private KP/public KP	3.6	3.9	3.7[c]	

Notes:
a Firms engaged in mining, manufacturing and energy sectors.
b Excluding depreciation.
c For 1992 only.
Source: *Journal of the Istanbul Chamber of Industry* (various issues) for factor shares; and Ozmucur 1993 for labour productivity data. Labour productivity (LP) is defined as net value added per employee, and capital productivity (KP) as the ratio of real net value added to real fixed assets.

cent in the 1985–9 period of wage repression. In the 1990s, the share of interest payments in value added also increased substantially in public firms, reflecting the policy switch toward domestic borrowing in market terms.

Table 10.7 also provides estimates of private/public factor productivity differentials based on earlier research by Ozmucur (1993). Value-added per worker in private firms was one and a half times higher than in public firms during 1985–9, and two times higher in early 1990s, mainly due to labour shedding in response to the wage shock. As expected, the public/private capital productivity differentials are much wider, because of higher capital intensity in mining and electricity sectors, in which public sector participation is greater.

The public/private productivity differentials point to the existence of a considerable scope for static efficiency gains in the industrial SOE sector, if proper reforms are implemented (OECD 1995). In the absence of disaggregated assessments of factor intensities, capacity utilization rates, labour redundancies and market conditions, caution needs to be exercised, however, in arriving at quick estimates of potential efficiency gains at the aggregate level.

Privatization in Turkey

General remarks

In terms of cross-country standards of progress in privatization, Turkey's reform effort has yielded limited results during the past decade (see World Bank 1995, Kikeri, Nellis and Shirley 1992, UNCTAD 1994). In the mid-1980s, the political enthusiasm for privatization was high, but an important opportunity was missed to forge a durable strategy on a sound legal basis. In 1990–3, the divestiture process gained visible momentum, generated a notable rise in revenues, but encountered legal obstacles and reversals with increased labour and political opposition (Sanver 1993). In response to the currency crisis, the 5 April 1994 stabilization programme accorded high priority to privatization, announcing ambitious targets for sales revenues and closures, most of which could not be achieved due to social and legal difficulties. However, the government was able to pass three important legislations in 1994 providing a more enabling environment for privatization, commercialization of remaining SOEs and increased private sector participation in infrastructure build–operate–transfer (BOT) projects. It may be noted that total privatization revenues from 1986 through 1995 amount to US$2.6 billion (in net terms).

In reviewing Turkey's reform experience in the past decade, three key aspects should be emphasized at the outset. First, privatization has been viewed and practiced mainly in its narrow sense, namely divestiture, with limited attention to other forms of private sector participation (with minor exceptions) in SOE management and operations. Second, the policy process has not been sufficiently concerned with capacity-building for the enhancement of the regulatory functions of the state with an eye to establish a competitive market system. Third, SOE reform and divestiture have not been effectively integrated to provide coordination and vision for policy choices and actions (Ertuna 1993).[7]

Against the backdrop of these general observations, the remaining parts of this section present a highly condensed overview of Turkey's privatization experience. The aim is to highlight the broad characteristics of what has actually transpired in the privatization process in an admittedly selective fashion.[8] Hence, a comprehensive review of the privatization controversy and micro-level research remains outside the scope of the present overview.

Legal-institutional arrangements

The institutional arrangements for privatization largely reflect Turgut Ozal's (prime minister, 1984–9 and president, 1989–93) style of political governance, which involved a heavy use of two techniques, namely extra-budgetary funds and decrees with the force of law (decree laws). These mechanisms were amply used to by-pass parliament and regular bureaucracy, centralize control within the prime ministry, facilitate adjustments in the legal framework and increase flexibility in revenue–expenditure management. Such an approach proved to be useful in trade and financial liberalization and implementation of large infrastructure projects, but eventually became too arbitrary and created resentment within the government establishment, thereby reducing elite support for structural reforms in the public sector. The process of privatization was initiated in such a spirit and style with high hopes of speedy implementation.

As noted earlier, Decree Law 233 (introduced in 1984) defined a new organizational framework for SOEs with a clause allowing their divestiture. In 1984, another legislation (Law 2983) created a new extra-budgetary fund agency, the Mass Housing and Public Participation Administration (MHPPA), which would be responsible for the divestiture process (as well as housing development) through the issue of revenue sharing certificates, equity stocks and operating rights. In 1986, Law 3291 established the legal framework for privatization and extended MHPPA responsibilities in the sale of assets and liquidation of units subject to the cabinet guidelines. Law 3291 outlined the procedures for the transfer of SOEs to the MHPPA and their subsequent restructuring and privatization. In 1990, the MHPPA was separated into two extra-budgetary funds: Mass Housing and Public Participation Administration (PPA) by Decree Law 414. The PPA was given the authority to execute the privatization process.

As a legal framework of privatization, Law 3291 remained in force until 1994. It contained, however, a number of features which prevented the applicability of commercial code to companies with more than 50 per cent public share, and limited the flexibility in labour adjustment. Moreover, the High Planning Council (HPC) was given burdensome responsibilities in the governance and control of large SOEs transferred to the divestiture process.

Such burdens definitely reduced the effectiveness of HPC in evolving a coherent medium-term policy framework. In the early 1990s, subsequent legal amendments (through decree laws) attempted to rearrange decision-making responsibilities for SOEs to be privatized, but such attempts created further legal uncertainties in the implementation process (Kilci 1994).

In the aftermath of the 1994 currency crisis, Law 3987 was enacted to authorize the government to carry out and speed up its privatization programme through decree laws. This so-called 'authorization law' was abolished by the constitutional court on the ground that privatization should be regulated by laws rather than decrees. In 1994, a number of new laws and decree laws concerning the privatization of the Turkish Electricity Board and telecommunication services were also abolished by the constitutional court (Tan 1996).

In response to such legal setbacks, a more comprehensive legal framework was legislated in November 1994. The new law on privatization (Law 4046) established the Privatization High Council as a policy-making body, and the Privatization Administration (PA) as a centralized implementation agency, both under the authority of the prime minister. The PA takes charge of the corporate governance of SOEs transferred to its portfolio of assets and units to be privatized subject to the guidelines set by the high council. The new law provides greater flexibility in the choice of privatization techniques, and emphasizes transparency in all transactions.

Furthermore, there are other notable features in the new legal framework. The key innovation is the recognition of labour adjustment issues and redundancy payments. The proceeds of privatization are to be used mainly in meeting the costs of divestiture, labour adjustment and financial restructuring of enterprises in the PA portfolio. For 'strategic' SOEs (defined as monopolies or enterprises important for national security and/or public interest), the state is allowed to retain a golden share with veto powers in corporate decisions. For specified monopoly enterprises and public services (such as railways, postal services, tobacco and alcohol, and telecommunications), the new law allows privatization techniques other than ownership transfer. Law 4046 stipulates the completion of preparatory work for the privatization of all state banks except the 'four main banks', namely the Central Bank, Agricultural Bank, People's Bank (for small enterprises) and Eximbank (for foreign trade) in two years.[9]

The new legal framework (Law 4046) has been supplemented by another legislative act (Law 4107, May 1995) for the privatization of telecom services, allowing the transfer of 49 per cent of ownership, of which 15 per cent is earmarked for the postal office and employees' fund, and 34 per cent for sales to the private sector. The telecom privatization law was partly amended in mid-1996 to strengthen the legal basis for valuation and bidding methods after the annulment of a number of articles by the constitutional court.

A major source of legal difficulties is the absence of explicit statements on privatization in the Turkish constitution. The constitutional court takes the position that privatization is not an unconstitutional practice. However, in its annulment of various privatization laws, the court has adopted certain views and interpretations which have effectively constrained executive action in this area.

In the absence of constitutional guidelines for the transfer of the state ownership and operational control, the constitution court tends to treat privatization as the 'reverse' case of the government takeover (national-ization) of private assets.[10] The constitution contains explicit statements regarding the protection of the property rights of private agents, and requires specific enabling laws for the transfer of private ownership (to the government sector) at realistic rates of compensation. In a similar vein (but in reverse direction), the court rulings stress the need for detailed laws, spec-ifying the conditions under which a particular mode of valuation and privatization (among a predetermined set of alternatives) would apply in the implementation process. The stated concerns of the court are the protection of the overall public interest, preservation of parliament's ultimate authority on matters of ownership transfer and avoidance of arbitrary administrative preferences in the privatization of government property and operations. Moreover, the court which considers certain infrastructure services (such as power utilities and telecommunications) as strategically important for national security and social welfare, expects case-by-case legislation for their privatization and regulation, and takes a critical view of their large-scale sales to foreign nationals and entities.

Notwithstanding the highly cautious stance of the constitutional court on issues of ownership transfer, government officials view the new legislative framework (as of mid-1996) as a more workable and sound legal basis for future privatization. Success will depend, however, on the choice of strategy and strength of implementation, besides other important factors such as the degree of public support and complementary policies for structural adaptation and social safety net.

Strategy and implementation

In the mid-1980s, after introducing the relevant institutional framework, Turkey missed an important opportunity to adopt and evolve a strategic approach to privatization. Based on sectoral assessments, a master plan proposal (prepared by Morgan Guaranty Trust during 1985–6) recommended priority listings and methods of privatization for a bundle of thirty-two SOEs (Aktan 1993, Kjellstrom 1990). Such an approach was considered unsuitable for local conditions and quickly abandoned. In subsequent periods, the objec-tives and methods of privatization have been subject to frequent turns and twists in response to changing political and market conditions.

At the outset, the main stated objective of privatization was to attain effi-ciency gains and better resource allocation in a growing market economy. However, in 1986 the High Planning Council added ownership dispersion as

Table 10.8 Privatization revenues, 1986–95 (US$ million)

	1986–93	1994	1995[a]	Total
1 Gross privatization revenues				
Block sale	956.0	7.8	312.9	1,276.7
Asset sale	30.5[b]	4.6	182.8	217.9
Public offering	430.4	2.8	0.0	433.2
International offering	0.0	330.0	0.0	330.0
Sale on ISE[c]	435.9	66.6	19.7	522.2
Total	1,852.8	411.8	515.4	2,780.0
2 Privatization revenues realized[d]				
Block sale	700.4	178.3	264.8	1,143.5
Asset sale	6.1	1.4	151.5	159.0
Public offering	422.0	2.7	0.0	424.7
International offering	0.0	316.3	0.0	316.3
Sale on ISE[c]	435.9	66.5	19.7	522.1
Total	1,564.4	565.2	436.0	2,565.6

Notes:
a   As of 31 December 1995.
b   Including US$14 million from the sale of incomplete plants.
c   ISE denotes Istanbul Stock Exchange.
d   Sale proceeds from privatization, including previous year's installments collection.
Source: Privatization Administration 1996a, 1996b.

another key objective. In later periods, the privatization objectives shifted toward fiscal concerns, namely revenue generation for the government and/or deficit reduction in the SOE sector.

Following a number of relatively minor asset sales and public offerings, an attempt was made to accelerate the pace of privatization through block sales of five cement companies and one aircraft catering company to foreign investors in 1989. These sales were not consistent with the 1986 guidelines of the High Planning Council, which emphasized ownership dispersion, and specified target groups of buyers. This inconsistency in government decision-making provided an opportunity for the political opposition to challenge block sales to foreigners in courts, creating a host of legal problems which were resolved in 1992. Foreign investors continue to own and operate these companies.

During 1985–9, total proceeds from privatization amounted to less than US$0.2 billion. In the early 1990s, the process gained momentum, generating sales revenues of about US$1.3 billion from 1990 to 1993. In the aftermath of the 1994 crisis, the announced programme was ambitious, but the implementation was stalled by legal difficulties connected with the revised framework (Authorization Law 3987), which was annulled by the constitutional court. With further legislative efforts, Law 4046 was passed, as noted previously, providing a sounder basis for privatization in 1995. However, the actual proceeds amounted to 10 per cent of the government programme target for privatization revenues in 1995.[11]

Table 10.9 Turkey: main privatization cases, 1986–95

Year/Company	Sector	Privatization 1985 revenue (US$ 1,000s)	Public share (%)[a]	Shares sold	Privatization method	Purchased by
1986–9						
Ankara Cimento	Cement	33,000	99.30	100.00	Block sale	SCF (F)[b]
Pinarhisar Cimento	Cement	25,000	99.90	100.00	Block sale	SCF (F)[c]
Subtotal		58,000				
1990–1						
Adana Cimento	Cement	45,077	47.28	47.28	Public offering	
Arcelik	Consumer durables	80,049	9.20	9.20	Public offering	
Cukurova Elektnk	Power generation	85,940	30.15	30.15	Public offering/block sale	Rumeli Elektrik (D)[d]
Erdemir	Iron and steel	151,020	48.60	22.71	Public offering	
Konya Cimento	Cement	27,180	39.87	31.13	Public offering	
Petkim	Petrochemicals	145,805	99.97	7.83	Public offering	
Subtotal		535,071				
1992–3						
Askale Cimento	Cement	31,158	100.00	100.00	Block sale	Ercimsan (D)
Corum Cimento	Cement	35,000	100.00	100.00	Block sale	Yibitas (D)
Denizil Cimento	Cement	70,100	100.00	100.00	Block sale	Modern Cim (D)
Gaziantep Cimento	Cement	52,695	99.73	99.73	Block sale	Rumeli Cim (D)
Ipragaz	Liquid gas	64,066	49.33	49.33	Block sale	Primagez (D)
Iskenderun Cimento	Cement	61,500	100.00	100.00	Block sale	Oyak-Sabanci (D)
Kepez Elektrik	Power generation	33,570	43.68	33.53	Public offering/block sale	Rumeli Elektrik (D)
Ladik Cimento	Cement	57,560	100.00	100.00	Block sale	Rumeli Cim (D)
Netas	Telecomms equipment	110,510	49.00	27.75	Public offering/block sale	NTL (F)[e]
Sivas Cimento	Cement	29,400	100.00	100.00	Block sale	Yibitas (D)
Sanliurfa Cimento	Cement	57,405	100.00	100.00	Block sale	Rumeli Cim (D)
Tofas	Automotive	26,655	39.00	17.87	Block sale/public offering	Fiat (F)
Trabzon Cimento	Cement	32,551	100.00	100.00	Block sale	Rumeli Cim (D)
Subtotal		662,170				

Table 10.9 (continued)

Year/Company	Sector	Privatization 1985 revenue (US$ 1,000)	Public share (%)a	Shares sold	Privatization method	Purchased by
1994						
Tofas	Automotive	330,000	21.13	16.67	International offering	
1995						
Havas	Airport handling services	36,000	60.00	60.00	Block sale	Yazeks (D)
Adiyaman Cimento	Cement	52,500	100.00	100.00	Block sale	Teksko (D)
Kumas	Magnesium processing	108,100	99.74	99.74	Block sale	Zevtinoglu (D)
Sumerbank	Banking	103,460	100.00	100.00	Block sale	Ipeks Tekstil (D)
EBK/Ankara	Meat processing	29,209	100.00	100.00	Block sale	
SEK/Istanbul	Dairy products	29,740	100.00	100.00	Block sale	Taciroglu (D)
Metas	Iron and steel	57,900	42.55	42.55	Block sale	Rumeli Hol. (D)
Subtotal		416,909				
Total		2,002,150				

Notes:
a At the time of offering.
b SCF: Societé Cement Français.
c F: foreign.
d D: domestic.
e NTL: Northern Telecom.
Source: Kilci 1994 and Privatization Administration Bulletins.

Table 10.10 Cumulative cash balance on privatization account, 1986–95 (US$ million)

	1986–95	(%)
A Resources[a]		
1 Privatization revenue	2,566	73.1
2 Dividend income	825	23.5
3 Foreign loans and grants[b]	6	0.2
4 Other cash inflows[b]	112	3.2
Total resources	3,509	100.00
B Uses		
1 Transfers to Treasury	558	17.7
2 ISE purchases[c]	134	4.2
3 Transfers to SOEs		
a Capital increase	1,830	57.9
b Credits	145	4.6
c Social aid and labour adjustment	29	0.9
4 Expenditures in privatization		
a Consultancy	34	1.1
b Bidding announcements/public relations	30	0.9
c Payments to related companies	367	11.6
5 Other cash outflows	35	1.1
Total uses	3,162	100.00
C Balance on privatization acount	346	

Notes
a   Cash proceeds.
b   Applicable only in 1995.
c   Denotes Istanbul Stock Exchange.
Source: *Privatization Administration* 1996b.

Table 10.8 shows privatization revenues from 1986 to 1995 and their breakdown by methods of sales. In order to highlight the characteristic features of major privatization cases, Table 10.9 gives a listing of divestitures with sales revenues above US$ 25 million from 1986 to 1995. The cumulative proceeds from twenty-nine major cases account for about 80 per cent of Turkey's total privatization revenue. Table 10.9 also shows that about 70 per cent of the revenues from major cases were realized through block sales (mostly to core investors) and international offerings, thereby indicating the limited contribution of the whole effort to ownership dispersion in the domestic economy.

In turn, public interest also relates to the use of revenues generated in the privatization process. Table 10.10 displays the cumulative cash balance in the privatization account. Although the contents of some expenditure categories (e.g. item 4c) are unexplained, the available cash flow figures (in US$ terms) indicate that the cumulative value of capital injections, credits and transfers to SOEs and their companies in the privatization portfolio is nearly equal to total privatization revenues (excluding dividend income). This evidence suggests that a greater caution needs to be exercised in official medium-term projections of overall public-sector finance, which tend to treat divestiture proceeds as an important source of 'net' revenue.

Implications and conclusions

In Turkey's historical development process, the SOE sector served as an institutional vehicle of industrialization, capacity-building, regional development, employment generation and income support to the agriculture sector. Eventually, the SOE sector became burdened, however, with the proliferation of non-commercial objectives, labour redundancy and political interference. In the post-1980 economic liberalization era, the government policy de-emphasized the role of SOEs in manufacturing development, and shifted the structure of public investment expenditures toward infrastructure sectors (mainly energy, transportation and telecommunications). Despite the diminished role of SOEs in industrial capacity expansions, their assets, operations and labour use are still significant at the national and sectoral levels, and thus provide an ample scope for opportunistic political behaviour in the public policy process.

In the present study, the authors provide a broad evaluation of the SOE sector as a whole (excluding financial state enterprises) from the period 1985–95, which is supplemented by a retrospective on the SOE reform process. The quantitative measures shown in the chapter are derived from the new official data base established in connection with Turkey's Seventh Development Plan (1996–2000), and therefore they may exhibit considerable differences from those provided in earlier research.

The present analysis brings out strong linkages between the aggregate financial performance of SOEs and the government's policy mix at the economy-wide level. The observed shifts in the overall SOE financial position are strongly connected with changes in policy stance on wages and income support to agriculture, government-imposed investment programmes and modes of deficit financing (impacting on interest burden), and also seem to be affected (in ways not precisely quantified) by import liberalization and inflation abatement concerns.

The implications of policy–performance linkages are mainly twofold. First, the observed operational inefficiencies at the enterprise level should not totally be attributed to managerial and technical weaknesses, because they may simply be reflecting costs imposed by public policy choices, which are not adequately compensated by budgetary transfers. Second, any reform process aiming at the commercialization and/or privatization of the SOE sector should squarely face the political task of transferring non-commercial functions (mainly income support schemes and job creation) to the general government (at the central and/or local levels), which requires adaptations in organizational, budgetary and incentive structures. This point has been totally missed in Turkey's reform strategy until recently, and seems to explain – to a considerable extent – insufficient public support for structural reforms in an environment of widely observed income and regional inequalities.[12]

Our retrospective on the institutional aspects of the SOE reform process highlights a number of important points. The commercialization of the SOEs has been unduly delayed until 1994, when the commercial code became partly applicable with the ban on the attachment and liquidation of SOE assets. The process of privatization has been hampered by *ad hoc* approaches to legal arrangements, heavy reliance on statutory decree with the force of law, insufficient dialogue with labour unions, political opposition and local business communities. Furthermore, the overall financial coordination of the SOE sector has been weakened as the number of SOE companies transferred to the portfolio of the privatization agency has grown steadily despite the limited progress in divestiture process.

As part of the reaction to the 1994 currency crisis, the legal-institutional framework of privatization has been substantially strengthened. The new privatization approach features more credible arrangements for labour adjustment issues, which enhance the prospects for accelerated reforms. In recent years, considerable experience has been gained in handling intermediate-size privatization cases. With an eye to sustain fiscal adjustment and restore credibility in structural reforms, Turkey seems to be ready for a bolder divestment effort starting from large enterprises in which investor interest is high.[13] In a complementary fashion, high priority needs to be accorded to the design of regulatory structures for private monopolies and rehabilitation of large loss-making SOEs in order to reinforce the efficiency-enhancing aspects of the reform process.

Notes

This chapter is a revised version of a paper presented at the Economic Reseach Forum (ERF) conference on 'State-Owned Enterprises in MENA', 15–17 May 1996 in Amman. The authors are indebted to Faik Oztrak, Zafer Yukseler and Ahmet Tiktik of the State Planning Organization and Metin Ercan of the Privatization Administration for most helpful discussions and valuable clarifications. Useful comments by participants at the ERF workshop are gratefully acknowledged. The views expressed in this chapter are personal and the usual disclaimers apply.

1 See OECD (1995) for a thorough review of the 1994 stabilization programme and related issues.
2 See e.g. Boratav and Turkcan (1993) for assessments of Turkish industrial policies, stressing the role of SOEs together with a critique of neo-liberal approaches.
3 The price distortions caused by these policies had adverse implications for sustainable growth in the longer run. See Hatiboglu (1995) for focused and novel assessments of methodological issues connected with the analysis of domestic terms of trade, productivity differentials and real income growth in Turkey.
4 For a comprehensive analysis of Turkey's SOE experience up to the mid-1970s, see Walstedt (1980).
5 For more detailed observations see World Bank (1993).
6 For the year 1995, the provisional estimates shown on Tables 10.3 and 10.5 for the SOE and total PSBR may have an upward bias. More recent data for 1995 point to the virtual elimination of the SOE's PSBR due to a sharper fall in operating expenses with the implication that the total 1995 PSBR may decline to 5.5–6.0 per cent of GNP. Because of heavier interest burden and widening social security deficit, the total PSBR is projected to rise to around 10 per cent in 1996.

7 In 1992, the government had considered the establishment of a more comprehensive and autonomous institutional framework (TOYOK) for the reforming of the SOE sector, but the draft bill was not enacted by parliament as it was found too cumbersome; for further details see OECD (1993: 25).

8 We draw heavily on Kjellstrom (1990), World Bank (1993), Kilci (1994), Aktan (1993) and Tan (1996). See also Sariaslan and Erol (1993) and various contributions on privatization (with a synthesis paper by Ziya Onis) in the special issue of the *Bogazici Journal* (Bogazici University) vol. 7, no. 1–2, 1993.

9 The public policy functions of state banks and SOEs are discussed and their contributions to industrialization process are emphasized by Senses (1994) in a balanced review of the new privatization law (no. 4046).

10 Our remarks on the constitutional aspects of privatization are based on the constitutional court opinions and annulment decisions reported in the *Official Gazette* no. 22645, 24 May 1996.

11 A notable case of divestiture in 1995 was the ownership transfer of the assets of KARDEMIR, the oldest iron and steel complex in Turkey, to the workers and local groups at the symbolic price of TL1. In the KARDEMIR case, the government assumed all past financial liabilities, the total sum of which (including obligations for severance payments) is unofficially estimated at approximately US$275 million.

12 The status quo bias in SOE governance may also be discussed in the context of 'non-neutral' distribution of gains or losses from the reform. The 'non-neutrality' argument has been examined in different frameworks, emphasizing, for example, differential political capability of pressure groups or uncertainty regarding the identity of gainers or losers from the reform as formally modeled by Fernandez and Rodrik (1991). In Turkey's highly polarized social setting, deeper institutional assessments are needed to explain delays in structural reforms along the theoretical lines of political economy models.

13 The rapid growth of the absorptive capacity of the Istanbul Stock Exchange is a supportive factor for more vigorous privatization efforts in the medium run. From 1989 to 1995, in percentage points of GNP, the stock market capitalization increased from 6.8 to 16.5, and total value traded (a measure of liquidity) had grown from 0.8 to 31.

Bibliography

Adaman, F. and Sertel, M. (1995) 'The changing role of the state from a Turkish perspective', paper presented at ERF Conference on the Changing of the State, 8–10 January, Rabat, Morocco.

Aktan, C. C. (1993) 'The privatization of state economic enterprises in Turkey,' *Bogazici Journal*, vol. 7, nos 1–2: 39–52.

Aricanli, T. and Rodrik, D. (eds) (1990) *The Political Economy of Turkey*, London: Macmillan.

Arslan, I. and Celasun, M. (1995) 'Sustainability of industrial exporting in a liberalizing economy: the Turkish Experience', in G. K. Helleiner (ed.), *Manufacturing for Export in the Developing World*, London: Routledge.

Ayubi, N. (1995) 'Etatism versus privatization: the changing economic role of the state in nine Arab countries,' paper presented at ERF Conference on the Changing Role of the State, 8–10 January, Rabat, Morocco.

Boratav, K. (1990) 'Inter-class and intra-class relations of distribution under Turkish adjustment: Turkey during the 1980s', in T. Aricanli and D. Rodrik (eds), *The Political Economy of Turkey*, London: Macmillan.

Boratav, K. and Turkcan, E. (1993) *Turkiye' de Sanayilesmenin Yeni Boyutlari ve*

KIT'ler (*New Dimensions of Industrialization in Turkey and SOEs*), Istanbul: Tarih Vakfi Yurt Yayinlari.

Celasun, M. (1994) 'Trade and industrialization in Turkey: initial conditions, policy and performance in the 1980s', in G. K. Helleiner (ed.), *Trade Policy and Industrialization in Turbulent Times*, London: Routledge, pp. 453–84.

Celasun, M. and Rodrik, D. (1989) 'Debt, adjustment and growth: Turkey: book IV' in J. Sachs and S. Collins (eds), *Developing Country Debt and Economic Performance: Country Studies*, vol. 3: 615–808, Chicago and London: University of Chicago Press.

Ekinci, N. (1996) 'Financial liberalization under external debt constraints: the case of Turkey', Working Paper 96/05, METU Economic Research Center, Middle East Technical University, Ankara.

Ertuna, O. (1993) 'Privatization of state-owned enterprises: a tool for improving competitiveness', *Bogazici Journal*, vol. 7, nos 1–2: 39–52.

Fernandez, R. and Rodrik, D. (1991) 'Resistance to reform: status quo bias in the presence of individual-specific uncertainty', *American Economic Review*, vol. 81, no. 5: 1146–55.

Hatiboglu, Z. (1995) *Economic Theory and the Turkish Experience*, Istanbul: Literatur Yayincilik.

Kikeri, S., Nellis, J. and Shirley, M. (1992) *Privatization: The Lessons of Experience*, Washington, D.C.: World Bank.

Kilci, M. (1994) *KIT'lerin Ozellestirilmesi ve Turkiye Uygulamasi* (*Privatization of SOEs and Turkish Experience*), State Planning Organization (DPT): 2340– IPGM: 442.

Kjellstrom, S. (1990) *Privatization in Turkey*, WPS 532, Washington, D.C.: World Bank.

OEDC (1993) *Economic Surveys: Turkey, 1992–93*, Paris: OECD.

—— (1995) *Economic Surveys: Turkey, 1994–95*, Paris: OECD.

—— (1994) *National Policies and Agricultural Trade, Country Study: Turkey*, Paris: OECD.

Onis, Z. and Webb, S. B. (1992) *Political Economy of Policy Reform in Turkey in the 1980s*, WPS 1059, Washington, D.C.: World Bank.

Ozmucur, S. (1993) 'Productivity and profitability in the 500 largest firms of Turkey, 1980–92', *Bogazici Journal*, vol. 7, nos 1–2: 63–71.

Privatization Administration (1996a) *Privatization in Turkey*, 4 January, Ankara: Press and Public Relations Department.

—— (1996b) *Privatization in Turkey*, 2 April, Ankara: Press and Public Relations Department.

Sanver, U. (1993) 'Kamu Ortakligi Idaresi Faaliyetleri, 1992–93' ('Activities of the Public Participation Administration'), mimeo.

Sariaslan, H. and Erol, C. (1993) *Turkiye'de KIT'lerin Ozellestirilmesi Sorunu ve Sistematik Bir Yaklasim Onerisi* (*The Problem of SOE Privatization in Turkey and a Proposal for a Systematic Approach*), TOBB (Turkey's Union of Chambers and Exchanges), Yayin no.: Genel: 266 Bom: 18, Ankara.

Senses, F. (1992) 'Labor market response to structural adjustment and institutional pressures', Working Paper ERC/1992–1, METU Economic Research Center, Middle East Technical University, Ankara.

—— (1994) 'Ozellestirme Yasasi Isiginda Ozellestirme, Kamu Girisimciligi ve Sanayilesme' ('Industrialization, public entrepreneurship and privatization in the light of new privatization law'), Working Paper ERC/1994–6. METU Economic Research Center, Middle East Technical University, Ankara.

State Planning Organization (SPO) (1995a) *Seventh Five-Year Development Plan, 1996–2000*, Ankara: SPO (in Turkish).

—— (1995b) *Macroeconomic Developments Before Seventh Five-Year Development Plan, 1990–94*, Ankara: SPO (in Turkish).

—— (1996) *Economic and Social Indicators. 1950–95*, Ankara: SPO (in Turkish).

Tan, T. (1996) 'Legal framework of market economy in Turkey', mimeo, Faculty of Political Sciences, Ankara University.

United Nations Conference on Trade and Development (UNCTAD) (1994) *Privatization in the Transition Process: Recent Experiences in Eastern Europe*, UN Publication no. E.94.II.D.25.

Walstedt, B. (1980) *State Manufacturing Enterprise in a Mixed Economy: The Turkish Case*, World Bank Research Publication, Baltimore and London: Johns Hopkins University Press.

World Bank (1993) *Turkey: State-Owned Enterprise Sector Review*, vols 1 and 2, Report no. 10014–TU, Washington, D.C.: World Bank.

—— (1995) *Bureaucrats in Business: The Economics and Politics of Government Ownership*, World Bank Research Publication, Washington, D.C.: Oxford University Press.

11 Productivity and profitability in the 500 largest firms of Turkey, 1980–94

Suleyman Ozmucur

Introduction

The Istanbul Chamber of Industry (ISO) regularly conducts a survey among the largest industrial establishments in Turkey. Every year questionnaires are sent out to 4,000 establishments. The establishments are ranked according to sales from production. The data for the top 500 are published in September (or in special) issues of the *Journal of the Istanbul Chamber of Industry*.[1]

There are several advantages to using data for the 500 largest firms (FHLF):

- 1994 data are available, compared to the 1991 manufacturing survey of the State Institute of Statistics (SIS).
- Although their number is small, they cover about half of the industrial value added.
- In addition to sales and employment, balance sheet data are also available since 1983.
- Net value-added data are also available, compared to gross value added (including depreciation and indirect taxes) in SIS manufacturing surveys.
- The industrial sector is covered; the mining and electricity sectors are also included. This enables an analyst to make comparisons with the manufacturing sector.

There are also disadvantages:

- Only the largest firms are covered, and this tends to introduce a bias into our data.
- The number is small. It is not possible to get twenty-eight sub-sectors as one can do with the SIS data.
- The coverage of 500 firms changes. There are about 200 firms which have been in the FHLF since 1980 (we should note that this is also a problem in SIS survey data).

In 1994, the FHLF generated 42.7 per cent of value added by Turkish industry. Their corresponding share was 37.9 per cent in 1982, 34.2 per cent in

1985 and 49.6 per cent in 1990. They account for an even greater proportion of value added by the manufacturing sector (44.1 per cent).

With 596,000 employees, the FHLF account for 17.8 per cent of total industrial employment. As expected, the employment contribution of FHLF is not as important as their value-added contribution.

In 1994, the value of exports generated by the FHLF reached US$ 8.4 billion. The corresponding figures for total and industrial exports were 15.6 and 15.3, respectively. They generated 53.5 per cent of industrial exports. The FHLF exported 61.7 per cent of their gross value added. The corresponding share for Turkey was 49.1 per cent. This clearly demonstrates the more pronounced export orientation of the FHLF. Export/gross product ratios are high due to a deep recession in 1994 (–6 per cent growth).

Seventy-nine public enterprises were included among the FHLF in 1980. The number of public establishments increased to ninety-one in 1990, and decreased to eighty in 1992 and seventy-one in 1994.[2]

In general, the percentage of firms making profits is higher in the private sector. In 1994, 90.2 per cent (387 out of 429) of private firms made profits. On the other hand, the same ratio was only 35.2 per cent (twenty-five out of seventy-one) in the public sector.

On average, the number of workers in a public firm is five times that of a private one. Similar ratios can be obtained for sales revenue (3.4), total assets (5.9), equity (6.8) and gross value added (4.0).

It may be helpful to give further information regarding relative sizes among the FHLF. The largest private firm ranks seventh among the 500, and the smallest public firm ranks forty-ninth. The ratio of largest to smallest firm sales from production is 275 (144 trillion Turkish Lira (TL) for TUPRAS and TL 522 billion for Isbir Sentetik Dokuma Sanayi).

The share of the public sector in total sales of the FHLF is 39 per cent, while the share in equity is slightly higher at 45.5 per cent. Other shares in total are given in percentage: total assets, 51.2; fixed assets, 57.5; workers, 50.8; wages, 56.5; net value added, 37.5; and profits, 26.2. The striking share in profit is a clear indication of the relatively high rate of profit in the private sector. The share in net profits is even higher.

Ninety-five per cent of the firms are in the manufacturing sector. These firms appear to create 91 per cent of the net value added. In sector 4 (electricity) there are four firms. They generate 7.9 per cent of sales, and 6.3 per cent of the net value added. They also employ 10.4 per cent of workers. They account for 35.3 per cent of equity and 35.2 per cent of fixed assets.

Profitability

The available data allow us to study three profitability measures.[3]

1   sales profitability = balance sheet profits/sales revenue
2   asset profitability (return on assets) = balance sheet profits/total assets

3   equity profitability (return on equity) = balance sheet profits/equity.

Table 11.1 and Figures 11.1a–11.1c illustrate profit rates for the FHLF. In general, the rate of profit is higher in the private sector. Average sales profitability is 7.6 for private and 1.9 for public sector establishments. The average return on equity is 41.1 for private and 4.1 for public sector firms. The asset profitability is 11.0 for the private and 1.2 for the public sector. These differences are due to higher asset and equity turnover rates in the private establishments. This can be seen very easily if profit rate is decomposed into two components (omitting 100's from both sides):

$$PA = P/A = (P/S) * (S/A) = \text{sales profitability} * \text{asset turnover}$$

or

$$PE = P/E = (P/S) * (S/E) = \text{sales profitability} * \text{equity turnover},$$

where

PA stands for asset profitability
PE, equity profitability (return on equity)
P, balance sheet profits
S, sales revenue
A, total assets
E, equity.

On the average, the equity turnover is 5.2 in the private and 2.8 in the public firms. Meanwhile, assets turnover rates are 1.4 and 0.8, respectively.

Figures 11.1a–11.1c may help us see the trend in profit rates. In the public sector sales profitability had reached its peak in 1985 with a rate of 10.8. A negative trend has been observed since then, reaching a rate of –10.1 in 1992 and –4.6 in 1994. However, this is largely due to a single firm (TEK, Turkish Electricity Institution). The TEK made large profits in 1985, the first year it was included in the FHLF. Since then it has realized negative profits. The private sector set the record in 1980 with a rate of 10.5. The rate has remained within the range of 6.1 to 9.8 per cent, with a negative trend during the 1987–91 period and a positive one after 1991.

With the exception of 1985, asset profitability (return on total assets) appears to be higher in the private sector. It reached the peak of 15.1 per cent in 1994. The average for the period was 11.0 per cent for the private sector while the public sector average was only 1.2 per cent.

The return on equity was higher in the private establishments, reaching a peak of 56.4 in 1993, while from the period 1980–94 the average was 41.1 per cent in the private sector, compared to 4.1 per cent in public enterprises.

Table 11.1 Profit rates in the largest 500 firms in Turkey (%)

	Sales total	Profitability Public	Profitability Private	Equity Total	Profitability Public	Profitability Private	Asset total	Profitability Public	Profitability Private
1980	7.3	4.8	10.5	28.3	16.2	50.7	—	—	—
1981	5.8	3.8	8.2	31.7	22.0	42.9	—	—	—
1982	6.0	5.5	6.5	31.1	25.3	37.6	6.7	4.8	9.4
1983	5.7	4.4	6.9	24.2	18.0	31.0	6.1	4.0	9.3
1984	6.7	6.4	7.0	24.5	20.6	30.7	8.7	7.9	9.6
1985	8.6	10.8	6.1	28.7	26.8	33.6	9.6	9.9	9.0
1986	6.9	7.8	6.1	24.6	19.6	35.3	7.5	6.7	8.8
1987	8.2	7.1	9.1	30.9	18.5	54.4	8.8	5.9	13.0
1988	7.5	6.3	8.5	27,.4	16.8	46.4	8.1	5.3	12.3
1989	6.3	4.4	7.8	20.7	10.1	39.0	7.3	3.8	12.2
1990	4.7	0.9	7.5	16.2	2.3	37.0	5.5	0.8	11.5
1991	−2.3	−12.0	4.8	−10.0	−44.5	24.8	−2.8	−11.3	7.5
1992	0.2	−10.1	7.2	1.0	−38.2	42.3	0.3	−10.0	12.0
1993	2.2	−7.7	8.1	12.3	−32.2	56.4	2.8	−7.3	12.9
1994	4.1	−4.6	9.8	20.4	−20.1	54.3	5.1	−4.4	15.1
Average	5.2	1.9	7.6	20.8	4.1	41.1	5.7	1.2	11.0

Note: There may be differences between figures given here and the rates provided by ISO. ISO gives rate of profit for those firms who make profits, excluding firms with losses. We include all of them with or without positive profits.
Source: calculated by author using ISO data.

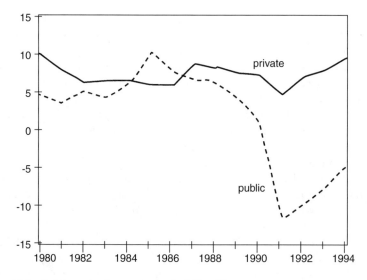

Figure 11.1a Public and private sales profitability (%)

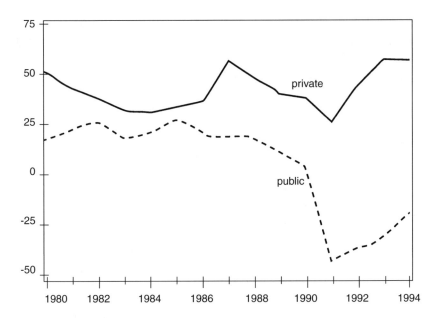

Figure 11.1b Public and private equity profitability (%)

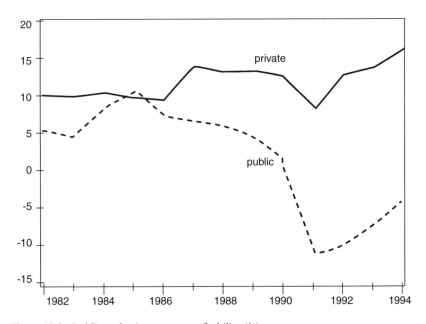

Figure 11.1c Public and private asset profitability (%)

Productivity

In the productivity estimate of the FHLF three productivity measures are used:

1   Labour productivity (net value added in 1987 prices/number of workers).
2   Capital productivity (net value added in 1987 prices/total assets in 1987 prices).
3   Total factor productivity (weighted average of labour and capital productivity).

Labour and capital productivity measures are given in Table 11.2a and Figures 11.2a and 11.2b. They are consistently higher for the private sector. For example in 1994, labour productivity was TL 15.7 million in the private and TL 9.1 million in the public sectors, while capital productivity was 0.24 in the private and 0.14 in the public sectors.

Labour (or capital) productivity gives the impression that net value added is created by that factor only. Total factor productivity tries to overcome this problem. Labour and capital productivity figures are weighted by their relative shares in net value added. However, there is a unit of measurement problem. Labour productivity is in million TL per worker, capital productivity has no unit (TL/TL). In order to make a meaningful comparison these productivity figures are put into index form and then weighted (using value shares of labour and capital in total) to obtain total factor productivity (Table 11.2b and Figure 11.2c).[4]

Factor shares in net value added

Distribution of net value added shows differences in the private and public sectors. The average share of wages in the private sector is 41.6 and 72.0 in the

Table 11.2a Labour and capital productivity

	Net value added no. of workers			Net value added total assets		
	Total	Public	Private	Total	Public	Private
1982	7.6	6.1	9.3	0.238	0.171	0.335
1983	6.3	4.3	9.0	0.185	0.122	0.279
1984	7.2	5.5	9.2	0.205	0.155	0.269
1985	7.9	7.3	8.7	0.192	0.158	0.256
1986	7.9	6.3	9.9	0.200	0.151	0.278
1987	10.0	8.1	12.3	0.224	0.170	0.301
1988	9.9	8.4	11.8	0.232	0.182	0.308
1989	9.1	7.6	10.8	0.233	0.181	0.305
1990	8.9	6.9	11.1	0.218	0.161	0.293
1991	9.0	5.8	12.7	0.212	0.138	0.302
1992	10.4	7.0	14.7	0.232	0.159	0.316
1993	12.3	8.7	16.0	0.228	0.166	0.290
1994	12.4	9.1	15.7	0.186	0.136	0.238
Average	9.1	7.0	11.6	0.214	0.158	0.290

Source: calculated by author using ISO data.

Table 11.2b Index of productivity (1985 = 100)

	Labour productivity			Capital productivity			Multifactor productivity		
	Total	Public	Private	Total	Public	Private	Total	Public	Private
1982	96.4	83.6	107.0	123.8	108.5	130.7	109.4	92.0	120.6
1983	79.5	59.0	102.9	96.2	77.4	108.7	87.0	63.6	106.2
1984	91.0	75.9	105.7	106.5	98.1	104.9	99.3	85.3	105.2
1985	100.0	100.0	100.0	100.0	100.0	100.0	100.0	100.0	100.0
1986	99.8	86.9	113.8	104.4	95.5	108.6	102.6	91.7	110.3
1987	126.7	111.7	140.5	116.4	107.5	117.4	119.9	109.2	124.2
1988	125.6	115.3	135.3	120.9	115.3	120.1	122.5	115.3	124.9
1989	114.9	104.6	123.7	121.1	114.9	119.2	118.2	109.2	121.0
1990	11.24	94.9	127.3	113.7	102.0	114.5	112.9	96.6	120.7
1991	113.8	80.1	146.1	110.6	87.3	118.0	113.2	77.9	133.7
1992	132.5	95.8	168.4	120.8	100.9	123.2	129.5	94.9	145.9
1993	155.4	119.7	183.3	118.7	105.1	113.3	144.0	120.;5	146.9
1994	157.0	125.4	180.5	96.8	86.3	93.0	113.4	122.1	129.9

Source: calculated by author using ISO data.

public sector. The average share of interest paid is 31.8 in the private and 39.7 in the public sectors. Average share of national income definition of profits is 26.0 in private and -12.0 in public sectors. A significant jump in the share of wages was realized in 1989 in both sectors. During 1991–3 the share of wages in the public sector was above 100 per cent. This coupled with an increasing share of interest paid led to a negative share of profits (Table 11.3, Figures 11.3a–11.3c).

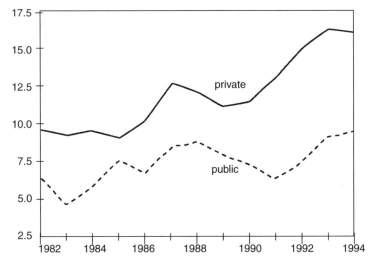

Figure 11.2a Labour productivity: net value added in 1987 prices/number of workers

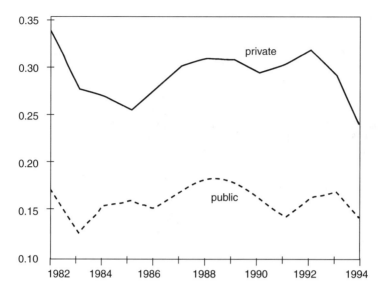

Figure 11.2b Capital productivity: net value added in 1987 prices/total assets in 1987
prices

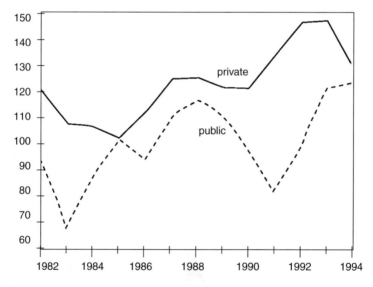

Figure 11.2c Index of multifactor productivity

Table 11.3 Distribution of net value added

	Private sector (400–430 firms)				Public sector (70–100 firms)			
	Wages and salaries	Profits	Interest paid	Rent	Wages and salaries	Profits	Interest paid	Rent
1982	42.3	26.1	31.0	0.6	66.4	10.4	23.0	0.2
1983	42.7	26.9	29.9	0.5	74.9	-2.6	27.5	0.2
1984	38.2	28.0	33.1	0.7	57.4	35.1	7.1	0.1
1985	39.4	23.7	36.2	0.7	41.3	43.9	14.6	0.2
1986	32.6	21.6	45.1	0.7	44.3	26.1	29.4	0.2
1987	29.5	34.9	35.1	0.5	40.5	17.4	41.9	0.2
1988	31.8	29.3	38.4	0.5	35.4	14.3	50.1	0.2
1989	39.1	30.0	30.4	0.5	55.5	3.9	40.4	0.2
1990	48.5	26.2	24.8	0.5	76.0	-14.7	38.4	0.3
1991	55.8	12.5	30.7	1.0	130.4	-99.2	68.4	0.4
1992	50.3	23.5	25.4	0.8	117.5	-82.0	64.2	0.3
1993	48.0	26.4	24.8	0.9	105.2	-63.2	57.7	0.3
1994	42.2	28.7	28.1	1.0	91.4	-45.3	53.6	0.3
Average	41.6	26.0	31.8	0.7	72.0	-12.0	39.7	0.2

Source: calculated by author using ISO data.

GDP growth, inflation, profitability and net value added growth

How do firms react to inflation and growth in gross domestic product (GDP)? There is a positive relationship between GDP growth and net value added growth in the private sector (Figure 11.4a). The correlation in the private sector is 0.64 (which is significant at the 5 per cent level). The corresponding figure in

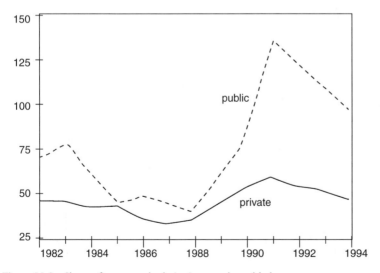

Figure 11.3a Share of wages and salaries in net value added

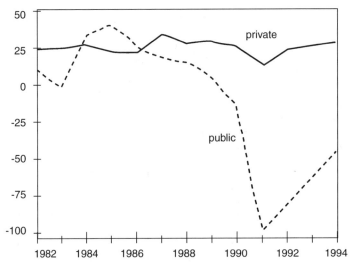

Figure 11.3b Share of profits in net value added

the public sector is only 0.24 (which is not significantly different from zero at the 95 per cent level of confidence).

There is a negative and a significant correlation between the rate of inflation and the growth rate of private net value added (Figure 11.4b); there is no such relationship in the public sector. During inflationary periods, the private sector cuts its production and increases the mark-up (Ozmucur 1995a).

There is no significant relationship between sales profitability and GDP growth (Figure 11.4c). On the other hand there is a positive and a significant

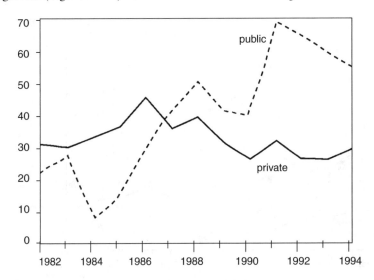

Figure 11.3c Share of interest paid in net value added

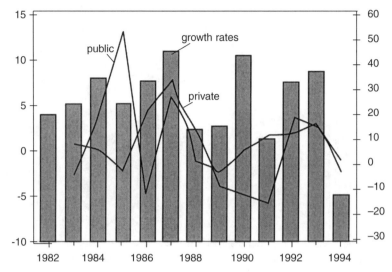

Figure 11.4a GDP growth and growth rates in net value added of private and public sectors
Note: correlation, private = 0.64, public = 0.24.

relationship between the rate of inflation and sales profitability in private sector (Figure 11.4d).

During inflationary periods, the private sector cuts its production and increases its sales profitability. During periods of expansion, the private sector increases its production and possibly profits (but not the profit rate). No such systematic behaviour is observed in the public sector.

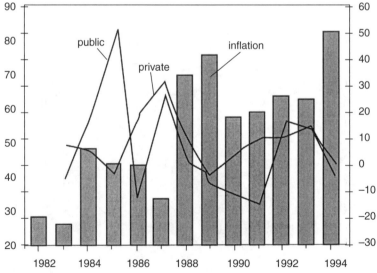

Figure 11.4b Inflation and growth rates in net value added of private and public sectors
Note: correlation, private = 0.56, public = –0.24.

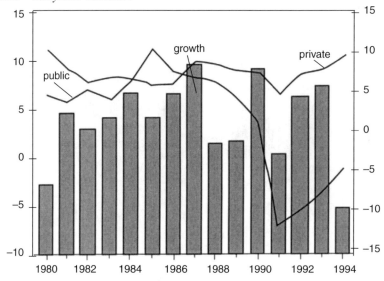

Figure 11.4c GDP growth and sales profitability

Note: correlation, private = 0.32, public = 0.16.

Factor shares and sales profitability

There is no relationship between the share of wages in net value added and sales profitability in the private sector (Figure 11.5a). On the other hand, there is a very high negative correlation between the share of wages in net value added and sales profitability in the public sector (Figure 11.5b).

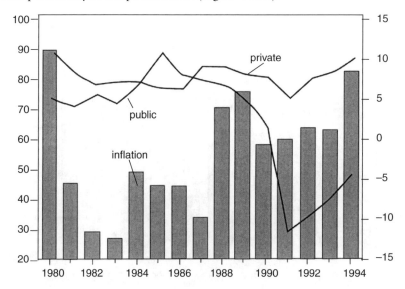

Figure 11.4d Inflation and sales profitability

Note: correlation, private = 0.53, public = 0.36.

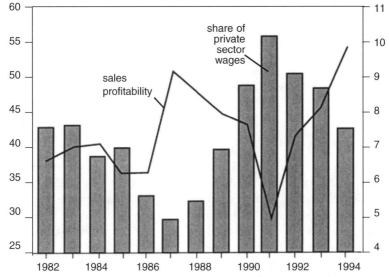

Figure 11.5a Share of wages in net value added and sales profitability in the private sector
Note: correlation = –0.40.

Similar conclusions can be derived for the share of interest paid. There is no relationship between the share of interest paid in net value added and sales profitability in the private sector (Figure 11.5c). On the other hand, there is a very high negative correlation between the share of interest paid in net value added and sales profitability in the public sector (Figure 11.5d).

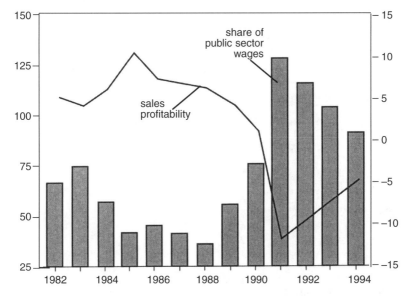

Figure 11.5b Share of wages in net value added and sales profitability in the public sector
Note: correlation = –0.96.

Wage rate and labour productivity

Is there a relationship between labour productivity and the wage rate? There is a positive and a significant relationship in the private sector (Figure 11.6a). This relationship is not observed in the public sector (Figure 11.6b), where the average wage rate may even be higher than labour productivity (Table 11.4).

Non-operational profits and sales profitability

As a consequence of large public deficits, real interest rates are quite high. High interest rates make it very difficult to invest. On the other hand, return on treasury bill rate and other instruments such as repurchased orders (REPOs) are very attractive (a comparison between the profit rate on equity and treasury bill rate is sufficient, 54 per cent as opposed to 100 per cent). Firms invest available funds in financial markets rather than on physical investment. There is a positive relationship between non-operational profits and sales profits in the private sector (Figure 11.7a, Table 11.5). No such relation is observed in the public sector (Figure 11.7b). Non-operational profits allow private firms to enjoy high profit rates without increasing production.

Macroeconomic indicators, profit rates and factor shares

Profit rates in the private sector are positively related to the budget deficit, while public sector profit rates are negatively related (Ozmucur 1996). There is a negative relationship between share of wages in net value added and real exchange rate in the private sector. In the public sector, there is a positive

Table 11.4 Average annual wages in the 500 largest firms in Turkey (TL million)

	Current prices			1987 prices		
	Total	Private	Public	Total	Private	Public
1982	0.8	0.8	0.8	4.0	4.0	3.9
1983	0.8	0.8	0.9	3.5	3.2	3.8
1984	1.2	1.1	1.3	3.3	3.2	3.5
1985	1.7	1.6	1.8	3.2	3.0	3.4
1986	2.2	2.1	2.4	3.0	2.8	3.2
1987	3.4	3.3	3.6	3.4	3.3	3.6
1988	5.6	5.1	6.4	3.3	3.0	3.8
1989	12.6	12.6	12.6	4.2	4.2	4.2
1990	24.9	24.7	25.2	5.3	5.3	5.4
1991	55.2	56.9	53.1	7.4	7.6	7.1
1992	95.7	100.2	90.1	7.8	8.2	7.4
1993	167.4	182.0	152.1	8.4	9.2	7.7
1994	271.5	301.9	240.1	7.5	8.4	6.6

Source: calculated by author using ISO data.

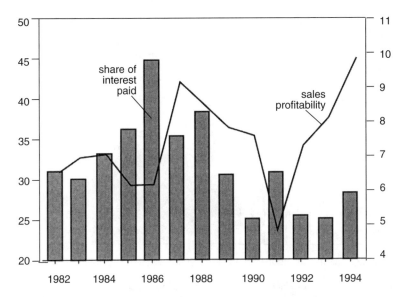

Figure 11.5c Share of interest paid in net value added and sales profitability in the private sector

Note: correlation = –0.21.

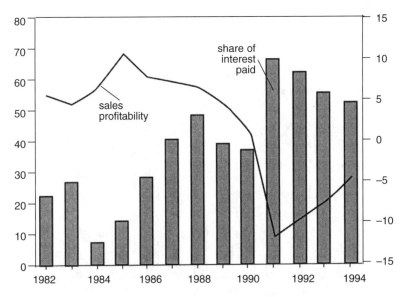

Figure 11.5d Share of interest paid in net value added and sales profitability in the public sector

Note: correlation = –0.83.

Figure 11.6a Wage rate and labour productivity in the private sector
Note: correlation = −0.85.

correlation between the share of interest paid in net value added and inflation, budget deficit and velocity (a proxy for the rate of interest). The relationship between the share of wages and the budget deficit is also positive in the public sector. On the other hand the budget deficit and the share of profits in net value added are inversely related.

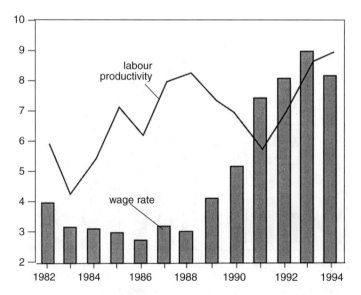

Figure 11.6b Wage rate and labour productivity in the public sector
Note: correlation = −0.38.

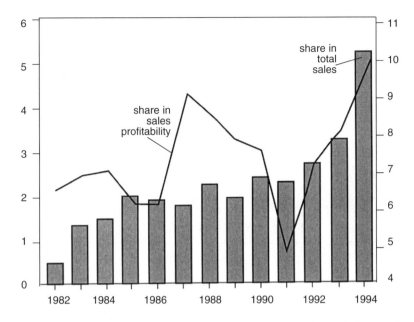

Figure 11.7a Share of non-operational revenues in total sales and sales profitability in the private sector

Note: correlation = 0.53.

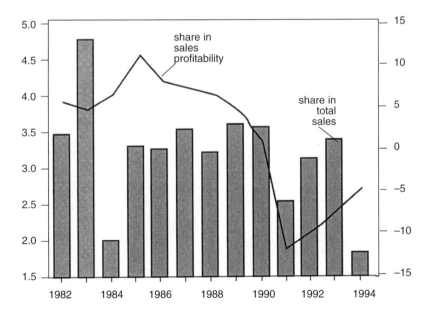

Figure 11.7b Share of non-operational revenues in total sales and sales profitability in the public sector

Note: correlation = −0.28.

Table 11.5 Share of non-operational revenue in total sales (%)

	Total	Public	Private
1982	1.8	3.4	0.4
1983	3.1	4.8	1.3
1984	1.8	2.0	1.5
1985	2.7	3.3	2.0
1986	2.6	3.2	1.9
1987	2.6	3.5	1.8
1988	2.7	3.2	2.2
1989	2.7	3.5	2.0
1990	3.0	3.6	2.5
1991	2.5	2.6	2.4
1992	2.9	3.1	2.8
1993	3.3	3.4	3.3
1994	3.9	1.8	5.4

Source: calculated from ISO data.

Financial structure and ratios

There is a marked difference between private and public firms as far as financial structure and ratios are concerned (Figure 11.8a–11.8d).

On the average fixed assets make up 51 per cent of total assets in the public sector (Akguc 1995). The corresponding ratio is only 28 per cent in the private sector (Figure 11.8a).

On the liabilities and equity front, the share of debt is higher in the public sector. On the average it is 64 per cent in the public sector and 60 per cent in the private sector. There is a marked increase in the public sector (Figure 11.8b).

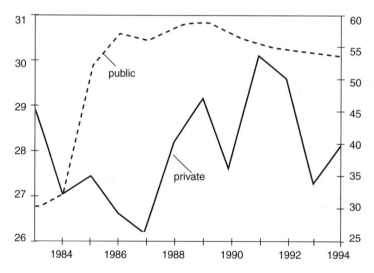

Figure 11.8a Share of fixed assets in total assets in the private and public sectors

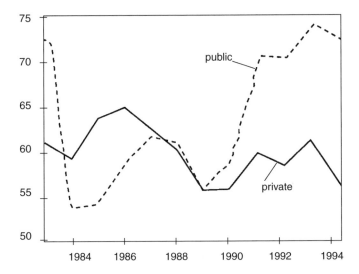

Figure 11.8b Debt/total liabilities in the private and public sectors

These are also reflected in high and increasing debt/equity ratios in the public sector (Figure 11.8c).

The current ratio (current assets/current liabilities) is very low in the public sector. The average is below one in the public sector, compared to 1.5 in the private sector (Figure 11.8d).

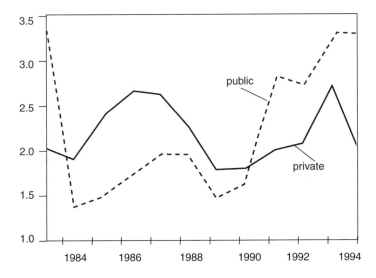

Figure 11.8c Debt/equity ratio in the private and public sectors

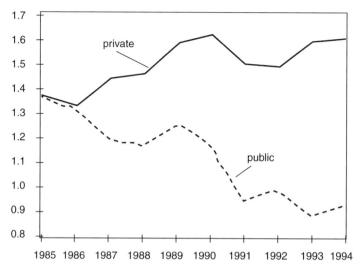

Figure 11.8d Current ratios in the private and public sectors

Conclusion

The significance of ownership is supported by data on the FHLF of Turkey. There are important differences in behaviours of private and public firms. Private firms follow market conditions closely to improve competitiveness and increase profit rates. Such a behaviour is not observed in public firms. There are also important structural differences among private and public firms. These differences in financial and economic ratios lead to a more satisfactory performance in the private sector.

Notes

The author is indebted to the discussant Mary Shirley and other participants as well as organizers of the Economic Research Forum (ERF) workshop which was held in Amman, May 1996.

1   ISO surveys started in 1967, covering the largest 100 (ISO members only). The number went up to 300 and then to 500 in 1980. For financial and economic indicators including productivity, see special issues of the ISO Journal and Ozmucur (1992, 1995b), and Akguc (1995).
2   Two very large establishments TEK (Turkish Electricity Institution) and TEKEL (State Monopolies) started to provide data in 1985. Furthermore, there may be some problems in evaluating public sector establishments. They may have provided data at the establishments or at the firm level. For example, State Coal Industries may appear as a single entity in one survey and as eleven entries in another.
3   For a survey on profitability, see Schmalensee and Willig (1989), Shepherd (1990), and Ozmucur (1992, 1993, 1995a, 1995b, 1996), among others.
4   For productivity calculations and their determinants, see Froutan (1991), Krueger

and Tuncer (1980), Nishimizu and Robinson (1984), Ozmucur (1992, 1995b), Ozmucur and Karatas (1994), and Yildirim (1989).

Bibliography

Akguc, O. (1995) 'Turkiye'nin 500 Buyuk Firmasinin Finans Yapisi', *Istanbul Sanayi Odasi Dergisi1*, Eylul, Yil, 30, Sayi, 354: 183–205.

Froutan, F. (1991) 'Foreign trade and its relation to competition and productivity in Turkish industry', World Bank Working Papers WPS 604, February, Washington, D.C.: World Bank.

Istanbul Chamber of Industry (ISO) *Istanbul Sanayi Odasi Dergisi*, Various issues.

Krueger, A. O. and Tuncer, B. (1980) 'Estimating total factor productivity growth in a developing country', World Bank Staff Working Paper, no. 422, Washington, D.C.: World Bank.

Nishimizu, M. and Robinson, S. (1984) 'Trade policies and productivity change in semi-industrialized countries', *Journal of Development Economics*, vol. 13: 177–206.

Ozmucur, S. (1992) *Productivity and Profitability: The Turkish Case*, Bogazici University Publications, no. 514, Istanbul: Bogazici University Publications.

—— (1993) 'Productivity and profitability in the 500 largest firms of Turkey, 1980–1992', *Bogazici Journal*, vol. 7, no. 1–2: 63–71.

—— (1995a) 'Pricing and income distribution in an economy with an important public sector', in C. Balim, E. Kalaycioglu, C. Karata, G. Winrow and F. Yasamee (eds), *Turkey: Political, Social and Economic Challenges in the 1990s*, Leiden, New York, Cologne: E. J. Brill.

—— (1995b) '500 Buyuk Firmada Mali ve Ekonomik Gostergeler: Karlilik, Verimlilik, ve Faktor Gelirlerinin Dagilimi, 1980–1992', *Istanbul Sanayi Odasi Dergisi*, Eylul, Yil, 30, Sayi. 354: 177–82.

—— (1996) *Turkiye'de Gelir Dagilimi Vergi Yuku ve Makroekonomik Gostergeler*, Istanbul: Bogazici University Publications.

Ozmucur, S. and Karatas, C. (1994) 'The public enterprise sector in Turkey: performance and productivity growth, 1973–1988', in F. Senses (ed.), *Recent Industrialization Experience of Turkey in a Global Context*, Westport, Conn.: Greenwood.

Schmalensee, R. and Willig, R. (eds) (1989) *Handbook of Industrial Organization* (2 vols), Amsterdam: North-Holland.

Shepherd, W. G. (1990) *The Economics of Industrial Organization* (3rd edn), Englewood Cliffs, NJ: Prentice-Hall.

World Bank (1995) *Bureaucrats in Business, The Economics and Politics of Government Ownership*, New York: Oxford University Press.

Yildirim, E. (1989) 'Total factor productivity growth in Turkish manufacturing industry between 1963–1983: an analysis', *METU Studies in Development*, vol. 16, nos 3–4: 65–83.

12 The relative efficiency of the public manufacturing industry in Turkey

An intertemporal analysis using parametric and non-parametric production function frontiers

Osman Zaim and Fatma Taskin

Introduction

The wave of privatization in both developed and developing countries initiated a number of research projects which focused on the analysis of performance of public and private enterprises using the criterion of productive efficiency. The theoretical arguments which explain the relatively poor performance of public enterprises compared to their private counterparts based their approach on the incentive and monitoring structures faced by their respective managers. In their study, Domberger and Piggott (1986) claim that the incentives and the constraints provided by the market promote productive and technical efficiency in the private sector whereas the public sector may face a different set of incentive structures which may not be compatible with the pursuit of efficiency in production. A related argument is presented in the property rights literature which ties the inherent efficiency differences to the very nature of the ownership structure and its effects on monitoring the managers. In his pioneering work Alchian (1965) argues that while the broadly dispersed and non-transferable ownership rights of public enterprises reduces the incentive of the public owners (voters or taxpayers) to monitor the performance of the public sector manager, the more concentrated and transferable ownership structure of the private sector generates incentives for shareholders to monitor managerial performance.

The purpose of this study is twofold. One objective is to show that two alternative approaches in the production frontier literature, commonly referred to as the non-parametric non-stochastic production frontiers and the stochastic production frontiers yield consistent and complementary results. The second aim is to evaluate and compare the performance of the public and private manufacturing sectors in Turkey by using these competing methods. Specifically, we will start with a non-parametric non-stochastic production frontier methodology to establish a manufacturing sector frontier for Turkey for each year between 1974 and 1991 based on data on twenty-eight subsectors where public and private sectors are registered separately. Once these frontiers are constructed, then examination of each subsector's distance to the frontier at each year for both ownership types will show the developments in efficiency through time. The results obtained from this approach can further be examined by two other model specifications, namely the time-varying stochastic production frontier and the efficiency effects model, both utilizing panel data. While the first specification allows one to determine how efficiency varies in time, the latter model will test whether there are statistically significant differences between average technical efficiency levels of public and private sectors.

The chapter is organized as follows. The following section of the study gives a brief summary of the developments in Turkish manufacturing industry emphasizing the role of the public sector and summarizing the results of previous empirical studies. The model specification are presented in the following section, after which there is a discussion of data source and results.

The role of the public sector in Turkish manufacturing industry

Prior to the 1980s, the main feature of the development strategies pursued by successive Turkish governments was their reliance on strong interventionist policies. During the early 1920s the strong sentiment against foreign business after the War of Independence led the government to provide substantial incentives for the creation of a local entrepreneurial class. However, the disruption of agricultural export markets during the Great Depression and the ensuing foreign exchange shortages accelerated industrial import substitution and proved to be a decisive factor in the country's turn towards statism. Hence, starting from the mid-1930s the state assumed the role of the entrepreneur class through the creation of public enterprises in a broad range of manufacturing activities. The state maintained its role as an agent of industrialization even after the emergence of the private sector in the late 1940s and with the introduction of central planning during the 1960s, its intervention on the economy as a whole reached peak level.

The industrialization policy of the import substitution period, characterized by heavy protectionist measures created a favourable environment for manufacturing investment.[1] The growth of output averaging 7.5 per cent during the 1965–80 period, increased the share of manufacturing in gross domestic product (GDP) from 14.1 per cent in 1963 to 19.1 per cent in 1979. In the same period, an increased public sector activity in capital intensive sectors such as basic metals, fertilizer, paper and petrochemicals resulted in a structural shift from the production of consumption goods towards the production of intermediate and capital goods. With these developments, the share of value added generated by the public sector enterprises in the large manufacturing industry increased to levels as high as 35 per cent towards the end of 1980s.[2] The increased importance of public production is also reflected in its share of employment and investment in the total large manufacturing sector (see Table 12.1).

Table 12.1 Share of the public sector in large manufacturing

Percent share of public sector in manufacturing	1976	1981	1986	1991
Value added	29	46	40	32
Employment	35	34	29	25
Investment	32	27	32	9

Source: computed from various issues of *Annual Manufacturing Industry Statistics*, State Institute of Statistics (Turkey).

By the late 1970s, Turkey's inward-oriented policies and continued reliance on the public sector as the engine of development caused growing fiscal and current account deficits. These shortfalls led to unsustainable levels of debt which resulted in the announcement of the 1980 stabilization and adjustment programme. The market-oriented adjustment programme, with an outward-looking development strategy, had the objective of liberalizing the economy. In this framework, autonomy given to public enterprises in price setting improved their financial position for a short period. However, this did not decrease their reliance on the government's budget. The initial guidelines for the reform programme stated that the government would abstain from expanding the public sector and hence, with this objective at hand, public investments were channelled away from manufacturing industry towards infrastructural sectors such as communication, transportation and energy. With the intention of alleviating the pressures on the government's budget, public enterprises in the manufacturing sector were directed towards commercial channels to borrow for their day-to-day financing requirements. This, increasing the debt service requirements of the public sector, led to even lower levels of investments in an attempt to reduce the public enterprise borrowing requirements.

The poor record of public sector investment was not compensated by the private sector. As one can follow from Table 12.2, total manufacturing investment reached its peak level prior to the debt crisis of 1977 and from then on it deteriorated significantly. Private–public breakdown of this declining total manufacturing investment shows that public manufacturing investment decreased faster than private sector investment. The reasons behind the decline in private investment were increasing interest rates, which resulted from financial liberalization and the crowding-out effect of government borrowing. Furthermore, heavy real currency depreciation and macroeconomic instability prevented private sector investment from sustaining the levels it reached during the previous decade, which had featured a heavy reliance on foreign borrowing.

The recent debates on privatization coupled with the poor financial performance of public enterprises initiated an academic curiosity on the sources of growth in the Turkish manufacturing sector, which resulted in a series of works on total factor productivity growth.

Earlier studies, inspired by the virtues of the outward oriented growth strategy of the liberalization episodes, attempted both to establish the links

Table 12.2 Index numbers for manufacturing investments (1988 prices, 1980=100)

	Total manufacturing investments	Private manufacturing investments	Public manufacturing investments
1974	88	125	49
1975	122	153	89
1976	134	174	92
1977	138	175	97
1978	116	155	74
1979	105	114	95
1980	100	100	100
1981	92	96	88
1982	82	95	68
1983	74	90	57
1984	70	92	47
1985	75	95	54
1986	75	104	44
1987	63	95	29
1988	59	94	23
1989	54	89	17
1990	84	146	19
1991	82	157	3

Source: computed from various issues of *Main Economic Indicators*. Turkey, State Planning Organization (Turkish Republic Prime Ministry).

between total factor productivity and trade regimes and also to evaluate relative performance of the public sector. In this respect one can cite the studies by Krueger and Tuncer (1982) and Nishimuzu and Robinson (1984). These studies, concentrating on the period from the mid-1960s to mid-1970s, reported significant trade policy effects on total factor productivity performance with the positive impact of export expansion and the negative impact of import tightening (Celasun 1994). Furthermore, Nishimuzu and Robinson, by comparing growth rates of total factor productivity in manufacturing for the period 1963–76 in Japan, Korea, Turkey and Yugoslavia found that they were lower in Turkey than in Korea and Japan but higher than in Yugoslavia (Nishimuzu and Robinson 1984). In addition, contrary to their expectations, Krueger and Tuncer (1982) detected relatively higher total factor productivity growth in the public sector, which is a finding supported by Yildirim (1989) and Uygur (1990) for approximately the same period.

The drawback of the total factor productivity methodology used in these studies is that, in this approach each economic identity (firm, sector or country) is compared to only itself in previous periods and not to an explicit common benchmark which makes it difficult to conduct direct multilateral comparisons. One other deficiency of the methodology is its inability to distinguish between technological progress and improvements in technical efficiency. The techniques used in this chapter, which are the subject of the next section, will provide alternative approaches.

Model

To investigate the intertemporal efficiency variations in Turkish manufacturing industry in general and the comparative position of the state in particular we will employ both non-parametric non-stochastic and stochastic techniques. Among the various approaches, we will particularly utilize:

- The Farrell output-based measure of technical efficiency
- The Time-varying Efficiency model of Battese and Coelli (1992) and
- The Technical Efficiency Effects model of Battese and Coelli (1995).

While the first model is a non-parametric non-stochastic technique, the other two are the applications of the stochastic production frontiers that use panel data. An appealing feature of using alternative specifications is the convenience it provides in checking for the robustness of the results and also in extracting complementary knowledge about the nature of the inefficiencies in public and private manufacturing sectors.

The foundations of the first methodology go back to Farrell (1957), where he showed how one can measure productive efficiency and its components allocative and technical efficiencies within a theoretically meaningful framework. His initial approach has been adopted and extended by Farrell and Fieldhouse (1962), Seitz (1970) and Afriat (1972). The methodology is based on the concept of output distance which is due to Shephard (1970) and is defined relative to the production technology S^t ($S^t = \{(X^t, Y^t): X^t$ can produce $Y^t\}$) as $D_0^t(X, Y) = \min \{\Theta : (X^t, Y^t/\Theta \in S^t)\}$. Here Y^t refers to the vector of outputs and X^t refers to the vector of inputs at period t. In other words, the distance function measures the reciprocal of the maximal ray expansion of the observed outputs (Y) given inputs (X). One advantage of the output distance function is its ability to provide Farrell measure of technical efficiency directly. Specifically:

$$D_0^t = \min\{\Theta : (X^t, Y^t/\Theta) \in S^t\}$$
$$= [\max \{\Theta : (X^t, Y^t/\Theta) \in S^t\}]^{-1} \tag{1}$$
$$= 1/F_0^t (X^t, Y^t)$$

where $F_0^t (X^t, Y^t)$ is the Farrell output-based measure of technical efficiency.

The output based productivity index may be computed by solving a linear programming problem for each year. Suppose that for each t, there are $k = 1,$ ...., K^0 observations on inputs, $X^{k,t} = (X_{k,1}^t ...., X_{k,N}^t)$ and outputs $Y^{k,t} = (Y_{k,1}^t ...., Y_{k,M}^t)$. By imposing constant returns to scale and strong disposability on the technology, for observation k^t we compute:

$$[D_0^t (X^{k,t}, Y^{k,t})]^{-1} = \max \Theta$$

subject to

$$\sum_{k=1}^{K^0} Z_k \, \Upsilon_{k,m}^t \geq \Theta \Upsilon_{k,m}^t \quad m = 1,\ldots,M \tag{LP1}$$

$$\sum_{k=1}^{K^0} Z_k \, X_{k,n}^t \leq \Theta X_{k,n}^t \quad m = 1,\ldots,N$$

$$z_k \geq 0 \quad k = 1,\ldots,K^0$$

where z_k is an intensity variable. This linear programming problem measures the output based Farrell technical efficiency of observation k^t relative to the constant returns to scale reference technology of the same period, namely period t. However, by imposing additional restrictions on the intensity variable z_k one can construct production frontiers that satisfy different scale assumptions. For example, the additional constraint,

$$\sum_{k=1}^{K^0} z_k = 1$$

if imposed on the linear programming problem (LP1), will yield efficiency scores relative to a variable return to scale production frontier.

One important pitfall of this method is that it assumes all the deviations from the frontier are due to inefficiency alone. However, if any noise is present (e.g. due to measurement error, weather, strikes and so on) then this may influence the placement of the production frontier and may result in exaggerated inefficiency scores. Nevertheless with the introduction of the stochastic production frontier approach, which is independently proposed by Aigner, Lovell and Schmidt (1977) and Meeusen and van den Broeck (1977) these deficiencies are alleviated. In this approach, the error structure that is assumed to be composed of two different components, one which captures the variation in output due to the factors which are not under the control of the firm and the other which represents the pure technical efficiency, provided a means to isolate the impact of random factors. The stochastic production frontiers, which are initially introduced for estimation of technical efficiency using cross section firm data, have been extended in various ways regarding both specification and estimation (see Greene 1993 for a recent survey of the frontier model literature). Particularly, realizing the potential advantages of panel data over a single cross-section data in stochastic frontier estimation, Pitt and Lee (1981) specified a panel data version of the Aigner, Lovell and Schmidt (1977) model. The initial panel specification, which is built on the assumption of fixed inefficiencies over time, is further extended by Cornwell, Schmidt and Sickles (1990), Kumbhakar (1990), Battese and Coelli (1992, 1995) and Lee and Schmidt (1993), so as to incorporate varying technical efficiency over time. Among the time-varying efficiency models we will employ Battese and Coelli (1992, 1995) specifications.

The time-varying model of Battese and Coelli (1992) is defined by:

$$\Upsilon_{it} = f(x_{it}; \beta) e^{(V_{it} - U_{it})} \tag{2}$$

and

$$U_{it} = \eta_{it} U_i = \{ e^{[-\eta(t-T)]} \} U_i, \quad t \in \Im(i); \quad i = 1, 2, \ldots, N$$

where Υ_{it} represents the production for the i'th producing unit at the t'th observation period; $f(x_{it}; \beta)$ is a suitable function of a vector x_{it} of factor inputs associated with the production of the i'th producing unit in the t'th observation period; and β a vector of unknown parameters. The V_{it}'s are assumed to i.i.d with $N(0, \sigma_v^2)$; U_i's are also assumed to be i.i.d. but non-negative truncation of the distribution $N(\mu, \sigma^2)$ where η is an unknown parameter to be estimated. Finally $\Im$ represents the set of T_i time periods among the T periods involved for which observations for the i'th producing unit are obtained. This model is constructed such that the non-negative observation specific effects U_{it} decrease, remain constant or increase as t increases, if $\eta > 0$, $\eta = 0$ or $\eta < 0$ respectively. That is, with the exponential character of the model technical efficiency must either increase at a decreasing rate ($\eta > 0$), decrease at an increasing rate ($\eta < 0$) or remain constant ($\eta = 0$).

The technical efficiency effects model of Battese and Coelli (1995) is similar in character to equation (2), except that the U_{it} are assumed to be random variables which are independently distributed as truncations at zero of a normal distribution with mean m_{it} and variance σ_u^2 where $m_{it} = g(z_{it}, \delta)$. Here z_{it} is a vector of variables which may influence the efficiency of a producing unit; δ is a vector of parameters to be estimated; and g(.) is a suitable functional form usually assumed to be linear.

Data model specification and results

The methods outlined are applied to construct manufacturing sector frontiers for Turkey for the period 1974–91 using data on twenty-eight subsectors (defined at three digits according to International Standard Industrial Classification) where public and private sectors are registered separately. In all the applications, one has to recall that the best practice is a common manufacturing sector frontier which is defined over subsectors in the manufacturing industry. Note however that, while constructing the best practice frontier, public and private production in each subsector are considered as separate observations. The implicit assumption that all industries utilize the same production frontier and that this frontier can be constructed from the observations on subsectors is similar in nature with ones employed by Caves (1992) and Torri and Caves (1992). In their approach to find the productivity differentials between the subsectors of two countries, the observations on outputs and inputs of subsectors of these countries are used together while constructing a stochastic production frontier.[3] A similar approach at a different aggregation level is employed by Fare *et al.* (1994) where a common best-practice world (production) frontier is constructed using the inputs (aggregate capital and labour) and outputs (GDP) of seventeen Organization of Economic Cooperation and Development (OECD) countries in the sample.

The data are compiled from *Annual Manufacturing Industry Statistics* (State Institute of Statistics 1974–91) which cover all establishments in the public sector and those establishments with ten or more employees engaged in the private sector. All three digit industries, except ISIC390 (other manufacturing industry) are included in the analysis. A nice feature of the data is that, except in few cases, both government and private activity coexist in all subsectors allowing for a comprehensive analysis of relative efficiency between public and private enterprises during the period 1974–91.[4] Table 12A.1 gives the list and the definition of these sectors included in the model.

Our measure of the aggregate output of a subsector is the real value of the output of the industry.[5] The three input proxies chosen are: number of individuals engaged in production, real value of the raw materials, fuel and electricity, and total capacity of power equipment installed at the end of the year in terms of horse power.[6] The usual difficulties associated with computation of the capital stocks at this disaggregate level forced us to use total capacity of power equipment installed as a proxy for the capital stock.

First a non-parametric non-stochastic frontier methodology is employed and linear programming problem (LP1) is solved to construct a manufacturing sector frontier for all the years between 1974 and 1991 under constant returns to scale (CRS) and variable returns to scale (VRS) assumptions. Then, geometric averages of the output distance functions are computed for each year across all the sectors and for different ownership types. These averages, which actually show the efficiency levels, are shown in Figures 12.1 and 12.2.

On the basis of these figures it is evident that technical efficiency in the Turkish manufacturing industry is in a declining trend.[7] Note that both diagrams show the same trend with higher efficiency scores in the VRS case compared to the CRS case. This is theoretically expected since the CRS frontier envelops the data most loosely of all scale assumptions and hence results in lower efficiency (higher inefficiency) scores compared to other scale assumptions. With respect to the level of technical efficiency for different ownership types, both diagrams are in agreement that there are two distinct periods: before and after 1982. Note that while until 1982 the public sector performed better than the private sector, the reverse is the case for the years after 1982 resulting in almost equal average efficiency scores when the entire sampling period is taken into account.[8]

The results reached from the non-parametric non-stochastic methodology

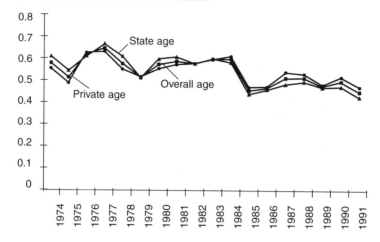

Figure 12.1 Geometric means of the efficiency scores obtained from non–parametric, non-stochastic methodology (CRS)

can be further verified by stochastic specifications. The stochastic production frontier for the panel data on the three digit subsectors of the Turkish manufacturing industry is defined by

$$
\begin{aligned}
\log \Upsilon_{it} = {} & \beta_0 + \beta_1 \log(lab_{it}) + \beta_2 \log(raw_{it}) + \beta_3 \log(cap_{it}) + \beta_4 [\log(lab_{it})\,]^2 \\
& + \beta_5 [\log(raw_{it})\,]^2 + \beta_6 [\log(cap_{it})\,]^2 + \beta_7 \log(lab_{it})\log(cap_{it}) \\
& + \beta_8 \log(lab_{it})\log(raw_{it}) + \beta_9 \log(cap_{it})\log(raw_{it}) + \beta_{10}\,t\log(lab_{it}) \\
& + \beta_{11}\,t\log(cap_{it}) + \beta_{12}\,t\log(raw_{it}) + \beta_{13}t + \beta_{14}t^2 + V_{it} - U_{it}
\end{aligned}
$$

where:

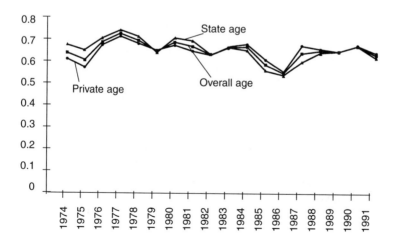

Figure 12.2 Geometric means of the efficiency scores obtained from non–parametric, non-stochastic methodology (VRS)

Y represents the real value of the aggregate output of a subsector;

raw represents the real value of raw materials fuel and electricity used by a subsector;

lab represents the number of individuals engaged in production in a subsector;

cap represents a proxy variable for capital stock which is defined as the total capacity of power equipment installed at the end of the year in terms of horse power; and

V and U are random variables whose properties we defined earlier for two alternative model specifications, namely the time-varying efficiency model of Battese and Coelli (1992) and the technical efficiency effects model of Battese and Coelli (1995).

The maximum likelihood estimates of the parameters of both the models are presented in Table 12.3. The first column shows the parameter estimates of the time-varying efficiency model and the second column is reserved for the parameter estimates of the technical efficiency effects model.

Table 12.3 Parameter estimates

Parameters	Time-varying Efficiency model	t-values	Technical efficiency Effects model	t-values
β_0	0.1467	(4.60)	0.025	(0.69)
β_1	0.0535	(2.09)	0.0870	(2.73)
β_2	0.8266	(38.34)	0.8438	(34.03)
β_3	0.0324	(2.25)	0.0041	(0.19)
β_4	0.0941	(6.04)	0.1009	(6.39)
β_5	−0.0075	(−1.32)	0.0112	(1.62)
β_6	−0.0024	(−0.58)	−0.0050	(−0.94)
β_7	−0.0810	(−7.14)	−0.0774	(5.60)
β_8	−0.1017	(−6.89)	−0.1340	(−9.39)
β_9	0.0843	(7.54)	0.0840	(6.22)
β_{10}	0.0067	(3.57)	0.0055	(1.99)
β_{11}	−0.0042	(−3.21)	−0.0024	(−0.46)
β_{12}	−0.0004	(−0.27)	−0.0008	(−0.47)
β_{13}	−0.0129	(−2.27)	−0.0151	(−2.37)
β_{14}	0.0011	(4.84)	0.0011	(3.37)
$\sigma_s^2 = \sigma_v^2 = \sigma^2$	0.2329	(8.84)	0.0490	(2.05)
$\gamma = \sigma^2/\sigma_s^2$	0.9040	(90.41)	0.0023	(0.20)
μ	−0.7788	(−5.27)	—	—
η	−0.015	(−2.52)	—	—
δ_0	—	—	0.0116	(0.86)
δ_1	—	—	−0.0933	(−2.73)

Source: author estimates.

Starting with the time-varying efficiency model, several hypotheses are tested to determine whether the structural production model and distributional assumptions on the error term are appropriate. The likelihood ratio testing procedure which simultaneously tests the significance of a group of coefficients is used. The structural tests include a test of null hypothesis of Hicks-neutral technical change; a test of null hypothesis that there is no technical change and a test of null hypothesis that the Cobb-Douglass production is the appropriate model. The tests on the distributional assumptions on the error terms included a test of the null hypothesis that the traditional average production function is a better representation of the data; that the test of the null hypothesis that time-invariant model applies; and finally a test of the null hypothesis that U_i's have half normal distribution. The log-likelihood function values of the restricted and that of unrestricted models together with the relevant test statistics are presented in Table 12A.2. As one can easily follow from this table, all null hypotheses are rejected, leading us to conclude that translog time-varying production frontier with non-Hicks-neutral technical change is the appropriate choice.

Before focusing on the efficiency issue, one also has to assess the economic plausibility of the estimated coefficients. Thus in Table 12A.3, the values of the production elasticities of the three inputs, returns to scale and the annual change in production due to technical change are listed, all evaluated at the sample means.[9] Most of the production elasticities have the expected positive signs. The production elasticity for labour is 0.1172 and for raw materials is 0.9326. The only exception is the capital elasticity which takes the value of –0.0075, which is not significantly different from zero at the 5 per cent significance level.[10] The estimated scale elasticity of 1.08 indicates a mildly increasing return to scale. Finally the last figure in Table 12A.3 denotes that the industry has experienced a rate of technical progress over the sample period of 0.81 per cent per year.

Now turning our attention to the parameters associated with the inefficiency error term U_{it}, namely γ, μ and η listed towards the bottom of the second column in Table 12.3, we see that all with t-ratios larger than 1.96 in absolute value are statistically significant. These significant t-ratios are not surprising, given the conclusions of the likelihood ratio test mentioned earlier. While validating the conclusions reached from the non-stochastic non-parametric methodology, a parameter which is of particular interest is η. Since the estimated value of η (–0.015) is negative and significant, this indicates that technical efficiency in the Turkish manufacturing industry decreases at an increasing rate. Then, one can easily conclude that both non-parametric non-stochastic and stochastic production frontier models are in coherence in showing that the technical efficiency is in a declining trend in the Turkish manufacturing industry.

To show the association between the efficiency estimates of the non-parametric non-stochastic methodology and the time-varying efficiency model, the efficiency rankings obtained from alternative models are compared. For the time-varying efficiency model, given the specification of truncated normal distribution of the error term relating to inefficiency, technical efficiencies of each subsector are estimated using a panel variant of Jondrow *et al.*'s (1982) formula for all the years between 1974 and 1991. Then, Spearman's Rank Correlation of the efficiency scores derived from non-parametric non-stochastic model and time-varying efficiency model are computed and reported in Table 12.4. A conclusion that emerges from rank correlations is that both methods are not only in coherence in showing the general trends but are also in agreement while ranking individual efficiency scores of different subsectors.[11]

The technical efficiency effect model is specifically formulated to incorporate the factors that influence the efficiency of the producing units and to test their significance. In this study the emphasis is on the efficiency effect of ownership structure in Turkish manufacturing industry. A dummy variable is introduced (which takes the value of 1 if the production takes place at the state-operated enterprises and zero otherwise) as a subsector specific variable in an attempt to identify the differences in predicted efficiencies between the subsectors of the manufacturing industry and the results are reported in the second column in Table 12.3.[12]

This model specification, as described in the model section, permits certain sector specific factors to shift the mean of the technical inefficiency error term U_{it}. For example the negative (and significant) sign of the coefficient related to the dummy variable ($d_1 = -0.0933$) which represents state production, indicates that the change in the ownership from private to state production will result in a decrease in the value of technical inefficiency effect and hence an increase in technical efficiency. However, a test of null hypothesis $\gamma = d_0 = d_1 = 0$ if failed to be rejected would mean that stochastic production function is not statistically different from an average response function where U_{it} is omitted. Thus a test of hypothesis that $\gamma = d_0 = d_1 = 0$ is conducted and the likelihood ratio test statistic is calculated to be 0.6423 which is less than the χ_4^2 critical value of 9.49. This means that all the observations are equally efficient and the deviations from the average response function can only be attributed to random effects implying that government ownership does not

Table 12.4 Spearman's rank correlation coefficients

Time-varying efficiency model	Non-parametric non-stochastic model					
	Variable returns to scale			Constant returns to scale		
	1977	1986	1991	1977	1986	1991
1977	0.614			0.529		
1986		0.661			0.636	
1991			0.614			0.629

Note: all values are significant at the 0.05 level.
Source: authors' computations.

contribute to inefficiency on the average. Note further that this conclusion is also consistent with the findings obtained from the non-stochastic non-parametric methodology where almost equal efficiency scores are obtained for both ownership sizes when averaged over time.

Conclusion

This study by using stochastic and non-stochastic non-parametric techniques of production frontier literature focused on issues such as how efficiency in the manufacturing sector changes in time and if public and private enterprises show different performances in their pursuit of efficiency. A non-parametric non-stochastic frontier methodology employed led to the conclusion that technical efficiency in the Turkish manufacturing sector is in a declining trend and that public and private enterprises, by differing in efficiency levels before and after 1982, averaged around the same efficiency level over the entire sampling period. This empirical result is re-examined by stochastic specifications, namely by time-varying efficiency model and efficiency effects model. The conclusion from the time varying efficiency model is that the technical efficiency of the Turkish manufacturing industry decreases at an increasing rate. However, the impact of government ownership on the average efficiency level is not found statistically significant in the technical efficiency effects model, mainly because of the relative poor performance of the private sector prior to 1982 which was compensated for in the years following when the private sector performance was superior relative to the public sector.

Notes

We wish to thank the editor and the participants of the ERF workshop on 'The Changing Size and Role of the State-Owned Enterprise Sector' held at Amman, Jordan, May 1996 for their helpful comments and suggestions.

1   The policies ensued carried typical elements, such as overvalued exchange rate under a system of strict exchange rate control, strict import controls through tariffs, quantitative restrictions, guarantee deposits on imports and generous tax and credit incentives for manufacturing investments.
2   Large manufacturing industry covers all establishments in the public sector and establishments with ten or more employees engaged in the private sector.
3   Compared to these studies our approach is appreciably less restrictive in the sense that we neither use a tightly-specified functional form such as Cobb-Douglass nor force matched industries from another country to share the same common production frontier. Furthermore, the alternative strategy of estimating production frontiers separately for each subsector using micro level data, that is, firm data, would have made within industry-comparisons possible at the expense of inter-industry comparisons. In this case this approach would suffer from the same shortcomings of the Total Factor Productivity approach where each industry is evaluated according to its own performance in the past without allowing for inter industry comparisons.
4   No government activity exists in the following sectors: manufacture of products of leather and leather substitutes ISIC(323), manufacture of furniture and fixtures

ISIC(332), manufacture of rubber products ISIC(355), manufacture of plastic products not elsewhere classified ISIC(356), manufacture of glass and glass products ISIC(362), manufacture of professional and scientific equipment not elsewhere classified ISIC(385). Also, in our data set, no private activity exists for petroleum refineries ISIC(353). This provides a balanced panel data with forty-nine observations for each year.

5 All nominal figures are deflated using two-digit manufacturing price index and are expressed in 1988 prices.

6 Since there is no price index for purchased inputs, nominal values are deflated by two-digit manufacturing price index.

7 The oscillations around the trend may be partly due to deflating both inputs and outputs by the same two-digit manufacturing price index. For example, the sharp drop in efficiency from 1984 to 1985 seems to be the result of deflating inputs (especially imported raw materials) with a price deflator which underscores the effect of real currency depreciation that exist during that period. Since this will overstate the real cost of raw materials, it will reflect itself as increased inefficiency in our indexes. Also, one should note that the declining trend in the levels of technical efficiency does not necessarily imply a declining trend in productivity growth. Nevertheless, it will have a dampening effect on the productivity growth that stems from technological progress. We thank Professor Merih Celasun who brought these points to our attention.

8 Geometric average of efficiency scores across all the years are 0.67 for the private sector and 0.68 for the public sector for the variable returns to scale case. The constant returns to scale frontier resulted in an almost equal efficiency score of 0.55 for both ownership types.

9 In empirical studies it is common to express variables as deviations around their means because of the convenience it provides in obtaining output elasticities at the mean level of inputs. In estimating the parameters of the translog production frontier we also adopted such a strategy. Hence $\beta_1 + \beta_{10}t$ for example directly provides labour elasticity.

10 This may have stemmed from using total capacity of power equipment installed as a proxy for the capital stock. During a period where energy prices are increasing, the energy-saving policies adopted by firms may have caused a low variation in power equipment installed in the time component of the panel data.

11 To give an example, both the time-varying efficiency model and the CRS non-stochastic non-parametric model are in coherence in depicting nine subsectors out of most successful fifteen subsectors consistently in 1974. The sectors which are found among the most efficient fifteen subsectors by both models in 1974 are: private manufacture of basic industrial chemicals (ISIC 351), private manufacture of other chemical products (ISIC 352), private manufacture of petroleum and coal derivatives (ISIC,354), both public and private manufacture of pottery china and earthware (ISIC, 361), public beverage industries, (ISIC 313), public tobacco manufactures (ISIC, 314), public petroleum refineries (ISIC 353) and public iron and steel basic industries (ISIC 371). A very similar ranking applies for the year 1991. For the year 1991 both models are in complete agreement in depicting ten out of fifteen most successful sectors. All subsectors that are listed as the most successful sectors in 1974 are also found among the most successful sectors in 1991 with the exception of public iron and steel basic industries (ISIC 371). However private beverage industries (ISIC 313) and private manufacture of electrical machinery apparatus (ISIC 383) are included among the successful sectors by both models.

12 The maximum likelihood estimates of the stochastic production frontier have been tested for all possible structural restrictions and the translog form with the non-neutral technical change is found to be the most appropriate form.

Appendix

Table 12A.1 Description of International Standard Industrial Classification codes

311	Food manufacturing
312	Manufacture of food products not elsewhere classified
313	Beverage industries
314	Tobacco manufactures
321	Manufacture of textiles
322	Manufacture of wearing apparel (except footwear)
323	Manufacture of leather and leather products (except footwear and wearing apparel)
324	Manufacture of footwear
331	Manufacture of products including furniture
332	Manufacture of furniture and fixtures
341	Manufacture of paper and paper products
342	Printing, publishing and allied industries
351	Manufacture of basic industrial chemicals
352	Manufacture of other chemical products
353	Petroleum refineries
354	Manufacture of petroleum and coal derivatives
355	Manufacture of rubber products
356	Manufacture of plastic products not elsewhere classified
361	Manufacture of pottery china and earthware
362	Manufacture of glass and glass products
369	Manufacture of other non-metallic mineral products
371	Iron and steel basic industries
372	Non-ferrous metal basic industries
381	Manufacture of fabricated metal products
382	Manufacture of machinery (except electrical)
383	Manufacture of electrical machinery apparatus, appliances and supplies
384	Manufacture of transport equipment
385	Manufacture of professional and scientific and measuring and controlling equipment not elsewhere classified

Table 12A.2 Hypothesis tests on time-varying efficiency model

Restriction	Model	Log-likelihood	χ^2	Critical value (5%)	Decision
None	translog	325.76			
$\beta_{10}=\beta_{11}=\beta_{12}=0$	translog (hicks-neutral)	315.26	21.00	7.81	Reject H_0
$\beta_{10}=\beta_{11}=\beta_{12}=$ $\beta_{13}=\beta_{14}=0$	translog (no-tech. change)	292.70	66.12	11.07	Reject H_0
$\beta_4=\beta_5=\beta_6=$ $\beta_{10}=\beta_{11}=\beta_{12}=$ $\beta_{13}=\beta_{14}=0$	Cobb-Douglas	265.35	120.82	18.31	Reject H_0
$\gamma=\mu=\eta=0$	translog (OLS)	76.95	497.62	7.81	Reject H_0
$\mu=\eta=0$		320.04	11.44	5.99	Reject H_0
$\mu=0$		323.15	5.22	3.84	Reject H_0
$\eta=0$		322.54	6.44	3.84	Reject H_0

Source: authors' calculations.

Table 12A.3 Key estimates derived from time-varying efficiency model

Description	Estimate
Labour elasticity	0.1172
	(0.0214)
Capital elasticity	–0.0075
	(0.0116)
Raw material elasticity	0.9329
	(0.0166)
Returns to scale	1.08
Technical change	0.0081

Note: numbers in parentheses are standard errors.
Source: authors' estimates.

Bibliography

Afriat, S. N. (1972) 'Efficiency estimation of production functions', *International Economic Review*, vol. 13: 568–98.

Aigner D. J., Lovell, C. A. K. and Schmidt, P. J. 1977. 'Formulation and estimation of stochastic production function models', *Journal of Econometrics*, vol. 6: 21–37.

Alchian, A. A. (1965) 'Some economics of property rights', *Ill Politico*, vol. 30: 816–29.

Battese, G. E. and Coelli, T. J. (1992) 'Frontier production functions, technical efficiency and panel data: with an application to paddyfarmers in India', *Journal of Productivity Analysis*, vol. 3: 153–59.

—— (1995) 'A model for technical inefficiency effects in a stochastic frontier production function for panel data', *Empirical Economics*, vol. 20: 325–32.

Caves, R. E. 1992) 'Determinants of technical efficiency in Australia', in R. E. Caves (ed.), *Industrial Efficiency in Six Nations*, Cambridge, Mass.: MIT Press: 241–71).

Celasun, M (1994) 'Trade and industrialization in Turkey: initial conditions, policy and performance in the 1980s', in G. K. Helleiner (ed.), *Trade Policy and Industrialization in Turbulent Times*, London and New York: Routledge: 453–84.

Cornwell, C., Schmidt, P. and Sickles, R. C. (1990) 'Production frontiers with cross-sectional and time-series variation in efficiency level', *Journal of Econometrics*, vol. 46: 185–200.

Domberger, S. and Piggott, J. (1986) 'Privatization policies and public enterprise: a survey', *Economic Record*, vol. 62: 145–62.

Fare, R., Grosskopf, S., Norris, M. and Zhang, Z. (1994) 'Productivity growth, technical progress and efficiency change in industrialized countries', *American Economic Review*, vol. 84: 66–83.

Farrell, M. J. (1957) 'The measurement of productive efficiency', *Journal of the Royal Statistics Society*, vol. A1, no. 25: 258–81.

Farrell, M. J. and Fieldhouse, M. (1962) 'Estimating efficient production function under non-increasing returns to scale', *Journal of the Royal Statistical Society*, vol. A125: 252–67.

Greene, W. H. (1993) 'The econometric approach to efficiency analysis', in H. O. Fried, C. A. K. Lovell and S. S. Schmidt (eds), *The Measurement of Productive Efficiency: Techniques and Applications*, Oxford: Oxford University Press: 68–119.

Jondrow, J., Lovell, C. A. K., Materov, I. S. and Schmidt, P. (1982) 'On estimation of technical efficiency in the stochastic production function model', *Journal of Econometrics*, vol. 9: 279–86.

Krueger, A. O. and Tuncer, B. (1982) 'Growth of factor productivity in Turkish manufacturing industries', *Journal of Development Economics,* vol. 11: 307–25.

Kumbhakar, S. C. (1990) 'Production frontiers, panel data and time-varying technical efficiency', *Journal of Econometrics,* vol. 46: 201–11.

Lee, Y. H. and Schmidt, P. (1993) 'A production frontier model with flexible temporal variation in technical efficiency', in H. O. Fried, C. A. K. Lovell and S. S. Schmidt (eds), *The Measurement of Productive Efficiency,* New York: Oxford University Press: 237–55.

Meeusen, W. and van den Broeck, J. (1977) 'Efficiency estimation from Cobb-Douglas production functions with composed error', *International Economic Review,* vol. 18: 435–44.

Nishimuzu, M. and Robinson, S. (1984) 'Trade policies and productivity change in semi-industrialized countries', *Journal of Development Economics,* vol. 1: 177–206.

Pitt, M. M. and Lee, L. F. (1981) 'Measurement and sources of technical efficiency in the Indonesian weaving industry', *Journal of Development Economics,* vol. 9: 43–64.

Seitz, W. D. (1970) 'The measurement of efficiency relative to a frontier production function', *American Journal of Agricultural Economics,* vol. 9: 43–64.

Shephard, R. W. (1970) *Theory of Cost and Production Functions,* Princeton, N.J.: Princeton University Press.

State Institute of Statistics (1974–1991) *Annual Manufacturing Industry Statistics* (various issues), Turkish Republic Prime Ministry.

State Planning Organization *Main Economic Indicators: Turkey,* (various issues), Turkish Republic Prime Ministry.

Torri A. and Caves, R. E. (1992) 'Technical efficiency in Japanese and US manufacturing industries', in R. E. Caves (ed.), *Industrial Efficiency in Six Nations,* Cambridge, Mass.: MIT Press: 31–119.

Uygur, E. (1990) 'Policy, productivity growth and employment in Turkey, 1960–89', MIES 90/4, Geneva: International Labour Office.

Yildirim, E. (1989) 'Total factor productivity growth in Turkish manufacturing industry between 1963–1983: an analysis', *Metu Studies in Development,* vol. 16: 64–95.

Index